T0402578

MARIANO
GUADALUPE
Vallejo

BEFORE GOLD
California under Spain and Mexico
VOLUME 7

ROSE MARIE BEEBE & ROBERT M. SENKEWICZ
Series Editors

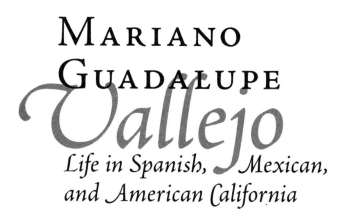

MARIANO GUADALUPE *Vallejo*

Life in Spanish, Mexican, and American California

ROSE MARIE BEEBE AND ROBERT M. SENKEWICZ

UNIVERSITY OF OKLAHOMA PRESS : NORMAN

LIBRARY OF CONGRESS CATALOGING-IN-PUBLICATION DATA

Names: Beebe, Rose Marie, author. | Senkewicz, Robert M., 1947– author.

Title: Mariano Guadalupe Vallejo : life in Spanish, Mexican, and American California / Rose Marie Beebe, Robert M. Senkewicz.

Description: Norman : University of Oklahoma Press, [2023] | Series: Before gold: California under Spain and Mexico; volume 7 | Includes bibliographical references and index. | Summary: "Draws on Mariano Guadalupe Vallejo's Recuerdos, his voluminous papers and correspondence, along with documents collected by members of his family over the decades, to illuminate the life and history of this military and political leader in Mexican California and to examine the broader experience of the nineteenth-century Californio community. Chapters consider Spanish versus Mexican rule in California, mission secularization, the rise of rancho culture, and the conflicts between settlers and Indigenous Californians, especially in the postmission era"—Provided by publisher.

Identifiers: LCCN 2022021901 | ISBN 978-0-8061-9076-1 (hardcover)

Subjects: LCSH: Vallejo, Mariano Guadalupe, 1808–1890. | California—History—To 1846—Biography. | Pioneers—California—Biography. | Mexicans—California—Biography. | Military governors—California—Biography. | Frontier and pioneer life—California. | California—History—19th century—Biography.

Classification: LCC F864.V2 B44 2023 | DDC 979.4/03092—dc23/eng/20220629

LC record available at https://lccn.loc.gov/2022021901

Mariano Guadalupe Vallejo: Life in Spanish, Mexican, and American California is Volume 7 in the series Before Gold: California under Spain and Mexico.

The paper in this book meets the guidelines for permanence and durability of the Committee on Production Guidelines for Book Longevity of the Council on Library Resources, Inc. ∞

1 2 3 4 5 6 7 8 9 10

To
ROBERT A. CLARK AND CHARLES E. RANKIN

We are forever grateful to them for their mentorship, support,
and especially their friendship.

Contents

Illustrations

Maps

Preface

As we were organizing our project to translate Mariano Guadalupe Vallejo's "Recuerdos" a number of years ago, Charles Rankin, then editor-in-chief of the University of Oklahoma Press, offered us a caution and an opportunity. The caution stemmed from the scope of the project. He told us that given the length of Vallejo's "Recuerdos," more than 400,000 words, the press would need to publish it in two volumes, and that most of the space in those volumes would necessarily be taken up by Vallejo's own words. As a result, we would be unable to include the number of annotations that we judged would be necessary to assist contemporary readers in contextualizing and understanding what Vallejo was saying. But, he continued, this presented an opportunity for us to offer comments on the "Recuerdos" and on Vallejo's life in a more organized fashion than conventional annotations would allow. He suggested we consider a companion volume of essays that would not only contain the material that would have appeared in our annotations, but extend our treatment into an examination of the significance of Vallejo's entire life and career. We immediately told Chuck that his suggestion appeared to us to be right on the mark.

This volume is the result of that conversation. We do not intend it to be a biography of Mariano Guadalupe Vallejo. Rather, we offer reflections on those aspects of Vallejo's life and career that we think have particular significance for the study of nineteenth-century California and what is now the American Southwest.

As we describe in our preface to the translated *Recuerdos*, Vallejo wrote his work in cooperation with Hubert Howe Bancroft's project. Bancroft was interested in the oral testimonies of people who had lived in Mexican California, but he was not especially concerned about their experiences after the American conquest in 1846. As a result, the testimonios his staff collected generally tended to conclude at the time of the American takeover. In his "Recuerdos," Vallejo managed to extend that final date by a few years, enough to give him time to mention the gold rush and criticize the California Land Act of 1851 in his final chapter. But the overwhelming majority of his material dealt with Alta California when it was part of Mexico. Vallejo, as a major participant in the region's military and political affairs, had much to say about life in Mexican California.

Yet in 1846 Vallejo's life was only half completed. When Bancroft contacted him in 1874, he had become one of the best-known people of Mexican origin in California. He had participated in a number of the founding events of American California, especially the 1849 Constitutional Convention and the first session of the legislature in 1850. He had testified as a star witness in a number of the land cases of the 1850s. Yet his renown did not save him from the troubles that afflicted many of his fellow Mexican landowners. The combination of seemingly endless legal expenses, a generalized American disdain for Mexican people, and poor financial choices made by himself and some relatives, especially his American son-in-law, John Frisbie, resulted in a tremendous loss of money and property. By the end of his life Vallejo was reduced to living in a home surrounded by only a few acres of his remaining land.

In this volume we offer essays that we believe shed light on Vallejo and the social realities he confronted in both Mexican and American

California. In the first essay, we situate Vallejo in the context of the activities of his father, Ignacio, who came to California as a soldier in 1773 and served at a number of missions, presidios, and pueblos during a military career that extended into the 1820s. Mariano followed his father into the military and quickly became an important participant in three sets of activities that defined public life from 1821 into the 1830s. First, the Mexican military presence in Alta California was not very substantial, and the soldiers who served there often found themselves not receiving the compensation they had been promised. This led to unrest within the military and a series of mutinies, one of which ensnared Vallejo himself. Second, Alta California's status after 1824 as a territory in the Mexican Republic meant that certain political posts, especially representatives in various assemblies, needed to be filled. Volunteers for such positions were not always plentiful, and the result was that military personnel like Vallejo were often conscripted as members of political bodies. Thus, Vallejo found himself involved in the political unrest that wracked the territory during the early 1830s. Third, as ranchos were granted to retired soldiers, including Vallejo's father, the Mexican footprint in California was being extended beyond long-standing mission boundaries. The rancheros needed laborers, and various military-led expeditions to obtain Indigenous laborers from among people who had left the missions or who were living in the Central Valley became more common. At the same time various Indigenous groups in the Central Valley raided horses from the ranchos and the missions, which also increased tensions between the Mexican-held regions and Indigenous territories. Vallejo himself led two expeditions into the Central Valley in 1829. He was one of the few people in California who was involved in both military and political unrest as well as struggles against the Indigenous peoples. This in itself made him a leading figure, and his experiences during this period throw significant light upon the development of society in Mexican Alta California.

In the second essay, we examine the beginning of Vallejo's role as a colonizer in the North Bay region. Here, as elsewhere in

California, "colonization" meant seizing Indigenous land, and Vallejo was an active participant in such endeavors. An 1833 journey to the Russian settlement at Fort Ross gave him familiarity with the North Bay and its Indigenous populations. The contact he made with various Indigenous leaders brought him into conflict with the local missionaries, and he was able to leverage both the contacts and the conflicts to establish an alliance with one important Indigenous leader, the Suisun Patwin chief Sem-Yeto, known by his Christian name, Francisco Solano. Vallejo's plans, and the plans of many other local Californios, were temporarily thwarted by the arrival from Mexico of a colonizing party led by José María Híjar and José María Padrés. The Californio leadership feared the influence of this group would make it impossible for them to take control of the lands that were going to become available when the missions were secularized. The ability to exploit land and labor was a crucial determinant of power in Mexican California. The conflict against the Híjar-Padrés party forced Vallejo and others to articulate more clearly the reasons they believed they, rather than the Indigenous people, were entitled to the mission lands.

The third essay deals with Vallejo's experiences with the Indigenous peoples of the North Bay and Central Valley. His relationship with Solano allowed him to struggle against a group he called the Satiyomi and other Indigenous groups who did not accept his claim to be the preeminent landowner in the North Bay. Vallejo's preoccupation with affairs in the north meant that he did not actively participate in the Californios' resistance against Governor Mariano Chico, who was imposed on them by the central government in 1836. After the expulsion of Chico, he did not offer significant assistance to the Californio successor, Juan B. Alvarado, in his struggles to assert his authority in the southern part of Alta California. Vallejo's reluctance to participate in these affairs resulted in a rupture between himself and Alvarado and was partially responsible for Alvarado's decision to grant land to a potential rival of Vallejo's, John Sutter, in 1840. The arrival in 1842 of Governor Manuel Micheltorena, whom Vallejo supported, and the resistance to his rule by many Californios only exacerbated the political tensions that had divided northern and southern Alta California since the mid-1830s. These tensions revolved around the distribution of power, specifically the power to direct the allocation of formerly Indigenous land.

In the fourth essay, we examine the American takeover of Alta California in 1846. This event was preceded by the Bear Flag revolt, in which a group of recently arrived Americans arrested Vallejo and held him as a prisoner at Sutter's Fort for a few months. Vallejo had already formed relationships with some American military personnel, notably Captain John Montgomery, who helped to secure Vallejo's release after the outbreak of war between the United States and Mexico became known in California. For the first few years of American occupation, these relationships worked very much to Vallejo's advantage. He served in the Constitutional Convention and the first legislature and became involved in a number of schemes to improve the value of his North Bay holdings by, among other things, locating the California state capital in that region. His early success in dealings with Americans gave Vallejo an overly optimistic assessment of his ability to prosper in U.S. California.

In the fifth essay, we examine the undoing of that overly optimistic assessment. We discuss Vallejo's dealings with the Land Commission and focus on a few of his minor land grants and on the land grant claimed by Guadalupe Vásquez, widow of American settler Mark West. In these cases Vallejo, as a Mexican, ended up being treated much more negatively than some Americans whose claims derived from his. These experiences symbolized the profound struggles in which most Mexican landowners were forced to engage, in what turned out to be a vain attempt to preserve their holdings.

In the sixth essay, we examine Vallejo's experiences as an increasingly landless Mexican in U.S. California. His finances were often handled by John B. Frisbie, who had married his eldest daughter, Epifania. Frisbie sometimes engaged in speculations of his own using Vallejo's money, and many of them did not pan out. Vallejo was forced to mortgage his house and to gain a little bit of disposable income by selling water from a spring on his property to the city of Sonoma. Frisbie took him on business trips to New York City and Mexico, but Vallejo himself profited little from these enterprises. By the mid-1880s he was sometimes dependent upon a small allowance that Frisbie, now living in Mexico, occasionally sent him. His financial decline was symbolic of a larger, racially based trend, as many of his old friends and colleagues were being forced to the margins of Anglo society.

In the seventh essay, we examine a claim that Vallejo made repeatedly in his "Recuerdos." He argued that the conventional American assessment of the Californios as an uncultured lot who had little regard for the education of their children was false. We examine the richly communal culture of Mexican California, a culture that Americans who were raised on "rugged individualism" could not appreciate. We also examine the many ways in which Californio authorities on the territorial and local levels attempted to set up functioning school systems and the tremendous importance they placed upon the education of their children. The failure of many of these efforts was due to the consistently poor condition of California's finances and the failure of the Mexican government to provide sufficient resources for the territory. Overall, Vallejo's insistence upon the importance of culture and education in early California was accurate and pointed out a much-neglected aspect of life in California before the gold rush.

In the eighth essay, we use the correspondence between Vallejo and his wife, Francisca Benicia, to examine how the hardships that many Californios were experiencing in American California affected the social dynamics of this family. In particular, we focus upon the efforts of Francisca Benicia to manage the family estate at the same time as she was raising a number of children without adequate income to provide for them. Her efforts were not always well received by her husband, who expected her to maintain a more traditional and passive role. But Francisca Benicia wanted to assume what she perceived to be the more assertive role that women played in American families. These contradictory desires on occasion caused considerable tension as the family struggled to adapt to an entirely new social milieu.

We hope that these eight essays throw light not only upon Mariano Guadalupe Vallejo but also upon the societies in which he lived before, during, and after the American conquest of California. We hope that the Bibliography and Suggestions for Further Reading we provide at the end of this volume enable interested readers to discover more about Vallejo and this formative era in California's history.

Finally, we thank Charles Rankin for suggesting that we write these essays, and we are extremely grateful to Albert Hurtado and James Sandos for their incisive comments on an earlier draft of them.

Acknowledgments

During the many years that Mariano Guadalupe Vallejo has been a major presence in our lives, we have been fortunate to benefit from much support and assistance from scholarly associations and communities. Our engagement with Vallejo began in earnest during the 2012–13 academic year, when Rose Marie received a fellowship from the National Endowment for the Humanities. She spent that year transcribing the "Recuerdos" and preparing a preliminary translation of many parts of it. The Huntington Library awarded both of us Mayers Fellowships in early 2016, which enabled us to consult a wide variety of primary source material relating to nineteenth-century California.

Our primary research home was The Bancroft Library in Berkeley. That institution houses Vallejo's "Recuerdos," his own and his family's papers, and many other documents created by people of Spanish, Mexican, Indigenous, and American descent that illuminate many aspects of Vallejo's activities. Bancroft Director Elaine Tennant, Interim Director Charles Faulhaber, Associate Director Peter Hanff, Curator of the Bancroft Collection Theresa Salazar, and Curator of Latin Americana José Adrián Barragán-Alvarez were unfailingly generous in allowing us access to these collections and helping us track down relevant material to complete our research. Collections Manager Lorna Kirwan provided invaluable assistance with obtaining images. Diana Vergil's office support was outstanding. Fellow researcher Kim Bancroft offered support and sage advice. We are tremendously grateful that all these professionals believed in this project and willingly helped us bring it to publication.

Tracking down information on Vallejo led us to many historical societies and archives. The staffs at these institutions were uniformly excited about the project, generous with their time and expertise, and willing to help us locate important documents and graphics. As he has done for us in the past, Peter Blodgett navigated us through the tremendous repository at the Huntington Library. At the Santa Bárbara Mission Archive-Library, Mónica Orozco, Brittany Bratcher, Bryan Stevenson, and Rebecca Vásquez helped us locate items in several important collections. At the California Historical Society, Marie Silva, Erin García, and Debra Kaufman skillfully guided us through those extensive holdings. The California State Parks repository at the Sonoma Barracks proved to be a rich resource to which Carol Dodge and Ronnie Cline provided us informative access. Patricia Keats assisted us in locating important sources at the Society of California Pioneers. George Miles gave us a thorough introduction to the Beinecke Library. Because the final phases of our research and writing occurred when most libraries and repositories were closed due to COVID-19, digital providers, notably the Internet Archive and the California Digital Newspaper Collection at the University of California, Riverside, were crucial resources.

At Santa Clara University, indispensable and wonderful financial support from President Michael Engh, SJ, enabled us to obtain and publish the large number of images we have included. We also benefited from timely encouragement from Provost Lucia Gilbert. In addition, Nadia Nasr, Erin Louthen, and Kelci Baughman McDowell of Archives and Special Collections provided their typical prompt and pertinent aid.

We also received outstanding support from staff members at a number of institutions we contacted electronically. These dedicated people included Marilyn Van Winkle at the Autry Museum of the American West, Marie Silva at the California Judicial Center Library, Sara Cordes at the California State Library, Jordan Leininger at Colton Hall, Kevin Kiper at the Diocese of Monterey, Holly Hoods at the Healdsburg Museum, Catherine Mills at History San José, Daniel Keough at the Los Gatos Library, Michelle M. Frauenberger at the Franklin D. Roosevelt Presidential Library and Museum, Tina Zarpour at the San Diego History Center, Dacia Harwood at the Santa Bárbara Historical Museum, John Cahoon at the Seaver Center for Western History Research in Los Angeles, Zayda Delgado at the Sonoma County Library, Jim Kern at the Vallejo Naval and Historical Museum, and Marcia Stock and Deya Terrafranca at the Ventura County Research Library and Archives.

We are grateful also for generous assistance from other scholars who helped us find sources, commented on earlier drafts, and supported us in a variety of ways. These include Antonia Castañeda, Iris Engstrand, Janet Fireman, Judy Fireman, Albert Hurtado, Molly McClain, Martha McGettigan, Louise Pubols, Rosaura Sánchez, James Sandos, Patricia Sandos, and Sam Stein. Tom Jonas's well-rendered maps greatly enhance these volumes.

At the University of Oklahoma Press, we appreciate the editorial advice of Charles Rankin, Adam Kane, and Kent Calder. Joseph Schiller provided excellent editorial assistance. Steven Baker's production process was, once again, peerless. We were fortunate to have the collaborative team of John Thomas and Kirsteen E. Anderson, who both improved the manuscript with superb copyediting. We are grateful for the creativity of Ariane Smith in book design.

We also are indebted to personal friends. Karen Valladao's financial gift was part of what allowed us to accept the Huntington Fellowship. Larry Gould put us in touch with Susan Futterman and Arnie Siegel, who provided excellent accommodations for our stay in Pasadena. Leslie Crail's delectable dinners always raised our spirits and satisfied our appetites. These and so many others were always at our side to lift us up at those times, familiar to all authors, when our energies ebbed.

Finally, we gratefully acknowledge the following repositories and private collectors who allowed us to use their resources to paint a more complete picture of Mariano Guadalupe Vallejo and his world: Raymond Aker; Archivo General de Indias; John Carter Brown Library; California State University, Monterey Bay; Cornell University Library; DeGolyer Library of Southern Methodist University; Georgetown University Library; Hartnell College Foundation; Indiana State Museum; Library of Congress; Museo de América; Museo Naval; David Newman; Oakland Museum of California; Peabody Museum at Harvard University; San Francisco Public Library; Santa Barbara Courthouse Legacy Foundation; Scientific Research Museum of the Academy of Arts of Russia; and University of Southern California.

All these people and institutions demonstrated to us yet again that scholarship is a community affair, and we feel deeply privileged to be members of communities that include each one of them.

Last but hardly least, we thank our two canine supervisors—first Ollie, then Cody—who never failed to remind us that a good day would always begin with a tummy rub and treats!

Abbreviations

CMD	California Mission Documents, Santa Bárbara Mission Archive-Library
DLG	De la Guerra Collection, Santa Bárbara Mission Archive-Library
DLGV	De la Guerra Collection: Vallejo, Santa Bárbara Mission Archive-Library
CHS	California Historical Society, San Francisco
HL	Huntington Library
MGV	Mariano Guadalupe Vallejo
SBMAL	Santa Bárbara Mission Archive-Library
TBL	The Bancroft Library

MARIANO
GUADALUPE
Vallejo

Soldado de cuera and *Mujer de un soldado*, 1791, by José Cardero
Courtesy of the Museo de América, Madrid. Inv. nos. 02285 and 02286.

CHAPTER I

"The State of the Country"
Vallejo and the First Decade of Mexican California

Mariano Guadalupe Vallejo was a leading figure in Mexican California (1821–48) and a man whose experiences after 1848 in many ways reflected the pain and travails of the Mexican population in American California, but his own Californio roots stretched back almost to the beginning of Spanish occupation. After Junípero Serra prevailed upon Viceroy Antonio María de Bucareli y Ursúa to remove Pedro Fages from his position as military commander of Alta California in 1773, Fernando de Rivera y Moncada was appointed to the position. Rivera y Moncada, a native of Compostela in northwestern New Spain, recruited people from that region for military service in Alta California. One of those recruits was Ignacio Vallejo, Mariano's father.

Ignacio Vallejo had been born into a locally prominent family in the town of Las Cañadas, outside of Guadalajara, in 1748. He apparently studied for the priesthood for a time, but gave it up, moved to Compostela, and joined the military there. He may have chosen that location because of the presence of some relatives, for a later nineteenth-century *Atlas mexicano* identified the local mountain range as the "Sierra Vallejo." The location, however, made him available for Rivera's recruitment and he signed up. The Rivera group, eventually totaling fifty-one persons, arrived in Baja California in early 1774. Rivera left most of them in Velicatá with José Francisco de Ortega as he himself hurried to Monterey to assume his command. Ortega, who had recently been promoted to *alférez*[1] and appointed commander of the San Diego presidio, organized the party's journey north. Arriving in San Diego on September 26, some members, including Vallejo, remained there with Ortega while others continued on to Monterey. Ortega reported to Rivera that some of the new recruits had proven difficult to manage and that he had placed one of them, Anastasio Camacho, under arrest. He also warned that others, including Monterey-bound Francisco Lugo, appeared to be on the brink of open rebellion.[2]

Ignacio Vallejo remained at the San Diego presidio until 1776. Ortega reported that Vallejo, along with former prisoner Anastasio Camacho, had performed very well during the Kumeyaay rebellion in 1775. Toward the end of 1776, Vallejo was sent to San Luis Obispo to serve as a carpenter. His skills came in handy, for before he arrived there, the local Chumash set a fire that destroyed part of the complex, although the church itself was not burned. Vallejo worked on the reconstruction of the mission establishment. He occupied a variety of positions over the next few years, serving as *mayordomo*[3] at Mission San Carlos in Carmel and as

---

1. "Alférez" (ensign); the lowest-ranked military officer, was approximately equal to today's rank of second lieutenant.
2. Vallejo gives a somewhat dramatic account of his father's youth in *Recuerdos*, 1:204–8. The 1884 *Atlas mexicano* is online at the Library of Congress, https://www.loc.gov/resource/g4410m.gct00091/?sp=31&r=0.147,0.563,0.7,0.366,0; Mason, *Census of 1790*, 22, 93; Fernando de Rivera y Moncada to Antonio María de Bucareli, March 20, 1774, Junípero Serra Collection, 408a, SBMAL; Bancroft, *History of California*, 1:231; José Francisco de Ortega to Fernando de Rivera y Moncada, October 3, 1774, C-A 1:154–57, TBL; Ortega to Rivera y Moncada, March 8, 1775, C-A 1:149–50, TBL.
3. A "mayordomo" was a foreman or supervisor. He served at a mission under a priest or at a rancho under the owner.

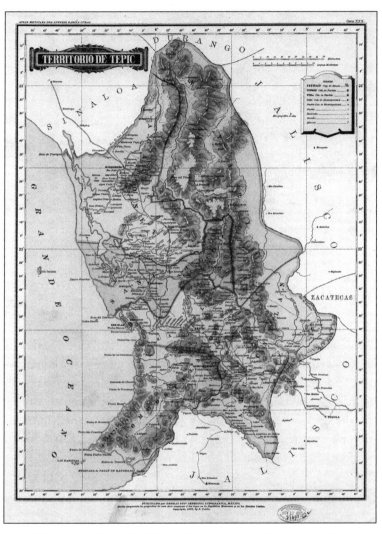

Map of the Sierra de Vallejo, from the 1884 *Atlas mexicano,* by
Antonio García Cubas. *Courtesy of the Library of Congress,*
http://hdl.loc.gov/loc.gmd/g4410m.gct00091

View of the Convent, Church, and Rancherías of the Mission of Carmel,
1791, by José Cardero. Ignacio Vallejo served as mayordomo
here in the late 1770s. *Courtesy of the Museo Naval,*
Madrid. AMN 1723 (4).

comisionado[4] at the Pueblo de San José. In both of these positions
he seems to have been involved in activities related to the construction and development of agricultural infrastructure. Although
his precise military status is sometimes difficult to ascertain, by
1786 he seems to have become an active member of the Monterey
military company, for in that year he was identified as a corporal
of the soldiers stationed at San José.[5]

4. A "comisionado" was a soldier appointed by the presidio commander to serve as a liai-
son between the presidio and the towns or missions in the vicinity. Duties might include
supervising the *alcalde* and exercising military and judicial authority. With secularization,
comisionados also became the temporary supervisors of former missions.

5. Rivera y Moncada, *Diario del capitán comandante Fernando de Rivera y Moncada,* 2:436;
Bancroft, *History of California,* 1:255, 299, 428; Engelhardt, *Mission San Luis Obispo,*
34–35; San Luis Obispo Marriage 50, November 30, 1776, in which Vallejo served as a
witness and was identified as a carpenter; San Luis Obispo Baptism 382, September 6,
1779, in which he was godfather and identified as mayordomo. Unless otherwise specified,
all sacramental records were taken from the Early California Population Project at the
Huntington Library.

However, his behavior created discord with the residents of the pueblo. In August 1786 Governor Pedro Fages ordered him to "separate himself completely" from the "daughter of González." She was probably María Gregoria González, daughter of José Manuel González, one of the original settlers of the pueblo. The year before, María Gregoria had married soldier Manuel Mendoza. The governor's order apparently did not stop Vallejo's behavior, and the pueblo residents renewed their complaints. In October 1787 Fages sent inspector Nicolás Soler to San José. Soler reported that Vallejo's "criminal relationship" with the married woman was affecting his ability to discharge his duties; therefore, he recommended that Vallejo be punished by being assigned to menial tasks or being sent to the countryside.[6]

Vallejo was assigned to serve on the mission guard at remote Mission Soledad, but by the mid-1790s he was back at San José. In late 1796 he became involved in the constant disputes between San José and Mission Santa Clara over the use of the land between them. Santa Clara missionary Magín Matías Catalá complained to the governor that Vallejo and another soldier, Gabriel Moraga, had insulted him during a heated discussion. The governor, Diego de Borica, apologized for their behavior but asked Catalá to remember that these soldiers "did not receive their education in the school for the nobility or in a Roman college." He said that he would order both men to go to the mission and personally apologize to the priest. Later, in 1797, Vallejo organized a group of twenty men from the San José area to be part of a military force that attacked a number of Indigenous villages in the East Bay across from San Francisco and took a number of prisoners. In 1799 Vallejo was appointed comisionado of the Pueblo de Branciforte near Mission Santa Cruz. He appears to have remained in that position

6. Pedro Fages to Ignacio Vallejo, August 11, 1786, C-A 44:12, TBL; Hittell, *History of California*, 1:531; Font, *With Anza to California*, 342; Santa Clara Marriage 103, July 2, 1785; Mason, *Census of 1790*, 35, 95; Nicolás Soler to Pedro Fages, October 17, 1787, C-A 4:132, TBL.

until 1805, when he was promoted to sergeant and returned to the Monterey presidio.[7]

By this time Vallejo was the head of a growing family. In 1791 he had married fourteen-year-old María Antonia Lugo, daughter of his old military companion, the disobedient Francisco Lugo. Their first child was born the following year. By the time Ignacio and María Antonia returned to Monterey from Santa Cruz around 1805, she had given birth to seven children. Their eighth child, Mariano Guadalupe, was born in Monterey on July 4, 1807.[8]

As the capital of the province of Alta California, Monterey was the residence of the governor. José Joaquín de Arrillaga held that post from 1802 to 1814. He was a Spanish military officer who had served in Baja California for two decades before arriving in Monterey. Throughout his tenure he was widely respected by leading military and religious figures alike. Soon after he arrived, he noted the dilapidated state of the soldiers' quarters at all four Alta California presidios, as well as the poor condition of the presidios' defenses and artillery. The latter was an obvious problem also noted by William Shaler, an American captain who visited Monterey in 1804. Shaler wrote, "The garrison is situated immediately in the vicinity of the anchorage, where they have no works capable of affording defense." Perhaps Vallejo's return to Monterey from Branciforte and his promotion to sergeant may have been influenced by the new governor's desire to bring a soldier with experience in construction to the presidio so badly in need of repair. Arrillaga also encouraged Vallejo to set himself up for an additional promotion. In 1806 Vallejo asked his brother Juan José, a priest in the Diocese of Guadalajara, to organize a legal process to prove his *limpieza de sangre*, or pure Spanish lineage. Three witnesses testified that they personally knew his parents and grandparents and were thus able to vouch for his ancestry. On the

---

7. Diego de Borica to Magín Matías Catalá, January 7, 1797, C-A 24:179–80, TBL; Ignacio Vallejo to Diego de Borica, July 13 and July 20, 1797, C-A 8:338, TBL; Milliken, *Time of Little Choice*, 289; Bancroft, *History of California*, II:499, 710–11.

8. Northrop, *Spanish-Mexican Families*, 1:350–52; Mutnick, *Some Alta California Pioneers*, 3:1178–80.

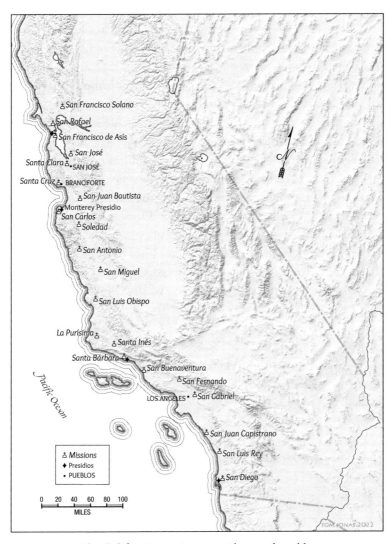

Alta California missions, presidios, and pueblos
Map by Tom Jonas

basis of this proceeding, Arrillaga promoted Ignacio to the rank of *sargento distinguido*,[9] the title he retained for the rest of his life.[10]

In light of Vallejo's role in constructing improved presidio defenses, it was probably no accident that his second son, José de Jesús, joined the Monterey company in the mid-1810s and focused on artillery. One of the main objectives of the presidio artillery was to provide protection from naval attacks. Indeed, when Monterey was attacked in 1818 by Hipólito Bouchard, a French privateer sailing under authorization from the forces of Argentinean commander José de San Martín, José de Jesús Vallejo manned a makeshift artillery battery on the beach. His brother Mariano, eleven years old at the time and nowhere near the battery himself, later recounted the family tradition, writing, "Don José de Jesús Vallejo aimed his culverins at the frigate. His volleys were so accurate that numerous holes were made on the water line." José de Jesús became so wrapped up in his success that he ignored an order to cease firing and only obeyed when his father personally came from his own post and commanded him to do so. The attackers were eventually able to put a landing party ashore beyond artillery range and take possession of the city. Young Mariano and his family had to evacuate and retreat inland. Years later he recounted the family's experiences as they fled:

> My good and venerable mother (may she rest in peace) found a spot for herself in a carreta lined with two cowhides on the bottom. Two other hides served as a canopy. After having eaten some unsalted beef jerky that was partially roasted, she surrounded herself with her entire family, which consisted of Juana, Magdalena, Encarnación, Rosalía, Salvador, and myself. A half dozen blankets she had received from Father Florencio at Mission Soledad were all we had for bedclothes. Some of us were seated, others were stretched out on the hides, some were crying

---

9. "Sargento distinguido" means distinguished sergeant.

10. Bancroft, *History of California*, 2:205–7, 615–16; Arrillaga, *Diary of His Surveys*, 16–20; José Joaquín de Arrillaga to José de Iturrigaray, July 19, 1806, C-A 23.339–40, TBL; Shaler, "Journal of a Voyage," 157; "Informe de legitimidad y limpieza de sangre de Don Ignacio Vicente Ferrer Vallejo," C-B 1, doc. 1, TBL.

because of the cold, while others were shivering, and my poor mother was taking care of everybody with infinite patience.

After Bouchard sailed south, the residents returned to Monterey, parts of which had been badly burned. Governor Pablo Vicente de Solá put Ignacio Vallejo in charge of rebuilding the pueblo. Six years later, in 1824, Governor Luis Antonio Argüello granted Vallejo Bolsa de San Cayetano, a tract of land outside of Monterey on which he had been keeping some cattle. This governor was a former soldier who had, in the 1810s, supervised the reconstruction of the San Francisco presidio, and he probably greatly appreciated Vallejo's construction expertise when he took up residence in Monterey in 1822.[11]

Given his father's and brother's careers as soldiers, it was probably preordained that Mariano Guadalupe would enter the military. He formally applied for enlistment as a cadet in the Monterey presidio company on December 31, 1823, and Governor Argüello immediately accepted him so that his service could begin the very next day. Mariano progressed steadily through the ranks, being promoted to corporal in 1825 and sergeant the next year. In July 1827 he was promoted to the rank of alférez and assigned to the San Francisco presidio—quite an achievement for someone who had just celebrated his twentieth birthday. His quick ascent was at least partially due to the fact that the Alta California military was already stretched quite thin due to the small number of people willing to serve in it. The fact that pay was both meager and irregular during the early years of Mexican independence was a major reason for the difficulties in recruitment. The situation at times got so difficult that convicted criminals were sentenced to serve in military companies as punishment. Vallejo participated in a legal proceeding in which the mayordomo of Mission San Gabriel was sentenced to six years of military service after being convicted of

11. Ignacio and María Antonia's eldest son, José Ignacio, was a sickly youth who died in 1826 from a "long illness" (San Carlos Death 2564, March 1, 1826); Uhrowczik, *Burning of Monterey*; MGV, *Recuerdos*, 1:176, 202, 204; Osio, *History of Alta California*, 30–39; Ignacio Vallejo to Luis Antonio Argüello, January 28, 1824, Vallejo Family Papers, C-B 441, box 6, folder 6, TBL; Aviña, *Spanish and Mexican Land Grants*, 39.

killing another man. Due to the lack of military officers, Santiago Argüello, who nominally held the rank of alférez at San Francisco, had been serving for some time at the San Diego presidio, and Vallejo's promotion was designed to have him fill Argüello's vacant post in San Francisco. However, this did not occur immediately.[12]

Military service was not the only occupation that suffered from a dearth of recruits in Alta California during its early years as a Mexican territory. Initially, there was also a considerable lack of interest in filling various political positions that Alta California's new status in the Mexican Republic required. The Mexican Constitution of 1824 designated Las Californias as a territory to be governed by an appointed governor complemented by an elected *diputación*.[13] José María Echeandía, an engineer in the Mexican Army, was appointed governor in 1825. The first governor appointed under the new constitution, Echeandía represented the liberal side of President Guadalupe Victoria's administration. He was instructed to initiate the preliminary steps of a process that was intended eventually to secularize all the Alta California missions. When he arrived in the territory, he decided to make his residence in San Diego, since he preferred the weather there to the cooler and more unsettled climate of Monterey. At the end of 1826 Echeandía ordered the selection of a body of electors who were to choose members of the Diputación. The electors gathered in San Diego in February to perform that task. Echeandía then headed north to the capital of Monterey, and the Diputación began to meet there in June 1827. By September, however, five of the original seven members had drifted away, so the Monterey Ayuntamiento[14] chose temporary replacements for them. The recently promoted Vallejo, who had not yet gone to San Francisco, was one of those chosen.[15]

---

12. MGV to Luis Antonio Argüello, December 31, 1823, C-B 1, doc. 3, TBL; Tays, "Vallejo and Sonoma," part 2: 216; José Mariano Estrada, "Hoja de servicio de Mariano Guadalupe Vallejo," December 31, 1827, C-B 19, doc. 55, TBL; MGV, *Recuerdos*, 1:292–93.

13. A "diputación" was an elected assembly.

14. An "ayuntamiento" was a municipal corporation in charge of administering and governing a town, similar to a town council.

15. Bancroft, *History of California*, 3:36; Geary, *Secularization*, 102–4; Tays, "Vallejo and Sonoma," part 2:216.

After Echeandía returned to San Diego, Vallejo served as treasurer and paymaster of the Monterey presidio. In addition, when Echeandía summoned the Diputación to meet in San Diego and Presidio Commander José Mariano Estrada went south to attend that meeting, Vallejo became the acting commander of the presidio. This was not an easy time for him, since a number of soldiers mutinied in early October because they had not been paid. Recently arrived Romualdo Pacheco was able to end the mutiny, and when Estrada returned early the following year, Vallejo resumed his role as alférez. He remained in Monterey and soon became involved in two controversial expeditions against Indigenous people.[16]

By the mid-1820s relations between Spanish soldiers and missionaries on the coast and the Indigenous people of the Central Valley, east of the foothill ranges, had been contentious for well more than two decades. Mission San José had been founded just west of the foothills in 1797, and by 1804 elements of most of the Indigenous groups in the surrounding vicinity had entered the mission. As was the case with all missions, not everyone chose to remain affiliated. In January 1805, Father Pedro de la Cueva, mission mayordomo Ignacio Higuera, two soldiers, and a small group of Mission San José neophytes went out to seek some people who had left the mission and were allegedly ill in the Asirin *ranchería*,[17] on the east side of the coastal foothills. They were attacked when they entered the neighboring Luecha territory, and Higuera and three of the neophytes were killed. In retaliation, a party under Luis Peralta went out to Luecha territory in January and again in February. The party killed at least ten people and brought back another thirty as captives. From then on, military expeditions toward the east to recover neophytes who had left the mission (always described as "fugitives") were a regular feature of life at

16. Bancroft, *History of California*, 3:66–67; Tays, "Vallejo and Sonoma," part 2:218–19; Osio, *History of Alta California*, 87–88.

17. A "ranchería" was an Indian village or settlement. The Spanish usually used the term to refer to a settlement of non-Christian Indians.

The Mission of S. José, California, ca. 1826–1827, by William Smyth. Courtesy of The Bancroft Library, University of California, Berkeley. BANC PIC 1979.016-D (sheet 2–3).

Mission San José. During the 1810s the Indigenous peoples of the valley retaliated by organizing their own expeditions to capture horses from the lands of Missions San José, Santa Clara, and San Juan Bautista, as well as from the lands of the Pueblo de San José. Colonial soldiers sometimes claimed that the main reason the Indigenous people wanted the horses was for their meat, but San José missionary Narciso Durán knew better. He told the governor in 1819 that they wanted the horses to battle more effectively against the Spanish and because of their usefulness in chasing game. When Vallejo himself captured the leader of a horse-raiding party almost two decades later, that person told him that the Indigenous people wanted horses "to attack our [Mexican] settlements.[18]

18. Milliken, *Native Americans at Mission San José*, 40–42, 58, 60–61; Bancroft, *History of California*, 2:34–35; Engelhardt, *Missions and Missionaries*, 2:612–13; Cook, *Colonial*

As these expeditions and raids were occurring, Indigenous groups were being incorporated into Mission San José from farther and farther away, sometimes forcibly and sometimes as part of their own survival strategies. Miwok- and Yokuts-speaking people from the Sacramento Delta region began to enter the mission in the first decade of the nineteenth century, and Miwok and Yokuts groups from the Central Valley itself appeared in mission registers during the following decade. By the 1820s six different languages were spoken at Mission San José, but Yokuts people from the San Joaquín Valley were beginning to predominate, both there and at Mission Santa Clara. Indeed, the Yokuts were dividing

Expeditions to the Interior, 267–80; Gray, *Stanislaus Indian Wars,* 33–36; Narciso Durán to Pablo Vicente de Solá, June 2, 1819, CMD, 1723, SBMAL; MGV, "Draft of the Circular on Indian Affairs," August 9, 1838, C-B 5, doc. 124, TBL.

themselves between the two missions, most likely seeking to ensure their prominence at both institutions. During the 1820s, Plains Miwok speakers entered Mission San José in large numbers as well.[19]

The arrival of so many people from outside the original mission territories increased tensions between these newcomers and people, often Ohlone or Coast Miwok, who could trace their ancestry to earlier Indigenous mission inhabitants at Missions San José and Santa Clara. This relatively veteran group was sometimes referred to in Spanish documents as "old Christians." Since the continuing forays into the interior always included these veteran Indigenous mission inhabitants as part of the expeditionary force, the incursions increased tensions between mission and nonmission Indians. In fall 1826, for example, Cosumnes Valley people attacked a group of mission Indians who entered their territory and killed perhaps twenty of them. In response, Mexican troops and a large group of mission Indian auxiliaries attacked the Cosumne ranchería at the end of November and killed more than forty men, women, and children before being forced to retreat.[20]

The 1827 arrival in the Central Valley of an American trapping party led by Jedediah Smith further inflamed this already unstable situation. Within a few weeks of the party's arrival at the American River outside present-day Sacramento roughly four hundred mission neophytes suddenly left Mission San José and headed into the valley. Father Narciso Durán at Mission San José assumed that the Americans were behind this departure. However, the exodus was organized by a veteran and high-status neophyte named Ssaches/ Narciso. He may have suspected that the Americans in the valley might persuade the Miwok and Yokuts people there to attack

19. Milliken, *Native Americans at Mission San José*, 4, 63–65; Skowronek, Thompson, and Johnson, *Situating Mission Santa Clara*, 239.

20. Sandos and Sandos, "Early California Reconsidered," 595, 605, 613–14, 621; San José Baptism 1663, April 1809; Milliken, *Native Americans at Mission San José*, 67; Cook, *Expeditions to the Interior* 166–60; Bancroft, *History of California*, 3:109–10; Ignacio Martínez to Alcalde of San José, October 26, 1826, Pueblo Papers, Object ID 1979-861-0744, History San José.

the mission. If that were to happen, he feared the possibility of an internal attack on the more seasoned neophytes like himself by the more recently arrived Miwok and Yokuts at the mission. The exodus could have been a way of attempting to protect this group. When no such attack materialized, most of the people who had left the mission returned within a relatively short time. In addition, soldier Antonio Soto, who had been sent out by San Francisco presidio Commander Ignacio Martínez to investigate, reported that the trappers were not stirring up the Central Valley Indigenous people against the Mexicans.[21]

The next year, however, Durán was faced with another, more serious desertion of neophytes. In the fall, a mission resident named Cucunuchi, whose Spanish name was Estanislao, and a group of Laquisamne people had refused to return to the mission after an approved visit to their ranchería on the Stanislaus River. They were being joined by a group from Mission Santa Clara under the leadership of a neophyte named Huhuyat/Cipriano. Durán asked Martínez to send out a group of soldiers to try to capture Cucunuchi/Estanislao and Huhuyat/Cipriano "dead or alive." Martínez sent out twenty men under the leadership of Soto to investigate. When Soto reported that Durán's concerns were not overstated, Martínez determined to dispatch a larger and more organized expedition in the spring.[22]

Martínez's determination was heightened by an event that occurred in late winter. Two mission Indians among a group that

---

21. Sandos and Sandos, "Early California Reconsidered," 603, 614, 617, 620–22; Weber, *Californios versus Jedediah Smith*, 28–34; Mission San José Baptism 1663, April 1809 (Ssaches/ Narciso). In the text, we give the Indigenous name of a neophyte, if recorded in the sacramental records, first, followed by the Spanish name the person was given at the mission. There is a good likelihood that the Indigenous name recorded in the sacramental registers bore little resemblance to the person's actual spoken name. The priest was simply trying to transcribe the sounds he was hearing from the Indigenous people at the baptismal ceremony—sounds he normally did not understand—into letter combinations that he hoped provided an approximate Spanish equivalent.

22. Mission San José Baptism 4471, September 24, 1821 (Cucunuchi/Estanislao); Mission Santa Clara Baptism 6297, May 6, 1815 (Huhuyat/Cipriano); Narciso Durán to Ignacio Martínez, November 9, 1928, in Cook, *Expeditions to the Interior*, 169; Osio, *History of Alta California*, 279–80.

was fishing in the valley were confronted by Cucunuchi/Estanislao and a group of his people. The younger of the two, a Yokuts neophyte named Guagmay/Benigno, who was from the same ranchería as Huhuyat/Cipriano, joined Cucunuchi/Estanislao. The older man, a mission *vaquero*[23] named Layum/Macario, had his "horses, saddles, harness, and clothing" taken from him but was allowed to return to the mission. He was told to inform Father Durán that those who had left the mission were planning to organize attacks on the mission lands.[24]

Martínez organized a force to go out into the valley to subdue the rebels. It was led by veteran Indian fighter José Antonio Sánchez. He and his initial detachment departed from San Francisco in May and picked up reinforcements at Missions Santa Clara and San José. His force ultimately consisted of thirty-four soldiers and more than sixty Indian auxiliaries, most likely recruited from the relatively veteran, non-Miwok and non-Yokuts segments of the Indigenous residents of the two missions. The expedition reached the vicinity of the Stanislaus River on May 7. Cucunuchi/Estanislao and his group were well dug in. Sánchez sent a party to seek a way to ford the river and perhaps outflank the Indigenous position. In the meantime, he decided to try to weaken the resolve of the Indigenous party by firing a cannon on their position. However, the cannon immediately malfunctioned and became useless. Cucunuchi/Estanislao appeared on the riverbank and urged Sánchez's Indigenous auxiliaries to desert. When Sánchez himself approached Cucunuchi/Estanislao and sought to talk with

---

23. "Vaquero" or cowboy; in Mexican California, generally described Indigenous people, frequently from Baja California, who tended the large stock herds under the direction of a mayordomo.

24. Narciso Durán to Ignacio Martínez, March 1, 1829, in Cook, *Expeditions to the Interior,* 169; Huhuyat/Cipriano's baptismal record indicated that he came from Pitemas. Guagmay/Benigno's baptismal record (San José Baptism 2694, February 11, 1814) said that he came from Josmite. Milliken, *Native Americans at Mission San José,* 5, indicated that these names referred to the same place, a spot not far from Cucunuchi/Estanislao's home location. Layum/Macario was probably baptized on January 30, 1809 (Mission San José Baptism 1626). He was also Yokuts, but from Cholvon, closer to the mission than Josmite/Pitemas.

him, one of Cucunuchi/Estanislao's men fired at him with a rifle, so Sánchez withdrew to a position farther away.[25]

The next morning Sánchez divided his forces and tried to approach the Indian fortification from multiple directions, but the Indian defenses proved to be more sophisticated and effective than Sánchez and his soldiers were expecting. An elaborate series of breastworks and trenches proved virtually impenetrable. In addition, during the battle that ensued, one of Sánchez's military parties was encircled by Indigenous defenders. Two soldiers were killed and two others were wounded. An additional soldier was captured. At the end of a few hours of fighting, Sánchez withdrew. On the following morning he began his retreat to Mission San José.

Martínez was deeply upset by Sánchez's defeat. Within a week he ordered the alférez of the Monterey presidio—Mariano Guadalupe Vallejo—to assume command of another expedition. Vallejo was a logical choice, for he had recently returned from a military expedition against the Yokuts ranchería of Joyima. Located on the San Joaquín River at the base of the Sierra Nevada foothills about eighty miles east of Monterey, this location was a hub of horse-raiding activity. Joyima was apparently the leading ranchería of a collection of Yokuts groups around the San Joaquín River and Tulare Lake that was raiding horses at ranchos and missions from Monterey to San Miguel. Monterey Sergeant Sebastián Rodríguez had undertaken two expeditions against the region in April and May 1828. Rodríguez stated that he slaughtered more than one hundred horses at Joyima so that the Indians would not be able to eat their meat. He reported that at least five Joyima Indians, two of his soldiers, and six Indian auxiliaries were killed in hostilities during the expedition and that he had captured and brought back at least eighty-five Christian and non-Christian Indians. At the end of May Rodríguez launched another expedition farther south

---

25. This paragraph and the next are based on Sánchez's diary. See Cook, *Expeditions to the Interior*, 173–74. See also Cook, *Conflict between the California Indian and White Civilization*, 229.

into the valley, but this foray was a failure and resulted in the death of one of his soldiers and the wounding of fifteen others.[26]

So the next year, when another expedition against horse raiders from Joyima was ordered, Alférez Vallejo was placed in charge. He set out from Monterey on April 22, with twenty-three soldiers under the general supervision of Sergeant Rodríguez, and thirteen settlers, led by Nicolás Alviso. Vallejo proved himself a harsh Indian fighter. Governor Echeandía reported toward the end of May that the expedition had killed forty Indian men and eight Indian women, a number far in excess of what Rodríguez had reported from his own expedition the previous year. Missionary Prefect Father Francisco Sarría bitterly complained to Monterey Commander José Estrada of "excesses" that Vallejo had committed on the military foray. Sarría also complained that some of the baptized Indians captured during the expedition were not being returned to their missions. Presumably, they were being forced to labor for soldiers or settlers.[27]

On the basis of this performance, Martínez decided that Vallejo was the man to defeat Cucunuchi/Estanislao. Less than a week after Sánchez returned from his failed attempt to subdue the

---

26. Cook, *Expeditions to the Interior*, 184–85. There are two copies of Vallejo's service record for 1830 in the Vallejo Papers: C-B 20, docs. 275 and 280, TBL. The first copy is signed by Martínez and contains an account of Vallejo's campaign against Cucunuchi/Estanislao. The second copy is unsigned, and one of the two pages contains an account of two expeditions into the Central Valley. We believe this second page is actually from Rodriguez's record and contains the account of his two 1828 expeditions.

27. José de Echeandía to the Minister of War, May 22, 1829, C-A 48:19–20, TBL; Cook, *Expeditions to the Interior*, 187; José Estrada to Francisco Sarría, May 22, 1829, CMD 3198, SBMAL. In his *Recuerdos* (1:163–67) Vallejo stated that his father had undertaken an expedition around Missions San Antonio and San Miguel against an Indigenous war party led by Chalpinich from "Joyuna" in 1818. Vallejo said that in the course of this campaign "those who were taken prisoner were executed since it was not possible to guard them, and it would have been highly inadvisable to set them free." Bancroft correctly observed that no other record of such a venture existed and suggested that Vallejo's account contained "some error of date" (Bancroft, *History of California*, 2:339). Since the missionaries criticized Mariano Guadalupe Vallejo for his campaign against the Joyima people in 1829, we surmise that the 1818 campaign he described in the *Recuerdos* was actually an edited version of what occurred eleven years later, and that the actual expedition was led in 1829 by a Vallejo whose first name was not Ignacio but Mariano.

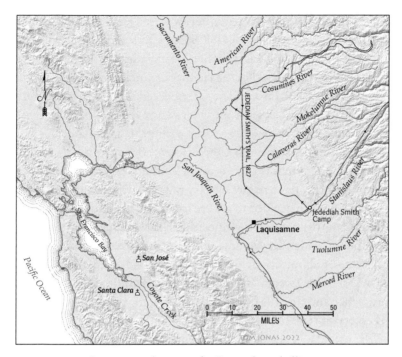

Locations relating to the Estanislao rebellion
Map by Tom Jonas

rebellion, Martínez put Vallejo in charge of another expedition. He ordered him to inflict "total defeat on the Christians who have risen up in rebellion and on the gentiles who are aiding them, teaching them a lesson once and for all." Martínez also made Sánchez second-in-command of the expedition.[28]

Vallejo wasted no time. He left Monterey on May 19, only three days after Martínez had issued his order. He collected men and supplies at Missions Santa Clara and San José. The total force consisted of about 104 soldiers and 50 or more Indian auxiliaries. Reflecting the urgency of the situation and the fact that a number of the rebels were Santa Clara mission Indians led by Huhuyat/

---

28. Ignacio Martínez to MGV, May 16, 1829, C-B 1, doc. 174, TBL.

Cipriano, the Santa Clara auxiliaries were led by Marcelo, a veteran Ohlone resident of Mission Santa Clara and a man who was very close to mission priest Father José Viader.[29]

Vallejo's party arrived in the vicinity of Cucunuchi/Estanislao's encampment on May 29. They discovered that the Indigenous group had moved away from where they had been when Sánchez had fought them a few weeks earlier. At the site of the former encampment however they discovered, as the rebels clearly intended, the remains of two of the soldiers killed in the earlier battle. The troops were met by a barrage of arrows from the dense thickets. Vallejo decided to set fire to the brush in hopes of forcing the Indians to abandon their positions. As the blaze was burning, he ordered his artillery to fire in the general direction of the Indian fighters. At about five o'clock that afternoon he ordered Sánchez to attack with twenty-five men, but the combination of Indian resistance and the still-burning fire eventually forced Sánchez and his party to retreat.[30]

The next day, Vallejo ordered a general advance. The troops were hindered by a series of pikes and trenches even more elaborate than what the Sánchez expedition had previously encountered. The trenches also afforded cover to Indian archers, who were able to wound a number of soldiers. A few Indians were killed or captured during this engagement. At nightfall, the soldiers stopped their advance.

The soldiers resumed their advance before first light the next morning and reached the Indian encampment. Most of the Indians had already left and had positioned themselves in a thicket. They refused to come out or surrender so the soldiers aimed artillery fire in their general direction. After more than an hour of fighting, with no chance of taking the Indian position or capturing the rebel

29. Shoup and Milliken, *Iñigo of Rancho Posolmi*, 91. On Marcelo's closeness to Viader, see MGV, *Recuerdos*, 1:188. Marcelo's Indigenous name was not recorded in the sacramental register, Santa Clara Baptism 1360, June 15, 1789.

30. This account of the expedition is taken mainly from Holterman, "Revolt of Estanislao." The diary of expedition member Joaquín Piña and Vallejo's report are in Cook, *Expeditions to the Interior*, 176–79.

appear before the Fathers, with the guarantee that they will protect them." The magistrates specifically named two Indigenous mission inhabitants, Mateo of Santa Clara and Cucunuchi/Estanislao of San José, as being engaged in this activity. In fact, Cucunuchi/ Estanislao had also successfully cultivated his own allies among the Mexicans. In 1837, Mission San José administrator José de Jesús, Mariano's brother, sent him out as the leader of a force to bring back eleven Indigenous people who had left the mission. Vallejo said the reason for the eleven leaving was that they had become "disgusted" with the way the *alcaldes*[33] were treating them. He identified Cucunuchi/Estanislao as one of those alcaldes.[34]

The scattered reports do not allow us to reconstruct these episodes fully. However, it certainly seems to be the case that by the years immediately preceding and immediately following secularization, hundreds of Indigenous people along with high-status neophytes such as Cucunuchi/Estanislao had gained considerable freedom of movement between the missions and their homelands in the valley. With ranchos already nibbling away at the extensive mission lands, and with would-be rancheros, often soldiers or the children of soldiers, eyeing additional lands, the missionaries did not feel that they could rely on their erstwhile military allies to hunt down "fugitives." The Indigenous people effectively took advantage of this situation. They tragically found these efforts thwarted, however, as a massive smallpox epidemic in the late 1830s killed thousands of people in the valley and a number of non-inoculated mission inhabitants, including Cucunuchi/Estanislao, who passed away on July 31, 1838.[35]

---

33. An (Indigenous) "alcalde" was the highest-ranking neophyte in the mission hierarchy. He was supposed to be elected by the neophytes, and he possessed a real, if limited, authority to supervise mission Indians and maintain order.

34. José Berreyesa, "Report on Encounters with the Indians," July 15, 1830, C-A 27:312–16, TBL; Engelhardt, *Missions and Missionaries*, 3:340; José Manuel Pinto et al. to Ayuntamiento of San José, August 21, 1836, C-A 29:122–23, TBL; José de Jesús Vallejo to MGV, August 21, 1837, C-B 4, doc. 301, TBL. Mateo's Indigenous name is not given in the sacramental records (Santa Clara Baptism 6344, December 9, 1815).

35. Mission San José Burial 5875, August 1, 1838.

Shortly after the legal proceedings that stemmed from the Cucu-nuchi/Estanislao expedition had been concluded, the Monterey presidio experienced another mutiny, as soldiers once again pro-tested their lack of pay. Vallejo recounted that around two o'clock in the morning of November 13, 1829, "Soldiers from the presidio company surrounded the house where I was living with my friends Don Juan B. Alvarado and José Castro." They told Vallejo that they had urgent mail to deliver. When he opened the door, "the house started to fill with armed soldiers. With their carbines posi-tioned across their chests, they suggested that I surrender." Vallejo, Alvarado, and Castro, along with a number of other presidio offi-cials, spent the next three days in jail. Some foreign merchants in Monterey, led by David Spence, negotiated their release. Most of them were allowed to remain in Monterey under the condition that they not oppose the mutiny. Vallejo and another officer, however, were placed on a boat and sent to San Diego. The leader of the revolt, Joaquín Solís, was eventually captured in February 1830 and sent back to Mexico.[36]

Vallejo was in San Diego only for a couple of weeks, but this short time proved important, for while he was there, he met Fran-cisca Benicia Carrillo, daughter of San Diego soldier Joaquín Car-rillo, a native of Baja California who had spent a number of years stationed at the San Diego presidio. After the capture of Solís, Vallejo was sent back north. He stopped in Santa Bárbara, where he assisted in the trial of Father Luis Martínez, accused of complic-ity in the Solís affair. Martínez was convicted and exiled to Peru, then eventually returned to Spain. In April 1830, Vallejo finally went to the San Francisco presidio and served as paymaster there. Meanwhile, his relationship with Francisca Benicia Carrillo was developing. He later recounted that her parents at first "resisted" his desire to marry her but eventually relented. In October he wrote a letter to the Mexican government, asking for permission

36. MGV, *Recuerdos*, 1:383–84; Bancroft, *History of California*, 3:69–85; Tays, "Vallejo and Sonoma," part 2:221–22.

to marry her. The same month he was elected to the Diputación for the session that was scheduled to begin in March 1831.[37]

Before the Diputación could meet, Echeandía was replaced as governor by Manuel Victoria at the end of 1830. Victoria had been appointed by the administration of conservative president Anastasio Bustamante, and he brought a much different sensibility to Alta California than his predecessor had. Whereas Echeandía had begun the process of secularizing some of the missions, Victoria abruptly halted that process and showed himself much more favorable to the missionaries than Echeandía had been. In March he announced that he saw no need to summon the Diputación into session. Vallejo and three other members, Antonio María Osio, José Joaquín Ortega, and José Tiburcio Castro, began a campaign to pressure Victoria into doing so. They eventually wrote letters to the Mexican government, denouncing Victoria and asking that he be replaced.[38]

Victoria angered a number of people in northern Alta California not only by his resistance to the secularization of the missions but also by his intervention in some judicial processes. A case against San Francisco soldier Francisco Rubio, who had been accused of sexually assaulting a young girl and murdering her and her brother, had been languishing since 1828. Victoria ordered that the case be reopened, and Rubio was convicted and executed in August 1831. Vallejo insisted that the signatures of the witnesses implicating Rubio were forged, that "all the inhabitants of San Francisco were certain this poor man was innocent" and that he had died because of Victoria's cruelty. In an unrelated development about a month later, San Francisco Commander Ignacio Martínez resigned from his position and Vallejo became acting commander.[39]

37. Tays, "Vallejo and Sonoma," part 2:222–23; Geiger, *Franciscan Missionaries*, 152; MGV to Benicia Vallejo, June 30, 1858, C-B 441, box 1 folder 3, TBL.

38. Tays, "Vallejo and Sonoma," part 2:224–25; Osio, *History of Alta California*, 106. Hereafter José Joaquín Ortega is referred to as Joaquín Ortega, the name he went by.

39. Bancroft, *History of California*, 3:190–92; MGV, *Recuerdos*, 1:422; Langellier and Rosen, *El Presidio de San Francisco*, 189.

The center of resistance to Victoria's administration was San Diego, where Echeandía was living, allegedly awaiting transportation back to Mexico. Victoria eventually headed south with an armed force, seeking to thwart the opposition, but his opponents also armed themselves, and the forces squared off on December 5, 1830, at Cahuenga, a mountain pass about ten miles northwest of Los Angeles. Victoria was slightly wounded in the battle, and he was soon deported from Alta California. Echeandía called the Diputación to meet in Los Angeles in January. Vallejo, who like many northerners, had not been aware of the full extent of the San Diego opposition to Victoria, hurried south to attend the session. He and Santiago Argüello were appointed to draft a defense of the anti-Victoria activities that would be sent to Mexico City. The Diputación appointed Pío Pico, its most senior member, as temporary *jefe político.*[40] After a week the Diputación adjourned and Vallejo went to see Francisca Benicia Carrillo in San Diego.[41]

Vallejo returned to Los Angeles in time for Pico's formal swearing in on January 27. As the next most senior member of the Diputación, Vallejo administered the oath to Pico. Pico's authority did not last very long, however. Echeandía soon challenged him and, with most of the armed men who had toppled Victoria behind him, gathered considerable support. Echeandía was able to supplement his forces with a group of armed local Indigenous people who had supported his moves to secularize the missions. Meanwhile, many people in northern Alta California rallied around Agustín Zamorano, a Mexican soldier who had accompanied Echeandía to California and was currently serving as commander of the Monterey presidio. Several missionaries in the north apparently supported Zamorano and offered some of their Indian auxiliary forces to him. It soon became clear that Echeandía was the leading

40. A "jefe" is a leader, head, or superior. The term may be followed by adjectives such as *militar, político, principal,* and *superior.*
41. Bancroft, *History of California,* 3:204 8; Tays, "Revolutionary California," 193; Tays, "Vallejo and Sonoma," part 2:226.

figure south of Santa Bárbara and that Zamorano had garnered the most support in northern Alta California.[42]

Even though he was a northerner, Vallejo stayed loyal to Echeandía. When the Diputación adjourned for a week in the middle of February, Vallejo started journeying toward San Diego to spend time with his fiancée, Francisca Benicia Carrillo. While he was passing through San Juan Capistrano, he received the formal letter granting him permission to marry her. The marriage took place in San Diego on March 6. Vallejo later offered in his *Recuerdos* a very melodramatic account of his wedding and the day after. He stated that at the reception Echeandía gave a toast that ended, "My young friend, times of unrest are not the best for getting married. The news I have received today makes it imperative that we move rapidly to the north, and you should accompany the expedition. . . . matters of military service take precedence over everything else." At six o'clock the next morning, Vallejo was summoned to appear before Echeandía and march away. With great sadness he separated himself from his wife of one day and departed. Actually, Echeandía did summon him, but it was to a meeting in San Diego. Vallejo remained with Echeandía in Southern California for the next months, as they prepared for potential conflicts with Zamorano. Word arrived in July that the Mexican government had appointed a new governor, José Figueroa, a Mexican military officer with considerable experience in Sonora and Sinaloa. The two factions in Alta California ceased their preparations for conflict as they awaited Figueroa's arrival.[43]

When Figueroa arrived in Monterey on January 14, 1833, he issued a general amnesty for everyone who had participated in the anti-Victoria movement of 1831 and the factional squabbles in 1832. Vallejo then hurried to Monterey, where he, Alvarado, and Osio met with Figueroa. Vallejo said that Figueroa "entered into

42. The most complete account of these complex political maneuverings is Tays, "Revolutionary California," 172–255; see also MGV, *Recuerdos*, 1:436; Harding, *Don Agustín V. Zamorano*, 90–156.

43. MGV, *Recuerdos*, 1:453–59; Tays, "Vallejo and Sonoma," part 2:227–31.

a discussion with us about the state of the country and the evils
leading it down the road to perdition, as well as the measures we
believed most appropriate for improving the situation of the territory and the condition of the neophytes." Figueroa impressed his
guests when he "took notes on what was being explained to him."
Vallejo summarized the meeting with the comment that all three
of them "were quite taken by the warm welcome they received."
Figueroa's sympathies were indeed more liberal than conservative,
and Bancroft speculated that his appointment may have been an
attempt by the Bustamante administration to move him even farther away from the country's political center. While this was going
on, Francisca Benicia, pregnant with their first child, remained in
Southern California. The child was born on March 14, after which
time she and the baby made their way to San Francisco. There,
they joined Vallejo, who was restored to his post as commander
of the San Francisco presidio. At the age of twenty-five he was
about to become a major actor in the political and military life of
Mexican Alta California.[44]

44. Bancroft, *History of California*, 3:234, 240–42; Tays, "Vallejo and Sonoma," part 2:231;
    MGV, *Recuerdos*, 1:463–65; Los Angeles Plaza Church Baptism 367, April 11, 1833. Unfortu-
    nately, the baby, Andrónico, did not survive his first year: Mission San Francisco de Asís
    Death 5334, January 21, 1834.

CHAPTER 2

"Terrible Cruelties and Injustices"
Indigenous Peoples, Missionaries, and Colonists

When Vallejo returned to the San Francisco presidio in early 1833 he possessed a set of experiences that no one else in Alta California could claim. He had engaged in two campaigns against the Indigenous peoples of the Central Valley. He had been a direct participant in the Diputación and in that body's struggles, in both northern and southern Alta California, to assert its own place in the territory's political developments. He had been directly involved in the three-way struggle among Echeandía, Zamorano, and Pico for the governorship. He had been the object of two mutinies by presidio soldiers. Thus, he was unique among the inhabitants of Alta California for being involved in such a wide variety of events.

It was significant that many of these events related to the military and political instability that accompanied Alta California's transition from Spanish to Mexican rule. Vallejo probably surmised that such instability was bound to increase as the Mexican government moved toward a dramatic reorganization of the mission system. For the next few years, he consciously turned his attention to the north, apparently animated by two desires. First, in the face of potential instability throughout the territory, he sought to create in the hitherto un-Mexicanized north a stronghold in which he might become preeminent. Second, by focusing on an area that contained the two youngest and least developed missions, he put himself in a position to profit from whatever changes Mexico might dictate concerning the missions' extensive landholdings.

The instructions Figueroa had received from the Mexican government upon his appointment were to pay attention to the area north of San Francisco, especially in light of the Russian presence there. Whether or not Figueroa told Vallejo of these instructions, Vallejo was very interested in publicly establishing himself as the point person in dealings with the northern region. On March 31, 1833, he wrote to Figueroa that he had heard the governor of Alaska was about to pay a visit to Fort Ross. Vallejo suggested that a motive for such a visit might be to examine the possibility of an alliance between the Russians and the Indigenous groups of the region, both those who had fled Mission San Rafael and the nonmission people of the Santa Rosa region. Vallejo stated that forestalling this effort would necessarily involve placing "some kind of settlement" in the region. On April 11 Figueroa ordered Vallejo to undertake an expedition to Fort Ross, with the ostensible purpose of procuring some needed supplies from the Russians. Vallejo later recounted that Figueroa had also given him "secret instructions with regard to high politics." This was true, for on the day before he formally ordered Vallejo to head to Fort Ross, Figueroa had sent him a confidential letter. He told Vallejo to scout out the land around Bodega Bay and Santa Rosa, to try to form good relationships with the Indigenous people of those areas, and to determine suitable locations for potential settlements in the region. He also instructed Vallejo to begin the process of identifying potential colonists: "I am also entrusting you with trying to find a few families who might want to move to the frontier. Tell them they will be given land, which they will own and cultivate, and they will be provided with as much assistance as possible. They should be prepared to leave as soon they are given the word." Vallejo left San Francisco around April 23 and returned shortly before May 5, when he submitted his report to Governor Figueroa.[1]

The fact that Vallejo oddly began his report to the governor with his departure from Fort Ross and his journeys through various Indigenous rancherías of the North Bay region indicated that the secret instructions were the issues raised in the confidential letter. Vallejo was above all interested in assessing the capabilities of the Indigenous peoples of the area and their relationships with the missions there and with the Russians. He reported that he first went to Bodega Bay and visited the ranchería of Tiutuye. The unbaptized Indigenous leader of the area, Gualinela, told him that a large group of mission and nonmission Indigenous people under the leadership of Pixpixuecas, a San Rafael mission Indian whose Spanish name was Toribio, was gathering to resist the San Rafael soldiers, who were marauding through the area and forcing the Coast Miwok people into the missions. Pixpixuecas/Toribio was an important figure at San Rafael. He and his wife, son, and mother had been baptized in 1820. He was from the ranchería of Licatiut, along the Petaluma River and was identified in the mission records as a chief (*capitán*) of that place. A bit north of Licatiut lay the ranchería of Petaluma, where Pixpixuecas/Toribio was also well connected, since Leluppi, the woman he married at San Rafael on the same day the family was baptized, had been born there. She was given the Spanish name Toribia.[2]

---

1. Bancroft, *History of California*, 3:325; MGV to José Figueroa, March 31, 1833, C-B 2, doc. 16, TBL; José Figueroa to MGV, April 11, 1833, C-A 20: 94–96, TBL; MGV, *Recuerdos*, 1:469; Hutchinson, *Frontier Settlement*, 219; José Figueroa to MGV, April 10, 1833, C-B 441, box 4, folder 4, TBL.

2. C. Hart Merriam Papers, vol. 1: Papers Relating to Work with California Indians, BANC FILM 1022, reel 7, V/21s/N5, p. 2, TBL; MGV, *Report of a Visit to Fort Ross*, 2–3; Goerke, *Chief Marin*, 134, Milliken, "Ethnohistory and Ethnogeography of the Coast Miwok," 6, 95–96; San Rafael Baptism 383, April 23, 1820 (Pixpixtaul/Anselmo, Pixpixuecas/Toribio's son); San Rafael Baptism 386, May 13, 1820 (Pixpixuecas/Toribio); San Rafael Baptism 387, May 13, 1820 (Leluppi/Toribia, Pixpixuecas/Toribio's wife); San Rafael Baptism 388, May 13, 1820 (Ottacacauic/Engracia, Pixpixuecas/Toribio's mother); San Rafael Marriage 107, May 13, 1820 (Pixpixuecas/Toribio and Leluppi/Toribia).

Misión de San Rafael en 1831, by Mariano Guadalupe Vallejo. Drawn for Edward Vischer in 1878. *Courtesy of the Library of Congress.* CA L-1131-2.

In his report, Vallejo contrasted his own ability to win the confidence of the Native people with their dislike of the priests and soldiers at the mission:

> I spoke persuasively to him [Gualinela]; I instilled him with confidence; I flattered him and managed to have his people speak with me even though they had previously fled in fear, leaving Gualinela there alone. I flattered and lavished attention on the chief in front of everyone, which helped gain his friendship. . . . When he spoke of the treachery of the soldiers, I observed that the natives had indeed been harassed and deceived as much by the soldiers as by the missionaries with their detestable and inconsiderate system of reducing these poor natives to Christianity, violently tearing them away from their homes and transporting them by force to strange lands.

Vallejo was clearly positioning himself and his soldiers (whom he said he had "forewarned" that they should "conduct themselves with moderation and gentleness") as potential replacements for the missionaries and their soldiers. He told the governor that he sent messages to all the inhabitants of the area, both "gentiles and Christian Indians," in which he assured them "that they would not be bothered if they remained peaceful." He claimed that his overtures worked. "They view me as a great captain," he proclaimed. As proof, "they promptly released several corporals who had been wrongfully pursuing them by order of the missionaries." He ended this section of his report with a vigorous denunciation of the mission system as a whole:

> Sr. Comandante General, it is necessary to confess the terrible cruelties and injustices perpetrated against the poor Indians by those entrusted with the administration of justice. The temporal and even greater spiritual harm done to these unhappy people has come from the missionaries who have debased the origins and fundamentals of our Christian doctrines. The result is that the natives now ridicule our attempt at evangelization, lose the truth of our religion, and ignore the true morality of our customs. At the same time, it is imperative to admit that these poor men had reason, as I stated before, to band together in such large numbers and remain in a hostile state. These are the inherent consequences of bad faith, of bad treatment and cruelty by the missionaries, and of the

bloodthirsty system that they introduced, wanting to convince others
that this method is an example of Jesus Christ. What monstrosities!

The overall message in Vallejo's report was clear: when the missions were secularized, Vallejo would be the perfect person to
assume Mexican command of the region.[3]

On his return from Fort Ross in May 1833, Vallejo once again had
to deal with a constant of presidio life in Mexican California: the
lack of pay and the low quality of food provisioned to the soldiers.
He quickly made trips to Missions Santa Clara and San José, seeking to buy supplies, but the situation did not markedly improve.
By September he was writing that the troops were exceedingly
hungry and subsisting on little but corn. The troops grumbled
against him. The governor allowed Vallejo to court-martial some
of them, and a few were transferred to other presidios. These episodes undoubtedly increased his desire to focus on the North Bay,
where he hoped to create an arena in which he would not have to
contend with such annoyances.[4]

Vallejo pressed this desire in other venues as well. On the same
day as he finalized his report, he wrote Figueroa a separate letter
in which he complained that, contrary to regulations, both male
and female neophytes were being routinely whipped at Missions
San Rafael and San Francisco Solano. Over the next few weeks, he
engaged in angry correspondence with the San Rafael missionary,
Father Jesús María Vásquez del Mercado. The missionary wanted
to punish a Coast Miwok neophyte named Ochacataval/Acisclo
for an offense whose nature was not entirely clear. The corporal
at San Rafael thought the punishment was too severe, however,
and kept the Indian under military control and away from the
priest. After a stern lecture to the missionary about the limits
of his authority, Vallejo told the corporal to turn Ochacataval/

3. MGV, *Report of a Visit to Fort Ross*, 4–5, 8–9.

4. MGV to José Figueroa, September 9, 1833, and MGV to Figueroa, September 11, 1833, C-B 2,
    docs. 169f and 169g, TBL; Figueroa to MGV, October 29, 1833, C-B 2, doc. 178, TBL; Figueroa
    to MGV, December 16, 1833, C-B 2, doc. 195, TBL.

Acisclo over to Vásquez del Mercado. When he returned from Missions San José and Santa Clara, he wrote Figueroa that whippings were also common at Mission San José. He said that when he objected, the missionary there had publicly proclaimed to him that the use of whips on the Indigenous people was entirely appropriate. In October, Vallejo told Figueroa that the missionaries were "tyrants" who saw no difference between the Indians being free versus remaining slaves.[5]

In August, Figueroa issued a provisional decree for the gradual emancipation of Indians from the missions. Meanwhile, Vallejo kept pressing his desire to establish himself in the North Bay region and, as Figueroa had instructed him to do in April, quietly gathered potential colonists. By October he had drawn together elements of ten families, approximately fifty persons in all, and sent them to establish settlements in two areas he had reconnoitered during his return from Fort Ross in the spring: a spot along the Petaluma River and at Santa Rosa. He told Figueroa that "Petaluma and Santa Rosa are equally suited for accommodating large numbers of inhabitants." The Petaluma spot was probably near Licatiut, the home of Pixpixuecas/Toribio, with whom Vallejo had established a decent relationship. Most likely Gualinela suggested to Pixpixuecas/Toribio that Vallejo, as a nonmission soldier, might be a useful contact. The Santa Rosa location was in the territory of the Cainamero, a southern Pomo group with whom Vallejo had communicated during his return journey from Fort Ross.[6]

Vallejo accompanied the expedition and remained in the Petaluma location long enough to plant some wheat for himself before returning to San Francisco. The fact that he left the region suggests that he believed he had established a good relationship with

5. MGV to José Figueroa, May 9, 1833, C-B 2, doc. 41, TBL; McNally, "Mariano Guadalupe Vallejo's Relations with the Indians," 98–99; Goerke, *Chief Marin*, 132; San Francisco de Asís Baptism 3482, March 29, 1808 (Ochacataval/Acisclo); Tays, "Vallejo and Sonoma," part 2:233; MGV to José Figueroa, May 31, 1833, C-B 2, doc. 52, TBL; MGV to José Figueroa, October 3, 1833, C-A 53:316–18, TBL.

6. Bancroft, *History of California*, 3:342–44; MGV, *Report of a Visit to Fort Ross*, 5–7; MGV to José Figueroa, October 3, 1833, C-A 53:316–18, TBL.

the Indigenous inhabitants at both Petaluma and Santa Rosa, the Licatiut and Cainamero, respectively, and that he did not have to worry about a negative reaction from the missionaries. He had previously assured Figueroa that Father Quijas at Mission San Francisco de Asís had told him that the matter of jurisdiction over various lands in the north could be resolved amicably in due course. Quijas had just arrived in California a few months earlier with a group of Mexican Franciscans from Zacatecas who had been assigned to take over the missions in northern Alta California. He knew virtually nothing about the missions north of the bay and was most likely simply trying to be accommodating to Vallejo, but the actual missionaries in the north, also newly arrived from Zacatecas, had other ideas. Father José de Jesús María Gutiérrez of Mission San Francisco Solano sent men and horses to the Petaluma River location, and men and hogs to Santa Rosa, in order to disrupt the settlement plans at both places. Vallejo's potential settlers were gone by January.[7]

By that time however Vallejo was already pressing on another front; namely, Pixpixuecas/Toribio. Apparently, Vallejo's overtures through Gualinela had had an effect on the Indian leader, who publicly softened his anti-mission position and even met Figueroa when the governor visited San Rafael in 1833. In addition, he accepted Vallejo's settlers later in the year.[8]

On November 16, Pixpixuecas/Toribio and his son Pixpixtaul/Anselmo appeared at Mission San Rafael with a group of fourteen Cainamero people from the Santa Rosa area, most of whom had been baptized but had apparently left the mission. A Cainamero man named Yitchan/Eulogio told Vásquez del Mercado that they wished to speak to him about "many important matters." Most likely the Indigenous groups suspected that their refusal to expel Vallejo's small colonizing party at Santa Rosa had upset the missionaries. Since there were hundreds of Cainamero and other

7. MGV to José Figueroa, October 3, 1833, C-A 53: 316–18, TBL; Bancroft, *History of California*, 3:255–56.
8. MGV to José Figueroa, January 1, 1834, C-B 2, doc. 255b, TBL.

southern Pomo residents at Mission San Rafael, Pixpixuecas/
Toribio most likely persuaded the Santa Rosa Cainamero that he
could help them smooth things over with Vásquez del Mercado
in order to prevent reprisals against the Cainamero and southern
Pomo mission Indians. Vásquez del Mercado was in no mood to
talk however. He initially told Yitchan/Eulogio that he would
speak to him the next day, but did not do so. On November 19,
ten of the Cainameros who had arrived with Pixpixuecas/Toribio
left the mission vicinity. Vásquez del Mercado reportedly soon
discovered the mission weaving room had been broken into and
all the blankets it contained had been stolen. He blamed the newly
arrived party and quickly arrested the six remaining people, who
included Pixpixuecas/Toribio and Yitchan/Eulogio. He also sent
out a party of twenty men who were able to capture the ten Cainameros who had left the mission. Then Vásquez del Mercado sent
the entire group to be imprisoned at the San Francisco presidio.
He claimed that the group's real aim was to scout out the mission
in preparation for a surprise attack, although it was unclear why
the group would have jeopardized such plans by stealing some
blankets.[9]

Vásquez del Mercado said he learned that Pixpixuecas/Toribio,
Yitchan/Eulogio, and another Cainamero named Bico/Mateo had
instructed three rancherías that they should attack the mission if
the prisoners were not returned from San Francisco by November
25, so he decided to order a preemptive attack. He sent out a force of
thirty-seven men with orders "to contain [the rancherías] in any way
possible." Vásquez del Mercado reported that the soldiers attacked
at a place called Pulia, a Coast Miwok settlement at the mouth of

9. José María Vásquez del Mercado to Comandante del presidio de San Francisco, November
   20, 1833, VA 1, HL. Vásquez del Mercado's list of the members of Pixpixuecas/Toribio's
   party is in VA 206, HL. San Rafael Baptism 1427, November 18, 1826 (Yitchan/Eulogio);
   José Sánchez to José Figueroa, November 21, 1833, VA 3, HL. The fullest account of the
   entire affair is contained in the legal proceedings that Figueroa initiated against Vásquez
   del Mercado: "Causa criminal contra el R. P. Fr. José María Vásquez del Mercado," C-A
   150, part 2, vol. 1, TBL. The quotations from Vásquez del Mercado in this section are taken
   from a letter he wrote to Figueroa on November 25, 1833, which is on pp. 701–4 of this
   document; Goerke, *Chief Marin*, 134–36; Bancroft, *History of California*, 3:323–24.

Salmon Creek on Bodega Bay. If Mercado was correct, then the attacking force may have gone there because the original group that fled San Rafael had headed there. The region was the home of Gualinela, an ally of Pixpixuecas/Toribio's, and the group may have sought refuge with him. They also may have wanted to steer any pursuing group away from their Cainamero home region around Santa Rosa. On the other hand, Vásquez del Mercado had only been in the North Bay for a few months and undoubtedly still had a weak grasp of Coast Miwok and Pomo place-names. Therefore, he may have been mistaken about where the attacking force went, and they may have traveled to Cainamero territory. In that event, they would likely have gone toward Jauyomi, the home of both Yitchan/ Eulogio and Bico/Mateo. Wherever the location was, a two-hour battle ensued. In that engagement, Vásquez del Mercado's forces killed twenty-one of the ranchería inhabitants and brought at least twenty more back to the mission as prisoners.[10]

Immediate denunciation came from Mexican authorities. Figueroa termed Vásquez del Mercado's actions "horrible." Stating that it was a "crime" to kill Indians who had not engaged "in any hostilities at all," he opened a criminal proceeding against the priest. The ranking military officer at San Francisco, José Sánchez, stated that the expedition the priest had sent out was "detrimental because the violence and rigor used against the Indians only insult and cause harm to the gentiles and intensify the resentment that is already present." Vallejo, as the San Francisco officer who had the greatest familiarity with the North Bay region, was ordered to release the prisoners at San Francisco and go to San Rafael to try to calm the Indians whom Vásquez del Mercado's expedition had inflamed. Vallejo took an armed force north with the released prisoners and secured the release of the remaining prisoners from the mission. These surviving prisoners reasonably assumed that

---

10. Merriam Papers, vol. 1; Papers Relating to Work with California Indians, BANC FILM 1022, reel 7, V/21S/N5, p. 2, TBL; Kelly et al., *Interviews with Tom Smith and María Copa,* 7, 12 ("pulya-lakum"). Milliken ("Ethnohistory and Ethnogeography of the Coast Miwok," 98) places Jauyomi on Mark West Creek. San Rafael Baptism 1437, November 18, 1826 (Bico/Mateo).

Pixpixuecas/Toribio had set them up for an ambush. They had already bound up Pixpixuecas/Toribio's mother and nephew and demanded action against him. Vallejo met with a number of mission Indian alcaldes at San Rafael and assured them that Pixpixuecas/Toribio had played no part in Father Vásquez del Mercado's decision to send soldiers against the newcomers. Vásquez del Mercado had told Figueroa that the attacking force had been led by two San Rafael neophytes. The alcaldes however told Vallejo that the person in charge of the attack was mission mayordomo José Molina, whose removal they demanded. When Vallejo returned to San Francisco, he wrote Vásquez del Mercado a strong letter demanding Molina's removal, which appears to have taken place.[11]

Believing that he had settled matters at San Rafael, Vallejo moved on to San Francisco Solano. There, he reported that he "preached an exhortation to the alcaldes and neophytes." He wanted to continue north into Cainamero territory, but Pixpixuecas/Toribio persuaded him that doing so was a bad idea. He told Vallejo that the Santa Rosa inhabitants, smarting from the deadly attack, would refuse to speak with any Mexican. Therefore, Vallejo, hoping that he had convinced enough mission Cainameros that neither Pixpixuecas/Toribio nor the Mexican authorities had been responsible for Vásquez del Mercado's actions, sent some Cainameros north to convey this message to their fellow Indians. He then returned to San Francisco.

Vallejo's visit to San Francisco Solano was significant for another reason besides these negotiations. For it was probably on this visit that he first met Sem-Yeto, a Suisun Patwin whose Spanish name was Francisco Solano.[12] Solano had been forced into the mission

---

11. José Figueroa to Rafael Gómez, December 5, 1833, C-A 38: 130–31, TBL; José Sánchez to José Figueroa, December 9, 1833, "Causa criminal contra el R. P. Fr. José María Vásquez del Mercado," C-A 150, pt. 2, vol. 1:718–21, TBL; MGV to José Figueroa, January 1, 1834, C-B 2, doc. 255b, TBL; MGV to José María Vásquez del Mercado, December 22, 1833, C-A 28:137, TBL.

12. MGV to José Figueroa, January 1, 1834, C-B 2, doc. 255b, TBL. Sem-Yeto was widely known by Indigenous and non-Indigenous people throughout Northern California as Solano, so that is how we refer to him.

system as a result of contacts between Suisun Patwin and mis-
sionized Ohlone in the early 1800s. In January 1804, a group of
fourteen residents of Mission San Francisco de Asís (thirteen of
whom were originally from the East Bay) went on an approved
excursion to the East Bay. From there they headed north, probably
in search of some relatives who had fled the mission and were living
among the Suisun. They never returned. Most likely they either
drowned crossing the Carquínez Strait or, if they reached the other
side, were killed by the Suisun. In 1806, mission Indians fleeing
a measles epidemic at Missions Santa Clara, San José, and San
Francisco may have carried the disease to the Suisun. In January
1807, three couples at Mission San Francisco fled to the Suisun
after the death of the five-year-old son of one of the couples. When
one man's wife either left him or was taken from him, the husband
returned to San Francisco. With the help of the missionaries, he
organized an expedition of mission Indians to recover his wife.
The expedition was a failure, as the Suisun killed twelve of the
expedition members and drove the others away.[13]

The Spanish determined to punish the Suisun. After the Car-
quín people on the south shore of the bay agreed to move to San
Francisco in 1809, there was no buffer left between the Suisun
and the Spanish. In May 1810 an expedition of Spanish soldiers
and Indigenous auxiliaries under the direction of Gabriel Moraga
marched against the Suisun. They killed a number of them and
burned part of a village, then returned to San Francisco with at
least eight boys and six girls as captives. Eleven children in this
group were baptized within a week after the troops returned to San
Francisco. The oldest girl and the two oldest boys, all around the
age of twelve, were apparently given some rudimentary religious
instruction prior to being baptized. The girl was baptized on June
20 and the boys on July 24. One of these boys, whose Indigenous

---

13. Milliken, *Time of Little Choice*, 180–11, 204–8; Milliken, "Ethnographic and Ethnohistoric
    Context for the Archaeological Investigation of the Suisun Plain," 4.

Indians Dancing at Mission San José, 1806,
by Georg Heinrich von Langsdorff. *Courtesy of
The Bancroft Library, University of California,
Berkeley.* BANC PIC: 1963.002:1023-FR.

name was recorded as Sina, was given the Spanish name of Francisco Solano.[14]

Solano grew up at Mission San Francisco de Asís. Twelve years after his baptism he married a woman from the Patwin village of Ululato named Cuyelme, who was given the Spanish name Anastasia. In 1824, along with a large group of Indigenous people originally from the North Bay, they were both moved to San Francisco Solano. Cuyelme/Anastasia died in March 1827. In October of that year Solano married Saquenmupi/Helena of the Aloquiomi group, located on the border of Patwin and Wappo territory near Pope Valley, about forty miles north of Sonoma. She died in 1830, and three years later Solano wed Coulas/Guida, a Topayto woman from the Lake Berryessa area, slightly to the east of Pope Valley. She died sometime after mid-1835.[15]

Francisco Solano's long tenure at Mission San Francisco de Asís helped to make him a leading Indigenous figure at Mission San Francisco Solano soon after his arrival. He was recorded as an "alcalde" by 1825, and he appeared in the mission registers as a godparent or marriage witness on a number of occasions. Yet, his name was clustered in very short time frames, followed by longer absences from the sacramental records. For instance, he was a godparent for three baptisms on October 23, 1825, but then did not assume that role again until March 3, 1826. After that, he attended a flurry of baptisms on June 7, 1826, then disappeared from the registers until December of that year, when he served as a witness for six marriages. He again witnessed marriages in July and December 1827,

14. San Francisco de Asís Baptisms: 4004, June 20, 1810, Geyunchole, given the name Cornelia; 4024, July 24, 1810, Sina, given the name Francisco Solano; and 4025, July 24, 1810, Geunsia, given the name Marcelino. Vallejo reported that Solano's Indigenous name was Sem-Yeto, meaning "brave hand," so this may well have been an honorific (*Recuerdos*, 1:50).

15. San Francisco de Asís Baptism 6192, June 16, 1821 (Cuyelme/Anastacia); San Francisco de Asís Marriage 1984, April 9, 1822, Francisco Solano and Cuyelme/Anastacia; San Francisco Solano Marriage 99, October 12, 1827, Francisco Solano and Saquenmupi/Helena; and Marriage 269, April 26, 1833, Francisco Solano and Coulas/Guida. Coulas/Guida was recorded in a census of Sonoma dated June 4, 1835: C-B 23, doc. 9, TBL. Milliken, "Ethnographic and Ethnohistoric Context for the Archaeological Investigation of the Suisun Plain," 12–13; Milliken, *Time of Little Choice*, 239.

June and July 1828, and June 1829. His periodic extended absences from the sacramental records suggest that he may have been away from the mission for considerable stretches. As we have seen in the case of Cucunuchi/Estanislao, such absences were not unusual for high-status mission residents. In addition, as was the case at other missions in the late 1820s and the 1830s, at San Francisco Solano a large number of neophytes could apparently come and go somewhat frequently. For instance, in June 1833 newly arrived missionary José María Gutiérrez complained that many neophytes there "flee from here to the mountains for fifteen, nineteen, or more days without giving me any notice."[16]

Solano's two marriages to women who came to the mission from Patwin regions a considerable distance from Sonoma give hints of his activity during those absences. While the missionaries undoubtedly assumed that he was recruiting candidates for the mission, he may well have been forging alliances that would enable him to become a leader of a consolidated Patwin force. The Suisun Patwins were surrounded by potentially unfriendly groups, including the Wappo and Pomo to the west and north, respectively. Both Saquenmupi/Helena and Coulas/Guida arrived at the mission roughly a year before their sacramental marriages to Solano. Neither was accompanied by her parents, who were referred to as "gentiles" in the marriage records and were never baptized. These marriages may well have been related to alliances Solano was forming with the rancherías of Aloquiomi and Topayto. When Vallejo met him at the end of 1833, Solano was already a powerful man. Solano quickly realized that Vallejo's desire to capitalize on the mission secularization, which the Californios were confidently expecting, afforded him an excellent opportunity to expand his influence and that of his people.[17]

---

16. Solano's position as alcalde is recorded in San Francisco Solano Baptism 155, October 23, 1825. The dates of Solano's presence at the mission are based on the following: San Francisco Solano Baptisms 155–57, 189, 191–94, and 209–18; San Francisco Solano Marriages 56–60, 68, 77, 80–81, 101–3, 150–52, 167, and 169; José María Gutiérrez to José Figueroa, June 16, 1833, C-A 38:133, TBL.

17. San Francisco Solano Baptism 371, October 12, 1827, Saquenmupi/Helena; San Francisco Solano Baptism 900, March 21, 1832, Coulas/Guida.

View of Fort Ross in 1828, by Auguste Duhaut-Cilly
Courtesy of the Sonoma County Library. Cdm/ref/collection/p15763co112/id7785.

46

At the same time, however, Vallejo and the Californios discovered they had to deal with fallout from political changes in Mexico City. When Antonio López de Santa Anna became bored with the official duties of the presidency to which he had ascended in early 1833, he returned to Veracruz and left power in the hands of Vice President Valentín Gómez Farías. An ardent liberal, Gómez Farías steered mission secularization through the Mexican National Congress. Unbeknownst to the Californios, however, the Gómez Farías administration also decided to combine secularization with an attempt to send a large number of colonists from mainland Mexico to Alta California.[18]

This effort was the culmination of three distinct strands of activity in New Spain and Mexico. Two of the strands had existed for decades, while one was comparatively recent. First, the governments of New Spain and Mexico had continuously desired to increase the population in the northernmost reaches of their territory. This desire led to intermittent, brief spurts of activity at the beginning of the colonization of Alta California, with the Portolá (1769), Rivera y Moncada (1773), and Anza (1774–76) expeditions. After the 1781 expedition that brought settlers to the Pueblo de Los Angeles, activity basically halted. A score of orphans from the Real Casa de Expósitos in Mexico City arrived in 1800, and after Bouchard's 1818 pirate raid, military reinforcements arrived in 1819. Yet, as the new Mexican Republic surveyed its northern border in the 1820s, it became increasingly suspicious of the expansionist entity it called the United States of the North.

Second, beginning in the 1810s, New Spain, and later Mexico, found itself powerless to do anything about the presence of a Russian colony some eighty miles north of the San Francisco presidio. Originally established as a base for otter hunting, Fort Ross had increasingly turned to agriculture and had quickly become an indispensable source of supplies for the Spanish institutions in the San Francisco Bay Area. The Russian presence irritated the government in Mexico City, but not sufficiently to lead to action.[19]

18. Geary, *Secularization*, 146; Bancroft, *History of California*, 3:328–30.
19. Bancroft, *History of California*, 3:247; Hutchinson, *Frontier Settlement*, 1–42, 217–18.

Third, one of the aims of the Mexican Republic in the mid-1820s was to make Alta California more robust economically, for which purpose President Guadalupe Victoria set up a committee, the Junta de Fomento de California, in 1824. This group, which included the last Spanish governor of Alta California, Pablo Vicente de Solá, heightened official interest in Mexico's far northwestern region. Secularization of the extensive mission lands offered a golden opportunity to strengthen the northwestern frontier against foreigners by making vast amounts of land available to attract a larger population.[20]

José María Padrés, an army officer and a friend of Gómez Farías's, was perfectly positioned to mold these general plans into a well-organized and attainable project. Padrés had served in Baja California in the mid-1820s, then had served a stint as Baja California's delegate to the National Congress, before becoming assistant inspector in Alta California. There, he had been known for his liberal ideas, which led to his expulsion by Governor Victoria. Vallejo remembered him well:

> Because he was a very refined and eloquent man with a strong presence, he soon found himself head of the faction. Even though the faction did not espouse known principles, it was preparing to strike a blow in California that would shake up the social relations existing at that time between the governing authorities and their subjects, and between missionaries and neophytes. What Padrés was intending to do was nothing less than secularize all the missions of Las Californias. . . . Since the young are always inclined to follow leaders who preach new doctrines, it was not difficult for Padrés to attract into his circle Don Juan B. Alvarado, Joaquín Ortega, Antonio María Osio, and the person who is writing down these lines.[21]

Working on Gómez Farías's behalf, Padrés organized a colonizing expedition to Alta California. The two of them convinced José María Híjar, a member of a prominent Jalisco family, to head the enterprise. Alta California Governor José Figueroa's request to

20. Reynolds, "Principal Actions," part 1:289–94.
21. MGV, *Recuerdos*, 1:503.

Rocky Beach with a Family of Sea-Otters,
ca. 1803–1807, by Georg Heinrich von Langsdorff. *Courtesy of*
The Bancroft Library, University of California, Berkeley.
BANC PIC 1963.002:1035-ffALB.

Agustín Zamorano
*Courtesy of the California
History Room, California State
Library, Sacramento, California.
Neg. 23903.*

be relieved of his command due to ill health provided a perfect
opportunity to insert the colonization effort into the center of Alta
California's political life. Híjar was appointed jefe político of the
territory, and Padrés was given the military command. After their
experiences with Manuel Victoria, many Californios favored split-
ting the civilian and military commands. Indeed, Alta California's
newly elected delegate to the National Congress, Juan Bandini,
had urged the government to consider doing so.[22]

As part of the colonization effort, a commercial enterprise called
the Cosmopolitan Company was created, and Juan Bandini, the
vice president, purchased a vessel, the *Natalia*. The company was
intended to exercise a large commercial role in the California the
colonizers intended to create. However, after the *Natalia* was
wrecked during a storm in Monterey in December 1834, the commercial aspect of the enterprise quickly faded away.

---

22. The legislative and tactical organization of the colony was a very complicated affair. The
definitive treatment is Hutchinson, *Frontier Settlement*, on which we are relying for the
overall story of the colony's experiences and travails in California.

The Californios were suspicious of the colonial enterprise from the beginning. The younger generation, born around the turn of the nineteenth century and now coming of age, had been following the secularization debates in the Mexican Congress as best they could. For years they had resented the missions' accumulation of large tracts of valuable land. They were determined to profit when this land inevitably became available as part of any secularization process. Ranchos such as Ignacio Vallejo's San Cayetano were already being granted from lands outside of mission jurisdiction, and everyone saw the opportunity of landownership. Led by Figueroa, who recently had acquired his own land near Los Angeles, the Californios decided they had to act.

Their first move was to try to prevent the colonists from settling near any mission lands. In August 1834, before any colonists had arrived, Figueroa went to the North Bay to scout out locations where he might be able to place them. He settled on a spot slightly north of Santa Rosa after negotiations with Chocheno, the local Cainamero leader. Vallejo had established a relationship with this former mission Indian, whose Spanish name was Daniel, the previous year. Chocheno/Daniel agreed to respect the Mexicans' intentions so long as the land he and his people occupied was left undisturbed. Figueroa named the settlement Santa Anna y Farías in honor of the Mexican president and vice president. He instructed Agustín Zamorano, a member of his party, to lay out the plaza and the surrounding blocks. Figueroa departed on September 1, leaving Vallejo in charge of constructing the first few town structures and preparing some land on the outskirts for eventual agriculture.[23]

Meanwhile, Híjar and Padrés had organized more than two hundred men, women, and children from a variety of occupations to form the new colony. Híjar and about half the colonists boarded

---

23. "Diary of the Expedition to the Other Side of the Bay of San Francisco, by General Figueroa," in Mathes et al., *Russian-Mexican Frontier*, 218–21; San Rafael Baptism 708, May 20, 1822 (Chocheno/Daniel, from Guiluc). On the location of the Cainamero ranchería, Guiluc, near Santa Rosa, see Merriam, *Ethnogeographic and Ethnosynonymic Data*, 76; Harding, *Don Agustin V. Zamorano*, 162.

the *Natalia* and arrived at San Diego on September 1, 1834. Híjar soon headed north overland to Monterey, while most of the colonists remained at Missions San Gabriel and San Luis Rey. Padrés and the remaining colonists boarded a second vessel, the *Morelos*, which docked in Monterey on September 24.[24]

When Híjar arrived in Monterey on October 14, he discovered that there had been a change in government in Mexico. Santa Anna had reassumed the presidency and had quickly decided that he did not want Alta California to be run by allies of the liberal Gómez Farías. So he sent a note by courier instructing Figueroa, whose health had somewhat improved, not to turn over political command to Híjar. When Figueroa informed Híjar of this communication, which the former had received on September 11, Híjar quickly countered by showing Figueroa his orders, which had also made him director of colonization and put him in charge of the secularization process:

Mexico City, April 23, 1834

Instructions in accordance with which José María Híjar, Political Chief of Upper California and Director of Colonization of Upper and Lower California, is to regulate his conduct:

Article 1. He will begin by occupying all the property belonging to the missions of both Californias, and the Military Commandant, under his responsibility, will, whenever he is called upon, provide the necessary assistance for doing so.

In the face of this dramatic development, the Californio elite promptly decided that the Híjar-Padrés colony was an even greater threat to their aspirations than they had feared. Therefore, they resolved to bring both the colonization and secularization processes under their control.[25]

Concerning colonization, they moved on two fronts. First, they arranged for the colonists already in Monterey gradually to be moved north to Santa Anna y Farías. The precise dates of these

24. Hutchinson, "Official List"; Hutchinson, *Frontier Settlement*, 267.
25. Hutchinson, *Frontier Settlement*, 273; Figueroa, *Manifesto*, 24.

relocations are unclear, but eventually a good number of people, including Padrés, went there. As was intended, conditions were rough in this new town. Supplies were scarce, and the Monterey government was disinclined to assist. They told the colonists that the missions, which were supposed to be the source of those provisions, were in bad shape and there was little that could be done. In addition, Vallejo, who was at Santa Anna y Farías, made things worse. Even though the site had been chosen because the Indigenous people in the vicinity were willing to have it there, Vallejo told the colonists that the danger of Indigenous attack was intense and that everyone had to be constantly on guard. He remembered, "We all had to sleep dressed, with our horses saddled, bridled, and tied up to wooden stakes driven into the ground at the foot of each soldier's and officer's bed." In the face of these uncertainties the colonists, as Vallejo intended, soon abandoned Santa Anna y Farías. After a brief stay at the San Francisco presidio, they ended up at Mission San Francisco Solano. There, Vallejo could easily keep a close eye on them since he already had been appointed comisionado for secularization. Vallejo shrewdly drew two colonists—José "Pepe" de la Rosa, a printer, and Antonio Ortega, a farmer—to his side, and they passed along information to him about the colonists' discussions.[26]

Second, the Californio leadership employed legal arguments against the colony. In Monterey, Figueroa and the Diputación engaged in a very public controversy with Híjar. Figueroa stated that, as far as he could see, Híjar's position as director of colonization was a function of his position as jefe político. Since he was no longer jefe político, it followed that he should no longer be director of colonization either. At one point Figueroa and the Diputación agreed that Híjar could be director, not of "colonization," but of the colony at San Francisco Solano, so long as he agreed to act subject to the political government of the territory.[27]

26. Bancroft, *History of California*, 3:279; MGV, *Recuerdos*, 1:596; Hutchinson, *Frontier Settlement*, 339, 369; Hutchinson, "Official List," 417; Koegel, "Canciones del país," 170–72.

27. Figueroa, *Manifesto*, 30, 62.

The main issue, however, was secularization. Figueroa argued that since "colonization" and "secularization" referred to different activities, the fact that Híjar claimed to be in charge of the former did not grant him any power over the second. The Californios feared that Híjar and Padrés had already decided who the secularization comisionados were going to be at each of the missions. They also feared that these officials, who would have a major voice in the distribution of lands, were all going to be colonists from Mexico, not Californios. As Vallejo later put it, "It did not take long, though, for us to discover that there were <u>twenty-one mission administrators among the colonists</u> who had been chosen by Padrés from among his Mexican friends and brought to California to act on their every whim. We, who had personal interests at stake (although the welfare of others did have something to do with it), rebelled against the idea of seeing the wealth of the country pass into strange hands, so instead of supporting Padrés's plan, we fought against it and the goals of that astute trickster."[28]

Figueroa and the Diputación vociferously argued that their opposition to Híjar and Padrés had little to do with their own interests. Rather, they insisted, they were only concerned for the welfare of the Indigenous people, the fruits of whose labor Híjar and Padrés were trying to steal. Figueroa told Híjar, "At all times the mission neophytes have been held to be the owners of mission property, for it has all been acquired by their personal work as a community under the direction of the Missionary Fathers who, as guardians, have administered and saved the existing wealth after maintaining, clothing, and taking care of the necessities of the Natives. . . . Thus, the farms, temples, real estate, cattle, and everything on the missions has been acquired by the constant work and privations of the Indians." The Diputación concurred, stating that "more than 20,000 Indians are the sole owners" of the mission property, and that such property was "the exclusive fruits of the arduous work of the mission neophytes and the sole

---

28. MGV, *Recuerdos*, 1:505.

José "Pepe" de la Rosa
*Courtesy of Ventura County
Research Library and Archives.
JDF-daguerre (Collections).*

inheritance waiting for them." Figueroa added, "Everyone knows that the Indians, by their skill and hard work, have acquired and preserved the property of the missions. They have subsisted on it, and they have possessed it ever since, either willingly or forcibly, they became Christians. Who, therefore, can take it away from them without attacking the social guarantees?" Vallejo claimed that the colony was led by "sinister men who wanted to seize power in order to become rich with the fruits of the labor of three generations of Indigenous people." In a nutshell, the Diputación argued, "Let the property of the missions be distributed to the Indians and for purposes beneficial to them, since they are the sole owners." As Figueroa stated, the territorial government had especial responsibility for "preserving the property of the most depressed class of its citizens."[29]

29. Figueroa, *Manifesto*, 31, 40–42; MGV, *Recuerdos*, 1:465.

Such alleged concern for the rights of the Indigenous people did not translate into a willingness to allow them meaningful agency. The Californios also insisted that the neophytes had been harmed by "a century of slavery" in the mission system. Accordingly, the Californios presented themselves as the successors to the failed missionaries. Since the Fathers had failed to assimilate the Indigenous people to Hispanic ways, the Indians were basically in the same underdeveloped state as when the missionaries had first encountered them. In fact, the settlers' assessment of what the assimilation process required was strikingly similar to that of the priests who had come before them: an allegedly benign but strict paternalism. Therefore, the Indians needed to be kept in a "state of dependence indispensable for preserving good order and obedience among them, so as to avoid the excesses and misconduct to which they are inclined because of their stupid ignorance." Figueroa had expressed similar ideas a year earlier in a letter to the government in Mexico City. He characterized California's Indigenous people as "very little civilized, and most of them are as savage as if they had just left the forests. They are as innocent as children, and it is necessary to lead them by the hand to civilization."[30]

This Indigenous people's alleged "lack of civilization" had important consequences. The Californios argued that, given Híjar's unfamiliarity with the California Natives, his efforts would inevitably fail. As Figueroa put the matter, the neophytes "have not yet left the abject state in which nature placed them, and since they are children on the road to civilization, who do not use their reason nor know their true interests, the government must perform the duties of a common father and provide them with every kind of protection. This is the duty of a just government." Neither Híjar nor any of the colonists was sufficiently acquainted with the California neophytes to provide the strong paternal presence that secularization would require. As Vallejo later wrote, the plans of Híjar and Padres would simply "reduce the neophytes to a state of peonage

---

30. Figueroa, *Manifesto*, 30, 49; Hutchinson, *Frontier Settlement*, 237.

similar to that which has contributed so much to the backwardness of the states of Tabasco and Oaxaca." Successful secularization required the guiding hand of people familiar with all aspects of the situation in Alta California. In Vallejo's words, the "distribution of land" should have been settled "between the Indians themselves and the settlers, based on their particular circumstances." Ironically, but tellingly, the Californio would-be rancheros ended up appealing to the same arguments that missionaries, whom they were vigorously denouncing, had used to justify their own actions for the previous sixty-five years.[31]

With little prospect of success, Híjar and Padrés proposed moving their colony to Baja California. The Californios, not wanting to have a colony anywhere in the Californias, rejected that proposal, so Híjar, Padrés, and many of the colonists remained at San Francisco Solano while Figueroa and the Diputación sought an opportunity to deport the leaders. A mini-revolt in Los Angeles at the beginning of March 1835, in which one of Híjar's lieutenants may have been peripherally involved, provided the pretext for action. Figueroa ordered Vallejo to arrest Híjar, Padrés, and a few others, and they were shipped back to Mexico. With the threat of the colony removed, the path was now clear for the Californios to divide up the mission lands. In the North Bay region, Vallejo was ready.

---

31. Figueroa, *Manifesto*, 47; MGV, *Recuerdos*, 1:538.

Portrait of an Indian boy, ca. 1853, by Isaac Wallace Baker
Courtesy of the Oakland Museum of California. A68.94.2.

CHAPTER 3

"Victory Was Now Turning in My Favor"
Conquest and Resistance in the North Bay

*F*or the next decade Vallejo focused most of his energy and activities on the areas north and east of San Francisco, interacting with two major sets of people. The first consisted of a variety of Indigenous groups in the North Bay region and in the southern Sacramento and northern San Joaquín Valleys. The second set, with whom he interacted much more intermittently, was the political and military leadership of Alta California.

The documentary record of Vallejo's interactions with the Indigenous peoples is somewhat thin. In dramatic contrast to his voluminous record keeping on many issues relating to his political and military careers, the primary documents concerning his military forays and his engagements with the natives of the Sonoma region are generally absent from the thirty-six volumes of documents he gave to Bancroft in the 1870s. This was surely not accidental. As we have seen, Vallejo had been severely criticized by both civil and ecclesiastical authorities for his actions in the 1829 campaigns against Joyima and Estanislao. The official report he had filed after the Estanislao expedition had been used against him and, from that time forward, he generally sought to keep his Indian campaigns out of the contemporary written record. The lack of these records means that Vallejo's *Recuerdos* is often the main account of his Indian campaigns from 1834 until the U.S. takeover.

The *Recuerdos*, however, is marked by consistent exaggeration of the number of Indigenous combatants against whom Vallejo and his forces battled. In addition, dates are often confused, events are presented out of chronological order, and the results of Mexican-Indigenous conflicts are presented in ways that consistently buttress Vallejo's claim to have been an effective and enlightened military commander. In this chapter, we attempt to present an account that is consistent with as much of the historical evidence and current scholarship as we have been able to gather.

There is more direct primary source evidence relating to Vallejo's interactions with Alta California leadership. As he became more involved in the north, that relationship became more distant and fraught. The people with whom he had grown up in Monterey, particularly Juan Alvarado and José Castro, became increasingly frustrated with his unwillingness to participate in military projects they regarded as essential to California's development and prosperity. Vallejo, for his part, became equally frustrated with what he regarded as the ineffectual nature of Mexican rule in California.

After his journey to the North Bay to return Pixpixuecas/Toribio and the other prisoners and to meet with the Indigenous people at Missions San Rafael and San Francisco Solano, Vallejo returned to San Francisco. He remained there for the first months of 1834, but he continued his preparations to solidify his presence in the North Bay. He wrote Figueroa on March 19, asking for a grant of land at Petaluma. As required by the colonization regulations decreed by the Mexican government in 1828, he presented a

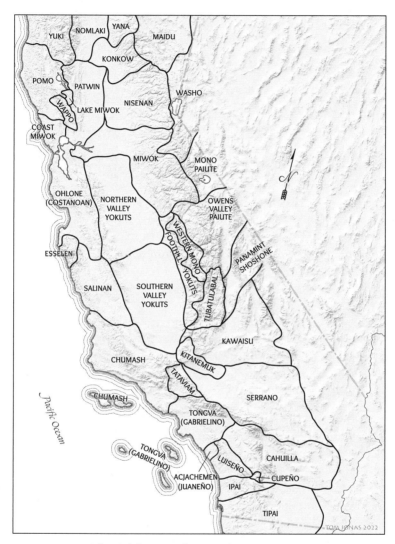

Alta California Indigenous language groups
Map by Tom Jonas.

Mission San Francisco Solano, ca. 1832, by Mariano Guadalupe Vallejo.
Drawn for Edward Vischer in 1878. *Courtesy of The Bancroft Library,*
University of California, Berkeley. BANC PIC 19xx.039:44b-ALB.

diseño (map) of the land he was requesting. The regulations also
required that the land not be currently under mission control.
Vallejo stated that the resident missionary at San Francisco Solano
had approved his request. This missionary was Father José Lorenzo
de la Concepción Quijas, who had replaced Father Vásquez del
Mercado and whom Vallejo had known when Quijas had been
at Mission San Francisco de Asís the year before. Quijas's seemingly conciliatory attitude toward boundary disputes at that time
probably encouraged Vallejo to assume that he would be amenable
to Vallejo's Petaluma plans. However, working at San Francisco
Solano apparently gave Quijas a different perspective. When he
finally did respond a few months later to Vallejo's request to put
his approval in writing, he adopted a more hardline position. He
said that part of the livestock and grazing lands of San Francisco
Solano were between the valleys where Petaluma and the mission
were located. He wrote that he could approve Vallejo's request

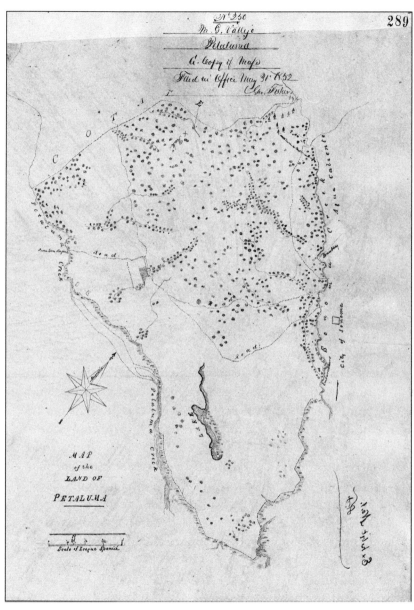

Petaluma, Diseño 250. Government Land Office no. 49, Sonoma County.
https://digitalcommons.csumb.edu/hornbeck_usa_4_a_sonc/16/

only if those lands were respected and the boundaries marked on Vallejo's diseño were scrupulously adhered to.[1]

The colonization regulations called for a grant request such as Vallejo's to be approved by the Diputación. Governor Figueroa convened the Diputación on May 1. Two days later Vallejo wrote him a note telling him that the San Francisco presidio was in terrible shape because its walls had collapsed during the last rains. The fairly obvious subtext was that San Francisco would soon have to be abandoned and that Vallejo was ready to go north to open its replacement. Once Quijas's letter had been added to the file, Figueroa submitted Vallejo's request to the Diputación on June 18. The grant was promptly approved on June 21.[2]

Within a few weeks Vallejo took a party of unknown size north. When his boats became mired in shallow water at the mouth of Petaluma Creek, he was attacked by a group of Indigenous people. Their identity is unclear, but their actions revealed that Vallejo had overestimated his success in assuring the people of the region of Mexican goodwill after the attack Father Vásquez del Mercado had organized six months earlier. After this minor skirmish Vallejo extricated his boats and sailed a few miles north to "Padre Ventura's landing" at Lakeville then traveled overland to Petaluma. There, he began preparations for setting up his fledgling rancho. His dealings with Pixpixuecas/Toribio and his visits to Petaluma the year before had allowed him to establish direct relations with the people at the nearby Indigenous ranchería of Licatiut.[3]

Vallejo stated in his *Recuerdos* that he became embroiled in his first hostilities with the local Indigenous people at this time. Reportedly, a Cainamero man stole a breeding horse from Vallejo's herd, then took refuge with the Satiyomi, a Wappo or Pomo group

---

1. The 1828 regulations supplemented earlier ones put into effect in 1824. Summaries of these regulations are in Bancroft, *History of California*, 2:515–16 (1824) and 3:34–35 (1828). The Petaluma related documents, including Quijas's letter of June 11, 1834, are in "Expediente sobre el paraje nombrado Petaluma." C-B 2, docs. 293 and 294. TBL.

2. MGV to José Figueroa, May 3, 1834, C-A 20:5–6, TBL; the Diputación's actions are recorded in C-A 60:121–23 and C-B 31, doc. 249, TBL.

3. MGV, *Recuerdos*, 1:596–604.

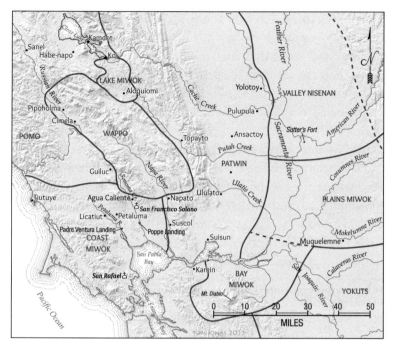

Indigenous locations in the North Bay region
Map by Tom Jonas

farther north. It is difficult to identify precisely who the "Satiyomi" were. The name is a Coast Miwok word originally used by the people of Licatiut to refer to a group north of Santa Rosa around present-day Healdsburg, but it seems Vallejo and the Mexicans expanded the term to refer generically to the Indigenous people living north of Sonoma. Whoever they were, Vallejo sent interpreters to them to request that the horse be returned and the man who had taken it be handed over. The Satiyomi refused and took one of Vallejo's emissaries prisoner, an insult that Vallejo was determined to avenge. He organized a military foray into Satiyomi territory, where an intense battle ensued. As Vallejo later recounted, "After three hours of fierce combat, . . . [my brother] Captain Salvador

Vallejo was covered in contusions, six soldiers were dead, thirty-two of my veterans were wounded, and thirty Indian allies were taken prisoner and then beheaded. Victory was now turning in my favor, for in addition to putting the enemy to flight I took 300 prisoners—men, women, and children."[4]

According to Vallejo's account, his brother Salvador pursued the fleeing Satiyomi all the way "into the mountains that today form part of Mendocino County. In a cave belonging to the Yubakhea and Bokhea Indians," he found and rescued a Cainamero who had been taken prisoner and tortured by the Satiyomi.[5] Eventually, two thousand Satiyomi gathered and attacked Mariano Guadalupe Vallejo at Valle de Tuche. Over two days Vallejo defeated them again and killed more than two hundred of them, but he realized that his supply lines, guarded by Sem-Yeto/Francisco Solano, were exposed. He was fortunate that Succara, the Satiyomi chief, did not attack either Solano or the supply lines. Instead, the Satiyomi were busily collecting additional allies and "the number of warriors who were arriving to join Succara's ranks kept increasing," so Vallejo sent an urgent message to Figueroa in Monterey. Figueroa soon arrived with four hundred soldiers. The size of the force convinced Succara to come to terms. It also persuaded the

---

4. MGV, *Recuerdos*, 1:605. Concerning the Satiyomi, Bancroft (*History of California*, 3:71) and Lothrop ("Indian Campaigns," 173, 181) identified them as Wappo, whereas Barrett (*Ethnogeography of the Pomo*, 219); Kroeber (*Handbook*, 233); and Merriam (*Ethnogeographic and Ethnosynonymic Data*, 74–75) considered them southern Pomo. McClellan ("Ethnography of the Wappo and Patwin," 235) believed that they were Wappo who moved into Pomo territory. The use of the Coast Miwok name indicates that Vallejo got his information about them from the Indigenous people in the Sonoma region. The information in the text and in this note was taken from a conference presentation by Glenn Farris, "Peace Treaty." We thank Dr. Farris for sharing this paper with us.

5. The location of these events cannot be ascertained with great confidence. Although "Yubakhea" and "Bokhea" may refer to Yuki groups, it is doubtful that Salvador Vallejo pursued the Satiyomi all the way into what eventually became Mendocino County. Vallejo probably included that reference to places far north of Sonoma at an early date in order to justify Salvador's later claim to Rancho Lupyomi in the Clear Lake region. However, any activity in 1834 probably occurred well south of modern Mendocino County. After 1856, the northernmost township of Sonoma County was called Mendocino and contained the old Rancho Sotoyome. We believe this is the general area where the events Vallejo describes occurred. See Thompson and Thos. H. Thompson & Co., *Historical Atlas Map of Sonoma County*, 10–11; MGV, *Recuerdos*, 1:605.

Cainamero, who were wavering in their allegiance to the Mexicans, to join the "Suisun, Sonoma, and Licatiut tribes who were already our followers."[6]

Besides the obvious exaggeration of numbers on both the Mexican and Satiyomi sides, Vallejo's account presents a number of difficulties. The lack of any record of a second Figueroa expedition to the north in 1834 led Bancroft to regard Vallejo's account as "either wholly unfounded or a gross exaggeration of some very trifling hostilities." Indeed, Vallejo's admission that he required Figueroa's help was quite uncharacteristic, for he normally presented his campaigns against California Indians as a succession of clear victories by himself. In our opinion, Vallejo constructed the Figueroa story to strengthen his claim that his leadership role in northernmost Alta California had been intentionally bestowed on him by the most popular governor of Mexican California, José Figueroa. Given that many Californios resented the preeminence Vallejo exercised in the north after 1834, Vallejo's narrative may have been a strategic maneuver to demonstrate that his power resulted not from his own desires, but from Figueroa's actions, which included coming to Vallejo's aid when the occasion demanded it.[7]

If the Figueroa part of the 1834 story represented Vallejo's attempt to justify his northern rule, another part of that story was probably more reflective of actual developments. Specifically, this campaign was the first time Sem-Yeto/Francisco Solano allied himself with Vallejo. As previously stated, they probably first became aware of each other when Vallejo went to Missions San Rafael and San Francisco Solano on his journey to reprimand Father Vásquez del Mercado at the end of 1833. Solano, who was actively forming alliances among many Patwin groups, was undoubtedly intrigued by this young, charismatic, and anti-mission officer. When Vallejo reappeared the next year, Solano made sure he was nearby. Once hostilities broke out against the Satiyomi, traditional adversaries of the Patwin, he volunteered the services of his men, but he

---

6. MGV, *Recuerdos*, 1:605–8.
7. Bancroft, *History of California*, 3:257.

stayed in the background, guarding the supply lines, for he wished to see what kind of field commander this young Vallejo actually was. This positioning probably also pleased Vallejo, who undoubtedly wished to assess the loyalty of Solano and his party as well. Both men were satisfied with the outcome. Although the Satiyomi did not directly attack Solano's men, Vallejo was pleased with his ally's performance and wrote later that, at one point, "I had no other recourse than to rely exclusively on Solano." When Vallejo formally founded Sonoma the next year, Solano brought more fighters and openly allied himself with the Mexican commander.[8]

Meanwhile Vallejo's power in the north was increasing. The Diputación passed regulations for secularizing the missions at the beginning of August 1834, and Figueroa promulgated them soon thereafter. The regulations called for the appointment of an official to take charge of everything except for the religious structures at each mission complex, and Figueroa appointed Vallejo to this position at Mission San Francisco Solano in October. Vallejo spent the next month attending to the arrival of the Híjar-Padrés colonists. As he intended, most of them soon took a profound dislike to Santa Anna y Farías and eventually relocated near Mission San Francisco Solano.[9]

Vallejo spent the winter and spring acting as Figueroa's agent at San Francisco Solano as relations between the colonists and the Californios deteriorated. After Híjar and Padrés were arrested and deported at the end of March, Vallejo was able to turn more of his attention to establishing his base at Sonoma. At the end of June 1835 Figueroa gave him formal permission to close the increasingly shabby San Francisco presidio, so he returned there and prepared to transfer its soldiers and operations to Sonoma. He had already appointed Ignacio Ortega, a member of the Híjar-Padrés party, as mayordomo of the Solano mission. Ortega, along with fellow settler Pepe de la Rosa, had become friendly with Vallejo and had acted as Vallejo's eyes and ears within the colony. The undisciplined

8. MGV, *Recuerdos*, 1:596.

9. Tays, "Mariano Guadalupe Vallejo and Sonoma," part 2:236; MGV, *Recuerdos*, 1:596.

behavior of Ortega and Salvador Vallejo quickly infuriated Father Quijas, who accused Ortega of "coarseness, incivility, and irreligion" and of giving "free reign to the infamous vice of lust." In mid-1835 Quijas left San Francisco Solano to take up residence at San Rafael. Vallejo was not unhappy with his departure, for it was Quijas who had insisted that Vallejo's Petaluma holdings were to be rigorously limited to the boundaries indicated in the original diseño. With the priest out of the way, Vallejo soon began to extend his rancho's boundaries. Undoubtedly not by accident, the original 1834 diseño was not included in the documents Vallejo eventually gave to Bancroft in 1875 or in any other archives that have since come to light.[10]

After closing down the San Francisco presidio, Vallejo rented some vessels from Englishman William Richardson, whom Figueroa had commissioned to establish some sort of base at Yerba Buena on the northwestern tip of the San Francisco peninsula. Richardson accompanied Vallejo as the latter transported his soldiers and supplies north. They traveled up Sonoma Creek to Poppe Landing, a spot slightly south of the mission. There, they were met by Solano and some of his people, who were expecting them. Solano had in his party a chief named, as Vallejo understood it, Pulpula. He was probably from an unmissionized ranchería on Cache Creek named Pulupula or Pulupetoy. According to Vallejo, in the course of a long welcoming ceremony, Solano told Pulpula, "The white man who is here with us can make it possible for us to annihilate the Satiyomi. I know that he is a man of his word. I can vouch for him. I also know that he is brave."[11]

At some point later that year Vallejo and his soldiers visited Solano's base territory near Suisun. The two engaged in an

10. Tays, "Mariano Guadalupe Vallejo and Sonoma," part 2:242–43; José Figueroa to MGV, June 24, 1835, C-A 53:406–8, TBL; Hutchinson, *Frontier Settlement*, 369, 421; Engelhardt, *Missions and Missionaries*, 3:582–84.

11. Miller, *Captain Richardson*, 46–49; Thompson and Thos. Thompson & Co., *Historical Atlas Map of Sonoma County*, 59; Barrett, *Ethno-geography of the Pomo*, map 2; Kroeber, *Patwin and Their Neighbors*, 262. There was only one baptism at San Francisco Solano of a person from Pulupetoy, and that took place on June 13, 1834, Baptism no. 1184. Vallejo also referred to a ranchería called Pulpula in the vicinity of Sonoma, but there is no evidence that such a ranchería ever existed in that location; MGV, *Recuerdos*, 1:599.

elaborate ceremony of riding together around the boundaries of the terrain. Vallejo later said that in his capacity as comisionado for Mission San Francisco Solano and as military commander, he was formally bestowing the land on Solano. More likely, he was signaling to "the large number of Indians" who were present that he and the Mexicans acknowledged Solano's possession of this territory and was thereby forging an incipient alliance.[12]

As Vallejo established a presence in the north, he experienced the same difficulties that missions, pueblos, and ranchos up and down Alta California were experiencing. Specifically, he found that Indigenous peoples north and east of the mission were already raiding significant numbers of horses and livestock. Vallejo enlisted the Cainamero people of the Santa Rosa region as allies against stock and horse raiders to the north, a strategy that proved reasonably successful as he was laying out the town and plaza of Sonoma. Toward the end of 1835, however, eight horses were stolen from Sonoma, and Vallejo was informed that they had been sold to a chief named Cotón or Cottre, whom Vallejo identified as the leader of the ranchería of the Guapos. In this instance, Ipui/Santiago, a Cainamero subchief, managed to recover four of the horses. But shortly thereafter, when Santiago took a party of people north in search of fish and seeds, they were attacked by the Guapos, who killed twenty men and two women. These two episodes made Vallejo determined to organize an expedition against the Guapos to punish them for the raids as well as their attack upon his Indigenous allies. The fact that the Cainamero party had been forced to trek north in search of sustenance revealed that Vallejo's presence in the region was already creating significant environmental consequences for the region's Indigenous inhabitants.[13]

---

12. Suisun grant, BANC MSS, Land Case Files, 2 ND, 60, TBL.

13. Cook, *Conflict between the California Indian and White Civilization*, 230. The most complete account of these 1835 episodes and Vallejo's campaign against the Guapos the next spring is found in Vallejo's report: MGV to Nicolás Gutiérrez, April 8, 1836, C-B 3, doc. 105, TBL. This letter is our major source for the details on the campaign in the following paragraphs. On Ipui/Santiago, see Milliken, "Ethnohistory and Ethnogeography of the Coast Miwok," 99; and San Rafael Baptism 1645, February 5, 1831.

The Guapos, like the Satiyomi, are difficult to identify precisely. Some authors identify them as a Wappo group, while others observe that Vallejo used Guapo interchangeably with Satiyomi, who are variously identified as either Wappo or Pomo. Vallejo was probably not concerned about being overly precise. "Guapo" is a Spanish word that at that time also meant "brave" or "fierce" and there is little reason to think that, in using this term, he was distinguishing a specific cultural or linguistic group of Indigenous people. He was probably simply characterizing the people against whom he fought on this particular expedition. In referring to them as "fierce," he was both complimenting them and, not incidentally, highlighting his own skill in defeating them. In his *Recuerdos* he wrote, "The Satiyomi were called Guapos because no other tribe of infidels was equal to them in terms of fearlessness or daring."[14]

The wet winter of 1835–36 prevented Vallejo from organizing an expedition against the Guapos before springtime. He organized his force at the end of March, and on April 1 he set out with approximately 150 men, perhaps 100 of whom were Patwin and Cainamero led by Solano. The remaining fifty consisted of Mexican soldiers along with some recently arrived foreigners. Vallejo acknowledged that Solano was able to guide the expedition so that it was undetected by the Guapos and was able to direct the men to a good spot for an attack upon the Guapo ranchería without being confronted or ambushed along the way.[15]

Vallejo wrote that the attack took place "southwest of the place known today by the name Gysers."[16] This placed the battle at or near Pipoholma, a Wappo settlement along the Russian River, located in a region that had long been home to both Wappo and Pomo groups. This village had been the site of intragroup tensions a few years earlier, when the Wappo had gathered some acorns slightly north of the creek that had served as the boundary between

---

14. R. Greengo and D. Shutler, "Historical Background," in Heizer, ed. *Archaeology of the Napa Region*, 230; Merriam, *Ethnogeographic and Ethnosynonymic Data*, 65, 74–75; Farris, "Peace Treaty," 11; MGV, *Recuerdos*, 1:674, 776; 2:1072.

15. MGV, *Recuerdos*, 1:674.

16. The correct spelling is Geysers.

them and the Pomo people. The Wappo people of Pipoholma left the acorns unattended overnight with the intention of returning to transport them home the next day, but the Pomo residents of Cimela stole the acorns overnight. This action was yet another indication of how severely Mexican incursion into the region had unsettled traditional food-gathering patterns. The people of Pipoholma organized a party and marched on Cimela. In the battle that ensued, two people from Cimela were killed and the Pomo eventually agreed to vacate the area. Indeed, the reason that Chief Cotón/Cottre, of Pipoholma, purchased the stolen horses may well have been to increase the village's defenses should the Pomo decide to return and contest the area.[17]

Vallejo recounted that he divided his forces, and he led a contingent that launched a frontal attack upon the village. Once the defenders came out to repulse this attack, another contingent led by his brother Salvador attacked them on their flanks. Surrounded, the Guapo surrendered after about forty-five minutes. Charles Brown, an American who was part of the expedition, later stated that when the Mexican-led force entered the village, Solano personally killed an infant boy and his pregnant mother. Furthermore, sixty-five men and more than one hundred women and children were taken prisoner and marched back to Sonoma. He stated that some of the prisoners "were divided among the different ranches of the mission," by which he probably meant the ranchos, including Petaluma, that were being carved out from the lands of the secularized Mission San Francisco Solano. The remaining people of Pipoholma were settled at Agua Caliente, about three miles north of Sonoma and twelve miles east of Petaluma—a location from which they could easily be conscripted for work at either location when needed.[18]

The success of this campaign, which promised to entrench Vallejo's position in the north, was counterbalanced by the specter of increased political instability in Alta California as a whole. Governor Figueroa, who had put an end to the provincial volatility

17. Barrett, *Ethno geography of the Pomo*, 265–66, 272, map 1; Sawyer, "Wappo," 258.
18. Brown, "Early Events in California," 12, 14, C-D 53, TBL.

that had followed Governor Victoria's expulsion, died in September 1835 after a brief illness. The emerging elite, grateful for Figueroa's initiation of secularization and his support of them in the face of the perceived threat from the Híjar-Padrés colony, was deeply shaken. According to Vallejo the news of Figueroa's death "had a chilling effect on everyone." He recounted that on the day of Figueroa's funeral in Monterey, "The escort accompanying the corpse was immense. It was the largest I had ever seen." For about three months afterward, José Castro, the senior member of the Diputación, served as the political chief, and Nicolás Gutiérrez, the senior military officer who had come to California with Figueroa, served as the military chief. In January 1836 the Mexican government ordered that the two commands be unified under Gutiérrez until the new governor, who would also hold both commands, arrived. That new governor was Mariano Chico, who arrived in Santa Bárbara around mid-April.[19]

In the midst of this political uncertainty, Vallejo decided to make a formal report to Gutiérrez. In the report he insisted that all members of the military expedition against the Guapos had behaved with moderation and that, because of Vallejo's success, the North Bay region was "secure." It appears that Vallejo was anxious to defend himself preemptively from any criticisms of him that arriving Governor Chico might hear in Monterey concerning either the behavior of his troops during the 1829 expeditions or the overall success of his campaign against Estanislao.[20]

Three weeks later Vallejo wrote another report to Gutiérrez, this one regarding three Castro brothers, Joaquín, Antonio, and Víctor. The brothers were sons of Francisco María Castro, who had come to California as a child with the Anza expedition in 1776. After a military career at the San Francisco presidio, Francisco apparently settled in the East Bay in the 1820s, and in 1834 Figueroa had granted the land on which he had settled to his children as Rancho San Pablo. The brothers had traveled from San Pablo and

19. Bancroft, *History of California*, 3:298–300, 414–16; MGV, *Recuerdos*, 1:627.
20. Bancroft, *History of California*, 3:421.

*El Funeral del Gobernador José
Figueroa*, a large mural painted
in the early twentieth century by
Dutch painter Theodore Van
Cina (1865–1940). *Used by
permission of the Santa Barbara
Courthouse Legacy Foundation.*

entered the North Bay region while Vallejo had been away on his
expedition against the Guapos. Apparently, they desired to avoid
detection, for they had taken a circuitous route around Sonoma.
While in the North Bay, they met with the "general" of the Cainamero. Since the Cainamero had lost twenty men and two women
in the Guapo attack a few months earlier despite their alliance
with Vallejo, some elements of the group were doubtless willing
to explore relations with other Mexicans. Vallejo had heard from
some San Rafael neophytes, who came to Sonoma shortly after his
return from the Guapo expedition, that the Castro brothers, using
strategies such as stealing necessities and snatching at least one
child from an Indigenous ranchería, were trying to force Indians
to go to San Pablo and work there.[21]

---

21. MGV to Nicolás Gutiérrez, April 24, 1836, C B 3, doc. 112, TBL. All the information about
the Castro affair in this and the following paragraph comes from this letter.

Vallejo was certainly anxious to prevent other rancheros from removing potential Indian labor from the region over which he was in the process of establishing control, so he sent out a squad of soldiers under Sergeant Antonio Peña. They captured the Castro brothers and brought them back to Sonoma, where they were kept under guard. When Vallejo questioned them, they simply replied that non-Christian Indians were "demons." In his message to Gutiérrez, Vallejo demanded strict punishment for the Castros. He said that behavior like theirs could spur an "uprising" among the North Bay people and destroy the "order" he had created by his "good treatment" of the unmissionized peoples of the region and his recent military "action" there.

Chico arrived in Monterey on May 1, 1836. On May 4 he sent Vallejo a letter, instructing him to travel to Monterey and to bring with him as many soldiers as he could spare. Fearing that Chico

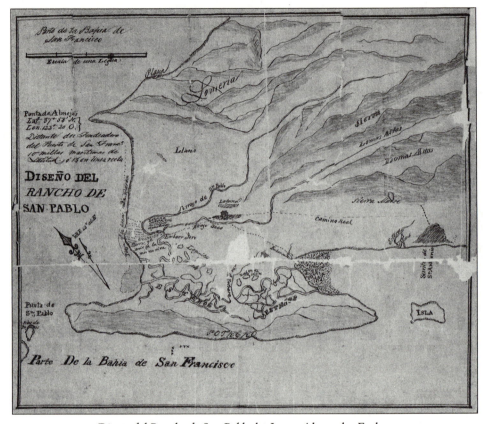

Diseño del Rancho de San Pablo, by James Alexander Forbes
Courtesy of The Bancroft Library, University of California,
Berkeley. Land Case Map D-216.

would keep the soldiers in Monterey for his own use, Vallejo
stalled as he planned his response. He later claimed that he did
not receive the letter until eight days after Chico had sent it. When
he did finally start out for Monterey, he met two Mexican merchants, Eulogio Celis and Federico Baker, in San José. He wrote
that they "advised me not to appear before the governor unpre-
pared." Reportedly, they told Vallejo that the new governor was

a "centralist" who had already indicated his willingness to use his executive power very strongly. Indeed, Chico's views reflected those of the conservative, anti-federalist group headed by Santa Anna that had assumed power in Mexico. So Vallejo returned to Sonoma determined to impress Chico with his own accomplishments on the northern frontier and make it more difficult for the new governor to strip him of any of the Sonoma soldiers. He gathered twenty-two soldiers and ten civilian militiamen to accompany him to Monterey. He also worked with Solano to assemble Indigenous people from a number of locations to join the delegation.[22]

When Vallejo had not appeared in Monterey after a week and a half, Chico fired off another letter to him. Meanwhile, Vallejo finalized his group, which eventually included, in addition to the soldiers and militia, eight Suisun, two Satiyomi (probably from among the Guapo whom he had recently defeated and relocated to Agua Caliente), two Napajo, and two Cainamero. The group arrived in Monterey on May 26. As Vallejo later recounted, he and his party "headed toward the door of the Señor Commander General's office. There, I stopped and ordered my men to line up in battle formation." When he knocked on the door, it was "opened by an old man dressed in a Japanese robe . . . with a green cap on his head. He was wearing green slippers embroidered in gold." After some awkward introductions, Chico retired and returned shortly wearing his military uniform. Chico asked why it had taken Vallejo so long to obey the order to appear in Monterey. Vallejo pleaded that the geography of the Bay Area and the lack of available boats made it difficult for him to get to Monterey as quickly as he would have liked. He claimed that due to Chico's unfamiliarity with Bay Area geography, he had to spend time explaining the location and breadth of both the Sacramento and San Joaquín Rivers to the new governor.[23]

In the course of the conversation. Vallejo informed Chico that his soldiers "relied solely on me, for I am the one who clothed, paid,

22. Mariano Chico to MGV, May 4, 1836, C-B 3, doc. 200, TBL; MGV, *Recuerdos*, 1:646–47.
23. Mariano Chico to MGV, May 17, 1836, C-B 3, docs. 205 and 206, TBL; MGV, *Recuerdos*, 1:648–49.

and maintained them." The message was rather explicit: if Chico wanted to keep Vallejo's soldiers at Monterey, he and the government would incur substantial additional expenses. Chico then had the various Indians appear before him, and he questioned them about their clothing, weapons, population, and methods of fighting. As Vallejo had intended, the Indians were an imposing sight.

The message the new governor was intended to receive was that Vallejo had created an independent and formidable military force in the North Bay. Since Chico was polite to him and especially curious about the numbers and military capabilities of the Indians he had brought, Vallejo was confident that his message had been delivered. Perhaps it had. In his confidential report to the Mexican minister of war, Chico called Vallejo "daring" and "possessed of a natural talent that is quite marked." His final judgment, however, was that Vallejo "is not to be trusted."[24]

Vallejo returned to Sonoma in early June. He quickly drafted a document purported to be a peace treaty that he had negotiated with a number of Indigenous groups. The treaty was calculated to solidify the impression Vallejo hoped he had given Chico of having successfully subdued a number of hostile tribes in the region. However, six of the seven groups mentioned in the treaty were actually Patwin, who had probably been recruited by Solano and had accompanied Vallejo on his expedition to the north. The most significant part of the treaty was section 5, which stated that the Guapos agreed to stay on their own land. This section basically ratified the arrangements that Vallejo had imposed upon the former residents of Pipoholma by prohibiting them from leaving the spot at Agua Caliente where Vallejo had placed them. Vallejo formally sent the treaty to Chico, who approved it at the end of June.[25]

Vallejo and Solano soon learned however that one of the latter's Patwin rivals had taken advantage of their absence in Monterey.

24. Tays, "Mariano Guadalupe Vallejo and Sonoma," part 2:248–49.

25. The supposed treaty is in C-B 3, doc. 119, TBL. A full list of the Indigenous groups it covered can be found in Bancroft, *History of California*, 3:71–72. Mariano Chico to MGV, June 27, 1836, C-B 3, doc. 217, TBL.

Zampay from Yolotoy had formed an anti-Vallejo and anti-Solano alliance with the Satiyomi chief Succara, and was attempting to bring some of the Napajo into the alliance as well. Ironically, Yolotoy, near the present Knight's Landing, was one of the rancherías mentioned in Vallejo's "treaty."[26]

Vallejo and Solano both acted to counter this threat. Vallejo attempted to bolster Solano's standing by creating an elaborately provisioned Indigenous military company to serve as the Indigenous leader's "honor guard." The force consisted of forty-four Indigenous men, both Suisun and loyal Napajo, who were outfitted with "long capes, cloth jackets, pants, linen jackets, shirts, military caps, shoes, knapsacks, hats, blankets, and pouches for provisions." Solano, for his part, journeyed through Patwin territory and shored up his alliances, including an important one with a Yolotoy man named Moti. Vallejo sometimes accompanied Solano on these journeys.[27]

Meanwhile, down south, Chico's centralist positions and overbearing personality quickly made him unpopular in Monterey and fostered opposition to him. The new governor was expelled before he had a chance to consolidate his position, but Vallejo took no part in these events because he was preoccupied with preparing for an expedition against Zampay. Gutiérrez reassumed command but soon created tensions with the Diputación by exercising what it considered arbitrary power. Vallejo's Monterey *compadres*[28] Juan Alvarado and José Castro assumed leadership of what quickly became an armed anti-Gutiérrez movement, and Alvarado visited Sonoma to request Vallejo's help. Vallejo took him to the place where Solano was gathering his forces for the campaign against Zampay. The Indian leader gave a speech in his own language, which Vallejo told Alvarado promised the support of the leader and his people. But no concrete support was forthcoming from either Vallejo or Solano and his followers, for Vallejo did not wish to disrupt the campaign he was already planning against Zampay.

26. MGV, *Recuerdos*, 1:674–75.
27. MGV, *Recuerdos*, 1:745–47.
28. "Compadre" means godfather, often used as a term of affection.

Nevertheless, Alvarado and Castro were swiftly able to overcome and expel Gutiérrez. They declared Alta California independent of Mexico, established a new government with Alvarado as governor, and appointed Vallejo as commander general. Vallejo traveled to Monterey with a detachment of soldiers to accept the office on November 11.[29]

When word reached Monterey in December 1836 that Zampay had begun to attack some of Solano's allies, Vallejo promptly sent a contingent of soldiers back to Sonoma on December 11 and returned there himself on December 25. He immediately began to organize an expedition against Zampay, but Solano, whose alliances had apparently not yet been solidified, persuaded him to wait. To solidify his ally's position further, Vallejo arranged for Solano to request a formal grant of Suisun as a rancho. In his capacity as military commander, Vallejo provisionally approved this request in January 1837 and promised to send it on to the government in Monterey for final approval.[30]

On the same day that Vallejo left Monterey, Alvarado headed to Southern California with fifty soldiers and a contingent of North American riflemen led by Isaac Graham. The Californios in the Los Angeles and San Diego areas were rejecting the revolutionary movement led by northerners, and Alta California was experiencing a rebirth of the regional rivalries that had wracked it in the early 1830s. In January 1837, Castro joined Alvarado in the south, and they soon asserted their control. Governor Alvarado remained in Santa Bárbara until May and organized a broad-based assembly that adopted a series of resolutions promising to unify the two factions. While all this turmoil was happening, Vallejo had to spend a good amount of time in Monterey, maintaining order and trying to smooth out rivalries among various factions in the capital. Consequently, not until May 1837 was he able to return to Sonoma and finalize plans to send out the expedition against Zampay.[31]

29. Tays, "Vallejo and Sonoma," part 3:348–51; Miller, *Juan Alvarado*, 45–52.
30. MGV, *Recuerdos*, 1:745–47; Suisun grant, BANC MSS, Land Case Files, 2 ND, 31–32, 60, TBL.
31. Miller, *Juan Alvarado*, 52–54; Tays, "Vallejo and Sonoma," part 3:352–54; MGV, *Recuerdos*, 1:772–77.

Once again, however, a rebellion against the new California government broke out in San Diego and Los Angeles. Alvarado, back in Monterey, instructed Vallejo to meet him at Santa Clara, where they had a series of tense exchanges on June 13–18. Alvarado once again pressed Vallejo to send some troops to help put down the rebellion in the south, but Vallejo insisted that he could not leave the north undefended. As he later wrote, "I explained to him that, even though I was determined not to abandon the patriots' cause, I suffered pangs of conscience over the prospect of depriving the frontier of its best defenders. I would be sending them to defend places in the south that were more populated than those of the north, and therefore they should have been able to defend themselves." Vallejo also complained to Alvarado about some appointments of southerners, especially of José Sepúlveda as captain of the civic militia, that Alvarado had made in his attempt to unify the south and north of California. Vallejo, by this time anxious to start the long-delayed expedition against Zampay, did agree to make a few soldiers available to Alvarado. As it turned out, however, the renewed rebellion in Southern California was tamped down without bloodshed, with the assistance of Andrés Castillero, who had been sent by the commander general of Baja California to try to calm things down. Castillero persuaded Alvarado that Alta California would not be adversely affected by the government and administration in Mexico City if the latter agreed to accept the Siete Leyes that codified the centralist administration in Mexico. Alvarado agreed, and Castillero headed to Mexico to seek confirmation of Alvarado's position as governor.[32]

Meanwhile, up north, the expedition against Zampay finally headed out at the end of June. It consisted of Mexican soldiers commanded by Salvador Vallejo and "auxiliaries" led by Solano, presumably consisting of his honor guard and others. Reflecting the delicacy of the situation, Vallejo instructed his brother to respect any Indigenous peoples he encountered on the way and to

32. Bancroft, *History of California*, 3:510; MGV, *Recuerdos*, 1:788–80; Miller, *Juan Alvarado*, 54–55; Osio, *History of Alta California*, 303–4.

do everything possible "to attract them to friendship with us."[33]

The expedition was a success. Solano's Yolotoy ally Moti led them to Zampay, and soldier Manuel Cantúa captured him, most likely in the vicinity of present-day Knight's Landing. Vallejo, who termed Zampay a "terrible man" who had killed at least seven friendly Indian leaders, wanted to execute him, but Solano dissuaded him. He told the Mexicans, "A dead Zampay could no longer be of use while a live Zampay could be used as a pawn or some sort of guarantee." He told Vallejo privately that he wanted to keep Zampay alive "so that he would have the pleasure of seeing Zampay every single day and of never letting Zampay forget that he had been his savior." In addition, he undoubtedly spread the word among the Patwin that he had saved their fellow countryman from execution by the Mexicans. Vallejo brought Moti to Sonoma as well, allegedly as a prisoner, but probably to protect him from retaliation from Zampay's supporters who were still in the Yolotoy ranchería.[34]

The thoroughness with which Solano had solidified his Patwin alliances against Zampay, along with Vallejo's capture of Zampay, caused Zampay's Satiyomi ally Succara to seek a pause in hostilities in order to try to devise another strategy against the Mexicans. As Vallejo narrated in his *Recuerdos*, Succara sent word to Vallejo that he was interested in seeking a truce. After preliminary negotiations Vallejo and Succara met outside of Sonoma. Vallejo drew up a formal treaty between the two of them that was supposed to last for a year and "put an end to the wars that both contracting parties have sustained between themselves for several years." Succara agreed to place a brother and two sons in Sonoma as hostages and to return Cainamero and Suisun prisoners. The Mexicans and the Satiyomi agreed to stay out of each other's territory without permission and to engage in regular exchanges of steers and cows (from the Mexicans) and bears (from the Satiyomi). After the treaty signing, both

---

33. MGV to Salvador Vallejo, June 25, 1837, C-B 4, doc. 250, and C-B 7, doc. 18, TBL.

34. MGV to Salvador Vallejo, June 25, 1837, C-B 4, doc. 250, and C-B 7, doc. 18, TBL; MGV, *Recuerdos*, 1:152, 748–49.

sides elaborately exchanged gifts and held three days of festivities. How many of the terms were actually adhered to is unclear, but the treaty allowed Vallejo publicly to proclaim once again his position as the preeminent Mexican authority in the north.[35]

One important aspect of Vallejo's narrative of these events was the role of Solano. The defeat of Zampay had cemented Solano's position as the major Indigenous leader of the region. As we have seen in his actions in saving Zampay from execution, he seems to have regarded his role as being to ensure that the Indigenous peoples received treatment from the Mexicans that would be commensurate with their own key role in the region. Vallejo seems to have realized this when he described the gifts that Succara gave him:

> Succara's gifts consisted of fishing nets, blankets made of bird feathers, dried fish, deer- and buckskins, and six young girls. I saved the deer- and buckskins for my soldiers to use. I handed over the young girls to Solano and gave him the feathered blankets, the fishing nets, and the dried fish. I did not divide everything evenly. I took the smaller portion of the gifts for myself and the *gente de razón*[36] because at that time I had very few soldiers, and Solano had several Suisun and Cainamero chiefs with him who were watching me like hawks. They were eyeing my every movement closely, and if they had discovered in me the slightest desire to appropriate the lion's share of the gifts for myself, this would have angered them. They would have displayed that anger by grabbing their bows and arrows to attack the gente de razón anew.[37]

For his part, Succara devised a new plan of attack within a few months of signing the treaty, embarking on a campaign in late summer or early fall of 1837. Vallejo's account was sparse regarding the details of the campaign, such as its length or the locations of battles, but it does not appear that Solano took part in this expedition against Succara. Vallejo said that, since his brother Salvador was away and Cayetano Juárez was sick, he placed Lázaro Piña,

35. M G V, *Recuerdos*, 1:799–801.
36. "Gente de razón" literally means "people with the capacity to reason"; that is, any non-Indian.
37. M G V, *Recuerdos*, 1:801.

who allegedly "just happened to appear to offer his services," in charge of the largely Cainamero vanguard of the Mexican forces.[38] When the expedition reached the Satiyomi force, it was met with a volley of arrows and rocks. As Vallejo reported, "The band of Satiyomi . . . hurled their projectiles too high and not one single [Cainamero] was injured." Nevertheless, the members of the vanguard "threw themselves on the ground as if they had been mortally wounded. Piña tried to make them get up, but not a single Indian moved." Vallejo continued:

> From the details my lieutenant provided, I realized that the Cainamero Indians had betrayed their leader and simply abandoned him. I had no doubt those traitors would provide the Satiyomi chief with all the details they knew regarding the preparations I had made to fight them. Therefore, I no longer believed it was prudent for me to take my reduced number of soldiers through the dense woods, because we would be forced to cut through there in order to reach the rancherías of the Satiyomi. So, I returned to Sonoma with the intention of organizing a new expedition.[39]

This episode revealed that Succara had successfully lured a number of Vallejo's Indigenous allies to his side. It is difficult to determine exactly who these people were. As we have seen, Vallejo used "Cainamero" to refer to the southern Pomo of the Santa Rosa region and the area to its north, which contained a cluster of different rancherías. A number of the people from this region had been killed or taken prisoner at San Rafael in the 1833 Vásquez del Mercado expedition, and Pixpixuecas/Toribio had advised Vallejo to stay out of the area. So alliances made with the Mexicans by residents of the region had probably always been tenuous at best. As a result, Vallejo's expedition against Succara was a failure.

Having pinned the blame for the failure of his Satiyomi campaign on treachery by the Cainamero, Vallejo was probably looking for an opportunity to publicly exercise his authority over them.

---

38. Piña was a sergeant but had been promoted to acting alférez. See Bancroft, *History of California*, 4:780.

39. MGV, *Recuerdos*, 1:824.

José Antonio Carrillo. *Courtesy of the California History Room, California State Library, Sacramento, California.*

The chance came in January 1838 when two Cainamero, Gaíñeco/ Tobías, a leader of the community of Guiluc near Santa Rosa, and Tola/Olegario, a stoneworker, went to Sonoma to speak with Francisco Solano. They told him that they had been involved in an altercation with two nonmission Indigenous people while fishing near Corte Madera. In the fight that ensued, they had killed them both, a man and a woman.⁴⁰

Gaíñeco/Tobías and Tola/Olegario were quickly arrested and locked up. Vallejo rapidly organized a formal legal proceeding, headed by Antonio Peña. Solano and Guecquez, the leader of the Patwin village of Ansactoy, testified against the two. At the end of the trial, Peña recommended that Tola/Olegario be executed and that Gaíñeco/Tobías spend five years in jail. It is not clear whether the sentences were actually carried out, but the jailing and trial of

---

40. Gaíñeco/Tobías was from Guiluc, in the Rincon Valley, slightly northeast of Santa Rosa; Merriam, *Ethnogeographic and Ethnosynonymic Data*, 75; San Rafael Baptism 696, May 20, 1822 (Gaíñeco/Tobías); San Francisco Solano Baptism 69, June 17, 1824 (Tola/Olegario); Tola/Olegario's origin is stated not in his baptismal record, but rather in those of his parents: San Francisco Solano Baptism 176, November 21, 1825 (Salajoupi/Atanacia) and Baptism 38, April 16, 1824 (Sixsema/Atanasio). These records state both of their origins as Guiluc.

the two leaders undoubtably sent a strong signal to the Cainamero about the emerging balance of power in the North Bay territory Vallejo was colonizing.[41]

By this time the political situation had taken yet another turn. In October 1837 word reached California that the Mexican government had appointed Carlos Carrillo as governor of California. The force behind this appointment was Carrillo's brother, José Antonio, who was the California delegate to the Mexican Congress. Carlos Carrillo took the oath of office in Los Angeles in December, but Alvarado and his allies, who believed that the 1837 agreement they had reached with Castillero was acceptable to Mexico City, determined to overthrow him. Alvarado and Castro went south, and Vallejo sent his brother Salvador and some soldiers to assist. As part of the operations, José Antonio Carrillo was captured and sent as a prisoner to Sonoma, where he and Vallejo had long conversations. José Antonio urged Vallejo to recognize his brother, whose title to the governorship, he assured Vallejo, would definitely be upheld by the Mexican government. Whereas Vallejo had virtually no relationship with José Antonio, Carlos, or their branch of the Carrillo family, his wife, Francisca Benicia, was from another branch of the same family. Given his increasingly ambiguous relations with Alvarado, he may well have calculated that his fortunes might improve under a Carrillo governorship, so he wrote Alvarado and urged him to recognize Carlos Carrillo as governor. Alvarado wrote back with an indignant refusal. A few weeks later, word was received that Andrés Castillero, in Mexico City, had secured the legitimacy of Alvarado's claim to the governorship, but Alvarado never forgot Vallejo's apparent abandonment of him. During the rest of the Mexican era, the relationship between the two men would never be repaired.[42]

Meanwhile, in the north, another Indigenous threat to Vallejo had already appeared in December 1837, although he apparently

---

41. "Causa criminal contra los indígenas Tobías y Olegario por haber muertos a dos gentiles mansos en esta población," C-B 5, doc. 21, TBL.

42. Miller, *Juan Alvarado*, 59–60; Tays, "Vallejo and Sonoma," part 3:361.

did not immediately realize its significance. During that month representatives from two Miwok rancherías on the Sacramento River, Ochejamne and Siusumne, arrived in Sonoma. They told Vallejo that they were being threatened by the Muquelemne, a Miwok group farther south that had been raiding horses from ranchos around Missions San José, Santa Clara, and San Juan Bautista for a number of years. They asked for Vallejo's protection, and in return they promised to be on the lookout for stolen horses in the Sacramento Valley region and to return them whenever the occasion presented itself. Vallejo agreed and, by his account, entered into a formal treaty with them.[43]

In March 1838 a group led by Ochejamne chief Huyumegepa and Siusumne chief Cumuchi appeared at Sonoma. They brought four horses they claimed to have recovered from the Muquelemne and named four other villages they said were partnering with the Muquelemne in the horse raiding. They also stated that three Christian Indians from Mission San José were heavily involved in the horse raiding and that a recent Mexican attack on the village of Sacayak, along the Muquelemne River, had been a mistake, because the Muquelemne had tricked the Mexicans into believing that that village was the center of the horse raiding. Grateful for this information, Vallejo asked Solano to organize a celebratory feast for them, which he did. It lasted eight days.[44]

However, Vallejo's dealings with the Ochejamne and Siusumne had a deeper meaning than he realized. In 1830 some Indigenous people who had escaped from Mission San José had taken refuge in Huyumegepa's village. When a Mexican military party and some Indigenous auxiliaries appeared and demanded that these people be returned, Huyumegepa refused. In the ensuing battle, the Ochejamne drove off the invading force. The Mexicans then enlisted some nearby American trappers and the combined force

---

43. The December 1837 treaty is referred to in "Notes by Vallejo on Indian Affairs," April 1, 1838, C-B 5, doc. 65, TBL; see Bancroft, *History of California*, 4:72.

44. "Notes by Vallejo on Indian affairs," April 1, 1838, C-B 5, doc. 65, and December 1, 1837, C-B 14, doc. 251, TBL; Bennyhoff, *Ethnogeography of the Plains Miwok*, 115. Sacayak was probably the ranchería of Sakayakumne. See Levy, "Eastern Miwok," 399.

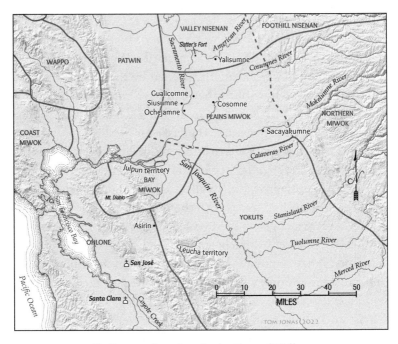

Indigenous locations in the Central Valley
Map by Tom Jonas

returned, defeated Huyumegepa's forces, and burned their village. The defeated Ochejamne were taken to Mission San José, where more than two hundred of them were baptized. Among them was Huyumegepa, who was given the Christian name Narciso. At some point after secularization, he and a number of other Ochejamne left the mission and returned to the village site, so he was not a person whose background made him friendly to the Mexican military or to the missions.[45]

45. José Berreyesa, "Sobre encuentros con los indios," July 15, 1830, C-A 27:314–16, TBL; Cook, *Expeditions to the Interior*, 187; Bennyhoff, *Ethnogeography of the Plains Miwok*, 29–31; San José Baptism 6362, January 18, 1831 (Huyumegepa/Narciso); Milliken, *Native Americans at Mission San José*, 69–70; Phillips, *Indians of the Tulares*, 1: 67, 96.

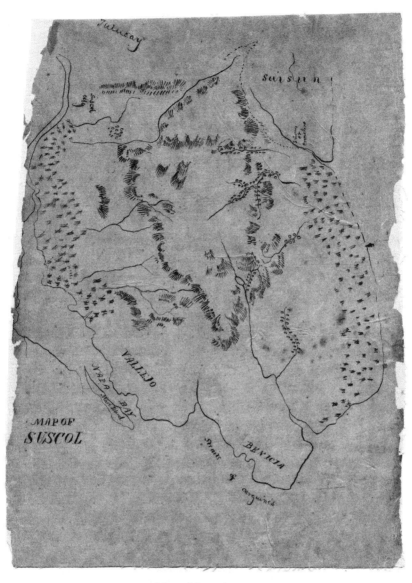

Map of Suscol, 1850
Courtesy of The Bancroft Library, University of California,
Berkeley. Land Case Map B-622.

The true meaning of the Ochejamne and Siusumne visit to Sonoma became clear in August, when a sixty-person horse-raiding party appeared at Rancho Suscol, some ten miles east of Sonoma. The party was led by Siusumne chief Cumuchi, who had been a member of the March delegation. Whereas that group had claimed to be anti-Muquelemne, the activities of the newer group revealed that the earlier visit had actually been a reconnaissance party. That group had realized that, given Vallejo's concerns with the victorious Satiyomi to the north and west of Sonoma, the best target for horse raiding would probably be east of that town, specifically at Rancho Suscol. The newer group however was unaware that Vallejo's concerns about the Satiyomi threat had dramatically abated. During the spring a serious smallpox epidemic had raged among the Indigenous people to the north, including the Satiyomi. The disease, which Vallejo later stated had killed "many hundreds" of people, had been introduced into the Columbia River region by Canadian trappers and from there had spread to Fort Ross. It was introduced into the unvaccinated Satiyomi region by one of Vallejo's soldiers as he was returning from a visit to the Russian outpost.[46]

The devastation of this epidemic meant Vallejo could relax his guard toward the north. So, when the horse-raiding party from the Central Valley appeared to the east, he was able to organize a swift response to it. Soon after the party appeared at Rancho Suscol, Vallejo surprised them and forced them to surrender some of their weapons. Fighting nevertheless broke out and Vallejo's forces quickly defeated the group. Cumuchi was captured, and he admitted that he and his people were cooperating with the Muquelemne. On August 9, Vallejo ordered his execution.[47]

46. MGV to the Comandante of San Diego, May 23, 1838, C-A 29:205–6, TBL; MGV to Alvarado, May 25, 1838, C-B 5, doc. 89, TBL. Cook estimated that the smallpox outbreak killed two thousand Wappo and Pomo people. See Cook, *Conflict between the California Indian and White Civilization*, 213–14; Cook, "Smallpox in Spanish and Mexican California," 184–86.

47. MGV to Alvarado, August 7, 1838, C-A 29:222, TBL; MGV, "Draft of a Circular on Indian Affairs," August 9, 1838, C-B 5, doc. 124, TBL.

At some point after this episode Vallejo became aware that representatives of the Castro brothers from Rancho San Pablo had again appeared in the North Bay and were attempting to seize Indigenous laborers, especially children, to work on their lands. Whereas in 1836 the Castros had focused their efforts on San Rafael, west of Sonoma, now they were focusing on the Suscol region to the east. Vallejo also learned that Solano was cooperating with the Castro representatives in this endeavor. He was furious that Solano was undermining his quest to establish exclusive control over the North Bay and its Indigenous population. In his *Recuerdos*, Vallejo later claimed that the Castro party had gained Solano's cooperation after they had gotten him drunk on potent Peruvian *pisco*,[48] but the reality was probably more complex. By this time Solano was undoubtedly aware of the deteriorating relationship between Vallejo and Alvarado. Therefore, he probably wanted to construct alliances with other Mexicans so that he might be able to preserve his own advantages in the region in the event that Vallejo were to lose a power struggle with Alvarado and his allies in Monterey. He knew full well that providing Indigenous laborers for areas where they were scarce was a tried-and-true way to win the favor of Californio rancheros. He undoubtedly also knew that Alvarado was close to the Castros and had visited them at San Pablo. Indeed, Alvarado would marry the brothers' sister Martina the following year.[49]

Vallejo reacted swiftly and strongly to Solano's activity. After gaining the support of nearby rancheros—many of whom had received their ranchos through his intervention—and obtaining extra ammunition from Fort Ross, he summarily arrested Solano and posted a substantial armed guard around the barracks where he was being held. Vallejo implemented his strategy so quickly and decisively that Solano's Indigenous allies were unable to thwart it. Solano soon agreed to abandon the Castros, to reveal where

48. "Pisco" is a type of brandy similar to grappa.
49. Tays, "Mariano Guadalupe Vallejo and Sonoma," part 3:349; Miller, *Juan Alvarado*, 67–70.

*Portrait of a Young Native
American Man, 1851,
by Harrison Eastman
Courtesy of the John Carter
Brown Library. Record 199.*

the mainly Napajo Indian children had been sent, and to assist in
their recovery and return. Vallejo, who had become the owner of
the only printing press in Alta California, then published and distributed a manifesto declaring that he had known nothing about
the sale of Indian children, that he had sent out soldiers to ensure
their return, and that he was acting in the interests of "justice . . .
in favor of a group of families who are crying over the absence of
their children, who were violently torn from their parents' arms
and homes." There was no mention of the manner in which Indigenous laborers were being treated on the ranchos of Vallejo and
of his supporters.[50]

Indeed, by this time Vallejo had significant support in the North
Bay region. Soon after the expulsion of Híjar and Padrés, Figueroa
put him in charge of colonization in the north, a position Vallejo
used to befriend an eclectic group of foreigners, many of whom
he favored with various land grants. These foreigners had come
to California in a variety of manners. Charles Brown, who participated in the 1836 campaign at Pipoholma, had deserted from

50. MGV, *Recuerdos*, 1:818–23; MGV to Prado Mesa, October 6, 1838, C-B 5, doc. 193, TBL; MGV,
Francisco Solano, gefe de las tribus de esta frontera, abusando del poder.

a ship that stopped in the port of San Francisco. George Yount entered California as a member of a trapping expedition. Mark West, a native of England, had wandered around Mexico as a carpenter before arriving in California and working for a few years for Thomas O. Larkin, U.S. consul to Alta California. Timothy Murphy, a native of Ireland who had spent some time in Peru, worked in California for Vallejo's brother-in-law John Cooper. James Black said he had become sick at sea and was left in California by a ship captain who did not want to take care of him anymore. By whatever path, they ended up in the North Bay, where Vallejo welcomed them and often helped to set them up with ranchos. He correctly calculated that most of them had little, if any, contact with other Californios, so their gratitude to him would lead them to support his efforts to establish himself as the preeminent authority in the north. Generally speaking, Vallejo's calculation was quite correct.[51]

The lessening of the Satiyomi threat from the north and the successful resolution of the issue with Solano and the kidnapped Indian children left Vallejo in a relatively strong position at the beginning of 1839. After a year of increasing tension between himself and Alvarado, Vallejo decided he had to let the people of Monterey know that he still possessed a potent Indigenous ally and that the tensions between him and Solano the previous year had been resolved. To that end, he wrote Alvarado on October 16, saying that Solano had requested permission to visit Monterey "with eighty men," and that he had granted permission. The letter was doubtless meant to rekindle memories in Monterey of Vallejo and Solano's 1836 visits to Governor Chico. Vallejo visited Monterey and met with government secretary Manuel Jimeno. Solano and a number of Indigenous people from the North Bay were part of Vallejo's entourage. As he had in 1836, Solano cut an imposing figure. Dorotea Valdez, a resident of Monterey, later recalled, "They wore feathers around their heads, and many of them had tattoos around their wrists, arms, and legs. . . . Solano and his Indians

51. Emparán, *Vallejos of California*, 50–51; *California Star*, March 13, 1847; Bancroft, *History of California*, 2:721, 731–32, 4:750, 5:772; Camp, *George C. Yount*, 85–152.

all rode fine horses. They had hackamores but few had saddles. Their hair was long and they carried bows and arrows. Their looks inspired fear in everybody."[52] It is not clear if this demonstration had any significant effect. In any event, Alvarado and his allies soon were able to capitalize on the presence of a newly arrived immigrant from Switzerland in an attempt to diminish Vallejo's influence.

The Swiss adventurer, John Sutter, arrived in Monterey from Hawaii on July 3, 1839, with a party of thirteen, including ten native Hawaiians. He met Governor Alvarado a few days later and expressed an interest in settling in California's interior valley. The governor, irritated at Vallejo's increasing independence in the north, gave Sutter the green light to reconnoiter locations in the Sacramento Valley, where he might act as a counterweight to Vallejo. Before he organized his formal expedition, Sutter decided to visit the northern frontier and form his own assessment of the situations at Sonoma and Fort Ross. Vallejo received him with surface cordiality and provided a vaquero as an escort for Sutter's visit to the Russian outpost.[53]

In mid-August, Sutter was ready. He and his party traveled through the Sacramento Delta region then north along the Sacramento River. He was passing through Miwok territory but he did not encounter any Indigenous people until he was about ten miles south of the present site of Sacramento. There, he met a number of people from the ranchería of Gualicomne whose leader was named Anashe. The Ochejamne leader Huyumegepa may well also have been present. Since a number of these people had been residents of Mission San José before secularization, they could communicate in Spanish, and Sutter's halting abilities in that language enabled some degree of interchange. After Sutter distributed various gifts, they encouraged his interest in locating his settlement slightly north of them, in Nisenan territory, so he put his people to work

52. MGV to Alvarado, October 16, 1839, C-B 8, doc. 216, TBL; Bancroft, *History of California,* 3:598–99; Beebe and Senkewicz, *Testimonios,* 37, 432fn.9.

53. Bancroft, *History of California,* 4:127–29; Hurtado, *John Sutter,* 52–59; Gibson, *California through Russian Eyes,* 459.

John Augustus Sutter, ca. 1852, by
J. H. Pierce. *Courtesy of The
Bancroft Library, University of
California, Berkeley.* BANC PIC
1980.043-FR.

erecting a primitive settlement at the confluence of the Sacramento
and American Rivers.

Vallejo was not happy about Sutter's presence. In a December
1839 letter to his brother José de Jesús about organizing an expedition from San José against Indians in the Central Valley, he
stated that the "new colony of foreigners" along the Sacramento
River was "very suspicious" and "reeks of poison." Sutter's was the
first European settlement in that part of the valley and it caused
groups there that previously had been raiding horses from ranchos
close to the coast to begin inland attacks against these newcomers. The Indigenous people in the valley knew that Sutter had
already visited Vallejo, so they naturally assumed that the two
men were going to be working together. Consequently, as they
were organizing their attacks on Sutter, they decided to attack
Vallejo as well, to prevent him from coming to Sutter's aid. They
struck in 1840, less than a year after Sutter arrived. He later wrote
that "in the spring of 1840, the Indians began to be troublesome
all around me." The fact he reported that the attacks came from
people "all around" him probably indicates that the attackers were
from areas close to New Helvetia; that is, the Miwok areas along

the Sacramento and Cosumnes Rivers. The attacks appear to have consisted of aggressive raids upon his growing livestock herds. Sutter recalled, "I was obliged to make campaigns against them and punish them severely." He went to the Cosumnes River, where he attacked a group he claimed consisted of two or three hundred people, killing thirty of them in surprise cannon bombardments. He stated, "After this lesson they behaved very well and became my best friends and soldiers."[54]

At roughly the same time, in April, Vallejo reported that "Ochejamne, Tagualme, and Lachysma" people appeared in the Napa Valley with "warlike intentions." They were most likely a horse-raiding party. Indeed, the makeup of the group was roughly similar to that of the horse-raiding party that had appeared in August 1838, being composed of Miwoks from the Sacramento and Cosumnes River areas. Vallejo said that he, his brother Salvador, and Solano led a group of soldiers and Suisuns after the intruders. Reportedly, they pursued them to the territory of the "Julpunes," which was in the delta about forty-five miles east of Sonoma. There, he reported, they captured Huyumegepa and twenty-one of his group.[55]

That Vallejo and his party were able to capture the Ochejamne chief and about two dozen of his fighters indicated that the battle must have been intense and bloody. This fighting, however, exposed rifts in Vallejo's Indigenous forces. Shortly after the group returned to Sonoma, the Indigenous infantry, which was probably largely

---

54. Bancroft, *History of California*, 4:133; Hurtado, *John Sutter*, 62–63; Hurtado, "John A. Sutter and the Indian Business," 59–60; Levy, "Eastern Miwok," 399; MGV to José de Jesús Vallejo, December 26, 1839, C-B 8, doc. 395, TBL; Sutter, *Diary*, 8–9; Hurtado, *John Sutter*, 73–74.

55. MGV, *Recuerdos*, 2:961; Cook, *Aboriginal Population of the San Joaquin Valley*, 68; Camp, *George C. Yount*, 146–47; Bennyhoff, *Ethnogeography of the Plains Miwok*, 22, 64–65, 144; Zollinger, *Sutter*, 74, believed that Sutter's attack at the Cosumnes River took place in May, which would have meant that the New Helvetia attacks occurred in April, at the same time as the attack at Sonoma. Bennyhoff (*Ethnogeography of the Plains Miwok*, 154n.22), makes a strong case that Yokuts were highly unlikely to have been in the party that appeared in the Napa Valley. So "Lachysma" was probably a mistake or an exaggeration on Vallejo's part. However, in another part of the *Recuerdos* (2:986), Vallejo used the term "Tagualme" as an older name for the Cosumnes River, so here he may have been referring to a Miwok group from that vicinity.

composed of local Coast Miwoks, attacked the Indigenous cavalry, which was probably mainly composed of Suisuns, as well as Solano himself. The reason was most likely related to the treatment the Indigenous foot soldiers felt they had received in the campaign. They had likely suffered far greater casualties than the Mexican soldiers or the Suisun mounted soldiers, and they resented bearing the brunt of the fighting. Indeed, in Yount's account of the battle, the Indigenous foot soldiers were in the thick of a series of intense hand-to-hand struggles, while the mounted soldiers were employed in more of a mop-up role. Exposing the foot soldiers to greater danger during the battle may have been deliberate, for the year before, a group of Coast Miwok people had complained to Governor Alvarado about Mexican encroachment on their land at Nicasio, about fifteen miles northwest of Mission San Rafael. Vallejo reported that Mexican troops under Lázaro Piña and a number of local rancheros put down the uprising and killed a number of Native infantry fighters.[56]

In October, some Miwoks from Mission San José arrived at Sutter's establishment. They showed Sutter passports they had received from José de Jesús Vallejo, the military commander of San José. They told him that they were going to trade with the Miwok village of Sakayakumne on the Muquelemne River. This was the same site that the Ochejamne and Siusumne had mentioned to Mariano Guadalupe Vallejo in March 1838, which might indicate that the people talking to Sutter were from the same groups that had come to Vallejo two years earlier. Indeed, their actions indicated that this group was intent on taking revenge for Sutter's actions at the Cosumnes River in the spring. Sutter gave the group permission to pass after telling them not to kidnap any women. Instead of heading for Sakayakumne, however, the group went north and raided the Nisenan village of Yalisumne, on the American River somewhat east of New Helvetia. They killed a

---

56. Camp, *George C. Yount*, 146–47; Goerke, *Chief Marin*, 141, 170–71; Carlson and Parkman, "Exceptional Adaptation," 243–44; MGV, "Sobre sublevación de tropa," Sonoma, April 16, 1840, C-A 30:5, TBL.

number of elders and small children and took the remaining inhabitants as captives. The fact that the Yalisumne were laborers for
Sutter indicates that this attack was probably a continuation of the
attacks on Vallejo and Sutter that had begun in the spring. Sutter
immediately set out after the raiders. He captured and executed a
number of them, though others escaped. In mid-October, Sutter
wrote José de Jesús Vallejo and brusquely told him that mission
Indians were no longer welcome in his domain.[57]

Meanwhile, Vallejo was determined to take advantage of the
unsettled conditions around New Helvetia. He later claimed that
the Indigenous people of the valley were becoming more troublesome. As he recounted, "The Indians were no longer satisfied with
just stealing horses and killing cattle. Instead, they would capture
the girls and boys of the peaceful Indians who were servants living
in the homes of the rancheros and *hacendados*[58] and sell them to
the Indians of the Sierra in exchange for some curious object that
struck their fancy." To that end, he sent larger forces against the
groups he thought had constituted the raiding party in April. He
dispatched José de Jesús Vallejo and Prado Mesa with troops to
"the southern part of the Sacramento Valley" and Salvador Vallejo
and José Sánchez to the area south of the Cosumnes River. The
group led by José de Jesús Vallejo and Mesa returned after three
weeks with six prisoners, including one whom Mariano Guadalupe
Vallejo termed "Califa, a daring Indian bandit who wielded a shot-
gun as skillfully as the best of our grenadiers." The other expedition was gone for five weeks and Salvador Vallejo was wounded,
but they returned with eighty prisoners. Mariano Guadalupe
Vallejo later said that his brother wanted to kill them all, but he
was able to save them. He reportedly sent them to San Francisco
with Francisco Sánchez, who "little by little . . . set them free."

57. Hurtado, *John Sutter*, 74–75; Bancroft, *History of California*, 4:137–38. Wilson and Towne,
     "Nisenan," 388, and Kroeber, *Handbook*, 394, plate 37, place Yalisumne in slightly different
     locations, with Wilson and Towne placing it closer to New Helvetia than Kroeber does.
58. An "hacendado" is an owner of an hacienda, or large estate.

This statement probably meant that they were actually distributed among the ranchos of Vallejo's allies in the area.[59]

In the early 1840s two events combined to encourage Vallejo to shift more of his focus toward the area north of Sonoma. First, the smallpox epidemic of 1838 had greatly weakened the Satiyomi, who had effectively blocked Vallejo's attempt to expand north of Santa Rosa. Second, in 1841 the Russians abandoned Fort Ross, which meant that Vallejo could attempt to extend his influence farther north without having to worry about Russian reaction. Fort Ross was technically purchased from the Russians by Sutter. However, he was not interested in the land but only in removing the tools, plows, and other agricultural and construction resources and bringing them to New Helvetia. That task was basically completed by the conclusion of 1841.[60]

Sutter continued to be a problem. As he gradually strengthened his position in the Central Valley, some of the Indigenous people there, such as the Ochejamne, were able to use New Helvetia as a counterweight to Sonoma and the Mexican establishments closer to the coast. Vallejo regarded Alvarado as a man who had done Sutter "so many favors" and began to criticize his performance as governor in a series of letters he wrote to Mexican officials beginning in January 1841. He bemoaned "the great difficulty in keeping the governor [Alvarado] and the Comandante General [Vallejo] of the *departamento*[61] united in action and in agreement." These efforts culminated when Vallejo sent Víctor Prudón to Mexico at the beginning of 1842 to lobby for changes in Alta California's government and the appointment of a new governor. He later stated his belief that California needed a Mexican governor who had "no family ties with the Californio families." He opined, "I always

---

59. MGV, *Recuerdos*, 2:984, 986–87; Bennyhoff, *Ethnogeography of the Plains Miwok*, 71, 154n.22; Hurtado, *Scotts Valley Band*, 40. We thank Dr. Hurtado for sharing his manuscript with us.

60. Hurtado, *John Sutter*, 99–100.

61. A "departamento," or department, was a government unit corresponding to a state or territory. Under the centralist Mexican government after 1836, Alta California, formerly a territory, became a department.

thought that in sparsely populated countries family ties were the cause of the law being mismanaged." This statement related to another criticism he had of Alvarado: that the governor favored his own family and friends in the administration of ex-mission property and the distribution of land grants. A governor fitting Vallejo's prescription, Manuel Micheltorena, was sent to California in 1842. However, he proved unable to prevent the unpaid soldiers he brought with him, whom the Californios derisively termed "cholos,"[62] from looting and robbery throughout the departamento. When the movement against Micheltorena gained strength in 1844, Vallejo refused to participate and remained, so he claimed, "neutral." His primary objective continued to be the consolidation of his power in the north.[63]

In 1843 Salvador Vallejo organized a large expedition farther north, to the Clear Lake region, approximately seventy miles distant from Sonoma. He later insisted that his activities at Clear Lake had begun a few years earlier. In January 1855 he told the Land Commission that he and his brother Juan Antonio had applied for a grant of land at Clear Lake in 1838 from the director of colonization of the northern frontier. That official was, of course, their brother Mariano. According to Salvador, Mariano approved the application in March 1839. Salvador claimed that he and Juan Antonio had occupied the land soon thereafter. Salvador stated he "placed on the land about one thousand head of cattle, between three and four hundred head of horses, and from eight hundred to one thousand head of hogs; that he built a house on the land the same year, and also corrals, and left an overseer and servants in charge of the place." A few months later he told the U.S. District Court for the Northern District of California that he first encountered the lake in the early 1840s. He testified that "in the year 1842 or 1843" he placed "a large number of horses and cattle and hogs" on the rancho

---

62. "Cholo" is a derogatory term for a mestizo.

63. Bancroft, *History of California*, 4:199; MGV to the Minister of War, December 15, 1841, in *Recuerdos*, 2:1029; MGV, *Recuerdos*, 2:893, 933, 1054, 1145, 1161. A full treatment of the many disagreements between Vallejo and Alvarado in the late 1830s and early 1840s can be found in Tays, "Vallejo and Sonoma," part 4:50–62.

and "built several houses there." He also said that the boundaries of the rancho had been agreed to by a local Indigenous chief named Minac. However, in the primary source documents relating to his 1843 expedition to Clear Lake, there is no mention of his having any rancho in the area in 1838, 1841, or 1842.[64]

Juan Bojorques, who participated in Salvador's 1843 expedition, said that it consisted of roughly eighty settlers and a good number of Indian auxiliaries. He reported that the purpose was "to bring Indians from the lake to be servants for him [Salvador Vallejo] and for the other settlers who were on the expedition." According to Bojorques, the expedition included an Indian from Sonoma who acted as interpreter. When they arrived at the village of Koi at the south end of Lower Lake, they did some trading and persuaded a chief to accompany them as interpreter. They continued up the eastern shore of the lake and entered the territory of a group whom this new interpreter could not understand, so they retraced their steps. They persuaded the chief of Kamdot, an island on East Lake, to cross over with some of his people. According to Bojorques, Salvador Vallejo told the chief that "he wished to place a rancho on their land, and the Indian answered that he could." Vallejo then said that he would like to take them to Sonoma to show them the place, but they refused to go. At the suggestion of expedition member Ramón Carrillo, Vallejo ordered the Indians into a temescal. About half of the group entered, and the chief approached Carrillo to ascertain what was happening. Carrillo immediately stabbed him with his lance and killed him. Indian auxiliaries chased down the other Indians who attempted to escape by swimming back to the island and killed them. They also blocked the entrance to the temescal and set fire to it. Bojorques said that the interpreter called to those inside and offered to free them, but they replied that they would rather "die by fire than be taken by the soldiers."[65]

64. Lupyomi grant, BANC MSS, Land Case Files, 247 ND, 3, TBL; *United States v. Teschenmacher*, 63 U.S. 392 (1859); Hoffman, *Reports of Land Cases*, 34–36.

65. Bojorques, "Sobre la historia de California," 24, 27, TBL. An older translation of the entire Bojorques manuscript is in Heizer, *Collected Documents*, 67–70. The identification of the rancherías at Clear Lake is in Parker, "Kelsey Brothers," 7–8.

The Temescal, by Charles C. Pierce

Reproduced by permission of the Huntington Library, San Marino, California.
Pierce Collection, no. 01787.

Fearing that a larger group of Clear Lake people would soon organize and attack them, the Mexican force and the Indian auxiliaries retreated. The withdrawal was haphazard and somewhat disorderly. Apparently fearing they would be ambushed if they returned to Sonoma by the same route they had taken north, they headed west. Eventually, they came to the Pomo ranchería of Sanel, about forty miles northwest of Koi, where they rested for three or four days. On their way back to Sonoma, they sacked an unidentified ranchería where, according to Bojorques, they took roughly three hundred prisoners, "children and adults, men and women." The Indians were given nothing to eat for the first two days of the four-day march to Sonoma "for their crime of being Indians." Fortunately, for the last two days the Indians were able to gather some herbs for themselves that they knew were good to eat and thus survive the march.[66] During this march Salvador was able to scribble out a note to his brother in Sonoma. He told him that the party had been received well by the Clear Lake people but that he suspected they were planning to kill the members of the expedition. When they refused to surrender their weapons, he ordered his soldiers and the auxiliaries suddenly to attack them. He reported that 130 "men and women" had been killed.[67]

William Heath Davis remembered that the ostensible reason for Salvador's expedition was that Indians had been stealing "cattle, horses, and sheep, and driving them to the Siskiyou country, where they traded them off to trappers and Indians of the interior." G. M. Waseurtz af Sandels, a Swedish traveler, happened to be visiting Sonoma when the expedition returned. He said he was told that the expedition had been launched because the Indians in the north had been stealing cattle. Sandels had been in California long enough to doubt this version, which he termed "a shallow pretext." He stated, "Whenever a ranch requires laborers, you hear of some Indian outrage, followed by the taking of prisoners by the Californians." He

66. McLendon and Oswalt, "Pomo: Introduction," 278, 282; Bojorques, "Sobre la historia de California," C-D 46:33, TBL. On Sanel, see Barrett, *Ethno-geography of the Pomo*, 171.
67. Salvador Vallejo to MGV, March 13, 1843, C-B II, doc. 342, TBL.

said that the prisoners were "mostly females and young children. They were huddled together like beasts, nearly naked."[68]

In his report to the governor, Vallejo put on paper the pretext that was prevalent among the Mexican residents of Sonoma: there had been a "criminal conspiracy" by various frontier tribes against "the white inhabitants." He stated he had sent Salvador out against nine distinct groups in the Clear Lake region. The attack, he reported, was successful even though the expedition had to surmount "every type of danger." He also admitted that the attack left 170 Indians dead. The governor fired back a note saying that the death of so many Indians had caused a public outcry and he had ordered an immediate investigation. Davis also remembered that "when the news of the massacre reached Yerba Buena, the people were horrified." There is no record that the investigation ordered by the governor was ever undertaken. Shortly after this expedition, however, Salvador did establish a rancho at Clear Lake, with headquarters very near the Pomo village of Habe-napo, which the coast Miwok called Lup-Yomi. In addition, observers noted that many Clear Lake Indians were working on ranchos in the North Bay region. Indeed, the forced recruitment of Indigenous laborers for the Sonoma-area ranchos was the major reason for the establishment and continuance of the Mexican presence in the Clear Lake region.[69]

Vallejo's activities in the North Bay were aimed at increasing his own power. In the Mexican California of the 1830s and 1840s, power meant land. Starting with Petaluma, Vallejo accumulated a good amount of land. Exactly when he began to develop Petaluma into a rancho is unclear. In his 1852 testimony before the Land

68. The quotations from Sandels are from a section of "The King's Orphan" published in Upham, *Notes of a Voyage to California*, 551–52; Davis, "Salvador Vallejo and 'Las Trancas,' His Hacienda," DA2 (164), p. 1, HL.

69. MGV to Manuel Micheltorena, April 1, 1843, C-B II, doc. 354, TBL; Micheltorena to MGV, April 26, 1843, C B II, doc. 366, TBL; Davis, *Sixty Years in California*, 34, 342; Merriam, *Ethnogeographic and Ethnosynonymic Data*, 120; 141; Barrett, *Ethno-geography of the Pomo*, 22, 194; Kroeber, *Handbook*, 232; Palmer, *History of Napa and Lake Counties*, 35, 49, 85; Hurtado, *Scotts Valley Band*, 42–45.

Commission Vallejo stated that he had been in possession of the land since 1834. George Yount told the commission that Vallejo had built a house there in 1834. Salvador Vallejo reported that the structure was a simple adobe residence and that he lived there most of the time whereas his brother Mariano would visit periodically. Yount said that about two hundred acres were cultivated with various crops, which according to José de la Rosa, were mainly wheat, but also included barley and beans. Mariano Guadalupe Vallejo said that he was constructing a larger house by 1836, and Salvador added that the construction costs of that larger dwelling amounted to about $80,000. John Cooper, Vallejo's brother-in-law, stated that, in addition to the house, the fledgling rancho contained "corrals, sowings, cattle, and horses." Yount added that Vallejo had as many as ten thousand head of cattle and horses at the rancho. It is clear that by the 1840s Petaluma was a thriving enterprise.[70]

As the California government accelerated the land grant process, Vallejo intensified his attempts to expand his holdings in the North Bay. After the achievement of political stability in the late 1830s, he wanted to obtain for Petaluma a formal post-secularization grant of the type that Governors Alvarado and Micheltorena were dispensing. The 1834 grant from Figueroa had been based on laws of 1824 and 1828. As we have seen, the 1828 law had required that lands granted not be part of any mission. The fact that missions no longer existed opened the possibility for Vallejo to seek additional territory that Father Quijas had claimed for Mission San Francisco Solano in 1834, so in 1843 Vallejo applied for a grant. He claimed he had lost the original title papers some time ago, but had worked with government secretary Manuel Jimeno to find the original *expediente*[71] in the archives. He used that document, he said, to prepare a formal request. But he alleged that during the chaos in Monterey following the Jones invasion in 1842, "The archives fell into the power of the invaders. From this

---

70. Petaluma grant, BANC MSS, Land Case Files, 321 ND, 6, 7, 10, 14, 18, TBL; Silliman, *Lost Laborers*, 45–50.

71. An "expediente" is a file or record.

general confusion . . . the papers were again lost, without hopes of obtaining them again." So he prepared a new petition for the land as well as a diseño showing the ten square leagues he was requesting. Micheltorena had not been in Monterey when Jones appeared and probably did not know that the only activity relating to the archives had been a quick search for recent Mexican newspapers to prove to Jones that war had not broken out. Therefore, on the basis of Vallejo's statement, Micheltorena granted him Petaluma on October 22, 1843.[72]

The next year Vallejo was back with another request. He said that a closer review of the boundaries of the grant on the "original diseño," which he reported was now in the government offices, revealed that the grant actually contained fifteen square leagues, rather than ten. He asked that these additional five leagues be granted to him and be viewed as compensation for the two thousand pesos[73] he was still owed for his service as commander general of the Departamento de Alta California. When Micheltorena agreed, Vallejo's Rancho Petaluma grew to more than sixty-six thousand acres.[74]

Petaluma was not the only large tract Vallejo was eyeing. Indeed, his interest in expanding his North Bay holdings predated his concern about Petaluma. On January 1, 1841, he wrote to the minister of war in Mexico City, complaining that the current Alta California government, headed by Juan Bautista Alvarado, was not attending to the soldiers. He specifically noted that the old Ranchos Nacionales,[75] which had been dedicated to the support of the troops, had all been taken over by various individuals and had become simply private ranchos. He stated that he had occupied the

---

72. Petaluma grant, BANC MSS, Land Case Files, 321 ND, 39, 42, 45, TBL; Hague and Langum, *Thomas O. Larkin*, 100.

73. In Spanish America a peso was a monetary unit equal to eight *reales*. In the first half of the nineteenth century, a peso was roughly equivalent to one U.S. dollar.

74. Petaluma grant, BANC MSS, Land Case Files, 321 ND, 50, TBL.

75. A "Rancho Nacional" was a rancho operated by the local presidio for the support of the soldiers and their families. After Mexican Independence, the Ranchos del Rey were renamed Ranchos Nacionales.

Suscol area on the northern shore of the Carquínez Strait, placing three thousand head of cattle and six hundred horses on this land, allegedly for the benefit of his own soldiers. But he stated that, in view of his many responsibilities as commander general, maintaining the stock was becoming increasingly difficult. He asked that this land be given to him as recompense for the back pay he was owed from 1824, when he joined the military, through his service as an alférez in the mid-1830s and as payment for the thousands of pesos of his own money he had expended to support the soldiers after he became commander general.[76]

Vallejo made a similar request to newly arrived Governor Micheltorena in 1843, when Micheltorena was still in Los Angeles, having not even arrived in Monterey yet. Vallejo had learned that the new governor was having trouble supplying his own troops with food and provisions, so he offered Micheltorena a deal. Vallejo claimed that he ought to receive Suscol as recompense for all he had contributed to the army while he had been serving Mexico as commander general of the Departamento de Alta California. He also offered that he would be open to purchasing the tract for five thousand pesos. Micheltorena, far from awash in funds and concerned that his unpaid troops might rob people in Los Angeles and thereby turn southern Alta California against his rule, indicated that he was receptive to this offer. To seal the agreement, Vallejo sent his brother-in-law John Cooper south in June, sailing a vessel filled with provisions. Micheltorena arrived in Monterey in August, and the following June allowed Vallejo to purchase Suscol for five thousand pesos.[77]

He also became interested in the land around Suisun, Solano's traditional home. As we have indicated previously, Vallejo had acknowledged Solano's possession of the area in 1835 and, in his

---

76. MGV to Ministro de Guerra y Marina, January 1, 1841, C-B 10, doc.10, TBL.

77. Suscol grant, BANC MSS, Land Case Files, 318 ND, 16–17, 48–50, TBL; Bancroft, *History of California*, 4:351. A number of these documents and other papers also appear in the supporting documents and arguments relating to the Supreme Court case *U.S. v. Vallejo* (66 U.S. [1 Black] 541); see, for instance, Frisbie, *Memorial and Accompanying Papers in Relation to the Soscol Rancho*.

position as military commander, had provisionally granted him the land as a rancho in 1837. Vallejo told the Land Commission that Solano constructed an adobe house for himself in 1835 and that eventually the rancho contained "several hundred houses for the accommodation of the tribe." He also said that Solano "cultivated the land extensively." In January 1842 Governor Alvarado formally granted the rancho to Solano. Since Solano was represented in these proceedings by Vallejo's younger brother Juan Antonio, the formal grant was probably part of a larger effort by Mariano Guadalupe Vallejo to enlarge his own holdings. Indeed, a few months later, he purchased the rancho from Solano and appointed Solano as his mayordomo. Most likely there was little change in the actual operations of the rancho, with Solano remaining effectively in charge.[78]

Indigenous people are thus represented, albeit briefly, in the documentary record of Rancho Suisun, but Suisun is a major exception. In general, the experiences of the Indigenous people who labored on the Vallejo ranchos or on most of the ranchos in California are not accessible in the written archives. Unlike the missionaries, Californio rancheros did not keep detailed accounts of the people who lived or worked at their establishments. Glimpses into their experiences can be obtained only from the occasional comments of contemporary visitors and from the work of archaeologists.

Contemporary visitors to ranchos tended to comment on the appearance of the adobe residence, the home's furnishings, the family's hospitality, and the extent of the rancho's agricultural and grazing lands. When they mentioned the Indigenous laborers, they tended to report on the numbers of people they saw. Visitors to Petaluma, for instance, tended to estimate the number of Indigenous people at anywhere from one hundred to one thousand. Since the number of rancho laborers most likely fluctuated seasonally, the number a particular visitor observed would have varied depending on when that person happened to arrive. Visitors, however, did not

---

78. Suisun grant, BANC MSS, Land Case Files, 2 ND, 31–32, 58, 60, TBL; MGV, *Recuerdos*, 1:749–50.

report on the laborers' activities in any great detail. Their silence was most likely because they observed standard activities that would have been seen on any rancho, such as planting and harvesting of crops and branding and slaughtering of herds. Compensation was most likely given in kind—food, shelter, and clothing—rather than in any form of money. Archaeological evidence seems to indicate that Indigenous people at ranchos, like those at missions or presidios, tended to use a mix of traditional and Spanish-Mexican tools and to consume a similar mix of foods.[79]

Vallejo did not comment often upon his treatment of the Indigenous laborers at his establishments. When he did, he tended to emphasize that he treated them well and that, when an occasion might offer itself, he tried to introduce them to the Spanish-Mexican ways of doing things, which he clearly regarded as superior. At one point he described the manner in which he tried to teach the Indigenous laborers the inappropriateness of theft, the necessity of punishment, and the basic principles of self-government: "Whenever one of the Indians in my employ would steal something from my home or from one of my workers, I would grab the culprit and lock him in a room. Then I would form a jury of his peers. If the crime was not very serious and if the accused was not a repeat offender, they generally would apply the sentence of twenty blows. In serious cases, though, the punishment would rarely be less than fifty blows upon the buttocks." In this case, just as when the missionaries described how they enforced discipline in their establishments, it is unclear what the recipients of these messages actually learned from them.[80]

Oral traditions can help us get closer to the experience. Vallejo's presence was very much remembered in the Coast Miwok traditions that Isabel Kelly recorded in her 1931–32 interviews with María Copa and Tom Smith. Copa, whose paternal and maternal grandparents were closely associated with Mission San Rafael, reported that Vallejo's activities throughout the North Bay region

---

79. Silliman, *Lost Laborers*, 56–59, 188.
80. MGV, *Recuerdos*, 2:905.

were remembered as ugly. She reported the tradition that Vallejo acted harshly toward his workers:

> My father's father was a Mexican; his mother was a Solano Indian.
> My grandfather was one of Vallejo's captains.
> He ran away with some of his Indian soldiers.
> Vallejo was mean to his men and abused them; he had those who ran away followed.
> These killed the cow and ate, and all went to sleep except one man who was to watch.
> They slept in an open spot. The sentry was no good, and Vallejo's men hid in the brush all around.
> My grandfather was named Copa. The others said to him in Spanish, "Do you surrender or do you die?"
> My grandfather said, "I'd better die. I don't want to suffer anymore. I shall die with my people."
> So they fought and all were killed. They piled the bodies like wood and burned them.
> One of Vallejo's soldiers told us about this later; he was there.[81]

Oral traditions are often difficult to corroborate precisely, but they do provide irreplaceable access to community memory. In this case at least, the memory of Vallejo's conquest and the resistance to it in the North Bay was brutal.

---

81. Kelly et al., *Interviews with Tom Smith and María Copa*, 75.

CHAPTER 4

"That the Bear Be Taken Out of the Design"

Vallejo and the First Years of American California

Archibald Gillespie arrived in Monterey aboard the USS *Cyane* on April 17, 1846. He identified himself as a merchant who had come to California to recover his health, but he was actually a naval officer who was carrying secret messages from Washington, D.C., to Thomas O. Larkin and John C. Frémont. Larkin, the U.S. consul in Monterey, had been appointed a "confidential agent" by President Polk. The letter to Larkin was from Secretary of State James Buchanan, who wrote that Larkin's major task was to try to prevent the Californios from allying themselves with any European power. He was also told to assure the Californios that if they desired "to unite their destiny with ours, they would be received as brethren."[1]

---

1. Hague and Langum, *Thomas O. Larkin*, 114.

Original Bear Flag
Courtesy of the California History Room,
California State Library, Sacramento, California. Neg. 1182.

In Monterey, Larkin introduced Gillespie to a number of people and persuaded former governor Alvarado to host a reception for him. It appears that some Monterey residents were not taken in by Gillespie's cover story. Angustias de la Guerra later said that "neither I nor Señora Spence [Adelaida Estrada] were deceived. . . . We found it difficult to understand why the U.S. government would send an entire warship just to bring an ill young man to California." She said that the two women shared their suspicions with military commander José Castro, but he rebuked them "for thinking badly of a man who was ill." She added, "He accused us, and all women in general, of thinking badly of others, which according to Castro was something that women did much more than men." Mariano Guadalupe Vallejo, on the other hand, later insisted that Castro was also suspicious and spent the reception at Alvarado's house plying Gillespie with "numerous alcoholic drinks with the hope that under the influence of wine mixed with pisco he would divulge the secret of his mission." Gillespie did not divulge his plans, however.[2]

The next day Gillespie headed off in pursuit of Frémont, who had entered Alta California in late 1845 with a detachment of soldiers on a surveying expedition. Claiming to be short of supplies, he reconnoitered the Monterey region before being ordered to leave by Commander José Castro in March 1846. In a deliberately provocative act, he raised the American flag on Gavilán Peak, just outside the capital of Mexican Alta California, before heading to the Central Valley and going north toward Oregon. When Gillespie caught up to Frémont, he delivered some written messages. They were mainly from his father-in-law, Senator Thomas Hart Benton of Missouri, concerning current affairs. However, what Gillespie handed to Frémont was much less important than what he said to him. He told Frémont of Larkin's appointment and brought the young army officer up-to-date regarding talk of impending war in both the United States and Mexico. Frémont quickly reversed direction and turned south, camping at the Buttes, about forty-five miles north of Sutter's Fort. There at the beginning of June he interacted with a number of Americans, including Ezekiel Merritt, a man who had been in California for a number of years and had regularly worked at Sutter's establishment.[3]

Frémont's return alarmed Castro, who was at Santa Clara preparing to gather and equip a force to fight Governor Pío Pico. A rumor was afoot that Pico was about to send a detachment north from Los Angeles to confront Castro and overthrow him, thereby endowing himself with both the military and political command. To counter Frémont's presence, Castro hurried to the North Bay where, with Vallejo's approval, he obtained a few hundred horses from San Rafael. He entrusted José María Alviso and Francisco

---

2. Beebe and Senkewicz, *Testimonios*, 263; MGV, *Recuerdos*, 2:1246–47.

3. Bancroft, *History of California*, 5:1–29; Hague and Langum, *Thomas O. Larkin*, 128; Castleman, *Knickerbocker Commodore*, 194–95; Warner, *Men of the California Bear Flag Revolt*, 76–82.

Arce with the task of taking them around the Sacramento Delta and through the East Bay region to Santa Clara. Merritt learned of this plan, and with a small group of Americans, intercepted them and took the horses to Frémont, who had moved his camp closer to Sutter's Fort. A few days later, Merritt led a group of about thirty-five men to Sonoma. Half of these men were would-be settlers who had arrived less than a year before. On June 14 they appeared in front of Vallejo's house and demanded entry.[4]

Their plans were exceedingly ill-defined. In subsequent years many of the participants insisted that they were reacting to a proclamation Castro had issued demanding that all Americans leave California within forty days. No such proclamation has surfaced. The closest approximation was a decree Castro had issued in March, after Frémont had left Gavilán. In that decree Castro had cried out that Frémont's actions merited "the loathing and hatred of the Mexicans." He urged the Californios, "Prepare yourselves to defend our independence so that united we can repel with a strong hand the audacity of ungrateful men who after receiving every manner of true hospitality in our country, reward the benefits they have acquired through our cordiality and benevolence with such ingratitude." Castro's proclamation was apparently transformed into a more aggressive document the more the Americans discussed it. By the beginning of June, Joseph Downey, a crewman aboard the USS *Portsmouth* in Monterey, wrote of Castro's "famous proclamation against all foreigners." Frémont probably took advantage of this exaggeration to stir up the Americans. He most likely calculated that their lack of organization and planning would make it easy for him to assume leadership of the group if it became advantageous for him to do so.[5]

The Americans certainly constituted a boisterous, disorganized, and motley group when they entered the Sonoma Plaza on June 14,

4. Salomon, *Pío Pico*, 96–97; Warner, *Men of the California Bear Flag Revolt*, 63–67.

5. MGV, *Recuerdos*, 2:1244–45; Downey, *Cruise of the Portsmouth*, 125. For Bear Flagger reminiscences, see Bancroft, *History of California*, 5:178–80, and Warner, *Men of the California Bear Flag Revolt*, 32–35.

Robert Baylor Semple. *Courtesy of The Bancroft Library, University of California, Berkeley.* POR: *Semple, Robert Baylor: 1.*

1846. In Vallejo's opinion they looked "ferocious." "Some of them were wearing on their heads coyote-skin caps without visors, some a knit hat without a crown, and some were wearing a red cotton bandana. With regard to the rest of the clothing covering the flesh of those thieves who were surrounding my residence, I will not attempt to describe it, for I recognize that I am incapable of properly completing that task." Due to fear of what would happen to his family if he left, he dismissed his wife, Benicia's, suggestion that he flee out the back door. Instead, he quickly dressed in his military uniform and opened the door. He asked the group who their leader was and received the response, "Here we are all leaders." He ended up dealing inside his house with Merritt; Robert Semple, an imposing six-foot, six-inch dentist who had arrived in 1845; and William Knight, an Indiana native who had spent some years in New Mexico before coming to California in 1841. After some time, John Grigsby, another 1845 arrival, joined the group, and he was eventually followed by William Ide, who had arrived in California with Grigsby. In the meantime, Salvador Vallejo, Jacob Leese, and Víctor Prudón joined the group. Vallejo served everyone wine.[6]

As the talks continued, the larger group of about thirty men outside became more impatient and agitated, and Vallejo credited Semple for calming them down. The people inside hammered out a "treaty" in which the Vallejo brothers and Prudón agreed not to oppose the government that the insurgent group intended to set up, and the insurgents agreed not to harm the inhabitants of Sonoma. But the larger group outside refused to accede to these arrangements. They demanded that the insurgent group take complete control of Sonoma and that the Vallejo brothers and Prudón be taken as prisoners to Frémont, whose camp by this time was close to Sutter's Fort. Mariano and Salvador, along with Prudón, were taken prisoner by a group of about ten insurgents, including Merritt, Semple, and Grigsby. Leese agreed to accompany them as interpreter.[7]

Before leaving Sonoma, Mariano Guadalupe Vallejo managed secretly to send Pepe de la Rosa to Sausalito to inform John Montgomery, captain of the USS *Portsmouth*, of what had happened and ask for his assistance. Vallejo had made Montgomery's acquaintance because he had been in Monterey when the *Portsmouth* sailed into the harbor there on April 22, 1846. At the same time, he met Lieutenant Joseph Warren Revere, who said he quickly learned that Vallejo was very friendly to the United States. The *Portsmouth* had left Monterey on June 1 and anchored at Sausalito to be nearer to Frémont, who was returning to the Sacramento region after Gillespie had caught up to him. Indeed, Montgomery sent Frémont a number of weapons and other military supplies at the end of June, before the news of war between the United States and Mexico arrived and before Commodore John Drake Sloat took

---

6. MGV, *Recuerdos*, 2:1249–51; Radcliffe, "Robert Baylor Semple, Pioneer"; Warner, *Men of the California Bear Flag Revolt*, 107–23, 139–45, 150–74, 174–95; Bancroft, *History of California*, 5.114–15.

7. Bancroft, *History of California*, 5:113–19.

possession of Monterey on July 7. When de la Rosa arrived at the *Portsmouth* on June 15, Lieutenant Henry Bulls Watson assessed him as "a Mexican and by no means, as I learn, a very reputable one." However, he was allowed on board after "he was recognized by the captain officially." De la Rosa's request was that Montgomery act, "in order that private property and defenseless women and children might be protected." According to Watson, Montgomery's initial reaction was that "the revolution was confined to California and must be settled among themselves." Montgomery told de la Rosa, "You will assure General Don Guadalupe Vallejo of my sympathy in his difficulties, but I cannot possibly interfere in the local politics of California."[8]

The prisoners and those who accompanied them spent the first night at Manuel Vaca's rancho. That night Vicente Juárez, disguised as a woman, was able to sneak into the encampment and offered to have an armed party attempt to rescue Vallejo. Not wanting to endanger his family in Sonoma by escalating matters, Vallejo refused. Then, however, the Americans did escalate, as Frémont sent an order that Leese should be treated not as an interpreter but as a prisoner. When they reached their destination, Frémont told Vallejo that "he could not intervene in our favor at that time, but he would try to help us later." Vallejo recounted, "That promise did not fill me with much hope." In his opinion, Frémont's camp was filled with an undisciplined rabble over whom the commander did not have sufficient control. As had been the case at Sonoma, Vallejo credited Semple, one of the group taking the men to Frémont, with calming down the crowd. This intervention allowed Frémont to send them to Sutter's Fort, where they were put in what Vallejo described as "a long narrow room" where they were "forced to sleep on the floor without a mattress or blanket." Vallejo especially resented this treatment by Sutter,

---

8. Revere, *Tour of Duty*, 31, 50; Downey, *Cruise of the Portsmouth*, 129; Watson, *Journals*, 143; Rogers, *Montgomery and the Portsmouth*, 36; Statement of Washington A. Bartlett, June 15, 1846, in "Documentary: The Bear Flag Movement," 81; Bancroft, *History of California*, 5:130–31.

whom he described as "a foreigner who had received many favors from me and my family but had relegated them to oblivion."[9]

During the early days of Vallejo's imprisonment, Montgomery tried to ensure that civilians in Sonoma, especially Vallejo's family, were safe.

On June 16 he sent a crew under Lieutenant John S. Misroon to Sonoma. Misroon received assurances from the insurgent leadership that Sonoma would not be plundered and that Vallejo and the other prisoners would not be harmed. He reported to Montgomery, "I then called upon the family of General Vallejo and moderated their distress by the assurances of safety for the General which I had received." Misroon also issued a safe-conduct pass to Benicia's brother, Julio Carrillo, so that he could travel to Sutter's Fort and personally assure Vallejo that his family was safe. When Carrillo arrived there, however, he was promptly arrested. At the beginning of July, Montgomery sent Lieutenant Washington Bartlett and Doctor Andrew Henderson to Sonoma to assist the Vallejo family and the other Sonoma civilians. Bartlett wrote to Vallejo and assured him that his family was safe and well.[10]

Meanwhile, William Ide assumed leadership within the insurgent movement at Sonoma. He drafted a declaration that accused the Mexican California government of military "despotism" that threatened the settlers with "extermination if they would not depart out of the country." Another crime of the California government was that it "seized upon the property of the missions," an odd statement because the overwhelming majority of the insurgents had never seen a functioning mission. Ide insisted that the aim of the insurgency was "a republican government." Ide's declaration was replaced with a more temperate one a few days later, but it is very doubtful that many of the insurgents read either one of them. At the same time, insurgent William Todd and a few others

9. MGV, *Recuerdos*, 2:1250–51; Bancroft, *History of California*, 5:119–21. For Sutter's part, he insisted that he was too lenient with the prisoners to satisfy Frémont. See Hurtado, *John Sutter*, 195.

10. John S. Misroon to John B. Montgomery, June 17, 1846, in "Documentary: The Bear Flag Movement," 88; MGV, *Recuerdos*, 2:1261–62; Tays, "Vallejo and Sonoma," part 6:226.

Francisca Benicia Carrillo de
Vallejo. *Courtesy of California State
Parks, Sonoma Barracks.*
No. 243-1-1403.N.

designed a flag for the movement. One feature of the flag was a
single star in the upper left, which was an obvious allusion to the
1836 flag of the Texas Republic. The major feature, however, was
a drawing of a bear (Mariano Guadalupe Vallejo said it looked
more like a pig!), which gave the Bear Flag movement its name.[11]

When word was received that José Castro and many local Californios were beginning to organize attacks on the Bear Flaggers,
Frémont decided it was time for him to assume command of the
movement, so moved his forces to Sonoma. By this time Benicia
Vallejo, already angered by the arrest of her husband and furious
at the refusal of the Sutter's Fort jailers to respect the safe-conduct pass Misroon had given her brother Julio, decided to act. She
secretly gathered up and sent some weapons to the local Californios who were organizing an anti-Bear militia in the countryside.
According to her husband, when her action was discovered, Fré-

---

11. Bancroft, *History of California*, 5:152; Warner, *Men of the California Bear Flag Revolt*, 62,
354; MGV, *Recuerdos*, 2:1255.

mont told her that she was "deserving of a very serious punishment for having supplied arms to the enemies of the government
of California." She replied:

> I have not given arms to the enemies, but rather to the friends, of the
> government of California. Those people under your command have no
> God and no laws. They have placed on the flagpole a rag that has a bear
> painted on it, and that is the same as saying they are thieves. If you want
> there to be peace on the frontier, order that the rag be taken down and
> raise the American flag. Under the protection of that flag we will be able
> to live tranquilly and perhaps even united, for many of my sisters are
> married to Americans, and you know that family ties are powerful.[12]

Benicia spent the rest of the time her husband was imprisoned
trying to protect her family. She told the naval officer Archibald
Gillespie that she had secretly locked up four pistols in the chest of
drawers in her room and was "keeping them to defend her honor
and the lives of her daughters in case some of the 'Bears' tried to
barge into their bedrooms." Rosalía Vallejo, Mariano Guadalupe
and Salvador's sister and Leese's wife, shared this concern for pro-
tecting local women from assault by Frémont's men. She recounted
in her 1874 testimonio:

> During the whole time that Frémont and his ring of thieves were in
> Sonoma, robberies were very common. The women did not dare go out
> for a walk unless they were escorted by their husbands or their brothers.
> One of my servants was a young Indian girl who was about seventeen
> years old. I swear that John C. Frémont ordered me to send that girl to
> the officers' barracks many times. However, by resorting to tricks, I was
> able to save that poor girl from falling into the hands of that lawless band
> of thugs who had imprisoned my husband.[13]

Benicia also attempted to raise her husband's spirits. In a series
of letters in June and July 1846 she reassured him, "Your children
and I are fine. Don't worry about the family." She reported that
Miguel Alvarado, the mayordomo at Petaluma, was taking care
of the harvest there, that the yearly slaughter of cattle at Suscol

---

12. MGV, *Recuerdos*, 2:127.
13. Beebe and Senkewicz, *Testimonios*, 29.

was proceeding, and that his own personal and business papers were secure. When she could, she sent him supplies of money, bread, and paper. Her husband very much appreciated her efforts. He wrote to her on July 22, "I am anxiously awaiting . . . to hear news from home." The uncertainty of his position, even after the American government had taken control of California, worried him. "Every day," he wrote Benicia, "we wait for the mail to arrive from Monterey. Maybe when it arrives we will be free to return to our homes."[14]

During the conflicts over these days, two Bears, Thomas Cowie and George Fowler, were captured and murdered by a Californio, Bernardo "Three-Fingered Jack" García. In retaliation, a Bear squadron under the command of Kit Carson shot three unarmed Californios: José de los Reyes Berreyesa and brothers Francisco and Ramón de Haro. Vallejo reserved his criticism for Frémont, writing, "Even if it were accepted that the order to murder Berreyesa and the Haro brothers did not come from Frémont, the responsibility for those murders lies with him. For in his role as leader he did not order that charges be brought against the murderers nor the punishment they deserved."[15]

After Sloat occupied Monterey on July 7, Vallejo assumed that, with the actual American government in control, he would soon be released. His release did not happen quickly, although Montgomery did act more directly to assist him. Secretary of the Navy George Bancroft had ordered Sloat to treat the Californios gently. A full year before war broke out, Bancroft told Sloat that, in the event of a conflict, he should adopt "the most friendly relations with the inhabitants." A few months later he wrote to Sloat: "You will do everything that is proper to conciliate towards our country the most friendly regard of the people of California." Vallejo's apparent friendliness to the United States made him a prime Californio candidate for such conciliation. Three days after Sloat took

14. Benicia's June and July letters, mostly undated, are in C-B 441, box 6, folder 5, TBL; MGV to Francisca Benicia Vallejo, July 22, 1846, C-B 441, box 1, folder 1, TBL.

15. Bancroft, *History of California*, 5:160–61, 171–74; MGV, *Recuerdos*, 2:1270.

possession of Monterey, Montgomery wrote him requesting that
the prisoners at Sutter's Fort be released. It is unclear whether Sloat
ever responded to Montgomery's letter, and in any event, he left
California on July 29, 1846. On that day, however, the new military
commander, Commodore Robert Stockton, wrote Mariano Guadalupe Vallejo to say that he had ordered his release. Montgomery
sent a message to Edward Kern, whom Frémont had left in charge
at Sutter's Fort, ordering him to release Vallejo and Julio Carrillo.
Montgomery told Kern that the two men were to be released "on
their parole of honor; not to take arms, instigate, or directly or
indirectly participate in any movement against the authorities of
the U. States in California, until regularly exchanged; and not to
leave their proper districts without permission from the officer in
command at this place until further notice."[16]

However, Frémont had instructed Kern not to release the prisoners except at his command, so Kern accordingly stalled and kept
them locked up. When Kern learned that Montgomery was sending Revere personally to release Vallejo and Carrillo, however, he
made the two men sign a more stringent statement than Montgomery had dictated as a condition for their release. Vallejo and Carrillo
had to promise not to "furnish supplies, carry communications, or
in any way assist any person or persons who may be opposed to the
United States of North America or the above named residents of
California [the Bear Flaggers], or leave any proper district without
permission from the commander at Yerba Buena, understanding
distinctly that if this pledge is not faithfully performed, my life is
forfeited wherever I may be found." When Revere arrived at Sutter's
Fort he brought with him a note from Montgomery, who was interested in assuaging and conciliating Mariano Guadalupe Vallejo.
Montgomery told Vallejo that all he needed was "simply a promise
of friendship to the United States or of strict neutrality in all differences pending between the existing and former governments of

16. Tays, "Vallejo and Sonoma," part 6:227; Castleman, *Knickerbocker Commodore*, 191, 195,
207 9; John B. Montgomery to Edward M. Kern, July 24, 1846, in Dunbar, *Fort Sutter
Papers*, doc. 32.

the Department of California, which will leave you fully at large to attend to your business concerns without hindrance or restraint." Kern released the two men to Revere. Vallejo, escorted by William Scott, a Bear Flagger, was back in Sonoma by August 6. The other prisoners were released on August 8.[17]

Vallejo was exhausted and decimated after his ordeal. He told Consul Thomas Larkin, "I left Sacramento half dead." While he was imprisoned, he had learned from Benicia that some of his Indigenous laborers were taking advantage of the opportunity to slip away. Even though most of her letters were aimed at trying to keep his spirits up, at one point she had to confess, "Not much can be done at the ranchos because the Indians are running away." He had also heard rumors that large numbers of "cattle and horses belonging to myself and others had been driven off" from his properties by Frémont's men. The fact that this turned out to be true compounded his suffering. He lamented, "I have lost more than 1,000 live horned cattle, 600 tame horses, and many other things of value which were taken from my house here and at Petaluma. My wheat crops are entirely lost." On September 9 Montgomery wrote to Vallejo that Stockton was in Yerba Buena. He said, "I desire much to have the pleasure of presenting you to him. I have made him acquainted with your friendly zeal and services, which I am persuaded he mightily appreciates and that he will be pleased to see you."[18]

Yet on the very next day Montgomery received disturbing news. A messenger sent by Kern at Sutter's Fort arrived, saying that a large war party of Walla Walla Indians from Oregon were marching through the Central Valley toward Sacramento. They were, it was thought, seeking revenge for the killing of the son of their

---

17. Hurtado, *John Sutter*, 196; statement signed by Mariano Guadalupe Vallejo and Julio Carrillo, witnessed by John A. Sutter, August 2, 1846, MGV's Release from Fort Sutter, CHS; Tays, "Vallejo and Sonoma," part 6:229; Kern to Montgomery, August 3, 1846, in Dunbar, *Fort Sutter Papers*, doc. 76; MGV, *Recuerdos*, 2:1312; Warner, *Men of the California Bear Flag Revolt*, 240–42.

18. MGV to Thomas O. Larkin, September 15, 1846, in Larkin, *Papers* 5:236; MGV to Larkin, July 23, to MGV, 1846, in Larkin, *Papers*, 5:154; Benicia Vallejo n.d. [1846], C-B 441, box 6, folder 5, TBL; John B. Montgomery to MGV, September 9, 1846, C-B 12, doc. 236, TBL.

chief. Montgomery immediately wrote Vallejo and asked him to make good on his offers of assistance to the Americans. He said, "The condition of the country, menaced as it is by a large body of armed Indians, in the neighborhood of Fort Sacramento, causes me to accept with gratitude the offer of your services with that of as many of the natives of California as you can possibly raise for the occasion." Vallejo immediately accepted, for it gave him the opportunity to demonstrate to the newcomers that the leaders in Mexican California, himself included, were organized, competent, and capable of attending to civic matters such as public safety. Salvador Vallejo also offered his help, and the next day Misroon wrote him accepting his offer "to superintend personally a body of Indians now in your employ for the sole purpose of maintaining a rigid system of observation around all of the passes leading from Sacramento to Sonoma in consequence of the approach of a large band of hostile Indians of the Walla Walla tribe."[19]

As it turned out, the threat was hardly grave. The Indigenous group, led by Chief Peopeo Moxmox, whom Vallejo knew as Macai, was relatively small and included women and children. They wanted to visit the grave of the chief's son, to ask for some sort of punishment for his killers, and to seek good trade relations. Everyone quickly realized that, as Vallejo later wrote, "The intentions of the Walla Walla Indians had been misconstrued, and their number had been exaggerated." Montgomery wrote to Vallejo after the perception of danger had passed and thanked him for "your assistance to the government of the United States in the recent emergency." Montgomery also indicated that he was well aware of Vallejo's position among the Californios and the leverage he could have in convincing his compatriots to accept the American presence. He complimented Vallejo and his men for having done "much towards allaying national prejudices and unfriendly suspicions among the various classes composing the societies of

---

19. Hussey and Ames, "California Preparations," 10–11; John B. Montgomery to MGV, September 10, 1846, C-B 12, doc. 237, TBL; John S. Misroon to Salvador Vallejo, September 11, 1846, C-B 12, doc. 238, TBL.

Californian Lancer, ca. 1846–1848, by William H. Meyers
Courtesy of the Franklin D. Roosevelt Presidential
Library and Museum. MO *1975.33a.7.*

California, and in hastening arrangements for the establishment of peace, order, and good government in the country." In a postscript, he renewed the invitation he had made on September 9 for Vallejo to visit him: "I am now living on board the ship and should be much gratified to receive a visit from you." Vallejo did go to Yerba Buena at the beginning of October and participated in a reception for Stockton on October 5. The Monterey *Californian* reported that a procession was formed to greet the commodore and that "General Mariano Guadalupe Vallejo, with several others who have held office under the late government, took their appropriate places in the line."[20]

---

20. MGV, *Recuerdos*, 2:1314–16; Heizer, "Walla Walla Indian Expeditions," 3; Hurtado, *John Sutter*, 199–201; John B. Montgomery to MGV, September 25, 1846, C-B 12, doc. 242, TBL; "Public Reception of Commodore Robert F. Stockton," *Californian* [Monterey], October 24, 1846; Tays, "Vallejo and Sonoma," part 6:230.

Vallejo continued his very public efforts to cooperate with the American authorities. After the surrender of the Californio forces at Cahuenga in January 1847, Frémont, who had been appointed military governor of California by Stockton, decided to appoint a legislative council to assist him in governing the region. Larkin informed Vallejo in a letter dated January 22 that Frémont had made Vallejo a member of that council and that it would convene at the end of March. Larkin and Semple both urged Vallejo to accept the appointment, but Revere urged caution. Warning Vallejo that tension was building between Frémont and the other American officers, he advised Vallejo to distance himself from the rivalry. Revere added that the Americans currently regarded Vallejo as a person who was "neutral and full of dignity," and that he should seek to preserve that perception. Vallejo eventually decided to accept the appointment, but the council never met. Indeed, Frémont's tenure as governor was quite brief. Army General Stephen Watts Kearny eventually assumed command in March 1847. He appointed Richard Mason to succeed him when he left California at the end of May.[21]

During this time, Vallejo continued to portray himself in the public arena as a willing participant in American California. In March 1847 he helped organize a public meeting in San Francisco to raise funds for the relief of the Donner party. By April, his efforts appeared to be bearing fruit. When General Kearny received reports of Indian raids on ranchos in a number of regions in California, he appointed Vallejo as subagent "for the Indians on the north side of the bay of San Francisco." Kearny said he was making this appointment because of "the well-known influence you possess over these Indians." John Sutter was given a similar appointment for the Sacramento region. As Albert Hurtado has remarked, with these moves the American military was signaling

---

21. Thomas O. Larkin to MGV, January 22, 1847, in Larkin, *Papers*, 6:16; Robert Semple to MGV, January 31, 1847, C-B 12, doc. 266, TBL; Joseph Warren Revere to MGV, January 29, 1847, C-B 12, doc. 265, TBL; "New Government," *California Star*, February 6, 1847; Harlow, *California Conquered*, 241.

that it intended to "develop a settler policy for Indian affairs that conformed to the interests of California's substantial ranchers and other large landowners."[22]

Vallejo realized the military's stance and was able to turn it to his advantage two months later. The episode began with an event that had been fairly common during the Mexican rancho era: a raiding party into Indigenous territory. In late June or early July 1847, a group of people from the North Bay area descended on an unnamed Indian ranchería about sixty miles north of San Francisco. They killed thirteen people there and took an additional thirty-seven as prisoners. Word of this affair reached Sutter's Fort during the second week of July. On July 24 the *California Star* published a letter, dated July 10, authored by "a gentleman residing at the Fort" who was "an officer of the Navy." According to the letter, "a party of Spaniards" from "Sonoma or vicinity" went to a group of "friendly Indians." The Indians received the party graciously and offered them food, but then the newcomers started to make prisoners of the Indians. In the ensuing struggle, ten or twelve were killed and the prisoners were then "tied together and driven to the settlements." Some children who were unable to keep up with the group were murdered on the road.[23]

On July 12, Sutter sent a message to Governor Mason. He reported that Samuel Smith, a resident of the upper Sacramento Valley, had just arrived and told him that the perpetrators of the deeds were not simply "a party of Spaniards." They were one Mexican and two Americans: Antonio María Armijo, Robert Smith, and John Egger. Armijo was the son of José Francisco Armijo, owner of Rancho Tolenas, which bordered on Vallejo's Rancho Suisun. Armijo had arrived in California from New Mexico in the late 1820s or early 1830s. Alvarado granted him Tolenas in 1840 as part of his efforts to restrain Vallejo's influence and power in

22. Bancroft, *History of California*, 5:539; Stephen W. Kearny to MGV, April 4, 1847, in 31st Cong., 1st Sess., House of Representatives, Executive Document No. 17, California and New Mexico, 296–97; Hurtado, *John Sutter*, 88–89.

23. *California Star*, July 24, 1847; Madley, *American Genocide*, 427.

the North Bay. Armijo had begun to engage in a series of boundary disputes with Vallejo almost as soon as he received his grant.
Robert Smith was an American who had arrived at Sutter's Fort
in 1845. His nickname, Growling Mad, was well earned. He had
apparently served in the California Battalion during the Mexican
War and was jailed for striking a ranking officer. Little is known
of Egger. The most likely scenario is that Armijo hired the two
Americans to go north and capture some Indians to work on the
family rancho.[24]

Mason ordered that the three men should be arrested. One was
apprehended at Sutter's Fort, another at Sonoma, and the third
at Yerba Buena. They were all in custody by early August. Very
soon after his son's arrest, José Francisco Armijo agreed to arbitration with Vallejo about whether a house he had constructed
was on his land or on Vallejo's Rancho Suisun. The arbitration
was a strange affair, since the person who was supposed to argue
Armijo's side was Vallejo's brother Salvador. The arbitration concluded with unanimous agreement that Armijo's house was on
Vallejo's land. It is hard to escape the conclusion that after his son's
arrest Armijo decided to end his boundary dispute with Vallejo
on Vallejo's terms. He was most likely hoping that Vallejo would
use his close relationship with the American military to assist his
son, which was exactly what occurred. The trial, scheduled for
September, was postponed until October, allegedly because of
Antonio María Armijo's poor health. Then the trial was moved
from Sutter's Fort to Sonoma. A jury impaneled by Vallejo and
Sonoma alcalde Lilburn Boggs found the three men innocent of
all charges, and they were released. Vallejo and Boggs told Mason
at the end of September that the prosecutor blamed the acquittal

24. MGV to Alcalde Jacob P. Leese, August 17, 1844, VA 81, HL; John A. Sutter to Richard B.
Mason, July 12, 1847, in 31st Cong., 1st Sess., Senate, *Executive Document No. 18*, 351; Suisun
grant, BANC MSS Land Case Files, 2 ND, 61, TBL; Warner, *Men of the California Bear Flag
Revolt*, 460–62.

on sloppy preparation of the legal case while Smith and Egger were prisoners at Sutter's Fort.[25]

One month later Vallejo sent the governor another letter, in which he showed himself very familiar with long-standing American attitudes toward Native peoples. He told Mason that he had "sought at all times the means of regulating the management of Indians, as well for their private benefit as to amalgamate them as far as possible with the whites." They were, he said, "a peculiar race." There was "no moderate way of inducing them to leave their miserable manner of living like brutes and, consequently, they are incompatible with our manners and customs." He suggested a number of measures to increase settler control over the Indigenous people of the north, including "that a military cavalry force should be established to be destined solely for the persecution and vigilance of the Indians, which force should at present consist of not less than fifteen men at this place." The Armijo affair and its aftermath indicated that Vallejo determined to use his close relations with the American military to reassert his authority over other settlers in the North Bay and to reestablish control over the Indigenous labor force on which he and the other rancheros depended.[26]

One year later, in April 1848, Vallejo informed Governor Mason that he wished to resign from the position of Indian subagent. He said that the task of gathering statistics about the Indigenous population was proving too difficult to carry out, and that the Indians were becoming increasingly hostile due to the constant encroachment of additional whites on their territories. He advised

25. Hurtado, *John Sutter*, 209–11; Joseph L. Folsom to Richard B. Mason, August 15, 1847, C-A 36: 90, TBL; *Mariano G. Vallejo v. Francisco Armijo*, Decision of Arbitration, August 16, 1847, C-B 12, doc. 312, TBL; Joseph L. Folsom to MGV, August 23, 1847, C-B 12, doc. 314, TBL; Richard B. Mason to MGV and John A. Sutter, August 19, 1847, Henry Halleck to James A. Hardie, September 10, 1847, and Henry Halleck to MGV, September 15, 1847, all in 31st Cong., 1st Sess., House of Representatives, *Executive Document No. 17, California and New Mexico*, pp. 384, 394, 395; MGV and Lilburn Boggs to Richard B. Mason, September 30, 1847, C-A 63:124–26, TBL.

26. MGV to Richard B. Mason, September 30, 1847, C-A 63:94–97, TBL. The original letter was in Spanish (C-B 12, doc. 317a, TBL), but it was translated into English for Mason by William E. P. Hartnell.

Mason that the recent removal of some soldiers from Sonoma had made matters worse, and recommended that no additional potential settlers be allowed into the area for the time being. This attempt to employ the American military to keep potential new American settlers away from what he hoped would continue to be his realm in the North Bay was unsuccessful. Mason replied that there was a greater need for the soldiers who had been stationed at Sonoma at the garrison in Baja California, where American troops were experiencing constant resistance from well-organized local groups. He added, "The number of American citizens, to say nothing of the Californians, north of the bay of San Francisco are sufficient to meet any Indian troubles that may arise from that quarter." He also refused Vallejo's request to resign because of "the difficulty of finding someone to take your place."[27]

In the midst of these events, Vallejo was also involved with some Americans in activities directed at increasing the value of the land he had acquired during the Mexican era. In 1846, Bear Flagger Robert Semple became convinced that the north shore of the Carquínez Strait was the perfect site for the major port of Northern California. Even though the American military had established its headquarters in the existing capital of Monterey, Semple correctly calculated that the San Francisco Bay region would quickly become the commercial hub of Northern California. The Carquínez Strait was close to the fertile regions of Sonoma and Napa, as well as on the water route to Sutter's Fort and the Central Valley, where a number of Americans had already established themselves. For these reasons Semple believed that this location was destined for prominence. Vallejo probably did not need much persuading, since he understood that a thriving city on the Carquínez would increase the value of his extensive North Bay lands. So, on December 22, 1846, he ceded to Semple half of a five-square-mile tract of Rancho

27. MGV to Richard B. Mason, April 15, 1848, C-B 12, doc. 342, TBL; Richard B. Mason to MGV, May 25, 1848, C-B 12, doc. 346, TBL; On the resistance of Mexicans in the Baja California peninsula to the U.S. invaders, see Moyano Pahissa, *La resistencia de las Californias,* 120–60.

Suscol that lay along the coast of the strait. Semple had sweetened his appeal by naming the proposed town Francisca, ostensibly in honor of Vallejo's wife. The actual reason for the name, however, was Semple's calculation that most Eastern merchants would know little of Northern California beyond the names of the Bay and Mission of San Francisco. Thus, they might well send merchandise to Northern California that was simply addressed "San Francisco," and Semple hoped this freight would be delivered to "Francisca." When the merchants at Yerba Buena learned of Semple's designs, however, they quickly prevailed on Alcalde Washington Bartlett to change Yerba Buena's name to San Francisco. Semple, who was still convinced of his proposed town's excellent location, settled for Francisca's middle name, Benicia.[28]

Semple told Vallejo in January 1847 that he saw further possibilities for the new town. When he was urging Vallejo to accept Frémont's offer to join the proposed legislative council, he argued that doing so would "give confidence to the people of the good intentions of the American people to place the old inhabitants of California on the same footing with themselves fully to carry out true Republican principles." He added, "Our interests too, though a secondary consideration, in relation to the location of the seat of government, are much at stake." Semple was anticipating that his town would quickly become the political and commercial center of California.[29]

Thomas O. Larkin shared Semple's enthusiasm for the location at least to some degree, and decided that he would like to participate in the venture. At the beginning of May 1847 Semple wrote Vallejo of Larkin's interest and argued that Larkin's involvement made a larger venture possible: "I am aware that the building of the city will greatly increase the value of your lands and should you be desirous to avoid the labor of making the city you could probably not entrust it to the hands of a more energetic man than Mr. Larkin." Vallejo, who had known Larkin for years, agreed. On

---

28. "An Ordinance," *California Star*, January 30, 1847; Bancroft, *History of California*, 5:670–71.
29. Robert Semple to MGV, January 31, 1847, C-B 12, doc. 266, TBL.

May 18, Semple returned his cession to Vallejo, and on the next day Mariano Guadalupe Vallejo and Francisca Benicia Vallejo deeded a larger tract to Semple and Larkin for $100.[30]

Vallejo remained interested in the proposed town. On August 9, he wrote Larkin that he had sent "some Indians" to the town to begin construction of a house, which he hoped would be "ready soon." By the end of November, the house, measuring 130 feet by 36 feet, was reported to be well under construction, with an expected second story to be added during the next year. The next year, 1848, was when the discovery of gold was made public, and Semple could hardly restrain himself. He wrote to Larkin of "the most flattering accounts from the mines." He continued, "Benicia will be no small business. . . . In a short time every person from Yerba Buena up will have the gold fever, and I am very confident that ships arriving on the coast with goods will take the fever and get as close to the seat of the disease as possible, which will be just here."[31]

Semple's dreams were never realized. By 1849 it was clear that San Francisco would be the major port, and Larkin's interest in the project waned. Benicia remained a small town that did not supply Vallejo with his hoped-for real estate bonanza. Indeed, the failure of Benicia foreshadowed Vallejo's experiences during and after the arrival of hundreds of thousands of Americans into his homeland. Vallejo was to discover that these newcomers were more numerous and much less accommodating than the military officers with whom he had been able to establish promising relationships.

As the American population increased and the U.S. government failed to establish California's political status, recently arrived military governor Bennett Riley faced increasing confusion resulting from a host of local councils and other ad-hoc legislative arrangements. He sought to channel the increasing uncertainty into

30. Hague and Langum, *Thomas O. Larkin*, 188; Robert Semple to MGV, May 4, 1847, C-B 12, doc. 287, TBL; various property transfer documents are in *California Star*, July 3, 1847, and C-B 12, doc. 291, TBL.

31. MGV to Thomas O. Larkin, August 9, 1847, in Larkin, *Papers*, 6:261; Bancroft, *History of California*, 5:672; Robert Semple to Thomas O. Larkin, May 19, 1848, in Larkin, *Papers*, 7:267.

*Customs House, San Francisco, ca. 1845–1851, by Fritz Wikersheim
Courtesy of The Bancroft Library, University of California,
Berkeley.* BANC PIC 1963.002:1304:04-ALB.

recognizable directions by calling a constitutional convention to
be held in Monterey at the beginning of August 1849. Electoral
districts to select delegates were created by adapting the Mexican
jurisdictional regions along the coast and creating new districts
in the interior. Not surprisingly, Vallejo was the elected delegate
from Sonoma. He was one of eight Californios elected and certainly the Californio best known by the Americans, most of whom
had settled in the northern part of the territory. When Robert
Semple was chosen as convention president, Vallejo and Sutter
were appointed to conduct him ceremonially to his chair. During
the proceedings Vallejo joined the rest of the Californios in resist-
ing the proposition that Indians should not be allowed to vote.
Being aware that many Californios were of mixed blood and somewhat darker complected than the Anglos from the East, they were
afraid that such a provision would be used to deny the franchise

San Francisco in 1847, from the Hill Back, by William Rich Hutton
Reproduced by permission of the Huntington Library, San Marino, California. Mss. HM 43214–43227.

to Californios in general. Therefore, the Californios unanimously favored a proposal that would have allowed taxpaying Indians to vote. In an awkward final compromise that was passed without a recorded vote, the convention allowed the legislature to enfranchise certain Indians by a two-thirds vote.[32]

Even though he did not speak as often as some other Californios, Vallejo did make two interventions. Both were designed to capitalize on the goodwill he had gained from his contacts with the military by highlighting the advanced social position and relative wealth he had attained in Mexican California. His first intervention came when the design for the state seal of California was under discussion—a design that included a grizzly bear and a miner. Vallejo introduced a resolution "that the bear be taken out of the design for the Seal of California or, if it do remain, that it be represented as made fast by a lazo[33] in the hands of a Vaquero." The two Spanish words in the resolution were intended to remind the delegates of California's Spanish and Mexican past. Over the ensuing years and decades, reminding Californians of their state's history would become an increasing element in Vallejo's public presence. The sardonic reference to the bear was probably designed to underline that he had been a prominent participant in that past. In fact, he had been so important that he had been the major target of the short-lived Bear Flag insurgency, which was the precise reason the U.S. military had paid special attention to him. He was hoping that publicizing his prominence again might produce the same result with these newer American arrivals.[34]

Vallejo's second intervention was a request that the convention appoint a three-member committee "to draft a code of laws for the state of California, to report at the first session of the legislature to be elected under this Constitution." This proposal followed an earlier discussion that had become entangled in the issue of whether

---

32. Harlow, *California Conquered*, 316–37; Bancroft, *History of California*, 6:276; Hargis, "Native Californians in the Constitutional Convention," 7, 12.
33. "Lazo" [sic] *laso*, means rope.
34. Browne, *Report of the Debates in the Convention*, 323.

the legislature should meet annually or biennially. When Vallejo introduced his resolution, he made a point of stating that, if the convention delegates were unsure whether there would be enough money to pay these committee members, then "he would pay it himself, willingly." Even though the proposal was defeated, Vallejo had, probably deliberately, underscored his considerable wealth. He was to discover that wealth and eminence would soon mark him, not for accommodation and respect, but for expropriation.[35]

The first statewide election took place only a month after the Constitutional Convention. The ballot was both to ratify the territorial constitution and to elect the first slate of state officers and congressional delegates. The abbreviated timetable meant that formal political organization was haphazard at best. A few people who had come to California with the idea of being elected to the U.S. Senate once the state was admitted to the union took the lead in this minimal organizing. One such person, former Mississippi Democratic Congressman William Gwin, had been a member of the Constitutional Convention. Another was a former Whig congressman from Georgia, T. Butler King, who had arrived in San Francisco in June 1849 to monitor events as a representative of the secretary of the navy. Since at that time U.S. senators were elected by state legislatures, both Gwin and King tried to build alliances with potential candidates around the state.[36]

Vallejo, who was running for state senator from Sonoma, found himself at least minimally involved in these machinations as he tried to gather allies, chairing a King rally in San Francisco on October 23. Vallejo's main opponent for the state senate seat was Jonas Spect, a Methodist clergyman. It first appeared that Spect had won, but late returns from Thomas Larkin's ranch in Colusa gave Vallejo the victory. Spect later claimed that he had been cheated.[37]

35. Browne, *Report of the Debates in the Convention*, 224, 393.

36. Cadwallader Ringgold to William Ballard Preston, June 19, 1849, in 31st Cong., 1st Sess., House of Representatives, *Executive Document No. 17, California and New Mexico*, 954–55.

37. Tennis, "California's First State Election," 364, 378, 382, 384; Emparán, *Vallejos of California*, 74.

Because of the delay in ascertaining the final Sonoma voting results, Vallejo arrived at the legislature in San José too late to cast his vote for senator. Still, he urged Pablo de la Guerra, who represented Santa Bárbara in that body, to vote for Frémont, despite the "real appreciation" he had for King. He told de la Guerra that Frémont had visited him and disclosed that he had never approved of the conditions under which Vallejo had been held prisoner at Sutter's Fort. The legislature elected Frémont and Gwin.[38]

Vallejo took his seat a few days after the senate election. One of his first moves was to have the town of Benicia included in a list of important ports in California to be forwarded to California's representatives in the U.S. Congress. One of his most significant efforts involved the preservation of the memory and practices of Spanish- and Mexican-era California in this new American state. On January 22, 1850, he introduced a resolution that "a special committee be appointed to report to the Senate the derivation and definition of the names of the several counties" that the legislature had set up. He was appointed to head that committee. The report, finished on April 16, was ordered to be published in both English and Spanish.[39]

Vallejo's report introduced a number of themes that would occupy his attention during his decades in American-ruled California. He wanted to ensure the Americans understood that the land they had conquered possessed its own history, tradition, and culture. He recorded the early Spanish explorations of Rodríguez de Cabrillo and Vizcaíno, as well as that the cities of Mendocino and Monterey were named for Spanish viceroys. Further, by starting his catalog of county names in the south, at San Diego, he was able to recount the 1769 Portolá expedition and the establishment of Spanish rule in Alta California. Though he mentioned a number of missions and often emphasized their wealth in crops and livestock, he was also careful to emphasize the role of the soldiers and presidios in maintaining them. His description of Santa Bárbara, for instance, mentioned the presidio but not the mission. His

---

38. Emparán, *Vallejos of California*, 74–75; *Journal of the Senate of the State of California*, 23–27.
39. *Journal of the Senate of the State of California*, 87–88, 104, 336.

accounts of the Indigenous people, such as Marín and Francisco Solano, emphasized their effectiveness as Indigenous warriors against the Spanish and Mexicans but also their ultimate acceptance of Mexican authority. He wrote, for instance, that after his battles, Marín "retired" to San Rafael. He characterized Solano as "a great chief, who also ruled various other tribes with great sway." But, Vallejo added, Solano also had to request Mexican assistance to put down an important Indigenous rebellion against his rule. The Spanish and Mexican eras, Vallejo insisted, were times of daring exploration, intrepid colonization, prosperous religious and social institutions, and successful submission of the Native peoples. Indeed, over the next forty years Vallejo would continue to insist in a variety of ways that the Americans needed to understand they stood on a foundation laid by their non-Anglo predecessors.[40]

Shortly after he submitted his report, Vallejo became involved in a second project that hearkened back to the Mexican era. Specifically, it was a continuation of the efforts he had undertaken with pre-gold-rush U.S. military officers to maintain the subordination of the Indigenous Californians and to preserve their availability as ranch laborers. State Senator John Bidwell, who had been ranching in Northern California since 1844, had declared in March 1850 that he would be introducing a bill for the "protection, punishment, and governance of the Indians." For its time, Bidwell's bill contained surprisingly enlightened elements. It provided Indians with justices of the peace, who were to be elected in various districts from an electorate of male Indians over the age of eighteen. The justices would have considerable power over Indian employment, especially relating to child labor, and could fine anyone who abused Indians or forced them to work in the mines. The law also contained some protections for various Indian lands, including hunting and fishing locations. Bidwell's bill was eventually considered on the senate floor but indefinitely postponed on March 30.[41]

---

40. Lamb, "Mariano Guadalupe Vallejo's Report," 57–60, 70–75.
41. *Journal of the Senate of the State of California,* 217, 224, 228–29, 257–58, 338; Gilles and Magliari, *John Bidwell and California,* 249–53, 291–93; Hurtado, *Indian Survival,* 129.

David Douglass. *Courtesy of the California History Room, California State Library, Sacramento, California. Neg. 1633.*

Subsequently, Elam Brown, an 1846 arrival who had been ranching in the East Bay for three years, introduced a bill in the assembly with few protections for Indigenous people in early April. This bill was passed by the assembly and sent to the senate. There, a committee composed of Bidwell, Vallejo, and David Douglass, a recently arrived native of Tennessee, was appointed to deal with it. The committee reconciled Brown's and Bidwell's approaches by scrapping many of Bidwell's protections for the Native people. The law allowed for the indenture of Indian children and for forcing any Indian who was "loitering or strolling" to be arrested and made to work. It seems clear that Vallejo and Douglass, working with Brown, dominated the committee that created the "Act for the Government and Protection of the Indians." As Albert Hurtado observed, the law "protected them very little and governed them

quite a lot." In the words of Michael Magliari, the statute "effectively preserved the Mexican rancho labor system in toto"—that
is, consistent with the labor system Vallejo had used at Petaluma
and Salvador had employed at Clear Lake.[42]

Another of Vallejo's legislative activities—the permanent location of California's capital—related to his land speculations with
Semple and Larkin. The facilities in San José were quickly revealed
to be entirely inadequate to lodge and accommodate the legislators,
and the wet winter of 1849–50 compounded the misery. Vallejo's
complaints were typical of what most legislators were experiencing. He told Benicia, "I am sick and tired of this place and I am
bored. The rains have been very heavy, and as a result, the mud in
the streets is unbearable. Besides, I am lacking the comforts that
old men like me greatly need. I am in a small room where five of
us are living together, with no other comfort than being able to
sleep under a roof. My eyes are bad, perhaps from stoking a very
small and very bad iron fireplace then having to go out into the cold
air." Given such conditions, discussions about finding a different
capital quickly surfaced. Early in the session, Vallejo confided to
Benicia, "Tomorrow I will be very busy trying to see if I can move
the capital to Sonoma or to Suscol near the mouth of the Suscol
estuary, where I have offered to donate some land." Eventually,
he offered "to lay out a city . . . upon the Straits of Carquínez and
Napa River, which in my judgment is the best location for the permanent seat of government." Vallejo tentatively named the capital
Eureka and proposed to donate land for the capitol building, the
governor's residence, various state offices, and institutions such
as a state university or college. He further promised to donate
approximately $370,000 for the initial financing of this enterprise.
The Senate Committee on Public Buildings and Grounds, chaired

---

42. Magliari, "Free Soil, Unfree Labor," 352; Bancroft, *History of California*, 3:11; Hurtado,
Indian Survival, 131; *Journal of the Senate of the State of California*, 1201, 1224, 1233, 1260, 1284.

by future U.S. senator David C. Broderick, urged acceptance of Vallejo's proposal in a referendum to be held in the fall of 1850.[43]

As all of this was occurring, Vallejo remained on the lookout for prominent individuals with whom he could establish the kind of relationship he believed he had been able to establish with the American military. For instance, on his way to the Constitutional Convention in Monterey he encountered in Yerba Buena former Indiana congressman Thomas Henley, who was apparently interested in opening a sawmill. Vallejo invited Henley to examine the wood that had been cut on his property. He gave Henley a letter of introduction to Benicia and told her, "Have José or Antonio take him to the old logging area that I bought from Alvarado in Petaluma, so he can see it. Tell them to take him along the best road." A few months later, as he was on his way to the meeting of the legislature in San José, he encountered James Jones, a lawyer who was in the running for appointment as a district judge. He invited Jones to visit Sonoma and borrow whatever law books he wished from Vallejo's personal library. A few weeks later, he invited Robert Hopkins, who was about to be appointed district judge for the Sonoma region, to rent one of the rooms in Casa Grande, Vallejo's house on the plaza, for his office. By the time the legislature adjourned in April 1850, Vallejo was in good spirits. His activities in the Constitutional Convention and the state's first legislature, along with the potentially influential contacts he believed he was making, gave him every reason to believe that he had negotiated the transition to American administration very successfully.[44]

43. MGV to Benicia Vallejo, February 28, 1850, C-B 13, doc. 37, TBL; MGV to Benicia Vallejo, January 28, 1850, C-B 441, box 1, folder 3, TBL; *Journal of the Senate of the State of California*, 498–505.

44. MGV to Benicia Vallejo, August 30, 1849, C-B 441, box 1 folder 2, TBL; MGV to Benicia Vallejo, December 30, 1849, and January 9, 1850, C-B 441, box 1 folder 3, TBL.

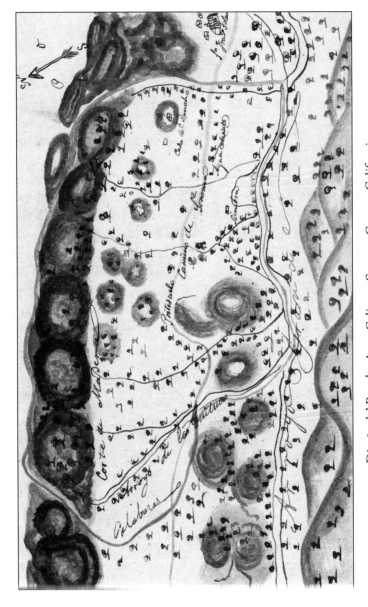

Diseño del Rancho Agua Caliente, Sonoma County, California
Courtesy of The Bancroft Library, University of California, Berkeley. Land Case Map B-662.

CHAPTER 5

"General, You Will Outlive These Vile Calumnies"

Land, Squatters, and Lawyers

B y the beginning of 1850, Vallejo was well aware that the tens of thousands of young American men who were swarming throughout Northern California brought with them concepts of landownership and usage that were radically different from those that had existed in Spanish and Mexican California. He knew that the Mexican-era ranchos did not conform to the American pattern of individual family farms and could become the object of pre-emption claims by various prospective American settlers in California. Probably encouraged by some Americans friendly to him, he attempted to consolidate his holdings into a more compact and defensible set of properties. Indeed, he had already begun to try to tighten his grip on the core properties around Sonoma and Petaluma. In the 1840s he had purchased Rancho Agua Caliente from Lázaro Piña, one of the soldiers of his company. This rancho was near where he had placed the residents of Pipoholma in 1836. Vallejo, in his capacity as director of colonization, had arranged in 1839 for Piña to be granted this rancho, and there may have been an understanding that Piña would hold it only until Vallejo was ready to take it over himself. Continuing on this track, in February 1849 he purchased Yulupa, just north of Petaluma, from Miguel Alvarado, another of his soldiers who had also served as mayordomo at Petaluma. In addition, he apparently tried to help his brother Salvador cement his own position by purchasing three hundred square *varas*[1] of Rancho Entre Napa immediately bordering Salvador's Rancho Napa.[2]

Suisun was the Vallejo property most distant from the emerging metropolis of San Francisco, so it was the land Vallejo was most ready to unload. Archibald A. Ritchie, a former sea captain with extensive experience in the China trade, was apparently interested in scouting out possibilities in the Benicia and Suisun Bay area. In early August 1850 he purchased a plot of land in Benicia. A few weeks later, the legal arrangements were finalized for Ritchie's purchase of Rancho Suisun from Vallejo for $10,000 in cash and an additional $40,000 in credit.

It is not clear whether Solano had any involvement in this transaction. In May 1852 Manuel Vaca told the Land Commission that Solano had died "about a year ago." Whether he cooperated with Ritchie is unclear, but it seems probable that the majority of labor at the rancho was done by the surviving Suisun Patwins, who had been living in the region for generations. In any event, Ritchie initially did very well. His laborers harvested a considerable amount of hay in 1851. In the next year he rented some oxen and wagons and purchased a group of mares and some stallions from Vallejo, indicating that he had profits to invest in his land. Success proved transient, however. By November 1852 he was immersed in

---

1. A "vara" is a measure of length, approximately thirty-three inches.
2. W. W. Robinson, *Land in California*, 110–13; Agua Caliente Grant, BANC MSS Land Case Files, 153 ND, 11, 32, TBL; Petaluma Grant, BANC MSS Land Case Files, 321 ND, 4, TBL; Silliman, *Lost Laborers*, 52; Entre Napa Grant, BANC MSS Land Case Files, 152 ND, 17, TBL.

(*above*) Las Trancas rancho, Salvador Vallejo's home in Napa
Courtesy of California State Parks, Sonoma Barracks. No. 243-x-3568

(*below*) Las Trancas adobe, home of Salvador Vallejo, ca. 1900
Courtesy of Sonoma County Library. Cstr_pho_024519.

considerable legal difficulty with squatters who were taking over parts of his land.[3]

Vallejo was already encountering serious difficulties of his own. The first set of problems revolved around the state capital that he had sought at the first legislature. In the fall of 1850, the voters approved the state senate committee's recommendation that the city of Vallejo become California's capital. In January 1851 Vallejo entered into a contract to have Edward Kellogg of San José divide this new town into lots. By the summer it was clear that preparations were not going well. One San Francisco newspaper, the *Evening Picayune*, referred to Vallejo as an "imaginary city."[4]

For its second session, the legislature met once again in San José, then convened at Vallejo for its third session in January 1852. It quickly became clear to everyone that Vallejo's promises had been dramatically unfulfilled, and the legislature decided after four days to move to Sacramento. Vallejo's son-in-law John B. Frisbie hurried to Sacramento and consulted with San Francisco lawyer Archibald Peachy, who was a member of the state assembly and of the law firm Vallejo had retained for his dealings with the recently formed California Land Commission. Frisbie told Peachy that Vallejo would be willing to donate to the state all of the uncompleted buildings in Vallejo, along with one-quarter of the land there. Alternatively, Frisbie suggested that Vallejo's bond for the remainder of the $370,000 simply be canceled, which was eventually what happened. The legislature actually did return to Vallejo for a brief time at the beginning of its 1853 sessions, when floods in Sacramento made it impossible to meet there. But it quickly removed itself to Benicia for a time before eventually settling on Sacramento as the permanent capital. Vallejo lost a considerable

---

3. Shumate, *Captain A. A. Ritchie*, 23, 25–26, 48–49; Suisun Land Case, BANC MSS Land Case Files, 2 ND, 57; Johnson, "Patwin," 351; Vallejo and Frisbie to Wells and Company, August 21, 23, 27, 1850, C-B 13, doc. 74, TBL.

4. *Journal of the Legislature of California for Its Second Session*, 645–47; "Agreement for the subdivision into lots of the town of Vallejo," January 27, 1851, C-B 13, doc. 138, TBL; *San Francisco Evening Picayune*, July 16, 1851, inserted into Vallejo Papers as C-B 13, doc. 179, TBL.

Henry Wager Halleck. *Courtesy of The Bancroft Library, University of California, Berkeley.* POR: *Halleck, Henry Wager: 1.*

amount of money as a result of this affair, close to $100,000 according to what Richard Henry Dana was told when he visited California in 1859. This loss was symptomatic of the financial difficulties Vallejo was already beginning to experience.[5]

Vallejo's problems with the state capital were soon dwarfed by his struggles to retain his lands. In 1851 Congress adopted the California Land Act. The statute established a California Land Commission and required Californios and others wishing to have their claims approved by the government to appear before the commission and prove their case. Championed by California Senator William Gwin, the law ultimately resulted in loss of land and financial ruin for most of the Mexican rancheros—which was its intention from the beginning.

The act had its origins in an 1849 report by Henry Halleck, a military officer who was then serving as California secretary of state. Through foregrounding some obviously fraudulent and ante-dated grants made in 1846 by the last Mexican governor of

5. John B. Frisbie to Archibald Peachy, March 31, 1852, C-B 13, doc. 228, TBL; John B. Frisbie to MGV, March 31, 1852, C-B 13, doc. 229, TBL; Emparán, *Vallejos of California*, 81–83; Dana, *Two Years before the Mast*, 384, 398–99.

California, Pío Pico, Halleck's report was calculated to give the impression that many of the California land grants were invalid. Halleck stated, "It has been alleged by very respectable authority, that certain titles to land were given by Governor Pico after the United States had taken possession of the country, and made to bear date prior to 7 July 1846. These grants have of course never been confirmed by the territorial legislature, for that body adjourned on 8 July, the day after our flag was raised at Monterey." Halleck moved on from that limited critique to attack what he regarded as the inappropriately informal system the Mexican government in California had used to grant lands. He argued, "A large number of land titles in California are very indefinite with respect to boundaries, the grants being for so many 'sitios,' 'creaderos,'[6] etc., lying between certain hills, streams, etc., as shown by rough sketches attached to the petitions. The sketches frequently contain double the amount of land included in the grants." He insisted that such a system was inconsistent with American ways: "Some of the land grants given by the Californian government contain conditions respecting their sale, etc., which are not only onerous to the holders, but contrary to the spirit of our laws." In forwarding Halleck's report to Washington, Governor Mason underscored Halleck's points concerning the illegitimacy of many of the grants: "I would call the attention of the government particularly to the representations made in this report respecting the claims of individuals to lands required for government purposes, and spurious titles to lands which evidently belong to the public domain."[7]

Gwin seized on Halleck's report, quoting it in a long speech he gave on the Senate floor on January 8, 1851. He went on to argue that mission land which had been secularized by Mexico should be regarded as the property of the state, and therefore as part of the American public domain, they should be open to bona fide

6. "Sitios" and "creaderos" [sic] "criaderos" mean plots of land and farmlands, respectively.

7. "Report on the laws and regulations relative to grants or sales of public lands in California," in 31st Cong., 1st Sess., House of Representatives, *Executive Document No. 17, California and New Mexico*, 118, 122.

American settlers. In an 1852 speech he made clear his positive feelings about these settlers. He denounced those who would "with mercenary rancor . . . pursue such settlers and denounce and stigmatize them in opprobrium as 'squatters.'"[8]

Missouri Senator Thomas Hart Benton opposed the Land Act. He was hardly impartial on the issue, since his son-in-law John C. Frémont was himself a claimant to a large Mexican land grant. Still, Benton accurately contended that the law was designed to "hold . . . every [Mexican] title to be a fraud against the United States, until the parties proved in three different courts, and one of them the Supreme Court of the United States, that they were not frauds against the United States." Though many claims were eventually upheld, the costs of the various legal proceedings at the Land Commission, the District Court in California, and the Supreme Court in Washington, D.C., drained the resources of many Californio landholders. As Elisha O. Crosby, a San Francisco lawyer who participated in many cases before the Land Commission observed, "Many of the claimants whose titles and rights were confirmed by the land commission were pretty well exhausted by the expense of that litigation." Faced with an unfamiliar legal system and forced into proceedings conducted in a language they did not understand well, Californio landholders were compelled to hire lawyers, often at exorbitant prices. One of these lawyers was Halleck, whose report had done so much to throw the legitimacy of the land grants into question. He had already put himself in a position to profit from that uncertainty by becoming a land-grant lawyer in San Francisco at the beginning of 1850. He joined a law firm organized by Frederick Billings, a Vermonter who had served as California's attorney general during the last days of military rule. In that capacity, Billings had evicted squatters from some land in San Francisco claimed by the military. He quickly realized that land issues were going to become very contentious in U.S. California. Together with Archibald C. Peachy, he formed

---

8. 32nd Cong., 1st Sess., *Congressional Globe*, 2037; Hargis, "W. M. Gwin: Middleman," 26–27.

a legal practice at the end of 1849 and persuaded Halleck to join. Since he was already very well known, they placed his name at the head of the firm. When the California Land Act was passed, they were ready.[9]

As soon as word reached California that the act had been signed into law, the firm printed and circulated a notice in Spanish advising all California landowners who held title from either Spanish or Mexican authorities that they had to present those titles to the Land Commission. The notice promised that the commission's procedures could result in an "immediate and final" confirmation of these titles, whereas failure to submit titles to the commission would result in the lands being irrevocably lost. The firm advertised itself as well situated to aid Californios. Completely ignoring Halleck's report and its influence on the act, the advertisement claimed that Halleck, as secretary of state, had been in control of the governmental archives and was quite familiar with the various documents in them that could assist the claimants. Peachy and Billings, for their part, were very familiar with the American court system and could therefore help claimants "in their defense" before American tribunals. The notice listed the names of twenty-five "references," all of whom had been residents of Mexican California. José de la Guerra y Noriega of Santa Bárbara headed the list, and Vallejo was included. This was not inappropriate as he had formed a close relationship with the American military government of which Halleck had been a part and had gotten to know Halleck somewhat better when they were both members of the Constitutional Convention. He had also served with Billings on the board of trustees for a proposed California university or college, which Vallejo hoped would end up in Vallejo, the capital city he intended to establish. The notice certainly had its desired effect, for the firm ultimately represented a large number of Californios before the Land Commission.[10]

---

9. Crosby, *Memoirs*, 71; 31st Cong., 2nd Sess., *Appendix to the Congressional Globe*, 55; Winks, *Frederick Billings*, 44–46.

10. A copy of the notice is in C-B 13, doc. 159, TBL; see also Bastian, "I Heartily Regret."

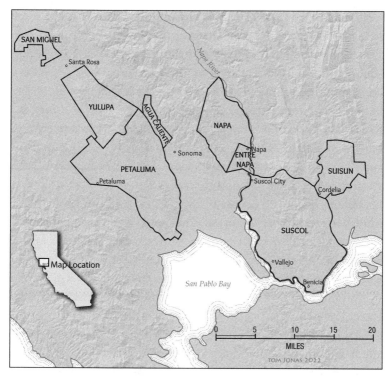

Mexican land grants in the Sonoma-Napa region
Map by Tom Jonas

Vallejo filed four claims in 1852 and was represented by Halleck, Peachy, and Billings in all of them. On May 31 he filed claims for Yulupa and Petaluma; on July 17 he filed a claim for Suscol; on September 11 he filed a claim for Entre Napa; and on March 2, 1853, he filed a claim for Agua Caliente.[11]

Vallejo had two distinct experiences with the Land Commission. His large grants were approved relatively easily, although

11. Hoffman, *Reports of Land Cases*, appendix, 35, 40, 46, 100; Yulupa Land Case, BANC MSS Land Case Files, 140 ND, 4, TBL; Petaluma Land Case, BANC MSS Land Case Files, 321 ND, 6, TBL; Suscol Land Case, BANC MSS Land Case Files, 318 ND, 6, TBL; Entre Napa Land Case, BANC MSS Land Case Files, 152, ND, 4, TBL; Agua Caliente Land Case [Vallejo], BANC MSS Land Case Files, 153 ND, 3, TBL.

it appears that Halleck, Peachy, and Billings had to spend some time and energy at the beginning of the process persuading him that his word alone was not going to be sufficient to sway the Land Commission. In September 1853, the firm wrote him, "It is very important that you should bring your witnesses here without delay to prove the boundaries of your Petaluma and Suscol Ranchos." Regarding Petaluma, Vallejo's lawyers asked for confirmation of both the original ten leagues granted by Figueroa in the 1830s and the five leagues added by Micheltorena in the 1840s. Halleck, Peachy, and Billings lined up an impressive group of witnesses on his behalf, including settler George Yount and surveyors James Hudspeth and Jasper O'Farrell. The Land Commission approved all fifteen leagues on May 22, 1855. The Suscol case took a parallel track. Roughly the same group of witnesses testified on his behalf and the commission approved Suscol on the same day it approved the Petaluma grants. The federal government, however, appealed both cases to the district court, necessitating further legal expenses to Halleck, Peachy, and Billings. As Paul Gates, a scholar generally favorable to the Land Act observed, Halleck's firm "charged fees that were substantially higher than those of his less successful competitors and, indeed, were all that the traffic will bear."[12]

Where Vallejo experienced legal difficulties was with his smaller claims and with a claim that was not his own. The smaller claims were Yulupa, Entre Napa, and Agua Caliente, and the external claim was filed by Guadalupe Vásquez, the widow of Mark West, an Englishman who had come to California in 1832 and had been granted Rancho San Miguel in the North Bay. Issues relating to these claims proved thorny and appear to have led to the fracture of his relationship with Halleck, Peachy, and Billings.

The ruling in the first case of Vallejo's to be decided, Yulupa, came on May 10, 1854. The Land Commission ruled that Miguel Alvarado had only been granted a part of this land and had been

---

12. Halleck, Peachy, and Billings to MGV, September 3, 1853, C B 441, box 4, folder 26, TBL; Hoffman, *Reports of Land Cases*, appendix, 35, 40; Petaluma Land Case, BANC MSS Land Case Files, 321 ND, 2–5, 7–8, 19–38, TBL; Gates, "Adjudication of Spanish-Mexican Land Claims," 234.

required to mark off his own property so that the rest of the land could remain the property of the Mexican nation. Because Alvarado had not done this, Vallejo's claim to the entire tract was invalid and his claim was rejected. A month later, the commission also rejected Vallejo's claim to Entre Napa. This much smaller claim was for a small part of the land that Vallejo claimed had been granted to Nicolás Higuera by Governor Chico in 1836. Because the evidence for Higuera's grant was inconclusive, the board concluded that Vallejo's claim should be rejected. Higuera had sold parts of his grant to other individuals as well, and Vallejo's portion of these transactions was fairly small, so he decided to let the Land Commission's decision stand.[13]

Most of Vallejo's difficulties revolved around San Miguel and Agua Caliente. Vásquez's husband, Mark West, had died in 1849, and she had asked Vallejo to administer the estate. When the Land Act passed, she gave Vallejo all the papers she had relating to the grant of San Miguel. Vallejo asked Halleck, Peachy, and Billings to represent her case before the Land Commission. The firm agreed and did some preliminary work. Since none of the West family had a sufficient understanding of the legal documents, the lawyers decided to depose Vallejo as their first witness in the case. He had already testified on a number of cases, including Rancho Suisun, which Halleck, Peachy, and Billings was handling for Archibald A. Ritchie, so the firm had confidence he would be a good witness. Vallejo gave a deposition on April 4, 1852. A few days later Frederick Billings followed up, asking Vallejo for the full names of West's wife and children and whether San Miguel had ever been the subject of a "judicial possession." The case was formally filed at the end of May.[14]

The election of Franklin Pierce in 1852 slowed the entire land claims process. The Whig members of the Land Commission were

---

13. Yulupa Land Case, BANC MSS Land Case Files, 140 ND, 16–17, TBL; Entre Napa Land Case, BANC MSS Land Case Files, 152 ND, 19, TBL.

14. Hoffman, *Reports of Land Cases*, appendix, 35; Suisun Land Case, BANC MSS Land Case Files, 2 ND, 58, TBL; Bowman, "Indices to California Land Cases," C-R 16, vol. 3, TBL; San Miguel Land Case, BANC MSS Land Case Files, 326 ND, 6–7, TBL; Frederick Billings to MGV, April 10, 1852, C-B 13, doc. 242, TBL.

replaced by Democratic appointees. It took the new commissioners some time to arrive in California and to familiarize themselves
with their responsibilities. As Halleck wrote to Pablo de la Guerra
in April 1853, "We received information of the removal of the commissioners and the appointment of new ones. When the latter
will be here, the Lord only knows; and even when they come they
must learn their duties and study some Spanish. So the wheels are
blocked again, for five or six months at least."[15]

In March 1853 Halleck, Peachy, and Billings filed its final claim
for Vallejo, Agua Caliente. The lawyers had realized early on that
this was a complicated case. Piña had left California and returned
to Mexico around 1846, and unsubstantiated rumors circulated in
California that he had been killed fighting the American invaders
there in 1847. Billings had asked Vallejo in 1852 if he knew whether
Piña was alive or dead, whether he had any heirs, and whether the
rancho had ever been formally granted to him. Billings also told
Vallejo that it was "necessary" for him to come to San Francisco
to clear up important matters about the Agua Caliente case.[16]

The manner in which Vallejo had acquired Agua Caliente was
only part of the complexity. There was also a concern about how
Vallejo had deeded part of the land. In 1846 he had agreed to give a
section of the grant to Andrew Hoeppner, a German who had been
employed by the Russians, in exchange for Hoeppner's teaching
his children to play the piano. Hoeppner fulfilled his part of the
bargain and assumed possession of the land in 1850. Before leaving
California, he sold the land in parcels to various Americans. After
a number of sales and resales, the tracts ended up in the hands of
three Americans with military connections. The first was Thaddeus M. Leavenworth, a Connecticut-born clergyman who came
to California as chaplain for the New York Volunteers and served
as alcalde in San Francisco under military rule in the late 1840s.
The second was Charles P. Stone, ordinance chief for the Pacific

---

15. Gates, "California Land Act," 401–2; Henry Halleck to Pablo de la Guerra, April 23, 1853, DLG 487, letter 10, SBMAL.

16. Thaddeus Leavenworth stated in 1858 that he thought Piña had died at the Battle of Chur-ubusco. See Agua Caliente Land Case [Vallejo], BANC MSS Land Case Files, 153 ND, 47, TBL; Frederick Billings to MGV, April 10, 1852, C-B 13, doc. 242, TBL.

Division of the Army, who was stationed at the Benicia Arsenal. The third was Joseph Hooker, a West Point contemporary of Halleck's who arrived in California in 1849 and had been stationed at Sonoma. These three men had also filed claims for their portions of the Agua Caliente property. Hooker was represented by Halleck, Peachy, and Billings, while Stone was represented by San Francisco attorney Julius Rose, a partner of well-known local lawyer Hall McAllister. Leavenworth elected to represent himself.[17]

Since the claims of the three Americans and of Vallejo depended upon the validity of the original grant to Piña and the validity of Piña's transferral of the land to Vallejo, Leavenworth and the two attorneys agreed to coordinate their efforts. All four claims were filed on the same day, March 2, 1853. The new commissioners began their work in earnest early in 1854. On February 14, Halleck, Peachy, and Billings informed the Land Commission that they were no longer representing either Vallejo or Hooker in the case, without giving a specific reason for their withdrawal. Apparently, they did not give either Vallejo or Hooker advance notice, for when their cases were called in April, Vallejo had not been able to hire another attorney and his case was postponed "for want of counsel." Both Vallejo's and Hooker's cases were called on July 18. It is not clear who, if anyone, represented Vallejo. Hooker had engaged someone he thought was a well-known legal figure in town, former Land Commissioner Harry Thornton, but he said he was deceived, for the person was not actually Thornton. Whatever legal representation Vallejo or Hooker had was apparently very ineffective, for in a mere two weeks the Land Commission rejected both claims on the basis of a lack of actual documentary evidence that Piña had ever received a formal grant from Governor Alvarado.[18]

17. Holden, "California's First Pianos," 35–37; Bancroft, *History of California*, 4:709–10; Lamb, *Extraordinary Life of Charles Pomeroy Stone*, 45–55; Shutes, "'Fighting Joe' Hooker," 305; Agua Caliente Land Case [Hooker], BANC MSS Land Case Files, 327 ND, 5, TBL; Agua Caliente Land Case [Leavenworth], BANC MSS Land Case Files, 333 ND, 6, TBL; Agua Caliente Land Case, BANC MSS Land Case Files [Stone], 325 ND, 6, TBL; *LeCount & Strong's San Francisco City Directory*, 187.

18. San Miguel Land Case, BANC MSS Land Case Files, 326 ND, 8–9, TBL; Agua Caliente Land Case [Vallejo], BANC MSS Land Case Files, 153 ND, 2, 5, 6, TBL; Agua Caliente Land Case [Hooker], BANC MSS Land Case Files, 327 ND, 14, 52, TBL.

The failure of Vallejo's and Hooker's claims caused the Agua Caliente claimants to follow two distinct paths. Leavenworth and Stone opted to continue their cases before the Land Commission. Leavenworth decided he needed a lawyer and engaged San Francisco attorney D. P. Belknap. Hooker appealed to the commission, arguing that the fact he had been deceived regarding the identity of his lawyer warranted that the rejection of his case be reversed. The board agreed and granted his request for a new hearing. By the beginning of 1855, Leavenworth, Stone, and Hooker were ready to present their cases to the commission. The lawyers for the three claimants coordinated their approaches. They admitted that the original grant papers were not in the archives, and stated that Piña had probably taken them with him to Mexico. But they produced from the archives a copy of an expediente recording that Piña had been granted the tract. Former governor Juan B. Alvarado testified that he remembered giving Piña this grant. On being asked how he could definitely remember the Piña grant when he had given out so many during his time as governor, he replied that Piña was "an officer of my guard." He said that Piña was "a worthy man and I remember the pleasure it afforded me to confer upon him the favor he asked." A month after this testimony, the commission confirmed all three claims on the same day, April 21, 1855. The confirmations were given despite the inability to locate the original grant to Piña, which had been the basis for the rejection of Vallejo's claim. In sum, after the withdrawal of Halleck, Peachy, and Billings, the commission treated Vallejo differently than the three American claimants. They were granted the land while Vallejo's claim, which was the foundation on which the Americans' claims rested, was denied. It does not appear that Vallejo was ever given the opportunity to refile before the Land Commission, as Hooker was. Instead, six weeks after the claims of the three Americans were approved, he incurred additional legal fees by filing an appeal to the district court. The backlog of cases in that venue was already considerable, and the case was not heard until 1858. Vallejo produced as many documents as he could and Leavenworth testified on his behalf. Using the same criteria the Land Commission had employed when approving the Americans' claims in 1855, the district court confirmed Vallejo's grant on July 13, 1859, more than four years after the other three grants had been confirmed.[19]

By that time Vallejo's relationship with his original attorneys was completely broken. In October 1854, the Land Commission's law agent reported that in delivering some documents to Halleck, Peachy, and Billings he inadvertently discovered that the firm had withdrawn from the Guadalupe Vásquez case. Vallejo was evidently unaware of this development, but given his earlier experiences in the Agua Caliente case, he was prepared to hire a replacement promptly. He selected San Francisco lawyer Benjamin S. Brooks, who had successfully argued John Wilson's claim for Rancho Guilicos in Sonoma before the Land Commission. Brooks took over the case very quickly but his case was unsuccessful before the commission, which rejected the Vásquez claim in April 1855. In his depositions at the beginning of that case in 1852, Vallejo had referred to two distinct grants obtained by Mark West, one consisting of one-and-a-half leagues in 1840, given by Acting Governor Manuel Jimeno, and the other for six leagues in 1844, given by Governor Micheltorena. The commission ruled that the authenticity of the documents detailing both grants had not been conclusively established.[20]

Shortly after that decision, José de los Santos Berreyesa published an article in the Spanish-language newspaper *Crónica* accusing Vallejo of having mishandled the case and thereby having defrauded the family. Berreyesa had long-standing disputes with Vallejo. As early as 1846 he and Vallejo's confidant Pepe de la Rosa had argued over who was entitled to hold the position of *juez*[21] in Sonoma. Guadalupe Vásquez published a response to Berreyesa, in which she said, "I have never had reason to mistrust

---

19. Agua Caliente Land Case [Hooker], BANC MSS Land Case Files, 327 ND, 14–15, 17–21, 40, TBL; Agua Caliente Land Case [Leavenworth], BANC MSS Land Case Files, 333 ND, 9, TBL; Agua Caliente Land Case [Vallejo], BANC MSS Land Case Files, 153 ND, 9, 65, TBL; Hoffman, *Reports of Land Cases*, appendix, 100, 102, 104.

20. Yulupa Land Case, BANC MSS Land Case Files, 140 ND, 16–17, TBL; San Miguel Land Case, BANC MSS Land Case Files, 326 ND, 13, 19, 63–66, TBL; Hoffman, *Reports of Land Cases*, 84, appendix, 5.

21. "Juez," meaning judge or justice of the peace, replaced the office of alcalde in some areas after 1836. A juez held combined municipal and judicial powers within the pueblo.

the irreproachable conduct of General Vallejo." Over the next year however she was persuaded to drop the attorney chosen by Vallejo, Benjamin Brooks, who had lost the case before the Land Commission. She hired a Sonoma firm, Ross and Temple, to represent her in the appeal of her case to the district court. Ross and Temple, in turn, enlisted San Francisco lawyer Elisha O. Crosby, who had already argued scores of cases before the Land Commission.[22]

During this time, Halleck, Peachy, and Billings remained Vallejo's lawyers in the Petaluma case. For after that grant had been approved by the Land Commission, the U.S. government appealed the decision to the district court. Vallejo had little choice but to retain the services of Halleck, Peachy, and Billings, given that this firm knew the most about the case. Once the district court affirmed the grant on March 16, 1857, Halleck proceeded to make it very clear there was no need for any more connection between his firm and Vallejo.

Eight days after the district court confirmed Petaluma, Halleck appeared in the same court as a government witness in the Guadalupe Vásquez case. He testified that in 1851 his law partner Billings had received from Vallejo the 1844 document from Micheltorena granting West six leagues of land and that he himself had received from John Frisbie the 1840 document signed by Jimeno granting West one-and-a-half leagues. He stated that he had come to believe the 1844 document was not genuine, and that was his reason for withdrawing from the case. He also stated that the 1840 document had been altered in an attempt to increase the grant to two-and-a-half leagues instead of one-and-a-half leagues. When asked who he believed was responsible for this fraud, he said that he did not believe Guadalupe Vásquez or her children could have forged or altered documents. He stated, "They are very ignorant people and I believe not one of them can either read or write." The implication

22. Bancroft, *History of California*, 3:660; "Guadalupe Vásquez statement," Sonoma, July 22, 1855, in Larkin, *Papers*, 10:173 (English) and C-B 13, doc. 393, TBL (Spanish); Munro-Fraser, *History of Solano County*, 663–64; San Miguel Land Case, BANC MSS Land Case Files, 326 ND, 73, TBL; Barker, "Elisha Oscar Crosby," 134–37; Crosby, *Memoirs*, 73; Benjamin Brooks to MGV, May 25, 1857, C-B 13, doc. 430, TBL.

was clear: Vallejo was responsible for the fraudulent 1844 document and also for the attempt to alter the 1840 document.[23]

Halleck's testimony created a sensation. The San Francisco *Herald* published a story about it the very next day. The *Sacramento Daily Union*, basing its report on the *Herald* story, headlined its account "Forged Land Title—Detected Perjuries" and exaggerated Halleck's testimony:

> Capt. Halleck testified in relation to the claim, that shortly after the organization of the Land Commission in the city, Gen. Vallejo came to his law office with a paper purporting to be a title to ten leagues of land. He looked at the deed, and feeling satisfied that it was not genuine, refused to have anything to do with it. Gen. Vallejo then left the office, but shortly afterwards came back with the title deed for what he said was two leagues of land. Capt. Halleck examined this closely, and then refused to lend his services towards the confirmation of that also, as he believed it was a forgery.[24]

Halleck himself tried to present a less sensationalistic account of his testimony. The next day the *Union* reported that the *Herald* had summarized a conversation between him and one of its staffers. The newspaper reported that Halleck stated, "No such interview as represented in our article of yesterday ever took place between him and Gen. Vallejo." But the damage had been done, and Vallejo felt the attack on his character deeply. Jasper O'Farrell, who testified for the West heirs in the Guadalupe Vásquez case, wrote Vallejo's friend Martin Cooke a letter in which he denounced Halleck for "the most ungentlemanly, unjustifiable, faithless, and untrustworthy proceeding I have ever heard of being acted by a lawyer (towards one who was his client) in trying to compromise Gen. Vallejo." Cooke showed the letter to Vallejo, who forwarded it to Frisbie. Knowing how deeply Vallejo had been hurt, Frisbie tried to assuage him:

> I read with great pleasure the letter of O'Farrell which you had the kindness to enclose. Such proofs of friendship and esteem from those who have known you long and well are peculiarly grateful, at a time

---

23. San Miguel Land Case, BANC MSS Land Case Files, 326 ND, 96, TBL.
24. "Forged Land Title—Detected Perjuries," *Sacramento Daily Union*, March 27, 1857.

when many, prompted by mean and mercenary motives, seek to blast the enviable fame which your life of distinguished public service has so well earned. But General you will outlive these vile calumnies and the record of your life will command the respect it so preeminently merits, and your name will stand prominent among those distinguished as benefactors and patriotic servants of the state. In this connection let me urge upon you most earnestly to relax no efforts to probe to the bottom of this West matter. . . . It is necessary for your protection against similar assaults in the future. The impression must not become current that your character may be assailed with impunity.[25]

Vallejo followed Frisbie's advice and dictated a statement for Guadalupe Vásquez, saying that she had never told anyone that the six-league document was fraudulent and that she believed Vallejo's only concern in the case was her own and her family's welfare. It is not clear whether Guadalupe Vásquez used Vallejo's statement in any way, but the commission decided the case on June 2, 1857, along the lines proposed by Ross and Temple, Crosby, and Halleck, finding the 1840 grant for one-and-a-half leagues was valid. Vallejo remained scarred by his experiences with Agua Caliente and the West heirs' cases. The Supreme Court did ultimately confirm his claim to Agua Caliente, but during the same session it rejected his much larger claim to Suscol, after that claim had been confirmed by both the Land Commission and the district court. Vallejo never used Halleck, Peachy, and Billings again. Benjamin Brooks handled most of his legal affairs in California for the next decades. But these experiences in the 1850s and the seemingly endless legal outlays they entailed were a stark illustration of the fragility of Vallejo's economic position in American California.[26]

---

25. *Sacramento Daily Union*, March 28, 1857; Jasper O'Farrell to Martin Cooke, April 7, 1857, C-B 17, doc. 418, TBL; John B. Frisbie to MGV, April 9, 1857, C-B 17, doc. 419, TBL.
26. "Declaración de la viuda de West," April 27, 1857, C-B 13, doc. 427, TBL; San Miguel Land Case, BANC MSS Land Case Files, 326 ND, 113, TBL; Yulupa Land Case, BANC MSS Land Case Files, 140 ND, 20, TBL; Hoffman, *Reports of Land Cases*, 174–75; Suscol Land Case, BANC MSS Land Case Files, 318 ND, 88, TBL.

CHAPTER 6

"He Is Very Poor"
Financial and Social Struggles

In his struggles to maintain his land and social position, and to provide for a growing family, Vallejo was closely linked for decades with one man, John B. Frisbie. Their relationship had its origins in the late 1840s and persisted until Vallejo's death in 1890. Frisbie was born in New York in 1823. He studied at the Albany Academy, then entered the law office of Henry G. Wheaton, a prominent local lawyer who served for a time as the district attorney of Albany County. Frisbie worked there for a number of years. After he was elected captain of the Van Rensselaer guards in 1846, he and his men joined the New York Volunteers, a California-bound group led by Colonel J. D. Stevenson. Frisbie and his group, Company H, arrived in California aboard the *Susan Drew*, which entered San Francisco Bay in March 1847. Company H was stationed in San Francisco for more than a year and performed a variety of duties, including administering the port and assisting the army quartermaster. In June 1848, fairly soon after the discovery of gold had become public knowledge, Frisbie was sent to the emerging gold country to

(*left*) John B. Frisbie
Courtesy of California State Parks, Sonoma Barracks. No. 243-x-3221.

(*right*) Fannie Vallejo Frisbie, ca. 1865
*Courtesy of The Bancroft Library, University of California,
Berkeley.* BANC PIC 1978.195:11-PIC.

try to bring back army deserters who had decided to abandon
their posts and prospect for riches. It is not clear whether he met
Vallejo or any members of the Vallejo family during the time he
was stationed in San Francisco, but given Vallejo's prominence
as a friend of the Americans and his position as adjunct Indian
agent, it is possible that the two men crossed paths. They certainly
became better acquainted with each other when Company H was
assigned to Sonoma in August 1848, but Frisbie spent only a few
weeks there because his company was ordered back to San Francisco and mustered out of service at the end of August.[1]

At some point Frisbie became acquainted with and enamored
of Vallejo's daughter Epifania. She had just turned thirteen when

---

1. Munro Fraser, *History of Solano County,* 349   511 Biggs, *Conquer and Colonize,* xv; Soulé and
   Nisbet, *Annals of San Francisco,* 775.

Frisbie arrived in Sonoma, but she had already gained a reputation among the Americans in the area as a girl who was "very handsome and will create a sensation." Frisbie also persuaded Vallejo to enter into a business arrangement with him. During his trip to the gold country, he had noticed that the few stores in operation at Sutter's Fort were doing a very profitable business selling supplies to soldiers and others who were rushing off to the placers. Having already been convinced by Robert Semple of the tremendous commercial possibilities of the Suisun Bay area, Vallejo partnered with Frisbie in setting up some stores to cater to potential miners on their way to "the diggings." By the next year the mercantile enterprise of Vallejo and Frisbie had opened stores in Sonoma, Napa, and Benicia. The store in Benicia was their principal establishment. A few years later, when the U.S. Navy was using it as a storehouse, it was described as a "long building . . . within 30 feet of high-water mark and a good dry landing on a sandbank." The stores sold supplies that Vallejo was able to gather from the Sonoma area and that Frisbie was able to obtain through his military contacts and activities in San Francisco. By August 1849 Frisbie had opened his own store in San Francisco, where he most likely purchased goods that arrived at the port, then sent them to the three stores farther inland. Since supply stores were scarce in the early days of the gold rush, Vallejo and Frisbie probably did fairly well. On the other hand, a restaurant that Frisbie operated was forced to close in December 1849. Along with other members of the New York Volunteers, Frisbie was involved in the planning for the Constitutional Convention, although he himself was not a member of that body. After the convention, he was an unsuccessful candidate for lieutenant governor.[2]

In the same year, 1849, Frisbie purchased Mare Island from

2. Emparán, *Vallejos of California*, 255, 258; Frisbie, "Reminiscences," 31–32, BANC MSS M-M 351, TBL; "Public Sale" (advertisement), *Daily Alta California*, December 28, 1849, and "Public Sale of Naval Stores" (advertisement), *Daily Alta California*, March 16, 1850. Some accounts of the company business may be found in C-B 13, docs. 59, 69, and 74, TBL, and in Vallejo and Frisbie to Thomas O. Larkin, October 30, 1848, in Larkin, *Papers*, 8:26. Biggs, *Conquer and Colonize*, 211; Bancroft, *History of California*, 6:177, 271.

William H. Aspinwall, ca. 1860–1870
*Courtesy of Division of Rare and
Manuscript Collections, Cornell
University Library. John Melmoth
Dow Papers,* RMC2007_0894.

Víctor Castro, one of the Castro brothers who had so vexed Vallejo
during the 1830s. He interested naval officers and investors, including Pacific Mail Steamship Company head William H. Aspinwall, in the place, and made a nice profit by selling it to them.
It eventually became an important navy yard. In August 1850,
Frisbie became a member of the founding board of directors of
the American-dominated, and thus misnamed, Society of California Pioneers. Frisbie was the principal speaker at the society's
gala event on January 1, 1851, and he made sure that Vallejo was
invited to give a toast in Spanish. As a local newspaper reported,
"Gen. Vallejo was called for most vociferously, and replied in a few
remarks and sentiment in his own native magnificent language,
to which the audience loudly responded. He is a popular man."[3]

Frisbie's business and social successes between 1848 and 1851
may have given him an exaggerated sense of his abilities. In this
regard, he was much like Vallejo, who had gained great confidence
in his ability to prosper in American California from his perceived

3. Hoffman, *Reports of Land Cases*, appendix, 43; Bancroft, *History of California*, 4:71, 6:630;
Emparán, *Vallejos of California*, 268; Soulé and Nisbet, *Annals of San Francisco*, 284; "Pioneers' Collation," *Daily Alta California*, January 3, 1851.

successes during those years. In any event, Frisbie's commercial successes and social connections impressed Vallejo. By this time his connection with Frisbie was evolving into a family relationship. Three days after the legislature adjourned in 1850, Vallejo was back in Sonoma, where he served as godfather at Frisbie's Catholic baptism. A year after his baptism, Frisbie married Epifania, who was a few months shy of her sixteenth birthday. During this time Frisbie no doubt informed Vallejo of his legal training. In July 1850 Vallejo made Frisbie his personal lawyer. Subsequently, Vallejo began to entrust Frisbie with additional financial responsibilities revolving around his enormous real estate holdings. The legal fees Vallejo had incurred to defend his land claims strained his finances. In addition, the large amount of livestock that had been stolen from Petaluma while he was imprisoned at Sutter's Fort and the large sums expended in his futile effort to make Vallejo the state capital compounded the weakening of his financial situation. Often guided by Frisbie, Vallejo undertook a number of ventures aimed at stabilizing his finances. Following up on his earlier projects with Semple and Larkin, Vallejo's earliest efforts centered on the Suscol property. In the early 1850s he began selling sections to various buyers, as Richie was doing with Suisun. Purchasers would usually make a down payment in cash and promise to pay the rest in installments with interest. But the chaotic nature of gold rush finances, which one San Francisco merchant termed "the inflation of an overdone business," meant that purchasers often failed to make the subsequent payments on time.[4]

For instance, in December 1852 Frisbie told Vallejo, "I have just called on the agent of Messrs. Clark and Curtis [who had bought part of Rancho Suscol] about paying their interest." Frisbie was told that they would pay the interest in a couple of days. He told Vallejo he did not believe that the late payments were the result of financial trouble, since Clark and Curtis were producing hay on their land and the current price for that commodity was very

---

4. Senkewicz, "Inflation of an Overdone Business," 65.

Pacific Mail Steam Ship Company's Steamer San Francisco, 1853
Reproduced by permission of the Huntington Library, San Marino, California.
John Haskell Kemble Collection. prijнк 00469.

good. The next month, Frisbie told Vallejo that Clark and Curtis still had not made their payments and recommended that Vallejo "annul the contract existing between you and them." Frisbie argued that Vallejo would certainly be able to find other buyers for this tract. Vallejo apparently gave Frisbie permission to threaten Clark and Curtis with foreclosure, for in April, Clark offered to pay Vallejo half of the $30,000 he owed in cash and the other half in installments at a 5 percent per month interest rate. Vallejo sent his associate Martin Cooke to San Francisco to see if he could extract any money from Clark. Cooke came back empty-handed, and Vallejo told Frisbie that entertaining other options for the sale of the property seemed to be the best approach. These types of failed transactions occurred and reoccurred, exacerbating Vallejo's difficult financial situation. Frisbie's own financial endeavors, which he undertook using money that most likely stemmed more from Vallejo's accumulated landholdings than from his own assets, compounded Vallejo's difficulties. For instance, in 1852 Frisbie used Vallejo's money to purchase a tract of land at Rancho Huichico in Napa County from Thomas O. Larkin. Some observers expressed concern about Frisbie's freedom to manage Vallejo's money. In 1851, lawyer Henry Halleck presciently wrote, "I fear Frisbie's speculations will utterly ruin the General."[5]

In March 1853 Frisbie sailed to New York in the company of his wife, Epifania, their one-year-old son Guadalupe, and Vallejo's young son Platón, who was going to join his brother Andrónico at school in Maryland. He also had business interests in mind. William Aspinwall had just sold Mare Island to the U.S. government, which intended to construct a naval yard there. Frisbie hoped he could sell some properties in the nearby town of Vallejo, which was still technically California's state capital, to Aspinwall. Arguing

5. John Frisbie to MGV, December 17, 1852, C-B 13, doc. 274, TBL; Frisbie to Vallejo, January 11, 1853, C-B 13, doc. 293, TBL; MGV to Frisbie, March 21, 1853, April 14, 1853, and April 29, 1853, C-B 441, box 1, folder 3, TBL; Henry Halleck to Pablo de la Guerra, September 29, 1851, DLG 487, letter 6, SBMAL; John Frisbie to Thomas O. Larkin, August 6, 1852, in Larkin, *Papers*, 9:119; William Eames to Thomas O. Larkin, April 29, 1853; Larkin, *Papers*, 9:252; John Frisbie to Thomas O. Larkin, September 19, 1853, in Larkin, *Papers*, 9:284.

U.S. Navy Yard at Mare Island,
California, 1857. Courtesy of the
California History Room, California
State Library, Sacramento, California.
City of Vallejo Picture Collection, folio
917.94 K9.

that the combination of Vallejo being the capital and the naval yard
locating there would increase property values, he offered a good
amount of land to Aspinwall for $50,000. He told Vallejo that he
thought Aspinwall was on the verge of accepting this offer when
G. W. P. Bissell, a San Francisco businessman who was Aspinwall's
partner in Mare Island, and Frederick Billings, Halleck's law partner, arrived in New York. According to Frisbie, Bissell and Billings
urged Aspinwall to reject Frisbie's offer, persuading Aspinwall that
"he may make a better deal by delay, thinking that perhaps you
will hereafter need the money more than at present." By this time
the Billings law firm was already representing Vallejo in five cases
before the Land Commission. Billings probably informed Aspinwall that the associated legal expenses were going to drain Vallejo's
finances considerably. Frisbie told Vallejo that Bissell's and Billings's
intervention had forced him to reduce the asking price, and he was
not inclined to go any lower. He assured Vallejo that "by playing
their own game (assumed indifference) we shall yet bring them to

our terms." He speculated to Vallejo that Bissell and Aspinwall's ultimate aim was to buy all of Rancho Suscol and urged Vallejo simply to hold tight. A month later he wrote Vallejo that Aspinwall had not increased his offer and that Bissell was about to return to San Francisco. He urged Vallejo not to enter into any negotiations if Bissell approached him. He was however unable to find another potential buyer, and shortly before he left New York, he confessed, "I find no purchaser in the Vallejo or Petaluma property."[6]

Vallejo's correspondence with Frisbie during these years was filled with various schemes to gain more money. In July 1854, guided by Frisbie, who had arranged to be the technical legal owner of Suscol, he sold off portions of that rancho to various American land developers, who intended to carve up the tract into smaller units and sell them to settlers. As usual, however,

6. Emparán, *Vallejos of California*, 263; William Eames to Thomas O. Larkin, March 15, 1853, in Larkin, *Papers*, 9:239; John Frisbie to MGV, July 2, August 3, and September 20, 1853, C-B 441, box 4, folder 13, TBL.

few of these sales involved the buyer paying the entire purchase price. Through all these maneuvers, the legal expenses kept mounting, and Vallejo and Frisbie were constantly trying to meet them. In July 1854, Frisbie reported that he still needed about $5,000 from some source, adding, "It is becoming exceedingly difficult to raise money." Vallejo was forced to sell more of his lands at Suscol to raise these funds. In November 1854, he sold a large section of the town of Vallejo to James Denver, Samuel Haight, and Samuel Purdy. A general banking collapse in San Francisco in 1855 squeezed the credit market in San Francisco and accordingly worsened Vallejo's and Frisbie's situations.[7]

Frisbie was also involved in railroad speculation, especially relating to a proposed line from the Carquínez Strait area inland to Marysville, California. He believed such a route would increase the value of the property at Rancho Suscol that he and Vallejo were seeking to sell. During his 1853 trip to the East, he wrote Vallejo, "Great efforts are being made here in behalf of the Benicia and Marysville railroad and I am strongly inclined to the belief that they will succeed in raising the capital necessary to the construction." However, his hopes never came to fruition. A few years later Frisbie was a commissioner selling stock in the San Francisco and Sacramento Railroad Company, in which he and Vallejo purchased twenty-five shares each, at ten dollars a share. The company did not lay very many miles of actual track. In 1858 he successfully lobbied the legislature to pass a bill facilitating construction of a line from Vallejo to Marysville. He optimistically predicted that this line would be constructed in "one or two years." Two years later he was still confidently predicting that the line's "immediate construction" was "beyond question," but this project, like so many others, never came close to completion.[8]

---

7. John Frisbie to MGV, July 25, 1854, C-B 441, box 4, folder 13, TBL; sale of land, November 22, 1854, C-B 441, box 4, folder 4, TBL; Senkewicz, *Vigilantes in Gold Rush San Francisco*, 33–37.

8. John Frisbie to MGV, July 2, 1853, C-B 441, box 4, folder 13, TBL; San Francisco and Sacramento Railroad Company stock sale, January 21, 1856, in Larkin, *Papers*, 10:236; John Frisbie to MGV, April 20, 1858, C-B 441, box 4, folder 13, TBL; *Statutes of California*, 265–67; John Frisbie to MGV, October 1860, C-B 441, box 4, folder 13, TBL; "Marysville and Vallejo Railroad," *Marysville Daily Appeal*, May 29, 1860.

Petaluma adobe in 1880
Courtesy of Sonoma County Library. Cstr_pho_015335.

In sum, the 1850s was a difficult decade for Vallejo. The bills from Halleck, Peachy, and Billings were substantial and certainly beyond his ability to pay in a lump sum. After the falling out over the San Miguel claim, the firm toughened its stance against Vallejo, placing legal attachments upon Rancho Petaluma and on Vallejo's Casa Grande in Sonoma. When the district court finally did confirm his Petaluma claim in 1857, Vallejo quickly sold the adobe and a portion of the land to William Whiteside. On the basis of this transaction, Frisbie was able to negotiate a $10,000 loan to Vallejo that enabled him to clear some of his debts.[9]

This was nowhere near the end of Vallejo's financial difficulties, however. After the district court confirmed his claim to Suscol in March 1860, the U.S. government appealed the case to the Supreme Court. This case represented a significant financial challenge for Vallejo. Beyond the additional legal fees, a loss would mean that he might have to repay individuals who had purchased large sections of the grant from him, which he simply did not have

---

9. Emparán, *Vallejos of California*, 78, 106; Frisbie to Vallejo, April 20, 1858, C-B 441, box 4, folder 13, TBL.

the cash on hand to do. Frisbie calculated Vallejo's financial worth at a substantial $338,000, but it was overwhelmingly tied up in land, with Rancho Suscol accounting for $200,000 of the total.[10]

In June 1860 Frisbie told Vallejo that it was in their interest to accept an offer to buy them out of some additional land claims. He explained, "We want money . . . and have a superabundance of litigation." A few months later Frisbie took a trip to the East. He hoped that a shipment of wheat he was sending to England—the first California wheat transported across the Atlantic—would give him a solid reputation among Eastern financiers. In that case he planned to borrow money "at Eastern rates of interest," rather than the higher rates prevailing in California. After a few weeks in New York, his enthusiasm over his prospects skyrocketed, as was typical. He told Vallejo, "It is my honest conviction, General, that there is an immense future almost within our grasp. Up to the present moment we have been going upstream but the tide is manifestly setting in our favor." He also assured Vallejo he was confident that the Supreme Court was going to dismiss the government's appeal in the Suscol case. His assessment of Suscol proved as unrealistic as his assessment of his financial prospects. In June he told Vallejo that, while he had made $12,000 from the sale of the wheat, that sum was "not as much as I expected." Compounding his troubles, rather than dismissing the Suscol appeal, the Supreme Court in fact rejected Vallejo's claim in March 1862.[11]

Frisbie had also been buying and selling Suscol land on the basis of Vallejo's claim. His initial reaction to the Supreme Court decision was to look after his own interests. He had been appointed a brigadier general in the state militia by California Governor Leland Stanford, whom he had first gotten to know when they worked together in the Wheaton Law offices in Albany in the 1840s. His militia rank apparently gave him some access to various legal administrators in the region. He was able to obtain some

---

10. John Frisbie to MGV, October 1860, C-B 441, box 4, folder 13, TBL.
11. John Frisbie to MGV, June 9, 1860; November 3, 1860; and June 18, 1861, C-B 441, box 4, folder 13, TBL; *U.S. v. Vallejo,* 66 U.S. 541.

land warrants from friendly local officials for the three thousand Suscol acres he owned and for an unspecified amount of land he had sold but on which he still held a mortgage. Yet, he did not take any parallel actions regarding Vallejo's properties and sales, even though Suscol accounted for a substantial proportion of Vallejo's worth. Frisbie told Vallejo that he had felt "indignation" at the "infamous outrage perpetrated by the government in its criminal violation of its solemn treaty" (referring to the 1848 Treaty of Guadalupe Hidalgo, which promised that "Mexicans now established in territories previously belonging to Mexico" would be able to retain their property). Vallejo opined that the U.S. government ought to be sued "to indemnify us for the flagrant violation of the treaty," which Frisbie agreed was a great idea, but nothing came from this suggestion.[12]

In addition, Vallejo soon became frustrated at his inability to get from Frisbie a clear picture of the effects of the Suscol ruling on his overall financial situation. After a few months of uncertainty, Frisbie sent him a fairly vague letter in which he acknowledged Vallejo's "pressing need of money." He said, "Believe me when I assure you that if it were in my power to offer relief you would promptly receive it. . . . General you can form no idea of my labors and struggling to save something from this property. My health is giving way, I am forced to all kinds of expedients to raise money to meet the indispensable disbursements that every day brings some key difficulty." Vallejo responded two days later and said, "I insist that you don't trouble yourself. Whatever you can do for me <u>now</u> is too late. I only want to know if I still have any right in the properties." In response to this direct question, Frisbie had to tell Vallejo that one of the properties in question had already been mortgaged and that another was tied up in legal proceedings. The only property that might have some value was a small property in the East

---

12. Tutorow, *Governor*, 1:12; Emparán, *Vallejos of California*, 267; "The Militia of California," *Sacramento Daily Union*, March 21, 1862; John Frisbie to MGV, April 20, 1862, and May 2, 1862, C-B 441, box 4, folder 13, TBL; Griswold del Castillo, *Treaty of Guadalupe Hidalgo*, 44–45, 72–77.

(*above*) Lachryma Montis Vineyard wine label, 1858
Courtesy of the California Historical Society. MS 2204_001.tif.

(*below*) *Lachryma Montis, Residence of Gen. M. G. Vallejo, 1857,*
by Stephen William Shaw. In Kuchel and Dresel's *California Views,*
vol. 1.2, no. 22, FL281075. *Courtesy of the California History Room,*
California State Library, Sacramento, California.

Bay in which Frisbie had a one-eighth interest but which, he told Vallejo, "I regard as our joint property, share and share alike." In any event, after the debts related to that property were calculated, Frisbie thought that it would be worth no more than $1,000.[13]

In the midst of all these difficulties, Vallejo had no practical recourse but to mortgage a vineyard he owned in Sonoma, which had given him great personal pleasure, and Lachryma Montis, the house he had recently constructed a slight distance off the Sonoma Plaza. Thomas P. Madden, a real estate agent and friend of Frisbie's, agreed to pick up the mortgage. However, he imposed an interest rate of 12 percent, and a depressed Vallejo told Benicia that he might have to sell "other properties that I have." While he sympathized with Vallejo's "great pecuniary embarrassments," Frisbie advised against "abandoning your homestead" and promised that he himself would pay the interest. These transactions crystallized the dire financial straits into which Vallejo had fallen. Benicia described the situation in a note to her son Platón: "He is very poor. Captain Frisbie has given bad accounts to your father, and the government of the United States has taken from him the Suscol properties and furthermore the little that remains to him is pledged to Mr. Madden and he also owes other people."[14]

In the meantime, Frisbie had headed to Washington, D.C. to lobby Congress to pass a bill allowing those who had bought Suscol land on the basis of Vallejo's claim to purchase those claims at bargain-basement pre-emption prices. The attempt failed in 1862, but it passed the next year. While the law removed the threat of future financial liabilities relating to Suscol for Frisbie and Vallejo, it did nothing to recover the losses Vallejo had already suffered. Toward the end of 1863 he wrote to Benicia, "I am tired, bored,

13. John Frisbie to MGV, November 2, 1862, and November 9, 1862, C-B 441, box 4, folder 13, TBL; MGV to John Frisbie, November 4, 1862, C-B 441, box 4, folder 13, TBL; Langley, *San Francisco Directory*, 252.

14. Emparán, *Vallejos of California*, 108; Benicia Vallejo to Platón Vallejo, April (no year), BANC MSS 76/79c, box 1, folder 19, TBL; MGV to Benicia Vallejo, July 19, 1862, BANC MSS 76/79c, box 1, folder 25, TBL; John Frisbie to MGV, November 9, 1862, C-B 441, box 4, folder 13, TBL.

and feeling hopeless, having to live with so much work and anxiety. This is not the life I lived ten years ago. I have been robbed by greedy men, unworthy of the trust I had placed in them." His anxiety continued and his disappointment in the people and the government in which he had placed so much confidence in the late 1840s regularly surfaced in his letters to Benicia. He said, "Ending up poor because the most powerful government in the world has taken over my most valuable properties is not my fault." In the same vein, most likely referring to Frisbie, he lamented, "I have suffered so much in so many ways; my business affairs, in the hands of rather unsuccessful people, have been in a continuous state of flux and are continuously at risk of being wiped out." Throughout his letters there was a gnawing realization that he had misinterpreted the American military's "conciliation" of him in 1846. He had assumed that similar deference would be the posture of many other Americans as well, but his experience before the Land Commission had proven otherwise. He confessed to Benicia and himself that he had been the victim of "a grand public movement that dragged down the fortunes of men like me who made themselves more visible."[15]

Until the summer of 1864, Vallejo continued to fear that he might have to sell the vineyard to pay the mortgage interest to Madden. However, his financial difficulties were temporarily alleviated in 1864 when a family squabble relating to the title of Rancho San Cayetano, which had been granted to his father, Ignacio, decades before, was finally cleared up. Thereby he received $15,000, some of which he used to pay down his debts to Madden. He then decided to accept Frisbie's invitation to go East with him. They visited a number of cities, including Washington, D.C., Philadelphia, Baltimore, Boston, and New York. Indeed, while they were in New York the procession carrying President Lincoln's body passed directly by his lodging at the Fifth Avenue Hotel. Vallejo's overall reaction to New York was quite similar to those of many other visitors before and since: "This city of New York is an immense

---

15. Gates, "Suscol Principle," 456 61; MGV to Benicia Vallejo, November 23, 1863; April 26, 1864; May 18, 1864; and July 20, 1864, C-B 441, box 1, folder 4, TBL.

"Funeral Honors to President Lincoln."
From *Frank Leslie's Illustrated Newspaper*, May 13, 1865,
pp. 120–121. *Courtesy of the Lincoln Financial Foundation Collection.*

place where everybody walks up and down the streets without knowing one another and without speaking to anyone. The hustle and bustle and confusion are such that the noise level is extremely loud. You have to speak by shouting, and even then, you cannot hear each other. I am tired of the trains. They run constantly, day and night, and are so crowded with people."[16]

The purpose of the trip is not entirely clear, although Vallejo wrote at one point, "The only reason I made the decision to go so far away and leave my family behind was because I needed to

16. Emparán, *Vallejos of California*, 102–3, 110–11, 212–13; MGV to Benicia Vallejo, April 26, 1864, C-B 441, box 1, folder 4, and March 20, 1865, and November 6, 1869, C-B 441, box 1, folder 5, TBL. The hotel was on Fifth Avenue and 23rd Street; for the route of the procession, see "Reception of the Remains," *New York Times*, April 24, 1865.

Plaza Sonoma, 1852. Courtesy of The Bancroft Library,
University of California, Berkeley. BANC PIC 1978.195.22-PIC.

see if I could arrange my business dealings with Frisbie and work together with him. I hope everything will work out for me." He did not specify what these "business dealings" were. Frisbie may have been trying to work out agreements with contacts he had acquired during his Suscol lobbying, or they may have related to something else entirely. In any event, Vallejo did not have fond memories of the trip. Toward the end of his stay in the East, he told Benicia, "I will be leaving for California, returning from visiting this country that I admire but do not love with my heart because the weather, just like the people in general, have treated me very badly and have been the cause of my ruin and that of my family." There is no indication that any profits for either him or Frisbie developed from this trip.[17]

The failure of the trip to produce any economic benefit apparently worsened Frisbie's situation. At the beginning of January 1866, he sent Vallejo a four-page summary of his own finances. His assets, mainly in land, amounted to $270,676, while his debts were $103,440. He told Vallejo that his most pressing necessity was to pay off his debts. He promised, "When the said indebtedness shall be fully paid I will convey the undivided half of the remaining portion of my said estate, real and personal, to you." Since the interest payments to Madden did not appear in Frisbie's list of what he owed and since he offered no time frame for gaining solvency, the meaning was clear: he could no longer afford to pay the interest on Vallejo's mortgage. Therefore, he arranged for Vallejo to deed the property to Madden, who agreed to let Vallejo live there for $150 a month. Madden also agreed to give Vallejo the right to repurchase the property for $21,000.[18]

In April 1867, two weeks after a fire destroyed his Casa Grande on the Sonoma Plaza, Vallejo learned that Frisbie had been able to patent some of the Suscol land he had been able to salvage after the

---

17. MGV to Benicia Vallejo, March 20, 1865, C-B 441, box 1, folder 5, and April 30, 1865, C-B 441, box 1, folder 4, TBL.

18. John Frisbie to MGV, January 3, 1866, C-B 441, box 4, folder 13, TBL; Emparán, *Vallejos of California*, 115.

Supreme Court decision. That news reminded Vallejo once again of the land he had lost, and he poured out his feelings in a letter to Frisbie's brother: "I saw in the papers that Frisbie and others have received patents, but Frisbie has told me nothing, which is very strange; but perhaps someday he will remember that I exist. . . . He knows what my family is suffering. He negotiates, receives money, and forgets absolutely that the 'bread of prosperity is to be divided among the poor who have produced that prosperity.'" He began to insist that Frisbie use some of the money to which he now had access to buy Lachryma Montis and the vineyard from Madden. He told Benicia that the funds Frisbie controlled had actually come from him. He said, "There are men who are entrusted with considerable interests, with no reservation and for such a long time that they become familiar with it and believe it belongs to them. Can you believe it?" He angrily told her that if Frisbie refused, the family should cut contact with him: "It will be necessary to take steps, and the first one should be for you and the entire family to be ready to leave Frisbie's house immediately."[19]

Frisbie first tried to improve his finances through additional railroad speculation. He succeeded in being elected to the state legislature in 1867 and pushed through a bill strengthening the position of the California Pacific Railroad, of which he was a vice president. This line was one of many successors of the Benicia–Marysville rail project, none of which had ever amounted to much, but construction of the railroad was not the actual intention of the bill. This fledgling company deliberately adopted a name, California Pacific, that was similar to that of the giant of the California railroad industry, the Central Pacific. As the California Pacific directors undoubtedly hoped, Central Pacific, not wanting to be confused with a nascent railroad that it judged would probably fail, bought it out in 1871.[20]

19. "Patents," *Napa County Reporter*, April 27, 1867; Emparán, *Vallejos of California*, 296; MGV to Benicia Vallejo, June 5, 1867 (emphasis in original), and MGV to John Frisbie, June 26, 1867, 76/79c, box 1, folder 25, TBL.

20. *Journal of the Assembly*, 1867–8, 452, 472, 739; Bancroft, *History of California*, 7:581–85; Hittell, *History of California*, 4:486.

Frisbie's profit from the buyout was increased by another successful move he made in 1870, when he organized the Vallejo Savings and Commercial Bank. Like other California banks, such as the Bank of California from which Frisbie had taken out a loan, the Vallejo Bank speculated in silver mining stocks and for a time was quite successful. Frisbie's improved financial situation finally enabled him to assist Vallejo. He purchased Lachryma Montis from Madden and deeded it to Benicia. Since the California constitution, reflective of Mexican practice and law, allowed married women to own property in their own name, this was a way of separating Lachryma Montis from any future financial difficulties that Vallejo might experience. Lachryma Montis eventually became an indispensable source of income for Vallejo and his family, because they were able to sell water from the spring on the estate to the town of Sonoma. Indeed, during 1874 and 1875, the years he collaborated with Bancroft, Vallejo was abnormally free from urgent and pressing financial concerns, although periodic fears were always present.[21]

Benicia, on the other hand, harbored considerable resentment that Frisbie, during his days of prosperity, was not doing more to assist her family. She shared her husband's belief that the money that Frisbie was using actually stemmed from Vallejo's assets. Simple justice demanded that he share a considerable portion of that money with them. She drafted a letter to him, which her children and her husband persuaded her not to send, where she thundered at him, "Didn't General Vallejo himself hand over some property to you without keeping a record of what you were doing, what you did, or what you are doing now? You do whatever you feel like doing when it comes to General Vallejo. Isn't it true that you are doing whatever you want to Guadalupe [General Vallejo]? Remember: Everybody knows that everything you have belongs

---

21. MGV to Benicia Vallejo, December 15, 1871, C-B 441, box 1, folder 6, TBL; "Real Estate Transactions," *Sonoma Democrat*, December 23, 1871; Munro-Fraser, *History of Solano County*, 225; Emparán, *Vallejos of California*, 120–21; MGV to Benicia Vallejo, November 16, 1875, C-B 441, box 1, folder 7, TBL.

Mariano Guadalupe Vallejo, 1878
*Courtesy of California State Parks,
Sonoma Barracks. No. 243-1-1421.*

to General Vallejo and his heirs, it doesn't belong to you. Isn't it true that you are still selling the lands and everything else, passing it all on to others and hiding the property from the General and from me?"[22]

What Benicia did not know was that Frisbie was investing a good amount of Vallejo's money into mining speculation. In 1876 the mining bubble burst and the bank failed. The consequences for Vallejo were serious. Initially, he was uncertain about the extent of his losses. He told his son Platón that Frisbie "scarcely told me in what or how he had lost everything. . . . He says that in his losses he involved me too. What a crime!" He was certain of one thing, however: "Frisbie ought not to have jeopardized or risked what was not his, neither in his speculations nor in the stocks." He wrote his daughter Epifania that he was having difficulty coming to terms with the fact that "all my property that I have in the hands of Frisbie on trust and in which I received $250 a month interest on $30,000 in money, besides the interest in the land and dwelling, have been lost in the speculations and the bank failure."

---

22. Benicia Vallejo to John Frisbie, August 26, 1873, BANC MSS 76/79c, box 1, folder 19, TBL.

Mariano Guadalupe Vallejo's calling card
*Courtesy of The Bancroft Library, University of California,
Berkeley. C-B 41, box 11, folder 6.*

Moreover, Vallejo found that Frisbie's financial losses reflected on him as well. In April 1877 he complained to Benicia, "I have been trying to obtain a little bit of money from my old friends (when I had money, I did all kinds of favors for them) to put my business affairs in good order. However, none of them has wanted to lend me even one single peso. They are a bunch of thankless ingrates, among them Mr. Brooks and Madden, whom everyone says are quite rich." Realizing that he was now experiencing more fully the setbacks that many of his fellow Californios had been suffering in American California, he told her, "We cannot hope to receive anything from our people. They are all poor, very poor." A few days later, he returned to the same theme in another letter to her. He lamented, "<u>Our people</u>, almost all of them, are so broke or poor. It is hard to believe that most of the time they have nothing to eat. There is so much poverty." Vallejo dabbled in various schemes relating to Baja California and a few other projects. Even though he was occasionally enthusiastic about "excellent prospects" relating to various business opportunities, nothing concrete ever materialized.[23]

Frisbie was likewise determined to seek other opportunities. The bank failure was hardly his first financial reversal, and he quickly determined to strike out again. He told Vallejo, "I have been casting about with the utmost solicitude to discern some enterprise in which I could embark to rebuild my broken fortunes." As he had done so often in the past, he focused on railroads, but this time his target was Mexico. He borrowed some money from his brother-in-law in New York and headed south. He persuaded Vallejo, whose former experience as a Mexican army officer he hoped would be useful, to accompany him.[24]

Vallejo's impression of Mexico City was ambivalent. He marveled at the Church of Our Lady of Guadalupe and at the cathedral and its sanctuary, which he called "truly stupendous and grandiose works of architecture." He said, "The ornate decor inside is astonishing. On the outside the construction is sumptuous and imposing. Both the inside and the outside are testaments to the men who founded them." But he was also overwhelmed by the atmosphere of the city: "One can't breathe the air here. It chokes you. The polluted air is truly unbearable." And he was appalled at the numbers and destitute condition of the Indigenous population. He claimed, "Mexico City has 300,000 inhabitants and of that number 260,000 are Indians who infest the streets, half naked. Some are completely naked and others wear ragged clothing and no shoes." He described "thousands upon thousands of Indian men and women carrying their children on their backs in a state of decrepitude in rags and tatters." He concluded, "It is such

23. Emparán, *Vallejos of California*, 139, 271; MGV to Benicia Vallejo, August 21, 1876, C-B 441, box 1, folder 7, and February 21, 1877, April 4, 1877, and April 6, 1877, C-B 441, box 1, folder 8, TBL.

24. John Frisbie to MGV, November 30, 1876, C-B 441, box 4, folder 13, TBL.

a miserable sight." In an interview with a Mexican newspaper, however, Vallejo adopted the posture that Frisbie wished, one that he hoped would help gain him access to the powerful of the city, saying, "I was born a Mexican; my ancestors were Mexican, and I have always maintained with my sword the honor of Mexico. I have both Mexican and American children, and I desire for my native land all the prosperity and progress enjoyed by the country of some of my children and mine by adoption. The day that Mexico has a railroad which, devouring distance, unites it with California, commerce and industry will flourish." Indeed, Frisbie and Vallejo obtained an audience with Finance Minister Matías Romero, whom they had met on their 1865 trip to the East when Romero was secretary of the Mexican legation in Washington, D.C., and also met with Porfirio Díaz.[25]

Vallejo and Frisbie left Mexico separately. Frisbie went to Washington, D.C., where he played a minor role in the U.S. recognition of Porfirio Díaz as president of Mexico. Frisbie later told Bancroft, and probably any Mexican official with whom he talked, that his role was instrumental in obtaining this recognition. He decided, on the basis of his relative success in these two national capitals, that he might have better success in Mexico than in California. Vallejo sailed to New Orleans, then traveled to Syracuse, New York, where a granddaughter of his had just married. When Frisbie finished his business in Washington, he and Vallejo returned to California. When they arrived, Frisbie began preparations to move himself and his family to Mexico.[26]

Before Frisbie left, Vallejo extracted a promise that his son-in-law would provide him with one hundred dollars per month. Vallejo told Benicia that, together with some rent they were collecting and the amount they were earning from the sale of water, they should be able to count on a total income of $150 a month.

25. MGV to Benicia Vallejo, June 7, 1877, August 30, 1877, C-B 441, box 1, folder 8, TBL. On the sanitation state of Mexico City at the time, see Agostoni, *Monuments of Progress*, 31–37; Emparán, *Vallejos of California*, 141.

26. Cosío Villegas, *United States versus Porfirio Díaz*, 147, 167; Frisbie, "Reminiscences," 12–14, BANC MSS M-M 351, TBL.

This was hardly a princely sum. He also requested a loan from his sister Encarnación, but he was disappointed when she did not quickly respond to that request positively. Subsequently, he continued to pursue a variety of possibilities to try to improve his monetary situation.[27]

He told Benicia that the trip to Mexico with Frisbie had given him something of a reputation as a railroad promoter, a perception on which he hoped to be able to capitalize. He reported, "Some Americans from New York want to establish or build a railroad from Acapulco to Mexico City, and they want me to go with them to obtain a permit from the Mexican government so that they can build it. Of course I accepted the proposition but before leaving, they have to give me $8,000 in gold, whether I obtain the permission or not." He even described in great detail how he was going to use the $8,000, including $2,000 for her and a $1,000 life insurance policy that would give her $40,000 if anything happened to him while he was in Mexico. He assured her that the Americans were "mulling over" his offer, but nothing came of it. He may well have suspected this outcome, for in the same letter, he complained that he had not yet received the hundred dollars that Frisbie had promised would be sent to him.[28]

During this time, he was staying at the Palace Hotel in San Francisco and he boasted that he had been able to negotiate a rate of one dollar per day. He realized that people who received letters from him written on Palace Hotel stationery would have a hard time believing that he was as needy as he claimed to be. However, he stayed there and kept looking for possibilities. At one point he appears to have decided that a parcel of land in the San Francisco presidio, currently property of the U.S. Army, had been granted to him by Governor Figueroa in 1834 and that he was entitled to it. The origin of this notion is not entirely clear, but he

27. MGV to Benicia Vallejo, January 27, 1878, C-B 441, box 1, folder 9, TBL; MGV to Benicia Vallejo, February 5, 1878, Melville Schweitzer Collection of California Miscellany, box 1, folder 2, CHS.

28. MGV to Benicia Vallejo, February 7, 1878, C-B 441, box 1, folder 9, TBL.

Palace Hotel, San Francisco, ca. 1875, by John James Reilly
Courtesy of the California History Room, California State Library,
Sacramento, California. STEREO-2361.

and his daughter María spent the two months before her wedding translating into English various documents that he thought would support his contention. Having María help him kept the expenses down. The longer they spent on this project, the more confident he became that he would be able to "present in court for my claims against the presidio." In typically confident terms he assured Benicia, "I am so busy with this matter regarding the presidio that I barely have a chance to eat. The matter appears to be going in a positive direction up to now, and I have hopes that I will win the lawsuit." However, in the absence of any real possibility of winning such a claim, he appears to have dropped the matter.[29]

Vallejo's financial difficulties continued. In 1880 he explained to his son Platón why he had been unable to visit him: "It is because during these times, one cannot go out without a pocket well stocked with what is called in Latin, numerata pecunia. In Sonoma, or rather at Lachryma Montis, impecuniosity is in full force and engrained in such a way that entire months go by and one doesn't even see a single peso. It is for that reason that I haven't fulfilled my promise to visit you." A year later he borrowed $1,500 from railroad builder Peter Donahue, pledging some lots in Sonoma as guarantee for the loan. But the lack of a regular income made his daily life more restricted than he would have wished. As he wrote in 1881, "I am very tired because of the business of the water. I have to get up at five o'clock in the morning to go into Sonoma to distribute it, and at seven o'clock in the evening to turn the machines back on. And, for what? Just to 'earn the daily bread' with much effort and fatigue." He still dabbled in various projects, holding out hopes of some quick gains. For instance, in 1883 he wrote, "Today or tomorrow I think I will be able to settle some other very important business that will produce (based on how it is prepared) some thirty or forty thousand pesos, or maybe more. I am delighted by the prospect that this might actually happen within a few months." Nothing ever actually did happen.[30]

In addition, Frisbie apparently did not consistently send the hundred-dollar monthly payment he had promised. Once he returned to Mexico, he quickly started to speculate in mining enterprises. With the reckless optimism that had guided so many of his previous ventures, he excitedly told Vallejo, "I deem my share in the El Oro and Real de Monte mines well worth a million dollars." He

29. MGV to Benicia Vallejo, February 5, 1878, Melville Schweitzer Collection of California Miscellany, box 1, folder 2, CHS; MGV to Benicia Vallejo, February 15 and March 18, 1878, C-B 441, box 1, folder 9, TBL.

30. MGV to Platón Vallejo, August 4, 1880, BANC MSS 76/79c, box 1, folder 27, TBL; MGV to Benicia Vallejo, August 19, 1881, C-B 441, box 1, folder 9, TBL; MGV to Benicia Vallejo, September 22, 1883, C-B 441, box 1, folder 1, TBL; Emparán, *Vallejos of California*, 155.

assured his father-in-law, "I shall be relieved from the pressure of poverty, which has borne so heavily upon me for the past few years." Yet five years later he had to admit, "Business affairs have not thrived with me." At the end of August 1885 Frisbie lamented, "No man has struggled harder than I have to make a success in life. Thirty years were wasted in California."[31]

Frisbie did send Vallejo one hundred dollars at the end of 1882, but when Vallejo twice asked Frisbie for money in the mid-1880s, the latter protested that he was too poor to send more than fifty dollars each time. Vallejo complained to Platón, "When Frisbie was here, I had a talk with him, without mentioning this unpleasant business regarding the predicaments in which I found myself. But he told me that he would not be able to help me at the present time because of his many commitments in Mexico." Actually, Frisbie was beginning to do better in Mexico. He became the paid lobbyist for the Southern Pacific Railroad in Mexico and escorted Díaz on an 1883 trip to the United States. Ultimately, however, connections not business ventures enabled Frisbie to do well in his new country. His association with U.S. senator Leland Stanford and railroad magnate Henry Huntington opened doors in the American expatriate and business communities in Mexico City. His daughter Sarah married the son of the American minister to Mexico, but unfortunately, she died after a difficult childbirth two years later. Frisbie was also able to gain possession of a ranch outside Mexico City. In the meantime, Vallejo was still struggling. Both he and Benicia knew their situation was grim. During an 1887 visit to Monterey, he wrote her, "And you, try to stay well. It is possible that one of these days we will get out from under the present circumstances."[32]

---

31. John Frisbie to MGV, December 29, 1879, April 14, 1880, June 30, 1885, and August 31, 1885, C-B 441, box 4, folder 13, TBL; MGV to Benicia Vallejo, December 28, 1882, C-B 441, box 1, folder 10, TBL.

32. Hart, *Empire and Revolution*, 124, 220; Schell, *Integral Outsiders*, 2–5; John Frisbie to MGV, October 13, 1885, and December 15, 1885, C-B 441, box 4, folder 13, TBL; MGV to Platón Vallejo, October 22, 1888, BANC MSS 76/79c, box 1, folder 28, TBL; MGV to Benicia Vallejo, September 12, 1887, C-B 441, box 2, folder 2, TBL.

Golden wedding anniversary photograph of
Fannie Vallejo de Frisbie and General John B. Frisbie, Mexico, April 1901
Courtesy of California State Parks, Sonoma Barracks. No. 243-x-3083.

Vallejo also became involved in a couple of legal conflicts during
his last years. At some point in the mid-1880s, he allowed himself
to become convinced that a lawsuit over his ownership of the San
Francisco presidio offered a solution to his financial difficulties.
The convincing was probably done by a San Francisco attorney,
Joseph M. Kinley. In January 1886 Kinley filed suit in San Francisco Superior Court on behalf of John K. Moore, who claimed
that, through a Mexican-era grant, he was the rightful owner
of more than one hundred acres in San Francisco. Moore was
not seeking the return of this land, but restitution from the current owners, who included the city and the U.S. military. At the

Mariano Guadalupe Vallejo, 1889
Courtesy of California State Parks,
Sonoma Barracks. No. 243-1-1424.

beginning of October 1886 Kinley filed a similar case for Vallejo, seeking not the property itself, but rather damages for Vallejo's having been evicted from the property by the American military authorities. Over Kinley's objections the suit was transferred from the Superior Court to the U.S. District Court, where it was eventually dismissed after Vallejo's death.[33]

The second legal conflict arose during 1886. Peter Donahue, from whom Vallejo had borrowed $1,500 in 1881, died in 1885, the year before Vallejo's loan became due. Vallejo was unable to pay it off. He told the heirs that he and Donahue had a verbal agreement that the debt would be canceled in exchange for Vallejo's giving Donahue's rail line right-of-way through some of Vallejo's property. Since Donahue's heirs were preparing legal action against him, Vallejo had to hire a lawyer, San Francisco attorney Henry Clement, to represent him. In 1889 Clement wrote to the attorney

---

33. "Judgment Roll in the Case of M. G. Vallejo versus O. O. Howard," U.S. Circuit Court 4152, 1890, BANC MSS 67/163c, TBL; "A Modest Little Suit for Four Hundred Million," *San Diego Union and Daily Bee,* January 16, 1886; "Suit on an Old Grant," October 12, 1886, and "Suing for a Portion of the Presidio," December 30, 1886, both in *Daily Alta California.*

of the heirs and said, "General Vallejo is far advanced in years and very poor." After recounting the many ways in which Vallejo had helped Donahue in Sonoma, Clement added a statement that summarized much of Vallejo's experiences in American California: "General Vallejo is not, and never has been, a businessman. He will sign anything his friends, or those he regards as his friends, ask him to."[34]

During the final decade of Vallejo's life, as he was buffeted by extreme financial difficulties and a series of legal issues, Bancroft's *History of California* was published. Vallejo believed that Bancroft's history had severe shortcomings. He was especially resentful of Bancroft's calling into question the occurrence of a large meeting that Vallejo claimed was held in Thomas O. Larkin's house in May 1845. According to Vallejo's account, José Castro proposed that California allow itself to be annexed by France. David Spence, supported by William E. P. Hartnell, spoke about the advantages of affiliation with Great Britain. A number of Californios, including Pablo de la Guerra and Rafael González, argued that California ought to declare its independence. Vallejo said that he offered a very strong speech in favor of annexation by the United States. He reproduced that speech, "more or less," in its entirety in his *Recuerdos*. According to Vallejo, Castro's partisans, fearing that Vallejo's rhetoric was about to persuade attendees at the meeting to follow his advice, walked out and deprived the junta of a quorum.[35]

Bancroft spent almost an entire page refuting Vallejo's account, writing, "I believe all that has been said of this meeting, including the eloquent speeches so literally quoted, to be purely imaginary. No such meeting was ever held, and no such speeches were ever made. There is no reason to doubt that Vallejo was disposed in 1846 to favor annexation to the United States. But in thus recording a formal meeting, with deliberate discussion of propositions to

34. Emparán, *Vallejos of California*, 164; Henry Clement to James G. Maguire, August 23, 1889, C-B 441, box 3, folder 27, TBL.

35. MGV, *Recuerdos*, 5:9–17. On Vallejo's disappointment with Bancroft, see our preface to MGV, *Recuerdos*, 2:1223–31.

deliver their country to a foreign power, I am very sure that General Vallejo's memory has been greatly aided by his imagination."[36]

Shortly after the publication of this volume of Bancroft's *History of California*, Vallejo was contacted by William Swasey, who had been employed by Larkin during the mid-1840s. Swasey pointed out this page of Bancroft's work and asked Vallejo whether he remembered that meeting. Vallejo replied that he certainly did, and that Bancroft was extremely "ungrateful" and had "no reason to doubt what I have told him or written for him in regard to the historical facts." Vallejo angrily told Swasey that if Bancroft thought Vallejo was trafficking in "myths or lies," then he should return the *Recuerdos* manuscript to him. A year after Vallejo's death, Swasey insisted in his book, *The Early Days and Men of California*, that Vallejo's story was true and that he had himself heard Vallejo's speech from an adjoining room in Larkin's house.[37]

This particular episode was very important to Vallejo, for in the twilight of his life he was swept into an Americanized version of pre-U.S. California. This version was a local variant of Manifest Destiny connected to the emerging Spanish Revival movement, which erased the Mexican history in California, a narrative against which Vallejo had struggled mightily in the 1870s. In this version of the California experience, not only was the American takeover inevitable, "Spaniards," who were intelligent and enlightened, actually welcomed it, for they realized the benefits that the Americans would bring to California. At the beginning of the decade, in 1880, the San Francisco publisher Alley, Bowen, and Co. released J. P. Munro-Fraser's *History of Sonoma County*. Vallejo had cooperated with the author in the preparation of this volume, and his portrait was prominently displayed as a full-page frontispiece of the book. Yet, the work anticipated the Spanish Revival orientation, and consequent neglect of the Mexican era, that would flower in the late nineteenth and early twentieth centuries. Its long subtitle spoke of

36. Bancroft, *History of California*, 5:62–63.
37. MGV to William Swasey, August 31, 1886, C-B 441, box 2, folder 2, TBL; Swasey, *Early Days and Men of California*, 57–58.

"Spanish and American Pioneers," and the chapter entitled "Early History and Settlement of Sonoma County" spoke of the "Russian, Spanish, and American occupation." After a listing of some of the early land grants in the Sonoma region, the reader was promised a fuller account of "the Spanish grants." Throughout the text, residents of Mexican Alta California after 1821 were usually referred to as Spaniards. In recounting Vallejo's version of the 1845 junta, the book went well beyond what Vallejo had put in his *Recuerdos*. He was described as a man whose ideas were "more enlightened and consonant with the times than those of the rulers of his country, both civil and military." Vallejo, the author wrote, "rightly judged that although foreign protection [a reference to Castro's argument that French protection would help California] might postpone, it could not avert the assumption of power [the U.S. takeover] which was beginning to make itself felt."[38]

During the 1880s, Vallejo found himself being drawn more and more into the interpretive framework that American occupation was inevitable and beneficial. In 1886, for instance, within the space of a couple of weeks he spoke at the Fruit Growers Convention in Sacramento, gave an address on the history of Yerba Buena Island, and planted a tree there during California's first Arbor Day celebration. In his address at the tree-planting ceremony he said, "My words fail to express my delight with the contrast between this island today and what it was in the older days in the possession of the Tuchayunes [the Indigenous group he said had once inhabited the island]. Surely, the wand of the higher civilization has passed over us, for all of which I have thanks."[39]

In November 1888 he was invited to Chico to be inducted into the local chapter of the Native Sons of the Golden West. The Chico newspaper termed him "the last of his noble race." In his remarks Vallejo made a joke about being arrested by the Bear Flaggers.

---

38. Munro-Fraser, *History of Sonoma County*, 57, 96. On Vallejo's insistence on the importance of California's Mexican era, see our Introduction in *Recuerdos*, 1:3–38.

39. Emparán, *Vallejos of California*, 172–73; "Arbor Day," *Daily Alta California*, November 28, 1886. On Vallejo's insistence on the importance of California's Mexican era, see our Introduction in MGV, *Recuerdos*, 1:3–38.

In a thank-you note to the group a few weeks later, Vallejo probably repeated what he had actually said in his speech: "I foresaw the rising tide of progress, the great and wondrous future of this Golden West, and when the <u>little bear</u> came to <u>hug</u> me at my home at old Sonoma, I gladly embraced the anticipated opportunity of cooperating with the American ideas, theory, and practice of vigorous growth and improvement of California." Less than a year before his death, Vallejo was contacted by an editor from *Century Magazine* and asked to contribute "a sketch of Spanish life" in California before the discovery of gold. He was unable to do so, but the request was fulfilled by his niece Guadalupe, whose romanticized essay about pre-U.S. California, which appeared in the magazine in 1891, announced the complete triumph of the views Vallejo had strongly rejected two decades earlier.[40]

It is impossible to say what Vallejo thought of this interpretation, for his correspondence of the 1880s was significantly more meager than earlier in his life. His gradually declining health and diminishing financial status no doubt contributed to his relative silence. But it is clear that he participated in articulating this Americanized version of California's past. Whether he was feeling resentment, resignation, or something else as he did so is impossible to say. We believe, however, that whatever emotions may have been racing through his heart, in his head he believed that what he was doing was the best way he could continue, in this land of his birth, to try to continue to serve the Californio and Mexican communities of the past, present, and future.

40. "Hale Fellow," *Chico Weekly Enterprise*, November 23, 1888; MGV to the Native Sons of the Golden West, Chico Parlor, January 10, 1889, C-B 441, box 2, folder 3, TBL (emphasis in original); R. U. Johnson to John Frisbie, August 17, 1889, C-B 441, box 4, folder 13, TBL; Guadalupe Vallejo, "Ranch and Mission Days in California."

CHAPTER 7

"If They Had Been Yankees, They Probably Would Have Behaved Quite Differently"

Community, Culture, and Education in Mexican California

By the time he composed his *Recuerdos* in the mid-1870s, Vallejo had for decades personally experienced the disdain most Anglo residents of California expressed for the Californio and Mexican communities. He had read Alfred Robinson's *Life in California* and knew firsthand that the opinion Robinson expressed about the Californios was widely shared: "The men are generally indolent and addicted to many vices, caring little for the welfare of their children, who, like themselves, grow up unworthy members of society." Robinson's opinions reflected prevalent American beliefs that stemmed from deeply rooted racism, Manifest Destiny, Protestant disdain for Roman Catholicism, and the still-persistent anti-Spanish Black Legend. In 1839

Zenas Leonard, who had spent a few years in California as a trapper, published his *Narrative*, which termed the Californios "very ignorant and much more indolent," with "little or no ingenuity" who "only seem to enjoy themselves when engaged in the chase." The most widely read book in the United States about California, Richard Henry Dana's *Two Years before the Mast*, published in 1840, termed the Californios an "idle, thriftless people." Lansford Hastings's influential 1845 *Emigrants' Guide to Oregon and California* characterized the Californios as "scarcely a visible grade, in the scale of intelligence, above the barbarous tribes by whom they are surrounded." Thomas Jefferson Farnham's 1846 *Life, Adventures, and Travels in California* stated, "The Californians are an imbecile, pusillanimous race of men and unfit to control the destinies of that beautiful country." In the same year, the *National Intelligencer* had stated that "the Spanish portion of the inhabitants [of Alta California] are a thieving, cowardly, dancing, lewd people, and generally indolent and faithless." Such attitudes were commonplace among the gold seekers who arrived in California in 1849 and they were reinforced by the fact that, when they arrived, they found that the smaller Pacific Rim Gold Rush of 1848 had already brought a number of Californios and people from Mexico and Peru to the diggings. The presence of many darker-skinned "foreigners" in what was now a U.S. possession produced great resentment that magnified the already existing notions of inherent Californio inferiority.[1]

These criticisms were diffuse and sometimes contradictory. As he reflected upon them and talked with other Californios about them, Vallejo seems to have organized them into two broad accusations. First, that the Californios were an uncultured people—undisciplined, dishonest, and intrinsically lazy. Second, that the Californios were an ignorant people—uneducated, disorganized, and inherently stupid. Rejecting these criticisms was a fundamental goal of his historical enterprise.

---

1. The Robinson, Leonard, Dana, Hastings, and Farnham quotations are from Langum, "Californios and the Image of Indolence," 183–85. The *National Intelligencer* quotation is from Pitt, *Decline of the Californios*, 16; See also Peterson, "Anti-Mexican Nativism" and Weber and Langum, "Here Rests Juan Espinosa."

CULTURE

In his discussions, Vallejo often drew contrasts between Californio and American culture. For instance, when he was describing the decision to evacuate women and children from Monterey during the 1818 Bouchard attack, he termed the separation of the women and children from their fathers and husbands "a heartwrenching scene." He wrote, "There were wives who refused to be separated from their husbands, mothers who insisted that their sons accompany them, and daughters who threw themselves into their father's arms saying, "Papá, why won't you let me die with you?" This kind of behavior "sprang from deep in the souls of the old Californios who believed love of family was far more important than any calculated plans or vile self-interest." Then he sardonically added, "If they had been Yankees, they probably would have behaved quite differently." At times his criticisms stemmed from more contemporary events. At one point in his manuscript, he mentioned the Crédit Mobilier scandal and a few other episodes for which the Grant administration was criticized in the 1870s. He wrote, "I cannot deny that it causes me great pain to relate such facts but—in fairness to the land that witnessed my birth, in fairness to the illustrious men of my native land whom American writers have outrageously slandered in order to portray the new rulers in a much more favorable light than the distinguished men who governed the country before it became part of the powerful federation of the United States of North America—I find myself impelled to seek revenge."[2]

At other points in his manuscript, the contrasts were more implicit. When he was describing the poor and irregular pay the Californio soldiers received, he argued that the soldiers refused to act dishonestly: "The garrisons in Las Californias teemed with soldiers of integrity and discipline. Even when months went by and their resources from the government failed to arrive, the soldiers

---

2. MGV, *Recuerdos*, 1:174, 380. Crédit Mobilier was a dummy construction company that Union Pacific set up to inflate construction costs on the transcontinental railway in order to reap tremendous profits. Several national politicians were implicated in the fraud.

never showed disrespect for the settlers' private property." The implicit criticism of American squatters in the 1850s would have been impossible for Vallejo's readers to miss. Whether the contrasts were direct or implied, the message was always twofold. First, Californio culture was not nearly so debased as the Americans thought. Second, and just as important, American culture was not nearly so advanced as they insisted.[3]

Vallejo insisted that Californio culture was, above all, communal, a point he made in the prologue of his work. The normal way for nineteenth-century historians, including those Vallejo had read, to begin their work was to create an image of themselves as solitary scholars drawn to a particular subject. Franklin Tuthill, whose *History of California* Vallejo had consulted, characterized his work as a solitary enterprise, the work of a single "historian" that "was written because there seems to be a demand for a History of California which should sketch the main events of the country from its discovery to the present time." In contrast, the first word of Vallejo's manuscript was "estimulado,"[4] a word that explicitly described a relationship between himself and others. He stated that eight different people who had lived in California before the American takeover, as well as "a number of other friends," had encouraged him to "undertake, for the second time in my life, the arduous and difficult task of writing the history of Alta California." Thus, from its very beginning, the manuscript pointed not only to Vallejo as author, but also to the involvement of the broader Californio community in the project.[5]

In Vallejo's view, the culture of the Californio community was open, tolerant, and forgiving. For instance, Vallejo stated that as the families journeyed to Mission San Antonio after the Bouchard raid, they took care of one another and were especially solicitous of the more vulnerable members of the community. Having been on that trek as an eleven-year-old child, he recounted that care was

---

3. MGV, *Recuerdos*, 1:282.

4. "Estimulado" can mean motivated or spurred on.

5. Tuthill, *History of California*, vii, 643; MGV, *Recuerdos*, 1:39–40.

given even to the wife of one soldier, Manuel Gómez, whom the Californios believed was in some sort of alliance with Bouchard. He remembered, "The women of Monterey, nevertheless, did everything they could to ease the remorse felt by Doña María del Rosario, the wife of the traitor." Lest his American readers miss the point, Vallejo made what he regarded as the lesson of this recollection quite explicit: "This fact should be enough, in and of itself, to prove to the world that the Californios of that time were generous souls and were not inclined to exact revenge."[6]

Vallejo also insisted that these community bonds were sufficiently intense to transcend class differences. For instance, he characterized former Monterey alférez Francisco Pacheco in this way:

> (Don Francisco Pacheco had given 5,000 pesos in cash for the rebuilding of the church in Monterey.) In honor of his undeniable courage and endless generosity, the people placed his body in a crypt facing the high altar of the church. When I visited Monterey in June of this year (1874), I found that the venerable remains of that long-ago champion of the people's rights and sincere and loyal friend were still there. Even though he was rolling in money and owned the San Felipe Rancho (which today belongs to his son-in-law Don Mariano Malarín), and the San Luis Gonzaga and Oresti haciendas, where he had immense numbers of cattle, he worked like a poor artisan and shared the fruits of his labors with the sick.

In the same vein, Vallejo approvingly quoted Alvarado's description of Alta California as a "one class" society.[7]

Vallejo largely attributed this unity to the significant number of intermarriages among the large Californio extended families, especially those families who, like his, could trace their California roots back to one of the early colonizing expeditions. As he supposedly had remarked in a conversation about the Californios with Franciscan missionary Narciso Durán, "Here we are all related to one another." Vallejo realized that these close relationships could, at times, complicate social organization. In the same conversation,

6. MGV, *Recuerdos*, 1:203.
7. MGV, *Recuerdos*, 1:132, 223.

reflecting upon his experience as military commander of California, he told Durán, "As long as a Californio is in control of California, the strict application of military regulations is something that cannot be put into practice." The reason was simple: "If one has the courage to resist the pleas of the men, he has no other option than to succumb to the cries and protests of the women." At another point he claimed that one of the reasons he had supported the appointment of Mexican officer Manuel Micheltorena as California governor in 1842 was that he had come to believe the territory should be governed "by a Mexican who had no family ties with the Californio families." He remembered, "In 1835 and 1839, when I attempted to act boldly in the pueblos of the southern part of the departamento, I had to abandon my plans for reform because at every instance my office was besieged by women relatives of mine who were coming to intercede for some guilty person or another."[8]

Yet this family-based culture did not inhibit all types of organization and structure. Vallejo was well aware that many Americans thought Californios were incapable of the discipline necessary for any kind of complex undertakings. Tuthill, for instance, had stated, "The people that made up the body of the population were dashing and careless, fond of fandangos, always ready for a dance, making the most of their religious holidays with bull-fights and bear-baitings, and almost universally given to gambling."[9] In Vallejo's view, this picture of undisciplined carelessness could not have been further from reality. In his description of the 1815 arrival of Governor Pablo Vicente de Solá, Vallejo quoted at length from a letter that Alvarado wrote him on September 29, 1874, describing the arrival ceremonies in great detail. Alvarado recounted the dress of the women at a welcoming dance for the new governor:

> The style of dress of the young women was that which was in fashion forty-seven years ago, when the first families founded the capital of Monterey in 1769. Their outfits consisted of an *enagua*, which is what the skirt or exterior garment was called. It was made of very fine white

8. MGV, *Recuerdos*, 1:874, 2:1054.
9. Tuthill, *History of California*, 153.

muslin, mid-calf length, and was decorated with gold sequins in a floral pattern around the hemline. The way the light reflected off the sequins created a brilliant burst of color for the eyes to gaze upon. The dancers' hair was cut in front and covered half their forehead. They called these bangs *tupé*. On each side of their face they would wear long ringlets they called *balcarrotas*. These ringlets reached to below their cheeks, which they colored with bean powder to make them rosy. The rest of their hair would be tied back and covered with a black silk net or one of a different color. They would wear a short, fitted, waist-length velvet jacket that was buttoned from the collar down to the waistband of the skirt. They wore long sleeves decorated at the wrist with fine white linen, upon which they would place gold bracelets. Their stockings were of flesh-colored silk. Their shoes, which were made of a double thickness of white satin, were called *del palillo* because they had high heels, much like the heels on ankle boots that are in fashion today, except the heels were made of a very porous, light wood. They would wear long earrings and strands of fine pearls, which were very abundant in this country because they were imported from Baja California. Around their waist they would tie a red silk sash. The ends of the sash, which were decorated with a five- to six-inch gold fringe, would touch the bottom of the skirt. The *rebozo*[10] was made of very finely woven Mexican silk in different colors (or a mix of colors). This was the elegant attire worn by the women of those times.

For Alvarado and Vallejo alike, the festivities indicated that the culture of Alta California was organized, well developed, and even continental European. According to Alvarado, when Solá arrived, "He said it gave him great satisfaction that customs from his native land, Nueva Castilla, were part of life in California, for they reminded him of the most cherished days of his youth." Alvarado then added his own comment on the ways some aspects of European high culture had been present in 1815 California: "Dances such as the Spanish contradanza, the minuet, and the jota aragonesa were danced here as they were in the Palace of Versailles in Paris. All the French customs were adopted in Spain and from there, the customs and fashions came to us." Then Alvarado added a conclusion that Vallejo and many former upper-class Californios

---

10. A "rebozo" is a shawl or wrap.

One of the first pianos to arrive in Alta California.
The family of José Abrego donated the piano
to the California Historical Society in the 1940s.
*Photograph courtesy of David Newman, great-grandson
of Abrego granddaughter Dulce Bolado Davis*

living in U.S. California in the 1870s shared: "The gringos ('gringos'
stands for Yankees) who claim to be the most civilized of people
are mistaken."[11]

For Vallejo, the summit of Mexican Alta California's European-
style cultural life occurred when Steven Smith brought three
pianos from the East Coast in 1843. One ended up in Los Angeles with Eulogio Celis and another one in Monterey with José
Abrego. Smith sold the third to Vallejo in January 1844. Reportedly, Abrego told Vallejo that Consul Thomas O. Larkin wanted to

---

11. MGV, *Recuerdos*, 1:132–33.

Eulogio F. Celis. *Courtesy of the University of Southern California Libraries and the California Historical Society.* CHS-6680.

borrow the piano for a dance that Larkin was hosting for Commodore Thomas ap Catesby Jones. Vallejo further stated that a young man in Monterey, Pedro Estrada, demonstrated a natural ability to play the instrument, and both Alvarado and Larkin thought that he ought to be sent to Mexico at public expense to develop that talent. However, led by David Spence, the Monterey Diputación rejected the proposal. For Vallejo, this was another example of the Californios' desire to bring traditional high culture into their region, and of many foreigners' unwillingness to believe that the Californios were capable of being this cultured.[12]

The piano that Vallejo purchased remained largely unused in his house until March 1846, when Vallejo hired Andrew Hoeppner, a German who had worked for the Russians at Sitka, to teach his children how to play it in exchange for part of the Agua Caliente rancho. Hoeppner apparently did his job, for Lieutenant Henry

---

12. Holden, "California's First Pianos," 35–36; Stephen Smith to MGV, January 31, 1844, VA 39, HL; Emparán, *Vallejos of California*, 250. Larkin described the dances for Jones and his crew in a letter to James Gordon Bennett, February 10, 1843, in Larkin, *Papers*, 2:6. In fact, Smith did not arrive with the pianos until May 1843, long after Jones had left: Bancroft, *History of California*, 4:395.

Wise of the U.S. Navy visited Sonoma in the summer of 1847 and reported that the children could play "remarkably well."[13]

Vallejo recognized that the piano and the other pieces of elegant furniture he purchased from Smith were traditional signs of refinement. Like the de la Guerra family in Santa Bárbara, the Vallejo family was anxious to demonstrate to the Americans that they had achieved a certain level of elegance and taste. For Vallejo, however, the defining feature of Californio life was the communal character of its culture and that is what he wished to emphasize in his historical project. An episode that occurred just as he was beginning to write his history helped crystallize for him the centrality of community. In the summer of 1874, as he was returning to San Francisco with Bancroft staff member Enrique Cerruti after they had interviewed some Californios in Monterey, their boat stopped in Santa Cruz. There, on the wharf, they happened to meet Francisco Rodríguez, who had been a soldier during the Spanish and Mexican eras. Rodríguez told Vallejo that he himself had been at Santa Cruz when Bouchard arrived, and he remembered that some people had thought this afforded them an opportunity to plunder the mission. They were stopped by Joaquín Buelna, the comisionado of Branciforte, and an anonymously composed popular poem commemorating that event soon made the rounds. Rodríguez recited the entire poem from memory for Vallejo and Cerruti, who was so impressed that he asked Rodríguez to recite it a second time so that he could write it down. In the course of this exchange, another old soldier named Pérez joined them. The encounter proved to be very emotional for Vallejo and the two old soldiers. Cerruti recalled, "The farewell was really sublime, and if my eyes did not then deceive me, I can assure you that the tears rolled down the cheeks of the two ex-soldiers and their ex-chief. General Vallejo laid one of his hands on the shoulders of Rodríguez and the other on the head of faithful Pérez and with dim eyes blessed them with all his heart."[14]

---

13. Holden, "California's First Pianos," 36–37; Wise, *Los gringos*, 109.
14. Cerruti, *Ramblings in California*, 133–35.

This chance encounter, and Rodríguez's recitation of the poem, re-enacted for Vallejo one of the primary social rituals of Spanish and Mexican Alta California. This was the production and recitation of improvised oral poetry, often in the form of *décimas*, poems with ten lines per stanza, sometimes with an introductory stanza of four lines. This literary form originated in Spain but gradually died out there after the Siglo de Oro. In contrast, it spread widely throughout Latin America and became a major form of popular culture. The literary form was flexible, and many regions would develop their own particular styles. Such oral poetry, sometimes written down and circulated throughout the locality, became an important means of knitting together various elements of the social fabric.[15]

We suspect that Vallejo was inspired by his chance encounter with Rodríguez. In any event, in his history he included a number of these poems as a way of demonstrating the manner in which this form of popular culture underscored the social bonds that he believed were such an important part of Californio life. The first poem that Vallejo reproduced was composed by Joaquín Buelna and described the same event as the poem Rodríguez recited had: the arrival of Bouchard and the potential sacking of Mission Santa Cruz. In Vallejo's telling, by reciting this poem Buelna persuaded those who had taken items from the mission to return them. Buelna was so pleased with this result that he composed another poem directed at men who had been flirting with his wife. It also had the desired result. Vallejo summarized the effect of the two poems in this way: "They did provide Buelna with political and domestic tranquility." Vallejo also described décimas and other poems written by or about Governor Solá and several other Californios. His point was that these poems served as important rituals. Even when opponents attacked each other, the use of this literary form meant that important norms of social cohesion were preserved and even strengthened. Hence, the communal nature of Californio culture was preserved.[16]

---

15. Trapero, *El libro de la décima*, 48–125.
16. MGV, *Recuerdos*, 1:198–201.

At the same time Vallejo was well aware that the literary quality of these poetic efforts was often poor: "The décimas are horrendous. They have no literary merit." Furthermore, "With the exception of one, all the poets who plied their craft in California during the Spanish period and even later, when the country belonged to Mexico, were mediocre. There were many poetic geniuses in California, but most of them lacked the opportunity to cultivate a relationship with the muses." That lack of opportunity related to another theme he explored in his history: Californios' consistent struggle to establish a functioning educational system for their children.[17]

EDUCATION

Vallejo was especially upset at the notion, apparent in the Robinson critique we cite at the beginning of this chapter, that the Californio community was wallowing in ignorance and was completely uninterested in educating their children. In his history Vallejo strongly insisted that the education of children had always been an important part of Alta California life. For him, the communal nature of Californio society was intergenerational. Not only did it encourage people to look out for each other in their current social situations, it also motivated them to do everything possible to improve the next generation through education. In the face of Anglo stereotypes of the carefree ignorance of the Californios, Vallejo maintained that Alta California had been marked by a desire for education on both the provincial and local levels.

He stated that all the governors during the Spanish era "took an interest in the education of the Californio youth, some more and some less. Don Diego de Borica (who was governor from 1794 to 1800 and died in 1801) took the matter of education very seriously." Borica, in partnership with the presidio commanders, attempted to ensure that the soldiers' children would receive a formal education, and the soldiers themselves generally cooperated in this endeavor.

---

17. MGV, *Recuerdos*, 1:201, 254.

Vallejo believed that the Spanish governor who did the most for education was the final one, Pablo Vicente de Solá. Insisting that this concern for education persisted during the Mexican era, he claimed that among the Mexican governors, Echeandía, Figueroa, and Alvarado made particular attempts to improve the quality of education in California. While he acknowledged that circumstances often prevented them from succeeding, he insisted that the yearning to improve education was never far from the surface. We believe that the documentary record supports Vallejo's claims.[18]

He was indeed correct that Borica and Solá made improving education an important part of their agendas. Borica became governor in 1794. During the 1790s, the non-Indigenous population of both Alta and Baja California was increasing, as more children were being born to the earliest generation of Alta California soldiers. Soon after his arrival, Borica asked the Monterey commander to inform him of which soldiers at the presidio could read and write. He promptly hired retired sergeant Manuel Vargas to open a primary school in San José, Alta California's oldest pueblo. He also instructed the presidio commanders to open similar schools staffed with retired soldiers. Indeed, Vargas moved to San Diego to assume control of the school at the presidio there the next year, and he was replaced at San José by retired alférez Ramón Lasso de la Vega. By 1796, there were twenty-seven students in the San José primary school and thirty-two students in the primary school at the Santa Bárbara presidio. Borica was quite involved in supervising their educational progress and periodically asked for written reports from the presidio commanders. If the commander reported good progress, Borica congratulated him and urged him to continue his efforts.[19]

---

18. MGV, *Recuerdos*, 1:135–38.

19. Rodríguez-Sala, *Los gobernadores de las Californias*, 309, 318–20; Diego de Borica to Comandante de Monterey, December 4, 1794, C-A 7:177, TBL; Bancroft, *History of California*, 1:642–44; Jones, *Los Paisanos*, 228; Ramón Lasso de la Vega to Diego de Borica, February 18, 1796, C-A 8:10, TBL; Felipe Goycoechea to Borica, February 25, 1796, C-A 8:101, TBL; Borica to Goycoechea, n.d. [1796], C-A 23:325, TBL; Borica to Goycoechea, October 28, 1796, C-A 55:7, TBL; Goycoechea to Borica, February 11, 1797, C-A 8:269, TBL.

Retired soldiers were employed as primary school instructors for one simple reason: there was no one else in the province to do this job. However, the dilemma that would continue to confound the educational efforts in California into the Mexican era was that many retired soldiers were simply not sufficiently literate to serve as teachers. For instance, in the mid-1780s, only fourteen of the fifty soldiers at the Monterey presidio, and only seven of the thirty soldiers at San Francisco were able to write. In 1791 the San Francisco presidio *habilitado*[20] reported that only two of the twenty-eight soldiers were literate. This situation continued to present difficulties. In 1806 Governor Arrillaga told the viceroy that it was painful for him to see that there was instruction for the Indians at the missions but not consistent instruction for the children of the soldiers and settlers at the presidios and pueblos. He asked that additional chaplains and five teachers be sent to Alta California.[21]

It does not appear that Arrillaga's requests were granted, and some schools seem to have opened and shut down depending on the availability of funding and of a suitably qualified retired soldier. In San José, for instance, the *juez de paz*[22] lamented that it was "painful to see so many children without a teacher" and urged that a school be built with public funds. It is not clear whether a building was constructed, but retired soldier Rafael Villavicencio was appointed schoolmaster in 1811 and was responsible for teaching reading, writing, and Christian doctrine for six hours per day. When Pablo Vicente de Solá became governor in 1815, the school in Monterey was run by retired corporal Miguel Archuleta, who apparently had been taught the rudiments of reading and writing by Soledad missionary Florencio Ibáñez.[23]

---

20. An "habilitado" was an officer in a Spanish regiment charged with its supplies or money, analogous to a quartermaster, supply master, or paymaster.
21. Bancroft, *History of California*, 1:642; report of José Argüello, May 12, 1791, C-A 15:293, TBL; José Joaquín de Arrillaga to Viceroy, July 15, 1806, C-A 25:337–38, TBL.
22. A "Juez de paz" is a Justice of the peace.
23. Statement describing a petition of the juez de paz. July 1, 1801, Pueblo Papers, doc. 1979-861-300, History San José; José María Estudillo to Comisionado del Pueblo de San José, July 4, 1811, and October 26, 1811, Pueblo Papers, docs. 1979 861 571 and 1979 861 576, History San José; Bancroft, *History of California*, 2:427; Geiger, *Franciscan Missionaries*, 125.

Vallejo portrayed Solá, the last Spanish governor, as an enlightened man who tried to improve the quality of California's educational endeavors. Solá took Vallejo and Alvarado under his wing, gave them a variety of fairly up-to-date readings to digest, such as contemporary Mexican newspapers, and introduced them to classics like *Don Quixote*. Vallejo also wrote that Solá brought two individuals with him to start better schools and also tried to start a school for girls in Monterey. Even though they were privately financed by Solá himself, it does not appear that any of these efforts enjoyed sustained success.[24]

Vallejo especially appreciated Solá's efforts because he knew from firsthand experience that the realities of frontier life—the lack of funds and of trained instructors—could severely constrain the quality of the education that was actually being offered. He was a student in Archuleta's Monterey classroom, and his memories of that experience were not pleasant. According to Vallejo, the classroom in Monterey "was usually long, narrow, and cold. Rough-hewn benches that were dirty from use were placed around the classroom. The walls were drab in color, full of cracks, and completely bare."[25] The day began with a ritual: "When the students arrived in the morning, they would walk the entire length of the room and then kneel before the cross or the printed image [of the Virgen de Guadalupe]. Then they would pray the *Bendito* aloud. After that they would go to where the schoolmaster was seated and in a stammering voice ask him for his hand." After reading aloud before the schoolmaster, the students would kiss his hand. The school used a version of the monitoring system that would be popularized and codified over the next few decades by Joseph Lancaster. Vallejo recounted that, after having greeted the schoolmaster, the student "would then go to his bench and sit down. After one of the older boys had shown him which lesson to study, he would begin reading his primer." The practice of penmanship could be especially brutal:

---

24. MGV, *Recuerdos*, 1:135–38.

25. Unless otherwise indicated, all of Vallejo's statements about his experiences in Archuleta's classroom come from chapter 57 of his *Recuerdos* (2:994–1007).

After the boy finished his page of handwriting practice, he would go and show it to the schoolmaster, trembling as he waited for the schoolmaster to pass judgment on his work. The schoolmaster would exclaim, "You rogue, you evil boy! You have left a blot of ink here!" The boy would respond, "Señor Maestro, forgive me today. I will do better tomorrow." Still, the relentless *dómine*[26] would wrap his fist around an enormous flat paddle and order the boy to extend his hands. The boy would beg and cry, but it was in vain. He would end up extending his trembling little hands that were trying to escape the blow. The schoolmaster was like a furious tiger thirsty for Christian blood. He would raise that terrible instrument of torture in the air and forcefully bring it down, two or three times, on the weak little hands of that six-year-old boy. These blows sounded like the thundering crack of a whip. Afterward, with disdain and anger the dómine would throw the piece of paper on the floor.

Since the examination of the students' handwriting practice was conducted much like a review of troops, that is to say, all the students would present their work in succession, the paddle never left the schoolmaster's hands and the sound of the blows would resonate up to 100 times in less than an hour or an hour and a half. But, there was more. On top of the table covered by a gloomy cloth, one could see another object that caused the boys to tremble and lower their eyes. This object was a long *disciplina*[27] made of hemp or wires. It was used for punishing major offenses such as laughing out loud, running in the street, playing hooky from school, [or] spilling an inkwell on the table.

Vallejo recalled that Archuleta used physical punishment so often that the students nicknamed him the "Potentate of the Beatings."[28]

After the student learned to read and write, he would advance to arithmetic, which Vallejo recalled was "nothing more than addition, subtraction, multiplication, and division. That was the extent of the technical nature of arithmetic back then." But reading, writing, and arithmetic were not the main subjects. That was, Vallejo insisted, "the study of Christian doctrine," and the book that was mainly used was the classic catechetical text by Gerónimo

---

26. "Dómine" means teacher or preceptor of Latin grammar; it is also used pejoratively to describe someone who mimics the behavior of a teacher but is not qualified to be one.
27. A "disciplina" was an instrument used for punishment or flagellation.
28. MGV, *Recuerdos,* 1:254.

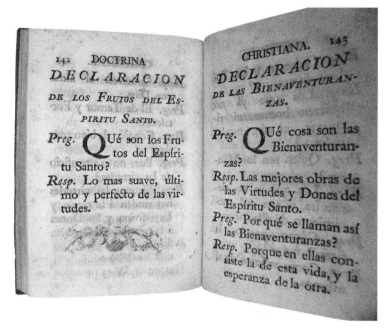

Catecismo y exposición breve de la doctrina christiana
por el P. Mtro. Gerónimo de Ripalda, 1808.
Courtesy of the Santa Bárbara Mission Archive-Library.

de Ripalda. For Vallejo, this catechism represented the traditional medieval Catholicism of the missionary priests that he came to reject. As he wrote, "Father Ripalda's catechism! Who among the old Californios does not know Father Ripalda? Is there anyone with even the slightest ability to reason and the freedom of conscience who does not detest that monstrous and fanatical code?" He added, "The boys suffered as they plowed through the horrible punishments that appeared on each page of this dark catechism. First they would learn the prayers, then the declarations, which are short, dry treatises in question-and-answer form—which was the perfect way for students to develop a sense of horror for any exercise requiring memorization. When a boy knew the catechism

from *cuerito a cuerito*[29] as we used to say back then, he was viewed
at school as a worthy boy, and at home he would be viewed as
another Seneca."

Vallejo admitted that there were some breaks in what he generally referred to as "torture for young children." For instance, he
recounted one episode in which the students forgot to cover the
inkwells and secure the classroom when Archuleta let them out
of school so that they could welcome a ship that had just arrived
in Monterey. When they returned, they found that some hens
had gotten into the classroom and spilled ink over all the sur-
faces. Archuleta sent everyone into the punishment room, where
he would decide whom to whip. But the boys covered the win-
dows, plunging the room into darkness, and engaged in a mini-
mutiny that forced the schoolmaster to flee outside. Through the
intervention of Governor Solá, the boys escaped with a minor
punishment.[30]

Vallejo presented the type of schooling he experienced in Monterey as particularly odious and as an example of old California at
its worst. Yet this type of education was typical in many frontier
areas of the Americas. For instance, American physician Daniel
Drake, who was born in 1785, spent part of his childhood in Kentucky. He remembered his own schooling in ways that were quite
reminiscent of the experiences that Vallejo described in Monterey.
Drake remembered, "After the master had taken his seat, the boys
were required, on entering the door, to take off their hats and make
a bow." The teacher was "a recent immigrant from the 'Eastern
shore' of Maryland, and an ample exponent of the state of society
in that benighted region. His function was to teach spelling, reading, writing, and deciphering as far as the rule of three; beyond
which he could not go. His attainments in that branch harmonized
as to quality and compass with his erudition in the others." The
school readings were generally taken from religious sources, often
the New Testament, and transgressions of various rules were met

---

29. "Cuerito a cuerito" means cover to cover.
30. MGV, *Recuerdos*, 1:239–41.

with corporal punishment. Drake said, "I was sometimes flogged or feruled, the summary punishment of those days." In short, the authorities in Alta California, like their counterparts in other frontier regions, cobbled together the best system they could, given the lack of resources and the educational norms of the eighteenth century.[31]

When Solá left California to assume his seat in the Mexican National Congress, his successor, Luis Antonio Argüello was consumed with tasks relating to California's status in newly independent Mexico, and educational efforts appear to have stagnated. Argüello's successor, José María Echeandía encountered a mixed situation. The school at San José was apparently continuing under the direction of a series of retired soldiers, including Joaquín and Antonio Buelna, José Antonio Romero, Matías Guerrero and Serafín Pinto. In addition, the school at the San Diego presidio was staffed by Antonio Menéndez, a Dominican priest who had been removed from Baja California as a result of Indian complaints against him. On the other hand, the Santa Bárbara presidio had a teacher, but, for a time, no students. The governor issued an order to Santa Bárbara parents, requiring that they send their children to school. In Monterey, the school was staffed for a time by José Tiburcio Castro, who was simultaneously serving as alcalde of the town. Echeandía told him that arrangement was unsatisfactory since it was impinging on his civic duties and he needed to find a full-time teacher as quickly as possible.[32]

Echeandía tried to put some order into this chaotic situation. In 1829 he composed an elaborate report on the status of the primary schools in California. He stated that there were eleven schools

---

31. Drake, *Pioneer Life in Kentucky*, 144, 149, 150; Manning, "Discipline in the Good Old Days."

32. Bancroft, *History of California*, 2:548, 574, 603; Antonio Suñol, "Cuaderno de recaudaciones de fondo de proprios y arbitrios en el año 1823," December 31, 1823, Pueblo Papers, doc. 1979-861-687, History San José; Serafín Pinto to Ignacio Pacheco, February 27, 1824, Pueblo Papers, doc. 1979-861-692, History San José; Serafín Pinto to Alcalde Constitucional de San José, February 27, 1824, Pueblo Papers, doc. 1979-861-693, History San José; Beebe and Senkewicz, *Testimonios*, 71; José María Echeandía to José Tiburcio Castro, January 20, 1829, MR 115, HL.

currently in operation, seven of them at missions: San Miguel (3 students), Santa Bárbara (44 students), San Buenaventura (36 students), San Fernando (20 students), San Gabriel (8 students), San Juan Capistrano (17 students), and San Luis Rey (35 students). Two were at presidios: Santa Bárbara (61 students) and San Diego (18 students). The final two were at the pueblos of Los Angeles (61 students) and San José (30 students). Echeandía also appended a note detailing the difficulties that the school projects had long been experiencing:

1.   The principal schools are the ones at the presidios and the pueblos. Even though in the past there were schools at the presidios, they became inoperative due to a lack of funds or because there were no capable people available to run them, until 1826 and 1827 when this government took extremely strong measures to reestablish the schools by providing them with a variety of ways to stay in operation. The same applied to the schools in the pueblos. Almost all the missions had schools. Very few have kept them in operation, but recently at some of the missions the schools have started up again. The decline of these mission schools has been due in part to a lack of qualified personnel who could provide the young neophytes with a modest level of instruction. Even for those students who are called de razón, it is difficult to find people who can teach them. The result is that at all the schools, progress is generally slow and gradual, and the level of instruction the students receive in reading, writing, and the doctrine is average.

2.   The funds from the municipalities and missions are available to cover any expense that is incurred regarding salaries of good teachers.

3.   At the missions, in addition to reading and the doctrine, the young neophytes learn how to sing Mass in addition to other hymns for church functions. They also learn how to play various wind and string instruments, which they learn how to do well.

4.   The Monterey presidio had a teacher who earned 30 pesos per month, which came from the funds of the municipality. Recently, the alcalde of that area took charge of the school for a short time until a teacher could be found for the school. It is believed that the reason why the school has languished is because nobody has received any notification about the need for a teacher.

5. The students at the missions do not attend school regularly because they are made to work sowing seeds, taking care of the birds, cleaning, harvesting, and other jobs that they do at the mission, especially at the ones with a small number of people.[33]

Echeandía was unable to follow up on this report, since he was replaced by Manuel Victoria the next year. Indeed, the political turmoil that wracked California until the arrival of the universally accepted Governor José Figueroa in January 1833 meant that education and schools were on the back burner for both local and territorial authorities. As a result, the number of functioning primary schools shrank. In a May 1834 report to Mexico City, Figueroa stated that there were only three such institutions in the province: at Monterey, Los Angeles, and Santa Bárbara. He lamented that they were all poorly funded and staffed by "inept teachers." After the expulsion of the leaders of the Híjar-Padrés party, Figueroa tried to place at least some of the members of the party as teachers in various locales. Florencio Serrano, for instance, was sent to San Antonio, but he reported that the "scandalous disorder" resulting from secularization made setting up a school impossible. The missionary, José María Vásquez del Mercado, and the comisionado, Manuel Crespo, were at odds over what the priest called the "stealing, robbery, drunkenness, and lust" of the local settlers. This controversy polarized the community and gave the residents many things of more concern to them than sending their children to school.[34]

Matters were equally chaotic at Monterey. Echeandía had not mentioned any school there in his 1829 report, but one started up in 1833. Anticipating that Figueroa would bring stability to the province, the local ayuntamiento had begun the process of reestablishing the school even before the new governor's arrival. The prompt action indicated the importance of the project to the leading citizens of the territorial capital. The ayuntamiento minutes recorded

---

33. Echeandía, "Estado sobre escuelas primarias," May 19, 1829, C-A 51:2–6, TBL.
34. José Figueroa to Secretaría del Estado, May 23, 1834, C-A 28:148–49, TBL; Florencio Serrano to José Figueroa, June 25, 1835, C-A 51:309, TBL; Engelhardt, *San Antonio de Padua*, 59–65.

that on January 8, 1833, "It was proposed that as soon as money becomes available, this issue will receive attention immediately." Indeed, issues relating to education are well documented in the surviving minutes of the Monterey Ayuntamiento. These minutes provide a very detailed case study of the way in which educational matters were a major and continuing concern in the capital of Alta California and give eloquent testimony to the importance placed upon educating the young.[35]

When Figueroa did arrive, he told the ayuntamiento on February 5 that he definitely wanted an elementary school initiated and that the means of paying a teacher "should not be an obstacle to establishing a school." Four days later Pedro del Castillo, who had entered California as an infantry sergeant around 1825, was appointed to coordinate the project. He proposed that the current residence of the Mazatlán troops, who had come to California as reinforcements after the Bouchard raid, be designated as the site for the school. He also recommended three people as potential teachers, and the choice fell upon Petronilo Ríos, a soldier who had come to California around the same time as Castillo. However, since Ríos was still in the military and could not accept, the ayuntamiento decided to appoint José María Aguilar, a local resident who had served as *síndico*[36] and as a member of the ayuntamiento, on a temporary basis. On March 16, the ayuntamiento drew up a formal job description for the new teacher. The highly detailed description most likely reflected issues that Monterey and other jurisdictions had had with previous teachers:

1. The preceptor should open the school at 7:30 in the morning and at 1:30 in the afternoon.
2. He will ensure that the children under his care attend school on a regular basis, and will notify their parents or the person responsible for the child if the child fails to attend school.

35. Unless otherwise indicated, all the material about the school in Monterey in the 1830s comes from "Libro de actas del ayuntamiento para el año de 1833," MR 251, HL.

36. A "síndico" was a public attorney or advocate/representative of a mission. Among Franciscans, the síndico was the person, usually a non-Franciscan, who managed the order's funds for the upkeep of its institutions, including its missions.

3.   He will also ensure that the children report to school with clean hands and that they maintain modest behavior when entering and leaving the school.

4.   On days when Mass is celebrated, he will attend with all the children, accompanying them to the church and seating them inside in the most appropriate place.

5.   He also will make sure that after his students leave school they will not play games that might be dangerous for them.

6.   To this end, he will appoint two or three boys who have good judgment to handle any misbehavior committed by the others and report to the teacher so that he can reprimand them or punish them based on their misdeed.

7.   The preceptor's first priority is to teach his students and explain to them with as much clarity as possible the Christian doctrine as it appears in the catechisms of Ripalda or Astete.[37]

8.   He will give them a weekly lesson on doctrine based on the ability of each child, who will recite the lesson from memory each Saturday.

9.   On Thursday afternoons, the teacher will read to the children articles from the Federal Constitution that he deems appropriate, starting from the beginning.

10. Based on the ability of each student, the teacher will give them daily lessons at an assigned hour in the morning and in the afternoon. Students will be reprimanded or punished for not knowing their lesson. The punishment shall not exceed two or three lashes.

11. With regard to the children who are learning to write, those who are just beginning to learn as well as those who are finishing, the teacher will make sure to correct their papers so that they can improve.

12. He will make sure that whenever a person deserving respect enters, all the children will stand up and remain quiet until the person who was inside leaves. And if it does not occur to this person to tell them to sit down, the teacher will order them to do so.

13. When the preceptor has some need or ample reason for not being able to be at school, he will inform the *señor alcalde* or the *regidor*[38] for the week, so that during the time the preceptor will be away from school another person can be appointed to fill his position at the school.

---

37. Gaspar Astete (1537–1601) was a Jesuit theologian. His most famous book was *Catecismo de la Doctrina Cristiana.*

38. The "alcalde" was a local magistrate, usually a member of the municipal council, and chief executive officer of a pueblo, possessing a combination of executive and judicial authority; the "regidor" was a member of the ayuntamiento.

14. The preceptor guarantees that to the best of his ability he will observe to the letter the requirements that are described in these instructions as well as demonstrate what his students have learned.

Shortly thereafter, Alcalde Marcelino Escobar presented a list of items that Aguilar requested for the school:

A pad for the table
Four reams of paper
Two pens for writing
One bottle of ink
Three benches to be used as seating for the children
One barrel for water
One chair and *pautas*[39] for writing practice

At the beginning of May, Aguilar told Castillo that he would not be able to continue doubling as a member of the ayuntamiento and as a teacher any longer. Castillo recommended the appointment of former soldier José Peña as the permanent teacher. Peña accepted on the condition that a house in Monterey be provided to him and his family, who were still living in San Francisco. A week later, Castillo reported that a house had been made available and that Peña would soon begin teaching. But he assured the ayuntamiento that Peña would not receive any salary until he actually started instructing students. It is not clear whether Peña ever did begin teaching. In any event, by January 1834 the ayuntamiento was again dealing with issues relating to the school. Aguilar was again pressed into service as a teacher, but by May he was pleading that he was overloaded with too many civic responsibilities. Juan Higuera, a former member of the ayuntamiento, took over but apparently did not last very long.

In November, the ayuntamiento, which was involved in a long and bitter controversy with the Híjar-Padrés colony, decided that it could end that dispute on its own terms by appointing Híjar as the school's teacher. Híjar declined to accept and told Governor Figueroa that the colony's membership included a number of

---

39. A "pauta" was a tool used to make lines on blank paper.

well-qualified teachers. After a month of indecision the ayunta-miento was forced to respond to complaints from Monterey-area parents over the continued lack of a functioning school. Acknowl-edging the "zeal" of the parents to have their children in school, it appointed colonist José Mariano Romero as teacher. He was probably the best credentialed of the teacher-colonists, for he had served on the faculty of a school in Mexico City. He did provide some stability to the school, but within a year of his appointment he became embroiled in controversy.[40]

In November 1835, the ayuntamiento wrote Romero: "Various complaints have been lodged against you regarding your responsibili-ties as stipulated in the contract you made with the public to provide instruction to the young people. Your failure to appear at school has forced this ayuntamiento to take the step of warning you that you are required to be at school during the hours stipulated and not to leave a child in charge in your place. This is what has prompted the dissatisfaction of the parents. I am communicating this to you for your information, as agreed to by this corporation."[41] The accusation of leaving a student in charge most likely meant that Romero had sometimes allowed an older student to act as a monitor and to direct some of the instruction. This system was employed at that time in Mexico City but probably was not well understood in California. Romero apparently contributed to the confusion by not being pres-ent at all times when the monitors were conducting instruction.[42]

Romero responded that the ayuntamiento's letter to him "destroys the good name and reputation I have acquired." He con-tinued, "No one who is accused is condemned without first hearing what he has to say. But in my case, no information was obtained from me, I was not summoned, and I was not even charged with the offence of which I know nothing about." He acknowledged that his method was new to the region: "This is the first time in

---

40. Híjar to Figueroa, November 5, 1834, C-A 60:263, TBL; Romero named preceptor, November 7, 1834, C-A 60:262, TBL; Hutchinson, *Frontier Settlement*, 195.

41. The correspondence between the ayuntamiento and Romero constitutes MR 347, HL.

42. Hutchinson, *Frontier Settlement*, 193–94.

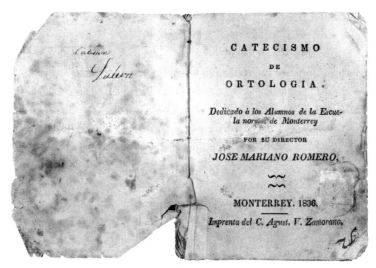

*Catecismo de ortología, 1836, by José Mariano Romero
Courtesy of the Seaver Center for Western History Research,
Los Angeles County Museum of Natural History.* GPF 932.

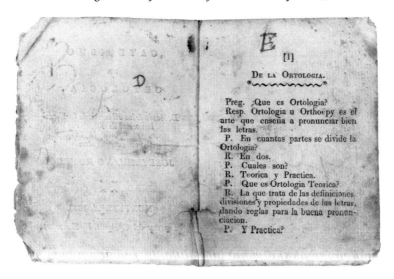

this territory that the teaching method I employ has been introduced; therefore, it is not unusual that the outcomes cannot be
assessed if the methods used to produce them are unfamiliar."
However, "The Illustrious Corporation knows that it can inquire
into the progress of the young people by visiting the school, but
ultimately, the method of instruction falls to me and to me alone."
He insisted that the students who were regularly attending school
were progressing very well and that those who were not making
progress were generally those whose parents had stopped sending
them to class. Finally, he reminded the ayuntamiento it had never
responded to his frequent requests for additional school supplies
that were "absolutely indispensable."

The ayuntamiento responded a week later. It first told Romero
that it had reviewed his complaint "with disgust": "What you have
been asked to do, which is to be at school during the regular hours
and not leave a young man in charge of the other students when you
are not there, is not a punishment imposed upon you, as you have
indicated. Your behavior has given the parents sufficient reason to
remove their children from school, which in turn, has prompted
this corporation to communicate with you officially in order to
remedy this situation." It agreed, "We will not interfere with your
method of instruction, since this has never been considered within
the scope of the corporation's responsibilities. But this corporation
will not turn a blind eye to your conduct with regard to the hours
you are supposed to keep at school."

In sum, it appears that Romero was allowed to continue to use the
monitor method as long as he remained present during school hours.
This arrangement proved to be workable, for Romero remained at
the school and his relationship with the ayuntamiento improved.
In February 1836 it provided new benches for the school, and in
April it decreed fines for families whose boys were not attending
the school. It also approved the establishment of a girls' school run
by María Dolores López. In 1836 Romero published a textbook,
Catecismo de ortología, which he dedicated to "the students of the
normal school of Monterey." Resentments remained, however. In

May 1836 Romero opposed the Monterey Californios who exiled Governor Chico, and he left California with acting military chief Nicolás Gutiérrez later that year. But these Monterey experiences demonstrated very clearly the importance that a number of Californio families placed upon the education of their children.

During his governorship Alvarado supported education but, due to extremely limited public funds, the financial support was never very significant. Vallejo blamed the lack of money on widespread smuggling, which reduced the revenues of the customs house. As a result, Alvarado's support was largely symbolic. He would, for instance, visit the school in Monterey and personally distribute medals to the top students. The Monterey school managed to survive. In the early 1840s there were two instructors. One was a Frenchman, Henri Cambuston. When American naval officer Philo White visited the school in early 1843, he found it in a "flourishing condition . . . conducted on a systematic plan, with judicious regulations for its governance." White counted about fifty boys in attendance and observed that they were "attentively occupied at studying, writing, etc." The last California governor sent by Mexico, Manuel Micheltorena, attempted to improve upon this situation. He issued regulations setting up additional schools and providing for the education of girls. Yet because his administration was almost instantly mired in controversy, little was actually accomplished.[43]

In 1844 Thomas O. Larkin, who had sent his oldest son to school in Hawaii, decided to supplement Micheltorena's fledgling efforts. He spearheaded a project to establish a bilingual school in Monterey that would cater to the children of American residents and wealthy Californios. Each subscriber would agree to pay one hundred pesos a year for three years, and that amount would entitle them to send two children to the school. The founders, who included Larkin, three other foreigners, and five Californios, stated that they would be requesting a Catholic teacher from the United States who would be responsible for teaching Spanish and English grammar, writing, and mathematics. The proposed school never got off the ground.

43. MGV, *Recuerdos*, 2:950; Miller, *Juan Alvarado*, 67; White, *Narrative of a Cruise*, 69; Eversole, "Towns in Mexican Alta California," 506, 538.

Larkin did make some preliminary inquiries in the Los Angeles area about potential interest in the school, but no one wished to send their children all the way to Monterey to attend it. Larkin wrote Alfred Robinson, who was in New York, to try to find someone to staff the school. He also wrote to ask his cousin William M. Rogers to let Robinson know if he was aware of any potential candidates. Robinson wrote back in January 1845 that he intended "immediately to advertise" for the position. But in May he had to confess to Larkin, "Your schoolmaster I have not advertised for yet, but intend to immediately so that he can obtain passage." But he added, "It is quite uncertain if one can be procured." The school never opened.[44]

However, Larkin's experiences in Monterey had taught him how much many Californios valued education for their children. One of his first communications to Commodore Sloat, one day after he had taken possession of Monterey, urged that Sloat pay the Monterey schoolmaster out of his own funds and thereby show that he supported education in California. Larkin advised the commodore: "Opening a school as the first act of your administration must be placed to your credit and honour as a thing of primary importance to the welfare of California, showing not only to the men of the country, but even to the mothers and children, that our government seeks their welfare, and intends that even the youngest in the land shall immediately experience the benefit from the change of flags. This act will and must be of much importance in bringing affairs with us and the natives to a prompt and happy conclusion."[45]

Larkin certainly had his finger on the pulse of life and the desire for a public school in Monterey. His note to Sloat provides more strong evidence that Vallejo's characterization of Californio culture as communal and concerned with education was far more accurate than the stereotypical and racially tinged assessments of many contemporary American writers.

---

44. "Petition to establish a school," in Larkin, *Papers*, 2:223–24; also in VA 87, HL; Larkin to Alfred Robinson, September 16, 1844, and May 6, 1845, in Larkin, *Papers*, 2:232, 3:174; Alfred Robinson to Larkin, January 20, 1845, and May 29, 1845, in Larkin, *Papers*, 3: 16, 204–205; John H. Everett to Larkin, November 8, 1844, in Larkin, *Papers*, 2:278–79.

45. Larkin to Commodore Sloat, July 8, 1846, in Larkin, *Papers*, 5:118.

Mariano Guadalupe Vallejo on his porch
Courtesy of Vallejo Naval and Historical Museum

CHAPTER 8

"I Need to Pour Out My Feelings with Someone Who Understands Me"

Family Letters

*I*n this final chapter we focus on the family experiences of Mariano Guadalupe Vallejo and, especially, Francisca Benicia Carrillo de Vallejo. During the almost fifty-eight years of their marriage, they exchanged at least 175 letters, of which he composed the overwhelming majority. Most of the letters were written while he was away from Sonoma and Lachryma Montis attending to various forms of business. As we have shown in previous chapters, many of Vallejo's experiences during the 1850s and thereafter were deeply unpleasant, as the loss of his land and money weighed heavily on him. During these years he often complained that he was lonely and that members of his family were writing to him much too infrequently. Yet the letters also pointed to a different side of his life, for they made clear that he often enjoyed being in San Francisco and other places, mixing with local dignitaries, being regarded as something of an elder statesman, and gradually becoming somewhat of a go-to authority on early California life.

Francisca Benicia's letters reveal that she was a very strong woman. Though she often resented his frequent absences, she quickly grew into her role as manager of a growing household. She became the one who sought to continue providing the necessities of life for her growing children despite constant financial uncertainty. She became what could be called a pioneering entrepreneur, providing needed goods and services to local hotels and seeking to turn the amenities of Lachryma Montis, such as the abundant water from a nearby spring, into profitable sources of income.

Much of the extended family dynamics of this remarkable couple has been admirably presented by Madie Brown Emparán in her irreplaceable volume *The Vallejos of California*. In this chapter we present a very small amount of their correspondence, selecting letters that throw light upon the social developments confronted by a Californio family during the first decades of American rule. Parts of that correspondence were unkempt, messy, and connected with the most private of matters relating to themselves and their children; thus, we have tried to respect the family's privacy. Also, in an attempt to try to remain close to the family experiences we do recount, we refer to Mariano Guadalupe and Francisca Benicia as they referred to each other in their letters, as Guadalupe and Francisca. The Vallejo children and their spouses (where relevant) are listed at the end of the chapter to assist readers in identifying references to family members.

❄ 1846

The first exchange of letters occurred when Guadalupe was imprisoned at Sutter's Fort in 1846. The themes in this brief correspondence were ones that proved to be lasting in many of the letters they would exchange over the next decades. Guadalupe was quite interested in keeping abreast of his businesses—in this case, the

Francisca Benicia Carrillo de Vallejo
Courtesy of California State Parks, Sonoma Barracks.
No. 243-1-1394.

state of affairs on the ranchos he owned. In her husband's absence, Francisca was forced to assume many responsibilities relating to the care and upkeep of the family's residence. In many ways, these preoccupations would continue to govern their lives. Guadalupe would spend much time away from Sonoma, at the Constitutional Convention, in the legislature, and before the Land Commission. During those times, Francisca assumed greater and greater control over matters at the family house. Guadalupe was not always happy with her choices, and Francisca sometimes resented his consistent willingness to pass judgment on matters about which she believed he was not properly informed.

1846[1]

Guadalupe Vallejo,

Your children and I are fine. Don't worry too much about the family because the señores are taking good care of us. We are sad because we don't know when you will return. My Mamá sends you many greetings. She says for you to take good care of Julio. Not much can be done at the ranchos because the Indians are running away. Alvarado is harvesting at Petaluma and Señor Eleuterio is slaughtering cattle at Suscol. Your papers are being well taken care of. I am sending you some money, a little bit of pinole, and bread. When you write to me, write more legibly because I can't read your handwriting.

Francisca Carrillo de Vallejo

Sacramento
July 12, 1846[2]

Francisca,

We are still fine. Since Salazar is heading back there to get some clothing, I am sending you this letter so that you can give everyone my greetings. Salazar will probably return right away and I hope he will bring me news about the family. Tell Rosalía that Leese received the few things he requested. I also received what you sent me, especially the corn tortillas.

We still don't have any news as to whether we will be set free soon, and this has us worried.

We send many blessings to all of you,

M. G. Vallejo

P.S. Julio is also fine and he sends greetings to the family.

---

1. C-B 441, box 6, folder 5, TBL.
2. C-B 441, box 1, folder 2, TBL.

Rosalía Vallejo, Jacob P. Leese, and their children.
Rosalía was Mariano's sister. *Courtesy of The Bancroft Library,
University of California, Berkeley.* POR: *Leese, Jacob Primer.*

Sacramento
July 22, 1846[3]

My dear Francisca,

By means of a vaquero who came from Napa on some errands for
Salvador and Julio, I know that the whole family is fine. And I also
know from the same messenger that Salazar should be arriving
very soon. I am anxiously awaiting his arrival to hear news from
home. We are all fine.

Even though Salazar may have already left to come here, I want
you to send me two quires[4] of paper, that is to say, ten folders,

3. C-B 441, box 1, folder 1, TBL
4. A quire is four sheets of paper folded to form eight leaves.

with one of the Indians from Suscol who knows the way (Petronio knows it well) because there is no paper here. If we wait much longer, we won't have anything to write on. Also, send me the small ivory chess set that is in one of the desk drawers, as well as some salt laxatives.

Have someone tell Alvarado to write to me and report on the work going on and the harvests. And tell him not to kill more than 100 fat steers at Petaluma for their tallow, and tell Señor Eleuterio no more than 150 at Suscol. Have them take the hides from Suscol to Sonoma.

Every day we wait for the mail to arrive from Monterey. Maybe when it arrives we will be free to return to our homes. Tell the mayordomos to keep a close watch. We know that the señora is at home and that all the girls are fine. We send them our greetings.

Julio is fine and sends his greetings to everyone, as do I. Take care of the children and give them an affectionate hug in my name, and don't forget about Rosalía and her children.

Your affectionate M. G. Vallejo wishes you happiness.

P.S. José has written to me and also to Andrónico, and he is sending you the attached letter with some drawings.

July 1846[5]

Guadalupe,

Señor Laugriano went into the granary and stole some things, and he was causing a commotion with the Indians. I told the captain about this and Laugriano was arrested. I am very afraid of him.

A man arrived here and showed me two letters and said they were about setting you free. He also told me that it was necessary for you to bring some men with you because there were some bad

---

5. C-B 441, box 6, folder 5, TBL.

people on the road who wanted to kill you and the others. Ask some good men to come with you.

I am fine and so is everyone here at home.

Francisca Carrillo de Vallejo

[P.S.] I am sending paper to you.

After his release from Sutter's Fort, Guadalupe spent a good amount of time trying to take advantage of the good relationship he had formed with the American military and with some of the more moderate Americans. His dealings with settler Robert Semple and Consul Thomas Larkin regarding the town of Benicia and his participation in the Constitutional Convention and the first legislature quite often kept him away from his family and their residence in Sonoma. Consequently, during this time of major transition Francisca found herself with increasing responsibilities at home and, more often than not, an absent husband. The situation did not sit well with her, and she let Guadalupe know her feelings when he was in San José attending the sessions of the legislature. In response, he let her know that his own living conditions in San José were far from desirable.

 1850

To Don M. Guadalupe Vallejo in San José
    Sonoma
February 8, 1850[6]

Guadalupe,

You tell me that I don't write to you in my own hand! You are correct. The letter I wrote you was in Don Pepe's hand because I was very busy. That is why I asked him to do it. You tell me that

---

6. C-B 441, box 6, folder 5, TBL.

you think about your family a lot. If that is true, then why don't you come home? Yes, I trust you. I imagine that you are busy. I am not ashamed of you, but I do believe that your government and your capitals keep you very occupied. . . .

Yes, I truly believe that you can go about your business without even thinking about your family because, if you did remember them and stopped to think about it, you would realize that your family needs you more than the government does. Don't you remember that you have the same obligations toward them that I do, and perhaps even more? Don't you remember that the family needs you to take care of them and advise them? Don't you remember that I get tired?

Why don't you come home and take care of your family and your interests? Don't you remember how much work you put into this ? Why are you letting all of this slip away, everything that has cost you the sweat of your brow, to go and earn one more peso? I don't want a single peso, nor hundreds of thousands of them, from you. Your family and I love you more than all the millions of pesos in the world.

Why are you working so much? Isn't what we have enough for you? Neither I nor your family want anything more. All the children think about you a lot. They didn't write to you because everyone who comes here from San José says that you are on your way home. But since so many weeks went by, they lost hope and started writing to you. Andrónico wanted to go with Captain Frisbie so he could see you. Uladislao, Jovita, and Benicia are waiting for you. They go outside every so often to see if you are coming.

My sister Vicenta arrived three days ago. Everyone here is fine.

I am always thinking about you,

Francisca Benicia de Vallejo

San José
February 28, 1850[7]

Francisca,

The books I have been waiting so long for, the ones that I wrote to you about in several letters, didn't arrive until today. Now I definitely can get ready to head home soon.

Don't believe that I am here because it is my choice. I am sick and tired of this place, and I am bored. The rains have been very heavy and, as a result, the mud in the streets is unbearable. Besides, I am lacking the comforts that old men like me greatly need. I am in a small room where five of us are living together, with no other comfort than being able to sleep under a roof. My eyes are bad, perhaps from stoking a very small and very bad iron fireplace and then having to go out into the cold air.

Take care of the family. Give them advice, and that way you will be fulfilling your duties as a mother and much more in my absence.

Why haven't you written to me again? And the girls, why don't they write to me? How can writing just one letter tire them out? And how is it that I am always able to write a letter?

Give everyone my greetings. Give Jovita and Uladislao a kiss. Tell Platón that I am very happy with his letters. Tell Andrónico to write to me as well, telling me everything he has been doing during my absence, such as the improvements at the house, and what is happening at the ranchos.

I am your
Guadalupe

1854

Guadalupe spent much of the 1850s dealing with issues that arose from the proceedings of the Land Commission, which forced him to

---

7. C-B 13, doc. 37, TBL.

spend a considerable amount of time in San Francisco. Meanwhile, in Sonoma, Francisca was dealing with growing children. In 1854, when the following letter was written, the two oldest boys, twenty-year-old Andrónico and thirteen-year-old Platón, were students at Mount St. Mary's school outside Baltimore, and Fannie was married to John Frisbie. There were six other children at home: Adela (age 17), Natalia (age 16), Jovita (age 10), Uladislao (age 9), Napoleón (age 3), and Benicia (age 1). Young Benicia would die during her sixth year, but two other children, Luisa and María, were born in 1856 and 1857, respectively. The Sonoma household was a crowded and bustling place, and Francisca felt that Guadalupe, in "that room where you are living," could not understand what she was going through.

Sonoma Springs
September 12, 1854[8]

Guadalupe,

I was sitting on my sewing chair waiting for you for quite a while, thinking perhaps that you wouldn't be coming, because the stagecoaches had arrived some time ago, and you weren't on any of them. Then, all of a sudden Billy came in with a letter from you in which you told me about the trouble we were going to have with Napoleón. I realized and understood very well how you must have felt during those moments when you were looking for him and couldn't find him. Oh my God! What would I have done if Napoleón had been lost! Guadalupe, take good care of Nápoles. From the moment I put him on the steamer, I have not been at ease, not even for an instant. The days seem longer to me than ever before. All I do is think about that little boy because I know he is so mischievous. If he doesn't see you, he is capable of wandering about until he finds you, and you might lose him again.

The rest of the family is fine. It's true that I had planned on

---

8. C-B 441, box 6, folder 5, TBL.

Lachryma Montis
Courtesy of California State Parks, Sonoma Barracks.
No. 243-x-3692.

going to San Francisco if you thought it would be a good idea. I would leave next Tuesday, if the captain arrived, as you say in your letter. I have all the girls here at the house so they can make their dresses. Tell Fanita that the girls are sending her two bonnets so that she can have them covered in green on the outside and lined in purple on the inside, or whatever she thinks is best. But don't put any flowers on the outside or perfume on the inside, and have the captain bring them when he comes back.

I will take care of everything that you have asked me to do, Guadalupe, as soon as you leave that room where you are living.

Tell Fanita to take care of Nápoles, or you take him with you wherever you go. It weighs heavily on me that I let him go with Don Pepe, with so much work that you have to do, and now Nápoles will create even more work for you.

Give Fanita all my love and give my best to the captain. Give Nápoles and Lupe many kisses. Have some coffee and toast prepared and enjoy it with the two of them in my name.

Benicia F. de Vallejo

P.S. Papá, since Saturday we have been in the house busily sewing our woolen dresses, the ones you told us to make for when we go to see you, Fannie, Nápoles, Lupe, and the captain, and to give each of you many kisses. Papá, if you see Felicidad, ask her why she tricked us, and the same goes for the captain. The other day he promised us that he would write to us as soon as he arrived in San Francisco.

Your affectionate[9] children,

Adela, Natalia, Jovita, Uladislao, Benicia

❋ 1858

In 1858, with a number of land cases still undecided, Guadalupe was called to Monterey. His mother had died in 1855, and she had willed her property—mainly Rancho San Cayetano, which her husband had been granted in the 1820s—to only two of her children, the unmarried Juan Antonio and María de Jesús, married to Víctor Fortoul. Juan Antonio was the original executor of the will, but when he died after falling from a horse in 1857, Guadalupe was named executor. He traveled to Monterey the next year and tried to straighten things out by including more of his siblings, especially his widowed sister Prudenciana, in the bequests. But Fortoul objected, and the case dragged on for a number of years. In the meantime, it became clear in Sonoma that Adela Vallejo wished to marry Levi Frisbie, John's brother, who was sixteen years her senior. Francisca and Guadalupe both objected, but Adela argued that she should not be bound by the Mexican custom of contracting matrimony only with the consent of her parents. She apparently also suggested that her own parents had not felt themselves bound to that custom when they had decided to marry in the 1830s, something Guadalupe vehemently denied. Adela then set a wedding date herself. However, when that date passed without a ceremony, Francisca informed Guadalupe of the situation and begged him to return quickly.

---

9. "Affectionate" is in English in the original letter.

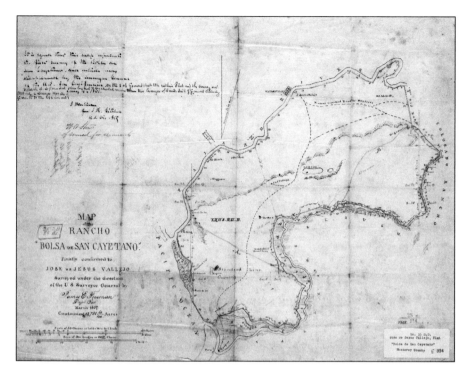

Diseño of Rancho San Cayetano
*Courtesy of The Bancroft Library, University of California,
Berkeley. Land Case Map E-994.*

Monterey
June 30, 1858[10]

Francisca,

The mail has been delivered three times already and I have been anxiously awaiting your letters, as well as those from the whole family. I suppose that either everyone is away or that they had

---

10. C-B 441, box 1, folder 3, TBL.

(left, to left of child) Prudenciana Vallejo Amesti
Courtesy of California State Parks, Sonoma Barracks. No. 243-x-3502.

(right) Juan Antonio Vallejo
Courtesy of California State Parks, Sonoma Barracks. No. 243-x-3542.

many commitments. But there is a well-known proverb that begins, "One who loves well, loves easily." So, my complaint is not necessarily with you, but you have asked me to forgive you several times. My complaint is more with Andrónico, Adela, Natalia, and Jovita. I will never forgive such negligence on their part with regard to their Papá, because all of them promised me that they would write at least one letter every week.

I know nothing about the marriage of Adela, to whom I wrote in response to your letter. If she is at home, tell her not to forget her promise and that I would like to hear her speak in her own defense. She is very unwavering in terms of her feelings, and even though those feelings are about the same thing (me), her argument lacks truth. I did not get married against the will of my wife's parents, even though they resisted at first. Before marrying, I

(*left*) Dr. Levi C. Frisbie
Courtesy of the Autry Museum of the American West,
Los Angeles, California. 200.1.3.34.

(*right*) Adela Vallejo Frisbie
Courtesy of the California History Room,
California State Library, Sacramento, California

never disrespected the family's domestic rules. I never saw my wife more than twice and I did not speak to her directly about getting married, but rather indirectly. I asked her parents for her hand in marriage by means of a letter written from 300 leagues away. I have never behaved in any other manner, and you yourself know that. In short, when you write to me, I would like for you to do so with no other purpose than to tell me what happens.

I presume that Jovita has probably returned to school. Her tuition is paid for.

You already know me. I see things differently than most people normally do. I love my family dearly, from my wife down to my youngest child. I sacrifice myself for them. We raise them, we educate them, etc., and that is the proof. If they are grateful, there is no doubt that they will not forget what we did for them, because few children can expect to receive gifts such as these from their parents.

Platón and Uladislao are in San Francisco. If Jovita and Benicita go to school, that will make four of them. Then you only have Natalia and two little girls left, which means that there is not much for us to do at home.

I will be finished here soon, and then I promise you that I will stay home for several weeks so that I can kiss the little ones and you, too.

Take care of yourself, take care of the children, and don't forget the one who loves you,

M. G. Vallejo

Lachryma Montis
July 14, 1858[11]

Guadalupe,

Adela's wedding came to nothing in the end. The doctor always had difficulties. I tried to make plans for this wedding three or four weeks ago, but there always was some sort of problem, and I think there always will be. This tires me out. Adela is more deserving of pity than anything else. Don't believe the stories you hear.

Jovita is still sick with a cough. Benicia is much better. Marillita is almost well. Andrónico, Adela, Natalia, Jovita, Napoleón, little Benicia, Luisita, Marillita, and I send you many hugs, many kisses, much affection, and many other things.

Come, come, come, come, come, come. You say that you love me and the family so much. If what you say is true, why do you leave me alone for so long now that the family needs your guidance? Remember, we are not talking about one or two children; there are many of them. You say that your duty and your obligations detain you. I don't know which obligation is more important to

---

11. Vallejo Family Papers, 243-366-314, California State Parks, Sonoma.

you, if it is taking care of your old sisters who no longer need to be taken care of or coming home to take care of your family. I cannot handle everything alone. I am very tired and very angry. The work in the orchards or the garden is so-so. Some fruit is beginning to ripen. They already harvested the oats. It is very hot in Sonoma.

I had written this letter two weeks ago and I didn't send it to you because I was embarrassed to have you see my bad writing. But I finally decided to write to you. You have every reason to be angry because the children don't write to you. Every day, I tell them to write to you. I think that Adela's wedding will be next week or whenever the doctor feels like having it.

I am very ill and sad because you no longer love me . . . . at all. What are we going to do? Patience.

Benicia F. de Vallejo

 1864

The late 1850s and early 1860s were a difficult time for the Vallejo family. The Supreme Court's rejection of the Suscol claim dramatically weakened their already fragile financial situation. In addition, the San Cayetano case, from which Guadalupe hoped to obtain some money, was still dragging on at the beginning of 1864. Francisca, who had a fourteen-year-old boy and two girls, ages seven and eight, at home, was much more proactive than her husband was about trying to devise ways to bring in additional income. Her female initiative seems to have greatly irritated Guadalupe. He periodically expressed his concern that his children, none of whom had married a Californio or a Mexican, were abandoning their ancestral ways in favor of what he regarded as the looser and less refined customs of the Americans. In March 1864, for instance, he groused to Francisca that Platón, then studying medicine at Columbia in New York, had not written to him in quite some time:

> It has been eight months since I have received a letter from him, and that silence has me very worried. In the last letter I wrote to him from Sonoma, I remember that I scolded him because he was not writing to

me. It is possible that he did not like that scolding, and that is why he has not written to me again. Nevertheless, he should not be so sensitive or so delicate, unless he is also thinking like an "American"; that is to say, acting totally independent, which would not surprise me.

The combination of all these difficult circumstances was extremely trying for Guadalupe. In April 1864 he let loose a barrage of pent-up anger and frustration in a letter to Francisca.

San Cayetano
April 26, 1864[12]

Francisca,

I wrote to you three days ago. I suppose you have received my letter and it probably seemed to you to be a bit serious and not very pleasant. When I was answering your letter, I was furious with the entire world, with all men, with the human race, with fate, and with everything ever written under the sun. I was in such a state when I received the letter you had written to me that, without pausing for an instant to reflect on it, I picked up my pen to answer it <u>truly believing that you had posted an advertisement in Sonoma so that the family bathrooms could be used by the public</u>, which made me go crazy. However, after rereading your letter, I saw that you were consulting with me and were waiting for my decision in order to do it or not, which tempered my rage. I was determined to write to you, but if there is anything in the letter that is <u>personal</u>, do not take offense, for I am repentant. This is not the time to aggravate the horrible circumstances in which we currently find ourselves. Useless complaints would only make matters worse, and this would lead to the total ruination of a family that is so dear to me and that should be as dear to you as well.

I have ended up poor because people have stolen from me. It is not because of any bad decisions on my part, even though people

12. C-B 441, box 1, folder 4, TBL.

have wanted to assert that. It is just bad luck and it has not been
in my power to remedy this. It almost seems like I was destined to
suffer those strokes of bad luck. As you know, it was not humanly
possible to correct them because this was the direct result of a
grand public movement that was supposed to drag down the fortunes of men like me who made themselves more visible.

Ending up poor because the most powerful government in the
world has <u>taken over</u> my most valuable properties is not my fault.
It is just that I have not been able to fight for them successfully
due to a lack of material force ($$) to counteract it. A capitalist
manages one or two million pesos and conducts his business in
China and Europe. He sends three or four clipper ships to those
places in search of valuable cargo and as soon as everything is on
board he sets sail. While sailing back to San Francisco in large and
expensive ships they get caught in a hurricane in the middle of the
ocean and they perish . . . ships, cargo, and men. Who is to blame for
this? A farmer, who is a speculator, plants a large amount of wheat,
barley, potatoes and uses all his money, and even his credit, on this
enterprise because wheat, barley, and potatoes bring a very high
price at market. However, after having made such an expenditure,
the seedlings begin to appear, but not a drop of water falls in the
winter. Who is to blame for this? Or if the harvest was good and
a fire destroys it all, or if the market goes down and the items in
question are no longer worth anything? Who is to blame for this?
Or if someone plants grapevines, orchards, etc., and the wine or the
grapes aren't any good? Who is to blame for this? Enough said with
regard to taking a philosophical approach to things. But referring
to our situation, it is true that lately we have suffered shortages up
to a certain point, painful shortages that we were not prepared to
experience. However, I have spent three years hoping to find a way
out of the predicament of that damned business at Suscol, which
in the end has humiliated me tremendously, causing me to be in
debt to those who have been working for me, and it is the reason for
the mortgage on the property. I came here to handle the business
regarding this property with the hope that I could come out with

at least $15,000, but I have not been able to accomplish this due to some complications that were not within my power to resolve. If I had been able to foresee this, I never would have come. I have suffered greatly, both physically and emotionally. I have been alone, totally alone, working hard to sell and get some money to bring back home. But that <u>damned money</u> has disappeared from the country, everybody is <u>hopping mad</u>, crying out, and wailing for it. I was in Monterey a number of days ago and, believe me, that place is pitiful. There are many families in the same situation, and if it were not for the fish, they would have died of hunger. I said to myself, "Thank God that there are geese, ducks, hens, and all types of vegetables to eat at my home." I was making comparisons between the two places, and it did give me some consolation. In my heart, I even wanted to share with them what my family had, which seemed like an abundance of food compared to what they had.

The greatest consolation I have received while being away is receiving mail from the whole family and holding it in my hands. Their letters do my heart good, they distract me, and they are a salve that has cured me somewhat. If only you had written to me as well, how happy I would have been! What satisfaction I would have received! How relieved I would have felt! I have been very carefully searching for what one could call <u>happiness</u> among some people. I have not been able to find it anywhere. I have asked (without people paying me any mind), heard, and discovered that in this detestable world everybody runs away from happiness. Gossip, scandal, murmurings, slander, lies, and evil itself reign everywhere. In the end, I have been nothing less than horrified by what I have discovered here. But God is great, God is good, the God of Napoleon!!!!!!!, that all-seeing and all-knowing God who <u>should take into account</u> our actions and how we have used our language!!!!!. That God—and our own conscience, I hope!—will punish those who maliciously or innocently have done wrong. I wish I hadn't known so much!

This is not a sermon, it is a letter written from the heart. I want you to read it with an open mind. I need to pour out my feelings

Napoleón Vallejo, ca. 1863
*Courtesy of The Bancroft Library,
University of California, Berkeley.*
BANC PIC 1978.195.08-PIC.

with someone who (<u>putting aside biased passion</u>) understands me. How happy I would be if, in the end, after so many years of <u>loathing and animosity toward me</u>, you could free yourself of that deeprooted hatred you feel for me and for the members of my family. Hatred and rancor produce nothing more than countless evils. I realize that loathing is natural, but even so, I follow the maxims of the men who have said, "One should seek peace and reconciliation when there are families that suffer because of the lack of reason on the part of their parents." My sons and daughters give me, up to a certain point, the greatest pleasure of my life. They know it and so do you. They express it in their letters along with the trust they have. Whether absent or present, they realize this and it pleases me to say it. I am tired of living without receiving any letters from you while I am away from home. It is an emptiness that I feel when I receive letters from Fanita, Adela, Natalia, Ula, Jovita, and Nap, but I don't see a letter from you. Do you understand? Andrónico has not written to me either.

I want to return soon. Give my regards to Ula, Nap, Lulú, and María, and many more to Don Pepe.

M. G. Vallejo

1865

In 1865 Guadalupe accompanied Frisbie on a trip to the East Coast. As we indicated earlier, the precise purpose of the trip is not clear, although it appears to have been connected with some business opportunities that Frisbie was seeking to develop. Guadalupe, who had never been out of Alta California, found the experience exhilarating, confusing, and depressing.

5th Avenue Hotel
New York
March 20, 1865[13]

Francisca,

I am still alive, but I don't know how I have been able to tolerate how cold it is in this country. However, a few days ago the temperature improved, and I feel like going outside for a few moments to get some fresh air. However, I must stay bundled up, otherwise I would be exposing myself to the illnesses that are so easily acquired here.

This city of New York is an immense place where everybody walks up and down the streets without knowing one another and without speaking to anyone. The hustle and bustle and the confusion are such that the noise level is extremely loud. You have to speak by shouting, and even then, you cannot hear each other. I am tired of the trains. They run constantly, day and night, and are so crowded with people. One is scared to ride on the trains because so many people are killed in the collisions that occur every day. Sometimes, when the trains travel on bridges over estuaries, the bridges collapse, and the passengers drown in their seats. At other times, two trains meet up as they are going down the same track. It is horrible to see how the people and the cars are ripped to shreds. This happened on a train that was going to Washington and, fortunately, I was spared. I have learned my lesson.

---

13. C-B 441, box 1, folder 5, TBL.

I have thought a lot about you and the family. However, when I realize it is necessary to travel on a steamer from San Francisco to here, six thousand miles in the middle of the ocean, and remembering that you get seasick so easily, I am happy that you are in our little house in Sonoma. I am extremely sorry that I have come here. I fear having to return by way of that damned ocean. It is so vast and the trip is so difficult. The only reason I made the decision to go so far away and leave my family behind was because I needed to see if I could arrange my business dealings with Frisbie and work together with him. I hope everything will work out for me, and if not, I will skin that mean bastard.[14] At least I will have seen something I can tell you about. However, I don't want you to think that I am very impressed by what I have seen, which is more than I expected before coming here. The country is an immense plain with ravines that are lower than the plain itself, without a single hill or mountain, filled with towns. It's true! I don't know why the sight of such a large plain is offensive to me. All the trees in the entire country are very small, similar to the two little oak trees in front of the henhouse. It looks like an orchard. The land is very arid. There are only small pine trees and oaks. The most beautiful thing I have seen is the Bay of New York at night. It is quite lovely because the bay is surrounded by more than two million inhabitants. It is a very small bay. All the cities are illuminated with gaslights that reflect on the water. In addition, thousands upon thousands of steamers also travel with lights. Just imagine that you are looking at a sky filled with stars on a dark night and there are also stars below, on the water. This is truly very beautiful. The fruit here has no taste. The grapes taste like boiled eggs.

The steamer leaves today and I would like to leave as well. I don't like this place, nor do I like the climate. It's true that there are very impressive things here, but I don't like them. Everything here boils down to being money hungry. I think the people are insane. It is a terrible state of confusion. Friendship is only out of

---

14. "Pelo mi indina rata."

Fifth Avenue Hotel, New York City, 1892, by Strohmeyer & Wyman
Courtesy of the Library of Congress. LC-DIG-stereo-1507698.

self-interest, and I didn't think of it like that before. Just thinking about that makes me unhappy. The madness they exhibit with regard to money is rabid <u>desperation</u>.

Take care of the children, and take care of yourself as well. I sent quite a bit of money for you with Platón. I hope it has been of use to you.

Platón already has a good position. We still have poor Ula to worry about. In a long letter I wrote to him, I gave him a lot of advice, primarily on the matter you told me about when I was home.

Goodbye, see you in about sixty days.

M. G. Vallejo

New York
April 10, 1865[15]

Francisca,

From Fanita's letters I have learned that you have been a bit ill, but that it isn't anything serious. I hope you are completely well by now. When you receive this letter, I will already be in Panama on my way back to California. My plan is to leave here on the 23rd of this month. Since I will be leaving soon, I don't want to go into too much detail. I will just say that I have visited many large cities and I have seen many things I have liked and admired. I will tell you all about it when I see you.

Take care of the children and give them my regards. Tell them I will see all of them soon if I don't drown during the voyage.

I am,

MGV

P.S. Give my regards to Don Pepe.

5th Avenue Hotel
New York
April 30, 1865[16]

Francisca,

Finally, on May 15, I will be leaving for California, returning from visiting this country that I admire but do not love with my heart because the weather, just like the people in general, have treated

15. C-B 441, box 1, folder 5, TBL.
16. C-B 441, box 1, folder 4, TBL.

me very badly and have been the cause of my ruin and that of my family. You already understand what I am saying.

So many things have happened since I wrote to you from Washington that I would need a ream of paper to tell you everything. And since I will be leaving soon, I will wait until I get home.

I hope that you and the children are well. Wishing you all good health, I am your

M. G. Vallejo

[P.S.] Give my greetings to Don Pepe.

5th Avenue Hotel
New York
May 28, 1865[17]

Francisca,

It is now going on one month since we should have left here for California, but so many significant things have happened with regard to public issues that everything has been turned upside down, paralyzing business matters, which when we first arrived had every sign of being handled successfully. But the war and the assassination of President Lincoln have caused everything to be delayed, thus detaining us longer than I wished to be here. Nevertheless, perhaps I will be able to leave by the first of June. I am tired and even more bored with this country. It is true that the weather has changed and the countryside looks better, but I don't like this climate. The air is bad and the people worse, which makes me tired of everything. I can no longer take care of my health.

I have hopes that I will be leaving here soon. If I should have the need to return some day, it will be in a very different manner: <u>you soon will understand why I am saying this to you.</u>

I need to write to Natalia, her letter is waiting to be answered.

_____
17. C-B 441, box 1, folder 5, TBL.

Kiss the children.

M. G. Vallejo

P.S. I wrote to Don Pepe quite a while ago and he didn't answer me.

 1866–1868

Guadalupe's failure to reap any financial benefit from his trip to the East with Frisbie meant that the family's financial situation remained dire. He spent more time in San Francisco, seeking any opportunity he could find, but nothing really developed. Francisca, still uncertain whether he truly realized the depth of the family's dire straits, wrote him in April 1866. He responded a day later, but the situation did not improve. Two years later, Francisca wrote him a letter that she dictated to Pepe de la Rosa. She was upset that Guadalupe did not understand that the reason she dictated the letter was because the task of keeping the family together was incredibly time-consuming. In the letter she poured out her own deep frustrations at the years of her often-absent husband's lack of appreciation for her efforts to generate money for the household in Sonoma.

Sunday
April 29, 1866[18]

Guadalupe:

Wherever you are, wherever you are living, I haven't received any news from you since you left home, not even once. Perhaps you haven't written to me at all, or maybe the letters got lost. Or it may be because you no longer love me. You need to come home so that we can talk for a bit. If you can't come, let me know so that I won't be waiting for you. Whenever you are able to come, please

---

18. BANC MSS 76/79c, reel 1, box 1, folder 19, TBL.

come. The house is completely changed. We have taken all the furniture out of your room and replaced it with other furniture. The rest of your things are in the room. The other rooms are set up and ready to receive visitors. We now have a little Fanita. Jovita is here. She is the one who manages everything in the house from top to bottom so that I don't have to do anything.

Napoleón and María were sick, but they are fine now.

Guadalupe: I don't want to trouble you about anything, but I am forced to do so. I don't have any money to buy what we need. You know that no one can be without shoes and other things. Napoleón is practically naked.

Guadalupe: I had written this letter several days ago but I didn't send it to you because I thought you would be coming home but . . . you were very busy.

San Francisco
April 30, 1866[19]

Francisca,

This Sunday morning, I received the letter you wrote yesterday. In spite of it being so short, the letter is very significant to me because I understand it. In the first place, I am here just as the magnetic force is always attracted to the pole. I came to San Francisco with a specific objective, or rather, to receive about four hundred pesos that a man from Pájaro owes me. Not only has he not sent me the money, but he also has not come or written to me. I planned to come for three days, and I have already been here for more than sixty. I came all dressed up and I am still that way. Of course, every day I am thinking about heading back to Sonoma, and each day there are new obstacles. General [Plácido] Vega has begged me to help him expedite his departure to Mexico, and I can't abandon him. It is true that nothing can be done without money, even though there

---

19. C-B 441, box 1, folder 5, TBL.

General Plácido Vega
Courtesy of The Bancroft Library,
University of California, Berkeley.
POR: *Vega, Plácido: 1.*

is some hope this week. That is how I have been existing, for a day, a week, a month, two months. Every day is filled with anguish, afflictions, increasing distress. My soul suffers as much as it can endure. When I see you, I will tell you a thousand things that, even though they might seem incredible, are true.

Platón arrived while I was reading your letter in my room. I was very sad. He gave me twenty-five pesos to send to you, and I can confirm that it is a gift from your son. Poor Platón is very busy, and he feels bad that he has not paid you a visit. There are so many sick people to care for, which makes it very difficult to travel up to Sonoma. He said he can barely go to Vallejo, not even for a short time.

I have not had the heart to abandon General Vega during his time of difficulties, nor can I refrain from helping him as much as I possibly can.

I will see you and the children soon.

Your,

MGV

P.S. Take my books and papers up to your room even if that means piling them up in a closet.

José "Pepe" de la Rosa
Courtesy of Ventura County
Research Library and Archives.
3466 (De-la-Rosa).

Sonoma
December 2, 1868[20]

Guadalupe,

The letter that I asked Don Pepe to write for me was not intended to humiliate you, as you seem to think. My intentions were very good and pure. If I asked Don Pepe to write for me, it was because I was very busy. Also, you know full well that I don't know how to write very fast. I also never thought that what I said to you in the letter was to be kept secret from Don Pepe because you, yourself, in my presence, have said the same thing to him about the bathrooms. He is an old man who has known the family for many years, and

20. C-B 441, box 1, folder 5, TBL.

he probably knows other secrets . . . and I will tell you again, there are no secrets in the letter I wrote to you, nor any bad intentions on my part, as you said in your letter. Because you are my husband, I was asking for your advice, in case you wanted to give it to me or it made you happy to give it to me. At the same time, I also was trying to be of help to you in some way or another. That was my intention. It pains me, Guadalupe, that you greatly disapprove of even the slightest comment on my part or if I tell you that I want something. It never would occur to me in my wildest dreams to offend you or humiliate you. Guadalupe! Guadalupe! What little regard you have for me after living together for so many years! It is very obvious that you look at me with indifference, [even] after so many years that I have spent attending to you as a wife, a friend, and a companion. Do you believe that I wanted to humiliate you or do something that would be an insult to your honor or mine? Never! Never! If telling you about things that are needed and what the family is lacking is offensive to you, then what am I supposed to do? Always the same issues, always the same difficulties: I think one way and you think otherwise. I want to do things correctly, and you tell me I'm doing things wrong. So, which one of us right? As soon as I realized that you didn't like my idea about the bathrooms; that is, that it didn't seem like a good idea to you, I didn't give it another thought. That was the end of it.

I am also going to tell you about the vegetable garden. I am delivering vegetables to the hotel, and eggs that the hens lay are going to the baker. I am informing you about this in this letter so that you will let me know whether or not you approve. I hadn't told you about this before because I didn't believe it would be necessary, but since you were so offended by the news about the bathrooms, that is why I am informing you now. If you don't like it, tell me, so I can stop making deliveries. I don't want you to think that I am also doing this to humiliate you. Don't think that I am so stupid, because if I wanted to humiliate you, there are any manner of ways in which I could do so. But I am not planning on doing that, nor do I want to do that, because that is not who I am.

You tell me in your letter that you would like for me to write about happy things and how I seem to want to make our life unbearable. But you are the one who makes your own life unbearable, and you do the same to mine. You blame me for any little thing I do, think, or want. Guadalupe: you need to view me in a different manner and not believe I am such a bad person. Don't disparage me so much, because you are only hurting yourself. It makes me so sad to think that you are so ill-disposed and angry with me for no reason. I am tired, sick, and angry because of this, and I can't find any solution. Let's leave all of this in God's hands, don't you think? When you come home, don't return angry. Come back happy because that is what I desire. Even though we are poor, if there is something you don't like, tell me so that I can do it the way you want. But don't mistreat me for no reason at all, because I can't put up with it. You are killing me, my heart is aching. I would rather die than see you angry.

Don't worry so much, manage your business dealings well, and don't get so upset if you can't get what you want. When you are able and your business dealings permit it, come and spend some time here, so that you can attend to the business matters here. It will also serve as a bit of a distraction for you. I think this would be good for you.

❄ 1869

At this time, Guadalupe was forced to confront an episode from his past. The person who forced him to do so was María Amparo Ruiz de Burton.[21] She was the granddaughter of José Manuel Ruiz, who had served as governor of Baja California in the early 1820s. At the conclusion of the Mexican War, when it became known that Baja California would remain part of Mexico, she and a number of other residents of La Paz who had been friendly to the Americans were taken to Alta California by Captain Henry S. Burton. He

---

21. Biographical information about Ruiz de Burton is taken from Sánchez and Pita, *Conflicts of Interest.*

(*above*) Casa de López, Old Town San Diego, California.
State Historical Monument No. 60. This was the home of Juana López,
the mother of Prudenciana Vallejo López de Moreno.

(*below, left*) Prudenciana Vallejo López de Moreno, 1857

(*below, right*) José Matías Moreno II, husband of
Prudenciana Vallejo López. He served as jefe político
de la frontera in Baja California and was secretary to Pío Pico.
*Images on this page are reproduced by permission of the Huntington Library,
San Marino, California. Helen Long Collection of Moreno Documents, box 19.*

and María Amparo Ruiz married in Monterey, and they settled in San Diego after he was named head of the U.S. military garrison there. She remained there when he was stationed in Fort Yuma at the end of the 1850s. María Amparo Ruiz and her husband moved to the East in 1859 and remained there for the next decade. Shortly after Burton died in 1869, she returned to California.

During her residence in San Diego, she became friendly with Juana López, a single mother, and her daughter, Prudenciana. Since María Amparo had largely been raised by her mother, they undoubtedly talked about their circumstances. In the course of those conversations, she learned that Prudenciana's father was Mariano Guadalupe Vallejo.

Juana López was actually a cousin of Francisca Benicia Carrillo's, for Juana's father and Francisca's mother were siblings. Prudenciana was conceived a few months after Francisca and Guadalupe were married.[22] It is not clear when Guadalupe became aware of her birth and whether or not Francisca ever explicitly learned of it. Given the close family relationship, however, we believe it is unlikely that Francisca was unaware of Prudenciana's existence.

In any event, Guadalupe and María Amparo Ruiz met in Northern California during the late 1840s and began corresponding regularly in 1851. María Amparo was a very direct woman, and when she became aware that he was Prudenciana's father, she urged him to acknowledge her. By this time, Prudenciana had married José Matías Moreno, who had been Governor Pío Pico's secretary in 1846 and had a rancho in northern Baja California.

Guadalupe took María Amparo Ruiz's advice in 1869, when José Matías Moreno and Prudenciana visited San Francisco. They stayed with Miguel Pritchard, who was secretary to the Mexican Consulate. Guadalupe met with her and acknowledged that he was her birth father. When she returned to the San Diego area, she wrote him a letter thanking him for doing so, and he responded

22. She was born at the end of May 1833, San Diego Baptism 6552. The ECPP transcription is slightly inaccurate. She was "hija ilegítima" (not "legítima"), as is clear on the original record, a copy of which is at SBMAL.

with a letter of his own. He combined heartfelt sentiments with a calculated attempt to maintain contact with her without Francisca noticing any letters from her. He also received a letter in reply after he informed María Amparo Ruiz that he had seen Prudenciana. Prudenciana and Guadalupe stayed in touch through third parties like María Amparo Ruiz and José Arce, a relative of Prudenciana's grandmother.[23]

Lachryma Montis
Sonoma Valley
September 24, 1869[24]

Señora Doña Prudenciana Vallejo de Moreno
My dear and beloved daughter,

I have just received your heartfelt letter, dated the 19th of last month. That you have written to me has pleased me so very, very much, and I reply by congratulating you on your safe journey and arrival in San Diego. The fact that Don Matías's health is improving each day gives me great satisfaction. May God will that he completely recovers his strength, and may he continue, as he has up until now, being the protector and father of such a fine and large family. Be good, my daughter, and always help your husband to take care of everything, and even more so now that he is ill. Be loving and kind to him, for he is such a worthy and good father. That way, you will fulfill your responsibilities as a wife and as a mother, and you and your children will receive blessings from Heaven and also from your father who sincerely loves you with all his heart.

Through you I am sending my warmest regards to Don Matías. Tell him not to fear because the climate and tranquility will help him recover his health soon. And <u>now more than ever</u> he should

23. Sánchez and Pita, *Conflicts of Interest*, 436, 459, 468, 479–80; José Arce to Prudenciana López de Moreno, July 26, 1872, HLG 936, HL.
24. HLG 905, HL.

Dr. Víctor Fauré. *Courtesy of California State Parks, Sonoma Barracks. No. 243-x-5270.N.*

count me among his many true friends, because his children are closely related to me, and you, dear Prudenciana, even more so. Tell him that I will help him however I can.

Shortly after you left San Francisco I paid a visit to the Pritchard family, where you were guests. They remember you fondly and asked me to give you their regards, which I am now doing with pleasure. Doña Avelina, in particular, sends her regards to all of you.

I don't want you to go to the trouble of sending me the "Cenzontle."[25] I am as grateful to you as if I had received it; but if you insist on doing so, send it to this address:

> Gen. M. G. Vallejo
> Port St. Orleans Hotel
> Care of Mrs. A. Haraszthy
> San Francisco

As soon as I return to the city I will remember your shoe size, no. 3, and also your glove size, no. 6, and that you do not have legs

25. A "cenzontle" is a mockingbird.

like a "Yankee." I will ask Doña Avelina about the last point <u>in case she knows something about it</u>. Or if she doesn't, what can we do? I will just have to guess.

Give my regards to your husband and kiss all the family for me. And you, receive the love and esteem of your father who loves you and gives you his blessing.

M. G. Vallejo

P.S. I am frequently away from here, and it would be better if you addressed my letters as usual but put them inside <u>another envelope</u> that says: "Víctor Fauré, MD" Sonoma.

He will give them to me or send them to wherever I am.

❊ ❊ ❊

September 14, 1869
Staten Island, New York[26]

. . . Good for you for having gone to see Doña Prudenciana. That is what you should have done thirty years ago! Doesn't it horrify you to think that for so many years you deprived her of all that affection which was hers by the laws of nature? . . . I don't want to preach to you, but honestly, of all your sins, my son, this is the worst one I have noticed in you . . . but better late than never . . . and since she surely has forgiven you, I hope that God will also forgive you! I was very moved by that part of your letter, and I also cried with both of you, even though from far away. . . .

M. A. de Burton

 1870

With economic prospects in California continuing to be bleak, in 1869 Frisbie moved his family back to his ancestral home in the Albany region of upstate New York. He did some lobbying

---

26. Sánchez and Pita, *Conflicts of Interest*, 302–3.

in Washington, D.C., in exchange for federal help relating to the town of Vallejo. He then returned to California, leaving his wife and children in New York. The next year, when he returned to visit them, he took Francisca with him. She found the trip and the reunion with her daughter and her daughter's family rewarding, and Guadalupe congratulated her on that.

May 5, 1870
Albany, New York[27]

Guadalupe,

We were having lunch with the whole family. I have been with Fannie for a few days. Guadalupe, ever since I left home I had wanted to write to you, but I couldn't do it. You know how long it takes for me to write a letter. I wish I knew how to write well and quickly so that I could tell all of you about what I have seen and heard. The day I left Sacramento I felt a bit sad, but I started to pray to God and to the Most Holy Mother of Light to give me courage and for all of us to come out safely from the danger we were about to face. I was already starting to see the hills and the mountain range, and I was thinking a lot about you and my children, when John arrived and told me there was a Spanish woman in the car. He wondered if I had seen her. I told him I hadn't, and it was already late. Then I heard a voice calling out "Cousin." I was startled and turned around to see who was calling me cousin. It was Rafaela Tempel and a brother-in-law of hers, as well as a niece and a nephew, who were this man's children. They were all traveling together to France. I then told her to come to my room. I was so happy. We started to chat. At various times my attention drifted to a mountain I would see. I was looking at everything. Then a porter came to prepare the bed, and my cousin went to her room to sleep. And then John came and told me to lie down and

---

27. C-B 441, box 6, folder 5, TBL.

(left) María Amparo Ruiz de Burton, portrait ca. 1874–1886
Courtesy of the California Judicial Center Library. PC 002.

(right) Henry S. Burton, husband of María Amparo Ruiz
*Reproduced by permission of the Huntington Library, San Marino,
California. Helen Long Collection of Moreno Documents, box 29.*

sleep and not to be scared. They gave me a small room, for me, all by myself. A short while later everyone was asleep. I undressed and put on my nightgown. It seemed impossible to me that I, too, was going to be able to sleep. I prayed and asked the Virgin to help me fall asleep. I couldn't sleep. The train didn't stop moving and swaying from side to side, making lots of noise and going fast. I finally fell asleep. Then the screeching of the railroad cars reminded me where I was, so I started to get dressed. I was already up when John arrived to tell me to get up so I could see the Sierra Nevada. It was such a beautiful landscape. I didn't get tired of constantly looking at the different hills, mountains, valleys, and water ditches made by the miners. The land had been excavated to make way for the carts to transport the gold.

When we arrived at the top of the Sierra at a place called Alta,
John told me, "This is the highest spot. Now we are going to begin
to descend the Sierra Nevada." And the train started to travel faster,
faster, faster, and faster, and even faster in the afternoon. John told
me we still needed to cross the highest mountain range, which was
called Rocky Mountain,[28] or the mountain of the rocks. It was getting dark, and everyone went to bed and the train kept moving and
moving and moving faster. We had very good food: roasted chicken,
a great many desserts, cherries and oranges, and anything else one
could wish for. As I was trying to remember everything, it seemed
as if I were in an enchanted world. I would close my eyes, and it
would seem as if some good angels were carrying me. The train
was moving so fast it appeared to be flying. I didn't tire of giving
thanks to God, to you, and to John for having made this trip possible for me. . . . . . so beautiful, so pleasurable, and so grand for me.
It seemed that my heart was bursting from my chest because of the
happiness I experienced when I would look at the mountains, the
hills, and the various places. We traveled four days and four nights
through a very ugly and desolate terrain. There was a lot of water
all around; small, dried grasses that could grow to the size of one
foot; and some small bushes that could barely grow. The ground
was the color of ashes, and different colors, too. The water from
all the rivers moves everything around, and it seems like someone
is stirring it up. It looks so dirty. There is water in abundance all
around. The rivers are not like those in Sonoma, Napa, and Sacramento. They come down from the large mountains filled with
water up to the level of the ground. Some of the lakes look like seas
(filled with boats, docks, the same as in San Francisco). I wasn't
able to see very well because the train was moving fast. When we
arrived at the river we changed cars there. We traveled by the area
where the Mormons live. On one side there is a very large mountain
range and on the other side a salt lake. In the middle there is a very
pretty town. It is a new town. Every so often, we would arrive at a

---

28. She spells it "Roquimauntin."

new town. The next day we began to climb the highest mountain range. When we were at the very top of the mountain range, my ears began to pop. I never tired of looking at the mountain peaks, so high and covered with snow. The rocks piled on top of other rocks looked like houses. I never tired of admiring God's splendor and the daring of the Americans. I can't find the words nor do I have the talent to describe how the Americans constructed this route and how God has made sure that it is safe . . . which is why the trains can cross such high bridges. They place some rocks and some poles together, and the cars run across them. Sometimes the car goes into a dark space; sometimes it seems like the car is flying in the air across the mountainside. Many parts of the route are covered with roofs to keep the snow from falling on the tracks and covering them. The more we traveled along, the more beautiful the countryside appeared to me. The rivers seemed bigger and mountains could be spotted from all directions as we were traveling down the mountain range, or the Rocky Mountains, all day long. Later, we ate dinner and went to bed. The train ran all night long. At dawn, we were on a plain that was so large you couldn't see where it ended. The train ran all day, and every so often we would pass by bridges, towns, mountains, land planted with corn, twenty or thirty railroad cars filled with firewood, coal, sheep, people, rocks, soil, iron, poles, planks, ice, sacks, large boxes, and I don't know what else because the cars are closed up like little houses. Some are like small corrals. They are different based on what they are used for. When we arrived at a city that is next to a river, which is called Omaha, we crossed over in a very large steamship and took on other cars. We traveled all day. I never tired of looking at the mountains, rivers, lakes, towns, and railroad cars. I thought the country that belongs to the Americans was very pretty. When we went on a bridge over the very large Mississippi River, I kept saying "Oh, oh, oh, how beautiful, what majesty, oh, God!" John took me by the hand, and we went out and stood to the side of the door of the railroad car. Then Mister Charles came, and he took me by the other arm. When we were about to cross the bridge, it was open because a boat was going to pass through. After the boat went by, the bridge closed, and then we crossed over. Just imagine how I must have been feeling! I couldn't say anything else except, "Sir, oh, how majestic, how beautiful, such a large river, I wonder how they made this bridge." Oh, I asked John thousands of questions. We had already traveled very far and I was trying to remember everything. I will never forget it. I thought about the boys[29] a lot. If you see any of them, tell them that I saw their rivers, mountains, valleys covered in green grass, and many, many trees and hills. When we arrived in Chicago, I thought the lake was very pretty, as well as the homes, the iron roadways, the ships, the people. Oh, so many things! The train then entered a very large house that was filled with trains pulling six or seven cars. All the cars inside the roundhouse were filled with people. Everybody was talking; some were going in, and others were leaving. We picked up our small suitcases and John said to me, "Follow me, Mother. I am going to introduce you to a gentleman." He told me that the man was an acquaintance of yours. He warmly welcomed us. He wanted me to stay with him so that he could take me to spend time with his wife. John told him that we didn't have time. He then took us to the car, the prettiest one of all. He gave me the main room in the car. We arrived at a town and stayed there. A short time later, John arrived in a buggy and took me to see Niagara Falls. It is very pretty but it didn't impress me that much. We crossed over the bridge and went to the country of Queen Victoria. I didn't like it very much because the houses are on the edge of a cliff. Then we went up on the train. We traveled all night. We passed through Syracuse at night. The next day, we arrived in Albany at seven o'clock in the morning. We were with Fannie and all her little children, hugging them and kissing them. They are all fine. I also am fine. Thanks be to God. Give my best to my children, relatives, friends, and countrymen, and take good care of yourself. Goodbye until the next time.

Benicia de Vallejo

---

29. She uses the English word "boys" in the original letter.

L. Montis
Sonoma
June 10, 1870[30]

Francisca,

I congratulate you on having arrived well and happy in Albany, where you found your daughter and grandchildren also well. Believe me, I am jealous of the pleasure all of you must have had upon seeing one another in a strange country so far from California, from which you never had left before. I can guess and imagine how you must have felt from the moment you left Sacramento, went up and down the Sierra Nevada, the immense plains up to Chicago, the speed of the trip and the sound of <u>tatatán, tatatán, tatatán, tatatán, tatatán</u>, day and night, that I told you about, the new and grand cities that you will have seen, etc.

All of this is miraculous, and you should be mindful of that. You should also consider that John's personal manner is nice and elegant, he is always good to our daughter, and he is good to us. This brings to mind the times when I have told you that not all men are alike, neither physically nor in terms of their sentiments or manner. There are some who are simply men and nothing else. And there are others who by their personal manner attract the will of the people, and they even are allowed to hide some of their faults. John is good and we should be proud of him.

I told Fannie in a letter what happened with Lulú and María, who suffered when you left California. They, as well as Andrónico, Adela, Natalia, Jovita, Platón, Ula, and Napoleón are fine, as am I. We all send you our regards.

Don't get sick. Give Fannie and her children a kiss and always believe that I am your

M. G. Vallejo

---

30. C-D 441, box 1, folder 6, TBL.

✳ 1873

Frisbie's financial situation improved in the early 1870s, as the Vallejo Savings and Commercial Bank he had founded prospered in the mining stocks speculation of the early 1870s. Frisbie was able to move his family from New York back to the town of Vallejo, where he was able to purchase a larger two-story house for them. He became a leading social figure in Vallejo and was able to entertain lavishly. Francisca, however, maintained that the financial success Frisbie was experiencing was due to the fact that her own family had been generous to him for decades. She was highly irritated that he was not repaying that generosity in a way she believed was commensurate with what the Vallejo family had given him. She poured out her feelings to him in a letter that she shared with her own children in 1873. In the end, her husband persuaded her not to send the letter.

August 26, 1873
Sonoma[31]

Señor Don Juan,

I pick up the pen, with pain in my heart and soul, but the great need I have to express myself is what has motivated me to write, even if my handwriting is poor. This letter is on behalf of all my children, the poor dears. If I am unable to help them in some way or another, it is not my fault, and I don't want them to think that I am petty or miserable. Today, August 26, 1873, we don't have any meat or bread in this house, nor even one cent with which to buy anything. For meals I have had to make do with beef tripe, which Don Salvador Vallejo picked up somewhere. For many days we have been eating beef and lamb tripe because we don't have any money to buy meat. Everything else is bought on credit at a store where we already owe about 350 pesos.

---

31. BANC MSS 76/79c, box 1, folder 19, TBL.

I am the cook. I am so hot. I suffer greatly. I have to wash the pots and the dishes two or three times a day. I don't have a cook. I have to wash all the clothes, and Lulú and María do the ironing, sweeping, and cleaning of the house. I don't even have a servant who can help me. I am everybody's servant. When a person is not used to that type of work, it becomes very burdensome. It is impossible for a woman of my age to be strapped to a washboard three or four days a week, and then, tired from that activity, go to the kitchen with hands that are sore and injured from doing the wash. And there, in the kitchen, her hands get cut or burned, and her feet get swollen from standing for so long. I am not going to mention every ache and pain or how much I am suffering because I would never finish.

I now must ask you, John, Why is there so much penny-pinching for me and for my children? Why are you letting us die from hunger? If it were not for the fruits and vegetables, I don't know what would have become of us. Luisa, María, and I need shoes. Where will we obtain them? We need a number of things. How will we get them? From whom can we get them? The General is ill. Uladislao and Napoleón are so poor that the little they earn isn't enough for the two of them. The General gives me so little money that there isn't even enough to buy soap. Why, Señor Don Juan Frisbie, why am I asking you about this? Are you not the one to whom a very large amount of property was turned over? Didn't General Vallejo himself hand over some property to you without keeping a record of what you were doing, what you did, or what you are doing now? You do whatever you feel like doing when it comes to General Vallejo. Isn't it true that you are doing whatever you want to Guadalupe? Remember: Everybody knows that everything you have belongs to General Vallejo and his heirs, it doesn't belong to you. Isn't it true that you are still selling the lands and everything else, passing it all on to others, and hiding the property from the General and from me? I have seen with my own eyes, and I have heard with my own ears what the General said to me, which was that he was going to hand over everything to Captain Frisbie. He said that he wasn't familiar with American laws and that he couldn't manage his property. However, he thought that Captain Frisbie was a very good man and a man of honor, and he would know how to manage everything well. And, he was our daughter Fannie's husband. The General told me so many things that I, too, thought this would be a good idea. Don't you remember when you came to Sonoma as a huckster, and General Vallejo bought you a blue blanket and a number of other items, and he lent you a room where you could put your belongings? Isn't it true that those were the only things you had in your possession? Do you remember?

Well, I certainly do remember. Do you remember when you started in Benicia? So many cattle, so many horses, so many people working. . . . You were the one in charge, you were the administrator, do you remember how much money you saved? Do you remember? I certainly do remember! Do you remember when you were going bankrupt and General Vallejo helped you out by giving you more property? I certainly do remember. And, I will remember for the rest of my life. . . . . . what a warm welcome you have given my family, how well you treat Andrónico, the way in which you help Platón, how well employed Ula is because of you, what a great reputation you gave Napoleón. Instead of giving these things to all of them, you took all of it away from them. You sold what Platón had . . . cattle, horses, a small house, some plots of land that his father had given him. You said that the other members of the family are good for nothing, they can't be trusted with anything, they are lazy, they don't know how to cope when they are given a job to do, they are passive, they sleep too much, they are very arrogant, they are always going for a stroll, they are indolent, they are spendthrifts, they are not worth anything, they barely have any talent, and they are of no use to anybody. The bad reports you were giving to the General about his children caused him to become angry with them. How many times have I had to defend them? How many times has the General wanted to throw them out of the house because you have said that my children are worthless? How many times have you found fault with my children and shared that with other people? When the General placed all the property in your hands, the children were very young. You were in a hurry to exchange the property the General gave you by selling it and buying something more to your liking. You really know how to grab what doesn't belong to you! Do you think that nobody is aware of this? Well, you are fooling yourself! We are all watching what you are doing. I can't put up with it any longer. I am suffering greatly from poverty and penny-pinching. I can never leave the house because I don't have one cent to my name. Nobody knows how much I am suffering or about the things I don't have. I feel worse for the General than I do for myself. He is always ill and doesn't know how to work. He is very frail. Why do you think we put up with you and the General lets you do what you do? It is because you are married to our daughter Fannie, and because of her little children. Do you remember when you told me that you had planted a tree and that the tree was in bloom? Then you told me that the tree had fruit, and the business was going well, and as soon as the fruit ripened, we would have enough to live on? What happened to the tree? It probably froze. Ice probably fell on it. The fruit is probably frozen. But even though the fruit may be frozen, you should be more grateful. You should remember how generous Guadalupe was with you when you were poor. He gave you a lot of money and a lot of property, and he gave you my daughter Fannie. And how have you repaid him? By making Fannie believe you are taking care of us, giving us alms as an act of charity; that everything you give to the General, to me, and to my children is done out of goodness, charity, generosity, and is given freely. You are just putting on airs by making Fannie and everyone else believe you are providing for us. You might make Fannie believe that, but the rest of the world, no! no! no! Do you remember when Fannie said that I was the biggest squatter, as you have led her to believe? That you told her everything she has belongs to you? She thought I was going to take it all away from her. Whenever you have the opportunity to speak about us, you say very bad things in front of other people, in front of the servants, even in front of your little girls. When they set the table, they say that their Papá gave their Grandpapá the rugs, that if it were not for their Papá, Grandmamá's house would not have any rugs . . . and other such comments, which are irritating and tiresome. They say that their Papá paid for Lulú and María's schooling, and that their Papá had to support a very large family. Who has told those children so many lies? You and Fannie! Why haven't you told them the truth, which is just the opposite? You have taken control of our property, and that is why you have enough money to pay for the girls' schooling and your rugs, as well as the trips you are always taking to New York and around the world, traveling with your family and spending <u>enormous</u> amounts of money so that people will say you are very rich. And then you come and take away the small amount of rent you had given to us, a paltry sum you would give to General Vallejo. How is it possible that you are so jesuitical?

Enough talking on my part. General Vallejo is very ill these days. I am very tired and very old, and soon we both will die. That is what you want! But, before that happens, <u>I</u> want to know how much property you have. I want it all laid out, everything, no <u>secrets</u> and nothing hidden! Then, when we know about everything; that is, when we are aware of everything we have, what is fair and what is ours . . . with nothing being hidden . . . what belongs to the General, to me, and to my children . . . when everything has been settled, then I want you to send me, on a monthly basis, an amount of money that is fair and that is mine by law. You do remember that this was General Vallejo's intention when he placed such a large amount of property in your hands. He didn't do that so you could keep it all for yourself. He turned the property over to you so that you could manage it well. That way, we would have enough to live on and to educate my children without having to ask for favors. I don't want to wait any longer. If General Vallejo wants to continue to allow you to manage the property as you have done for more than twenty years, I want to know everything! The first thing that needs to be done is to eliminate all secrecy, nothing is to be hidden. General Vallejo's property shouldn't be hidden from anybody—not from me, not from the public, and not from my children. General Vallejo's property shouldn't be hidden from anybody, and least of all from those of us who are his heirs. General Vallejo hasn't stolen anything from anybody. Everything he turned over to you, and even much more land, had been given to him by the Mexican government. However, he refused to take more land for himself. He gave it to those who came to populate the area on this side of San Francisco Bay. Don't you remember that? We had so much property when you came. Everything you saw, managed, and still manage was not stolen. The government steals first and then men do . . . one of those men was General Frémont . . . and then you. Do you remember when you didn't know where to keep the gold? Do you remember that you put the gold in one or two suitcases, then you took the suitcases full of gold to San Francisco? And then . . . you kept secret what you did with the money. And then you would say that you had gone bankrupt. No! no! no! It isn't possible to go bankrupt so many times, but you knew where you could get hold of more money. Even though you kept falling, you always had the means to pick yourself up again. The General would believe you and everything was done. I very much want to speak with you after you have received this letter.

I started writing this letter during the month of August, and as of today, October 8, I still haven't finished it. I write so poorly and so slowly that everyone who read this letter forgave me for that. In the end, I am happy that I said something. I know full well that nobody is going to listen to me. Everything written in this letter is the absolute truth.

Adela: I was writing this letter to John Frisbie, but your Papá didn't allow me to send it to him because he said that John would get mad, that he wasn't well, and that there are countless other considerations and issues [the General] has with him. However, he doesn't seem to have any issues with those of us who are suffering. I have a general awareness of what is going on and I am the one who has nothing. That is why I have mentioned everything that I remember and everything that I have witnessed. John is already rich and we are poor. He was given the property so that he could

Patio of the Hotel Iturbide, Mexico City. *Vistas Mexicanas, 175.*
Courtesy of DeGolyer Library, Southern Methodist University. Ag1985.0372.

manage it well. Yes, he did manage it well, but he did it for himself and he left us poor . . . poor . . . poor . . . old, and sick. Yet, we still have the obligations of supporting and educating two daughters. And it's fine if he casts us, the old people, to one side, because we have benefited greatly from that "so and so" John.

Francisca María Felipa Benicia Carrillo de Vallejo

October 27, 1873

Sonoma
October 27, 1873

[P.S.] I finished writing this letter at 10 o'clock tonight, so that everyone can read it, but I have to obey your Papá. If I were an American woman, they wouldn't treat me like that, but I am a Spanish woman and that is why they do what they do.

1877

In the spring of 1877, Guadalupe accompanied Frisbie on a trip to Mexico City. His impressions of that country and its capital were complicated. He admired much of the colonial architecture he encountered yet was repelled by some of the unhealthy and unsanitary conditions he encountered in Mexico City, conditions he often blamed on its Indigenous population. On his return trip, Guadalupe sailed from Veracruz to New Orleans then traveled by rail to Syracuse, where he was able to visit his daughter Adela, whose own daughter had just married Dennis McCarthy, a Frisbie family friend. During his journeys from Mexico City to Syracuse, he often commented on his impressions of Mexico City.

Hotel Iturbide, No. 75
May 28, 1877[32]

Francisca,

Last night, Sunday, I arrived in this city, tired and quite battered about after traveling on land and water for eighteen days, but I am well and healthy. The crossing from New Orleans to Veracruz took seven days and the heat was excessive. Veracruz is a very beautiful city, but it was extremely hot, which caused me to suffer greatly. Yesterday we left for Mexico City and traveled by train for three hundred miles through the most picturesque mountains in the world. The train from Veracruz to Mexico City is truly stupendous because of its construction and the route it follows. It is truly something miraculous. I have to write quickly because the mail is leaving very soon. Give my many regards to Lulú, María, Doña Carmelita, and Natalia. I will write a longer letter next time.

M. G. Vallejo

32. C-B 441, box 1, folder 8, TBL.

Hotel Iturbide
June 7, 1877[33]

Francisca,

I am finally in the capital of the Mexican Republic, our former native land. We arrived on May 27, so I have been here for eleven days.

The first impression I had of this place made me feel that it was a bad omen. It produced a sadness in me, and a sense of melancholy took hold of my whole being. It wasn't until today that I was able to conquer it by a supreme effort and <u>necessary</u> determination, since the situation doesn't lend itself to any other alternative.

The general aspect of the city, having been within it, seems sad to me. Add to that its inhabitants on the streets and it seems sinister. There is no similarity between our habits and customs in California. The contrast is greater than one can imagine. I am surprised and it pains me.

I was very sick during the first six days. Besides the difficulties of the trip and all of the noise, one can't breathe the air here. It chokes you. The polluted air is truly unbearable. In addition, the sight of thousands upon thousands of Indian men and women carrying their children on their backs in a state of decrepitude, in rags and tatters, thousands upon thousands of donkeys carrying grasses and clay pots that get in one's way on the streets, and others carrying coal, is such a miserable sight.

On the other hand, the cathedral and the sanctuary are truly stupendous and grandiose works of architecture. The ornate decor inside is astonishing. On the outside the construction is sumptuous and imposing. Both the inside and the outside are testaments to the men who founded them. However, it makes one feel pity, sadness, and a sense of compassion to see so many people scattered about on the glazed floor tiles amidst the immense naves, massive

---

33. C-B 441, box 1, folder 8, TBL.

Cathedral of Mexico City, 1880, by William Henry Jackson
Courtesy of the Library of Congress. LOT 3160.

columns, and opulent altars. Seeing people seated on the floor here and there as they listen to Mass <u>contrasts</u> with the glorious music, so stupendous that it enraptures and is an ecstasy worthy of another civilization.

There is so much good here, but also so many bad things that I can't describe now.

Tell Carmelita that I have looked everywhere for her husband, and I can't find a trace of him, but I will continue doing everything possible.

I think a lot about you, Lulú, and María. When I think about Jovita I feel a deep sadness in my heart. Poor thing, whenever I have dreams about her, I dream that she is unhappy.

Today I am going to visit the president.

My eyesight is bad, and I can't write any more.

Goodbye, Francisca. Give my best to our children, to Doña Carmelita and Ricardo, and also to the Italians.

Your husband,

M. G. Vallejo

[P.S.] Everything here seems warlike. There are troops everywhere; thousands of armed men inundate the streets and plazas.

Hotel Iturbide, No. 75
Mexico
July 30, 1877[34]

Francisca,

The steamer *City of Mexico* arrived at Veracruz yesterday. We are planning to leave on it today if the men from the government resolve the business we have pending before the ministries regarding the railroads. If the decision is favorable, it is probable that we will stay here another twenty days to get it all settled properly. But if it is not favorable, we will leave on this steamer and head straight to Washington, and from there to California. I pray to God that it will be resolved soon, for a thousand reasons. The first is that I can't have peace of mind being away from the family. And the second is because in this land one can't live with any sense of security. The entire country is in an uproar. It is a diabolical labyrinth, a frightful "pandemonium" with no hope of salvation. The society is horribly corrupt down to its very foundations. What a pitiful country, yet so rich and so beautiful!

The population of Mexico City is 300,000 inhabitants, but <u>250,000 are full-blooded Indians</u> and they wander around the streets as if they were on their rancherias. Some are naked and

---

34. C-B 441, box 1, folder 8, TBL.

others are half dressed. Think of them as if they were the likenesses of Isidora and Bill, and Vicente and Jesusa.

It is eight o'clock in the morning and General Vega is coming into my room with another general by the name of Ballesteros, along with General Palomares. This situation will keep me from writing at greater length. General Vega is fine and sends affectionate greetings to the whole family.

I have asked him frequently about Domínguez, Carmelita's husband, and he tells me that it has been many years since he has heard anything about him, despite the fact that he has tried to find out something. He believes he was killed in a battle near Guadalajara.

Give many, many greetings to the whole family, to Carmelita and Ricardo, and also to the Italians.

Doña Carolina is sending some little Mexican souvenirs to you. I am bringing them. She is sending a rebozo to Jovita.

Frisbie already knows how to speak Spanish, even though it is a bit jumbled.

Goodbye. I send to you and the girls the affection of your husband.

M. G. Vallejo

Hotel Iturbide
August 30, 1877[35]

Francisca,

The steamer on which we were supposed to leave for the United States at the end of July sank before arriving at Veracruz, so we have had to wait another twenty days. There was no other way to leave Mexico. This city really is one which you "get out if you can." This country is so very backward in terms of its roads or its means of communication with the world.

It makes me sad, and I am very embarrassed to tell everyone that this entire country is ripe for conquest. The few white people who

_____
35. C-B 441, box 1, folder 8, TBL.

are here are subject to the control of the immense multitude of Indians, as well as to <u>others</u> who are half black and are at the head of public affairs. They mistrust all white foreigners who come here because they think that when the white race becomes the majority, they will no longer have a place in society. As soon as they hear the word "emigration" they start to tremble, as if they had been electrified by fear or anger. But they will not be able to stop the hand of fate. It is necessary for other people to come and conquer them.

Mexico City has 300,000 inhabitants, and of that number 260,000 are Indians who infest the streets, half naked. Some are completely naked, and others wear ragged clothing and no shoes. They are loaded down with coal, mats, and pots. The Indian women sell tortillas and all types of food, leading one child by the hand while holding another child who is nursing. There are many good things in this city just waiting for another type of people to come and give it new life. It is necessary for at least five million white families to emigrate to this country.

This country has many elements of prosperity and wealth, but they can't be exploited today. Even though the lands are very fertile, agriculture is in its infancy, and the Mexicans don't have the means to export products to other countries of the world. The mines are very rich, more so than those in California. Even though some of the mines are being worked, their exploitation is held back due to the instability caused by continuous revolutions.

When I go out on the street, I become acutely aware of the stench caused by so much filth and misery, and so many Indians. I have so many things to tell you when I return, God willing. I think you will be shocked when you hear what I have to say. I don't want to tell you about it in a letter.

I have only seen one sewing machine in the dressmakers' shops. The seamstresses sew by hand, seated on very low benches, and so do the men in the tailor shops. Some of them are more bent over than Don Pepe.

I have thought about Carmelita a lot when I have seen the poor women sewing without machines. I asked them why, and they told

Cargadores, 1880.
Mexican street scenes by William Henry Jackson.
Courtesy of the Library of Congress. LC-D418-8559 *and* LC-D418-8556.

me that "machines are not allowed because they would take work away from the poor people." They don't use, and I haven't seen, <u>one single broom</u> with a handle to use for sweeping. And they give the same reason: it is because the Indians would stop earning money from the sale of their straw and cane brushes. Everything here was made or built by the old Spaniards. There is nothing from <u>our</u> contemporaries.

Adela and Jovita have written to me and it pleases me to see their letters. Fani has not written to me, nor has Andrónico. Fani must think that because she is now a grandmother, this releases her from her duties as a daughter, but it doesn't. She hasn't written to her husband either. There have been times when John has felt very sad. Even though she may act this way out of pride, she is no better than her father (by a long shot)[36] nor her husband, who has always treated her well. Jovita is suffering, but the world is an evil place and it is necessary to suffer in order to be reborn. She should be and she deserves to be happy. Arpad wrote me a very flattering letter. I haven't answered him yet. I can't forget how he treated Jovita.

In Veracruz yellow fever is destroying the population. Thirty to forty people die every day; therefore, I am afraid of that disease.

The mail is about to leave, and I don't have any time to write more. This letter is going on an English boat. The train is already leaving and I am taking my letter to the American minister.

General Vega just came into my room. He sends greetings to you and to the whole family.

Give my regards to everyone.

Your,

M. G. Vallejo

---

36. "By a long shot" is in English and in parentheses in the original letter.

Mexico
September 26, 1877[37]

Francisca,

The attached letter will inform you about the situation in the city and port of Veracruz. We were supposed to leave for California from this port. The outbreak of yellow fever is devastating the population, and even the passengers who are <u>only</u> transferring from the boat to the train are dying. Frisbie wants to leave, but I have refused. Now that the disease is worse than ever, he has told me that we must leave. That is why I wrote him the attached letter. I would rather go by land to Acapulco and from there travel to La Paz to see if I can settle <u>something</u> regarding the issue related to Margarita, but not with her, rather with her parents.

Give my regards to Lulú, María, Natalia, and Atila and family.
Believe me that I am always your

M. G. Vallejo

[P.S.] Don't forget to give my regards to Doña Carmelita.

The following letter was written on stationery with the letterhead of the Consulate General of the United States of America.

Mexico City
October 17, 1877[38]

Francisca,

I will leave for California via Syracuse on the first steamer that arrives in Veracruz. There is no longer any yellow fever. Frisbie went on ahead, "risking his neck," but he arrived safely, thank God.

---

37. C-B 441, box 1, folder 9, TBL.
38. C-B 441, box 1, folder 8, TBL.

He was determined and very much needed to be in Washington during these days. That is why he left.

Give my many regards to everyone, Lulú, María, Carmelita, Natalia and family, and Atila. Send them also to Fannie and family, Platón and family, Andrónico, Jovita and children, Ula, and Napoleón and his wife.

When I left Vallejo, I weighed 231 pounds. I weighed myself four days ago in Cuernavaca and I weighed 191 pounds. 231 − 191 = 40.

I have shrunk from not eating, or rather from eating poorly. I am so skinny I can barely walk, but I am handling it because it would be crazy to die among these people.

Your husband,
M. G. Vallejo

Syracuse
November 24, 1877[39]

Francisca,

Yesterday I arrived in this city, and I met up with Adela, which gave me immense pleasure. I also saw Adelita, who is married to a young man named McCarly.[40] He seems like a very nice fellow. According to what everybody says, he has a very good character and fine manners. May God bless them, and may they be happy.

Today marks nine days since I left Mexico City, traveling on the ocean and on the continent by way of New Orleans, day and night, without resting for a single moment. But I am here now, and I am just waiting for John to return from Washington so that I can then return to California as soon as possible.

I am beginning to regain my health. In Mexico I lost forty-one pounds and I was very sick the entire time, but I never wanted to tell you. Thank God that I left that country! It kept me physically and

---

39. C-B 441, box 1, folder 8, TBL.
40. This is apparently how Vallejo heard the name McCarthy.

morally ill. My tongue is tired from so much talking and at times scolding many people whose opinions are so different than mine.

I am writing from the house of Adelita's husband. Adela is also writing to the doctor at this very moment. All three of us send you and the girls our greetings.

Goodbye until next week or a bit later. Give my regards to Natalia, Atila, and family.

M. G. Vallejo

Syracuse
December 8, 1877[41]

Francisca,

Today, Saturday, we were supposed to have left for California, but John has not yet returned from Washington. Lynch told me last night that he would be coming tomorrow, Sunday. Therefore, we won't be leaving until next week—that is, if there is no obstacle to get in the way of our trip.

It is freezing cold here. Everything is covered with snow, but the house where I am a guest belongs to Adela's son-in-law, Adelita's husband, and he as much as the others (of course)[42] take excellent and loving care of me. Of course, the heaters that are used in the winter keep the house at a good temperature from top to bottom.

Adela has just told me that she received, at this very moment, a letter from Lulú in which she tells her, among other things, that everyone at home is fine.

It is possible that we will travel together to California, but I can't say so for sure since Adela is waiting for letters from the doctor.

I have so much to say about things in Mexico that the ideas don't all fit in my head. It feels like my brain is melting or my skull is exploding from thinking so much about that unfortunate country.

---

41. C-B 441, box 1, folder 9, TBL.
42. In English and in parentheses in the original letter.

Fannie Vallejo Frisbie
Courtesy of California State Parks,
Sonoma Barracks. No. 243-x-3074.N.

So many illusions dispelled! And to think that none of this can be remedied by the Mexicans themselves is a great loss. It is necessary for a new civilization to pull them along or make them disappear.

Goodbye. Give my regards to everyone.

M. G. V.

※ 1878

Fairly soon after he and Guadalupe returned to California, Frisbie decided to move his family to Mexico. The move happened in stages, with Fannie and her daughter leaving California toward the end of March to meet Frisbie in Chicago, so that they all could travel to Mexico together. In a letter to Francisca, Guadalupe described in great detail the emotional farewell. At the same time, he and his youngest daughter, María, were busy translating documents for his hoped-for presidio lawsuit. María was engaged to James Harry Cutter, son of a locally prominent San Francisco public official. Guadalupe could not help but contrast Fannie's behavior with the looser adherence to traditional social norms exhibited by María and her fiancé, Cutter.

Thursday
Palace Hotel
San Francisco
March 21, 1878[43]

Francisca,

Fannie and her daughter little Fannie left this morning to meet up with Frisbie in Chicago and from there to leave for New Orleans on their way to Mexico. We were together in their rooms last night until one o'clock in the morning, and many relatives from both sides, as well as many friends and acquaintances, came to say goodbye to them.

When the moment came for Fannie to leave, she could not control herself, and she threw herself into my arms, screaming and crying, thinking of nothing else but her mother and her father. She was screaming like a woman in despair: "Papá, Papá, I will never see you again, nor mother either. Ay! Papacito, I am going to Mexico . . . I will never see both of you again!!!" She was out of control, crying and screaming, so much so that it was necessary to close the doors of the rooms.

In the midst of her expressions of sorrow, she asked me to give you her regards and commend her to God. In the end, it was a very tender scene in the presence of the entire family and other people, who also were crying.

This morning, we all went to accompany them to Oakland where, as the train was pulling away, the scene from last night was repeated. They finally left and we lost sight of them.

Today, at eight o'clock in the evening, I received a telegram from the summit of the Sierra Nevada, and Siqueira tells me that they are fine and send their greetings to everyone.

I think María and Lulú will leave here on Saturday, and it is possible that Doña Carmelita will also leave.

---

43. C-B 441, box 1, folder 9, TBL.

It is good that you have received the "check"[44] for $100. Don't forget that I want to be able at least to pay the hotel bill. María's stay here has doubled the amount of our expenses and, believe me, I can't find a solution to this.

I received the $40 you sent me, and I still have the money in my pocket to pay the hotel.

Jovita continues to be about the same. She seems very depressed. I find this to be very sad because she will be giving birth soon, and she says that Arpad is behaving himself, even though it causes her embarrassment to say so.

María and the young man Cutter have angered me. They are silly and imprudent and believe they <u>already</u> can do whatever they want to do in my presence. I truly do not think the same way they do. <u>Others have already gone out to hunt and they have not gotten married</u>. "There is many a slip between the cup and the lip."

Goodbye,

Your,

M. G. Vallejo

 1881

Francisca also discovered that the new order of things was passing her by in ways that she found deeply painful. In the early 1880s Archbishop Alemany decided that, given the increasingly decrepit state of the old mission, Sonoma needed a new church. He decided to sell the mission. Francisca was heartbroken, since her mother and six of her children who had died very young were buried there and would have to be moved to the family cemetery outside Lachryma Montis. She reflected that this was just one more of the many sufferings that she and Guadalupe were forced to endure. Their children, she told him, did not know everything that had happened to them. And, she added in what was most likely a veiled reference to Guadalupe's daughter Prudenciana, she did not know everything that "happened to you in the past."

---

44. "Check" is in English in the original letter.

(*left*) María Vallejo Cutter and (*right*) James H. Cutter.
*Courtesy of the Autry Museum of the American West,
Los Angeles, California. 2002.1.7.17 and 2002.1.3.16.*

San Francisco
December 29, 1881[45]

Guadalupe,

I received your little letter dated the 25th, in which you bring up such important and sad memories, which have no remedy. This broke my <u>heart</u> and I started to cry, but then I started thinking that "if there is no remedy to be had, then it is better to just forget," even if one doesn't want to, because if we don't forget, we will die of sheer sadness. Nobody knows the things that have happened as you and I do. Our children don't even know, nor do I know what happened to you in the past.

---

45. C-B 441, box 6, folder 5, TBL.

If my Mamá and my brother Juan were here, I wouldn't feel so sad. But this business of having to move the dead is terrible. May God give us strength and courage to do it. My poor Mamá, she was such a good Catholic. Do you remember that she always went to sweep the church, and that she herself begged Father Quijas to bury her next to the Holy Water? And now we have to remove her from there. It is a disgrace, it is fate. It seems that the priests are intentionally doing this. They are always looking for ways to hurt you, and it is all because we are poor. They no longer have any interest in you. These priests have no feelings, they have no heart. Even though you did favors for them when you were rich, now that you are poor they don't know who you are. And, besides, they are taking away what you have. They are scoundrels. For them, the church is a store, a butcher shop, and a bakery. Yet, even that is better, because if things aren't being run properly, the police will handle it.

These priests do whatever they want, and they do it with hypocrisy, sanctity, and lies. There are no police here who watch over things. There are so many things I want to say against the priests! But what do I gain by doing so? <u>Nothing. A person could inform the bishop. What a bishop!! He is worse than all the priests put together. He has a withered-up heart that is dry, dry</u>. No! no! no! That man doesn't know anything about a mother's love. He knows nothing. The woman who gave birth to him was one of those women who take water to the priest's house, and she gave birth to him there. In the darkness of the night, the baby was then taken to a convent. When they arrived at the convent, an old priest opened the door. He received the baby, took him to a small, dark room, and left him there until the next day. At nine or ten o'clock the next morning the extremely old priest remembered that he had left the boy there. He saw that the baby was alive, and he rushed out of the room. He picked up a rag and part of an old coat and soaked them in dirty water. He formed the cloth into the shape of a nipple and placed it in the baby's mouth. That is how they fed him. The old priest gave him the name José Alemany. When he was older, he

Mariano Guadalupe Vallejo outdoors at Lachryma Montis, 1885
Courtesy of the Sonoma County Library. Cstr pho 007325.

used to play with skulls and other parts of the dead. They raised him and educated him within the confines of the convent, where he would play at saying short Masses and giving short sermons. He never had a relationship with a woman. He did, however, love an extremely old Irish woman. If some woman had fallen in love with him, she probably was some disgraced nun who was going through life like the wandering Jew. I imagine him as ugly, indecent, and probably old, stuck in the middle of a poisonous tarantula's nest. Don't you imagine him as some sort of clever animal: a panther or a hyena, a hawk or a cat? I can't compare him to a bear or a lion because they aren't that mean. I can only compare him to another priest, but there is nobody as evil as he is.

Yes, he has a withered heart. He has no soul, and he does not possess that all-encompassing, pure, holy, and selfless love. Only a father of a family and a mother like me can appreciate the love of our children and the love of our parents in that way. There are no words to describe this! Only God can.

You will help me rebury my dear Mamá and all our children who died. When they are all together, I will be happy. Goodbye.

Benicia de Vallejo

✳ 1890–1891

Guadalupe and Francisca passed away a year apart, on January 18, 1890, and January 30, 1891, respectively. During their final hours, they were both attended by many of their children and grandchildren.[46] Their funerals occurred at the new church that replaced the mission, which was at the time being used as a warehouse for a store across the street. Guadalupe and Francisca were buried side by side at Mountain Cemetery, not far from Lachryma Montis.

---

46. Natalia Vallejo de Haraszthy to Platón Vallejo, June 19, 1890, and January 7, 1891, BANC MSS 76/79c, box 1, folder 15, TBL.

The Vallejo Children

This listing of Guadalupe's and Francisca's children and their spouses, with the addition of Prudenciana López, is intended to help readers understand the references in the correspondence between Guadalupe and Francisca in this chapter. The children are listed in birth order.

Andrónico Vallejo (1833–34) died in infancy.

Prudenciana López (1833–1920) was an out-of-wedlock daughter of Mariano Guadalupe Vallejo and Juana López. She was raised in San Diego by her single mother. Prudenciana married José Matías Moreno (ca. 1817–69) in 1851. Vallejo acknowledged her as his daughter at the urging of María Amparo Ruiz de Burton in 1869.

Andrónico Vallejo (1834–97) spent most of his life as a music teacher in Vallejo.

Epifania (Fannie, Fanita) Vallejo (1835–1905) married John Frisbie (1823–1909) in 1851. They moved to Mexico in 1878, and both Fannie and John died there.

Adela Vallejo (1837–95) married Levi Frisbie (1821–92), brother of John Frisbie, in 1858. Her parents initially opposed the marriage, but eventually gave their approval. Adela and Levi's daughter Francisca Adelaida (Lily) married Dennis McCarthy in Syracuse, New York, in 1878. Lily died in 1881.

Natalia Vallejo (1838–1913) in 1863 married Attila Haraszthy (1835–86) in a double ceremony with her sister Jovita, who married Attila's brother Arpad. After Attila's death, Natalia spent most of her time in Sonoma.

Plutarco Vallejo (1839–41) died in early childhood.

Platón Vallejo (1841–1925) entered medical school at Columbia in New York in 1860 and returned to California in 1864. He worked at Mare Island and with the Pacific Mail Steamship

Company before starting his own medical practice. In 1867 he married LILY WILEY (1852–85). He became very involved with his father's work while Mariano was composing his "Recuerdos" for Bancroft. Platón wrote his own reminiscences in 1914.

GUADALUPE VALLEJO (1843–47) died in early childhood.

JOVITA VALLEJO (1844–78) married ARPAD HARASZTHY (1840–1900) in 1863 in a double ceremony in which her sister Natalia married Arpad's brother Attila. The marriage was a difficult one, and at times Jovita insisted that another member of her family stay at the house when Arpad was there. She died shortly after the birth of her third child. Uncertain about whether her marriage had been officiated by a Catholic priest, Archbishop Alemany of San Francisco refused to allow her burial in a Catholic cemetery until he received formal documentation about the wedding.

ULADISLAO VALLEJO (1845–?) fought in Mexico as a young man for Benito Juárez against Maximilian. He then did odd jobs at various locations in California and Baja California. Through his father's influence, he was appointed tax collector in Sonoma in the 1880s, until in 1887 he absconded with a good amount of the tax money. He eventually ended up in Guatemala, where he married MARÍA ORANTES. The circumstances and date of his death are uncertain.

PLUTARCO VALLEJO (1847–48) died in infancy.

BENICIA VALLEJO (1849–53) died in early childhood.

NAPOLEÓN (NÁPOLES) VALLEJO (1850–1923) attended Santa Clara College, then worked as a railroad agent and telegraph operator. After marrying MARTHA BROWN (1854–1917) in 1875, he worked as a traveling salesman for the Haraszthy family company. He divorced Martha in 1890 and soon afterwards married KATE LEIGH STOKES (1872–1900). After Kate's death, he remarried Martha Brown in 1911.

BENICIA VALLEJO (1853–59) died in early childhood.

LUISA (LUISITA) EUGENIA VALLEJO (1856–1943) married RICARDO DE EMPARÁN (1853–1902), the Mexican consul in San Diego, in 1882. After her parents' deaths, she and her family moved into Lachryma Montis. Luisa was very active in public affairs and was instrumental in having Lachryma Montis designated as a state historical monument in 1933.

MARÍA (MARILLITA) IGNACIA VALLEJO (1857–1932) married JAMES HARRY CUTTER (1854–1925), son of a former San Francisco harbormaster, in 1878. The couple lived in San Francisco, where James worked in a variety of business enterprises.

Biographical Sketches

José Abrego (ca. 1810–78) came to Alta California in 1834 with the Híjar-Padrés colony. He became a merchant in Monterey and held a variety of political offices, including as treasurer of the territory from 1839 to 1846. After the war he continued working as a merchant in Monterey until his death. One of his sons, Abimael, married Adelaida Leese, daughter of Mariano Guadalupe Vallejo's sister Rosalía Vallejo. (Bancroft, *History of California*, 2:686; Northrop, *Spanish-Mexican Families*, 2:1; Hutchinson, "Official List," 410)

Joseph Sadoc Alemany (1814–88) was born in Catalonia, Spain. He entered the Dominican Order and served as a missionary in parts of the United States. He was appointed bishop of Monterey in 1850 and archbishop of San Francisco in 1853. He served in the latter position until he resigned in 1884 and returned to Spain, where he died. (McGloin, *California's First Archbishop*)

Juan Bautista Alvarado (1809–82) was born in Monterey to José Francisco Alvarado and María Josefa Vallejo. His father died shortly after his birth, and his mother then married José

Raymundo Estrada, brother of José Mariano Estrada. Alvarado served as secretary of the Diputación from 1828 to 1834 and was a member of that body for the following three years. He led the revolution against Nicolás Gutiérrez in 1836 and served as governor until 1842. He was also a leader in the movement against Micheltorena in 1844–45. (Bancroft, *History of California*, 2:693–94; Alvarado, *Vignettes*, vii–xiv; Sánchez, "Juan Bautista Alvarado," in *Nineteenth-Century California Testimonios*, 76)

José María Alviso (1807–46) was the son of Juan Ignacio Alviso and María Margarita Bernal. He married María Galindo in 1833, but she died the following year. In 1836 he married Manuela Cantúa. He served first as a soldier at San Francisco, then as a member of the militia at San José. He died a few months after the Bear Flag revolt. (Bancroft, *History of California*, 2:695; Northrop, *Spanish-Mexican Families*, 1:23)

Nicolás Alviso (1792–1834), the son of Francisco Javier Alviso and María Duarte, was born at Monterey. He served as a soldier at the Monterey presidio and participated in several expeditions against Indigenous people in the Central Valley. He was married to Bárbara Butrón. (Bancroft, *History of California*, 2:695; Northrop, *Spanish-Mexican Families*, 1:18)

Francisco Arce (ca. 1822–78) was a native of Baja California. He came to Alta California in 1833 as a youth and received his education in Monterey. He served as clerk and secretary for various government officials in Monterey. During and after the Mexico-U.S. war, he lived in both Baja and Alta California, before finally settling in Alta California. (Bancroft, *History of California*, 2:699–700)

Miguel Gerónimo Archuleta (1779–1822) served in the military in San Francisco and Monterey, where he became a schoolmaster. (Bancroft, *History of California*, 2:700; Northrop, *Spanish-Mexican Families*, 2:12–13)

Luis Antonio Argüello (1784–1830) was born in San Francisco. His father, José Darío Argüello, was then serving with the military at the Santa Bárbara presidio. Luis entered the military at an early age and quickly rose through the ranks. In 1818 he became captain of the garrison at San Francisco. Selected as acting governor in 1822, he held that office until the appointment of José María Echeandía in 1825. After leaving office he filled several military positions and died at San Francisco. (Bancroft, *History of California*, 3:9–13)

Santiago Argüello (1791–1862), younger brother of Luis Antonio Argüello, was born at Monterey. He entered the military at an early age and served at Santa Bárbara from 1806 to 1817 and at San Francisco from 1817 to 1827, before being transferred to San Diego, where he served as commander and as a member of the Diputación. He retired from the military in 1834 and served as alcalde of San Diego in 1836, acting against Alvarado. He was commissioner of Mission San Juan Capistrano from 1838 to 1840 and prefect of Los Angeles from 1840 to 1843. He received several land grants and died in 1862 on his rancho, Tijuana, near the California-Mexico border. His wife was Pilar Ortega. (Bancroft, *History of California*, 2:702)

José Joaquín de Arrillaga (1750–1814) was born at Aya, Guipúzcoa, Spain. Entering the army at an early age, he served in northern Mexico and Texas in the 1780s and 1790s. He was appointed lieutenant governor of the Californias in 1783 and served as interim governor from 1792 to 1794. In 1804, when the governments of Alta and Baja California were separated, he was appointed the first governor of Alta California and served until his death. (Bancroft, *History of California*, 2:204–7)

José de los Reyes Berreyesa (1785–1846) was the son of Nicolás Antonio Berreyesa and María Gertrudis Peralta. In 1805 he married María Zacarías Bernal, who bore thirteen children.

He served as a soldier at San Francisco and, for a brief time, as a teacher in the same location. He also served as secretary of the ayuntamiento at San José. He was killed by Americans during the Bear Flag movement. (Bancroft, *History of California*, 2:718; Northrop, *Spanish-Mexican Families*, 1:73–74)

JOSÉ DE LOS SANTOS BERREYESA (1817–64) was the son of José de los Reyes Berreyesa and María Zacarías Bernal. He joined the military and served as a sergeant at Sonoma. During the Bear Flag revolt in 1846 he was serving as alcalde there. His father was one of three people murdered by the Bear Flaggers on June 28 near San Rafael. (Bancroft, *History of California*, 2:718; Northrop, *Spanish-Mexican Families*, 1:74)

JOHN BIDWELL (1819–1900), born in New York, was one of the leaders of the first North American overland party to California in 1841. He worked for John Sutter for a few years and was tangentially involved in the Bear Flag movement. After the Mexico-U.S. war, he served with Mariano Guadalupe Vallejo in the first session of the California State Senate. He remained in California for the rest of his life. (Gillis and Magliari, *John Bidwell*)

FREDERICK BILLINGS (1823–90), a native of Vermont, arrived in California in 1849. He formed a very successful law partnership with Archibald Peachy and Henry Halleck. After the Civil War he returned to Vermont and became president of the Northern Pacific Railroad. (Winks, *Frederick Billings*)

JUAN BOJORQUES (1811–91) served for many years as a soldier at the San Francisco presidio. He moved to Sonoma in the 1830s, where he served under Mariano Guadalupe Vallejo. (Bancroft, *History of California*, 2:723)

DIEGO DE BORICA (1742–1800) was a Spanish colonel who served as governor of California from 1794 to 1800. He was widely respected and placed great emphasis upon trying to improve educational opportunities in the province. (Bancroft, *History of California*, 2:724)

HIPÓLITO BOUCHARD (ca. 1785–1837) was born in Saint-Tropez, France. By 1811 he was sailing and fighting on behalf of the revolutionaries in the La Plata River region in what is now Argentina. In July 1817 he was given command of the *Argentina* and set out to circumnavigate the globe. By August 1818 he had reached Hawai'i, and from there proceeded to raid the coast of Alta California. On his return to South America, the *Argentina* was used as a transport vessel for San Martín's 1820 expedition to Perú. At the conclusion of the campaign, Bouchard received some land in Perú, where he settled. He died there in January 1837, killed by one of his slaves. (Ratto, *Capitán de Navío*; Uhrowczik, *Burning of Monterey*)

HENRY S. BURTON (1819–69) was born in New York and graduated from West Point in 1839. He served in the Second Seminole War in the early 1840s. As an officer of the New York Volunteers, he served in Baja California during the Mexico-U.S. war. After the peace treaty was signed, he escorted a group of Baja Californians who had supported the American troops to Alta California and married one of them, María Amparo Ruiz, at Monterey in 1849. He later served in the Civil War. (Bancroft, *History of California*, 2:737)

HENRI CAMBUSTON was a native of France who came to Alta California from Mexico in 1841. He was a schoolteacher in Monterey and became involved in a series of quarrels with legal authorities and Prefect José Castro. In 1848 he married Gabriela Soberanes, daughter of José Feliciano Soberanes and María Antonia Rodríguez. He died toward the end of the 1850s. (Bancroft, *History of California*, 2:740; Beebe and Senkewicz, *Testimonios*, 42–45)

José Manuel Cantúa (1814–46) was a soldier in the San Francisco company in the 1830s. He was at Sonoma in 1844 and with Sutter in 1845. He was killed at Olompali. (Bancroft, *History of California*, 2:741)

Carlos Antonio Carrillo (1783–1852), a brother of José Antonio Carrillo, was born at Santa Bárbara. He served in the military at Monterey and Santa Bárbara from 1797 to 1825. In 1828 he served in the Diputación, and he was a delegate to the Mexican Congress from 1831 to 1832. He served again in the Diputación in the mid-1830s. In 1837 he was appointed governor of Alta California, but he was never able to force Alvarado from office. (Bancroft, *History of California*, 2:743)

José Antonio Carrillo (1796–1862), a brother of Carlos Antonio Carrillo, was born in San Francisco. He served in the Diputación from 1822 to 1824, as Echeandía's secretary in 1826, and as Los Angeles alcalde in 1827. He was exiled to Baja California in 1831 following a quarrel with Los Angeles alcalde Vicente Sánchez. From 1831 to 1832 he opposed Governor Victoria and favored Pío Pico. After serving as a delegate to the Mexican Congress, he opposed Alvarado in 1837 and was jailed at Sonoma as a result. He participated in the resistance to the North American invasion in 1846, signed the Treaty of Cahuenga in 1847, and attended the Constitutional Convention in 1849. (Bancroft, *History of California*, 2:745)

Julio Carrillo (1824–99) was a son of Joaquín Víctor Carrillo and María Ignacia López and a younger brother of Francisca Benicia Vallejo. After the American conquest of California, he lived in the Santa Rosa region. (Northrop, *Spanish-Mexican Families*, 2:46–48)

Ramón Carrillo (1821–64) was a son of Joaquín Víctor Carrillo and María Ignacia López, and a younger brother of Francisca

Benicia Vallejo. He moved to the Sonoma region with his mother in the late 1830s. In 1846 he was involved with the Californio resistance to the Bear Flaggers and was accused of complicity in the killings of Thomas Cowie and George Fowler. After fighting against the Americans in southern California, he remained there after the war. In 1864 he was murdered at Cucamonga, most likely by Americans who blamed him for the killings of the two Americans. (McGinty, "Carrillos of San Diego," part 3, 285–93)

JOAQUÍN CASTRO was the son of Francisco María Castro, a soldier who settled at San Francisco before 1800 and was granted the San Pablo rancho on the eastern shore of San Francisco Bay in 1823. Joaquín lived at San Pablo and served in various civic and military offices. He and his brothers Antonio and Víctor were accused by Vallejo of trying to force North Bay Indigenous people to become laborers at San Pablo in the 1830s. (Bancroft, *History of California*, 2:751–52; see also chap. 3.)

JOSÉ CASTRO (1808–60), the son of José Tiburcio Castro, served in the Diputación in the 1830s and spent four months as acting governor after the death of José Figueroa in 1835. He took part in the resistance to both Mariano Chico and Nicolás Gutiérrez in 1836, and served again as acting governor after Gutiérrez's expulsion. He took an active role against Micheltorena in 1845. After Micheltorena's exile, he became military commander and led part of the resistance against the Americans. He fled to Mexico in 1846, returned to Alta California in 1848, and then returned to Mexico in 1853. He was appointed military commander of Baja California in 1856, an office he held until he was killed in 1860. (Bancroft, *History of California*, 2:751–52)

MANUEL DE JESÚS CASTRO (1821–1904) was the son of Simeón Castro and María Antonia Pico. Born in Monterey, he served as secretary to the prefect of Monterey from 1842 to 1844. He was one of the instigators of the revolt against Micheltorena. He was made prefect of Monterey in 1845 and supported Pío Pico against José Castro. After a fight with José María Flores in 1846, he fled to Mexico in 1847. From 1852 until his death, he lived mainly in San Francisco. (Bancroft, *History of California*, 2:753)

MAGÍN MATÍAS CATALÁ (1761–1830) was a native of Catalonia who was ordained in the Franciscan Order. He went to Mexico in 1786 and to Alta California in 1793. After a brief stay at San Francisco, he moved to Mission Santa Clara in 1794, where he worked until his death. He suffered greatly from rheumatism. Toward the end of his life, although he could only hobble feebly as he visited the sick, he insisted on continuing his work, gaining a reputation as "the holy man of Santa Clara." (Geiger, *Franciscan Missionaries*, 42–46; Engelhardt, *Holy Man of Santa Clara*)

EULOGIO CELIS (?–1868) was a Spaniard who arrived in California in 1836 in the employ of Mexican-based merchant Enrique Virmond. He became a businessman, generally in southern Alta California. In 1843 he married Josefa Argüello, daughter of former governor Luis Antonio Argüello and Soledad Ortega. He returned to Spain with his wife in 1853. After his death his wife returned to California. (Bancroft, *History of California*, 2:755; Northrop, *Spanish-Mexican Families*, 1:47–48)

MARIANO CHICO (1796–1850) was born in Guanajuato, New Spain. He served in the Mexican Congress and was appointed governor of Alta California in December 1835. Arriving there in April 1836, he was expelled by the Californios only three months later on July 31. In 1846, he served as governor of Guanajuato and participated in the war against the North American invasion. (Bancroft, *History of California*, 2:759; *Diccionario Porrúa*, 752)

JOHN B. R. COOPER (1791–1872), a native of Alderney Islands in the English Channel, arrived in Massachusetts as a young boy. He first came to California in 1823 as master of the Boston vessel

Rover. Settling in California as a merchant in 1826, he married Mariano Guadalupe Vallejo's sister Encarnación the next year and became active in public affairs. He received several land grants during the Mexican period. He divided his time between living in Monterey and making trading voyages in the Pacific. (Woolfenden and Elkinton, *Cooper;* Bancroft, *History of California,* 2:100–101)

THOMAS COWIE (?–1846), a native of Missouri, first came west in 1843 and then helped drive some horses and mules back east. Moving to California permanently in 1845, he became involved in the Bear Flag movement in 1846. On his way to get gunpowder for the Bear Flaggers. he was captured by a group of Californios and killed. (Warner, *Men of the California Bear Flag Revolt,* 65–66, 242–46)

NARCISO DURÁN (1776–1846) was born in Catalonia, Spain, and joined the Franciscan Order. Arriving in Alta California in 1806, he served at Mission San José until 1833. He became president of the missions in 1825, but his stand against the emancipation of the Indigenous Californians made him unacceptable to Mexican officials, who forced him to step down in 1827. Nonetheless, he was elected president again in 1830 and was appointed commissary prefect in 1836. He remained in that office the rest of his days. (Geiger, *Franciscan Missionaries,* 68–75)

JOSÉ MARÍA ECHEANDÍA, a lieutenant colonel of engineers, was engaged in surveying the boundaries of the newly created Federal District in Mexico when he was appointed political and military governor of Baja and Alta California in 1825. Because he disliked the chilly and foggy climate of Monterey, he made his headquarters in San Diego. Little is known about him outside of his service in Alta California. He returned to Mexico in 1833 and was reported to be practicing his profession as an engineer in the 1850s. He died sometime before 1871. (Bancroft, *History of California,* 3:243–45; Hutchinson, *Frontier Settlement,* 124–25)

ESTANISLAO was the Spanish name given to Cucunuchi (ca. 1793–1838), a twenty-eight-year-old Laquisamne man, when he was baptized in 1821 at Mission San José. He became an Indigenous alcalde there, an indication that he enjoyed the favor of the local clergy. Along with some companions he refused to return to the mission after visiting his ranchería following the 1828 harvest. His forces defeated those of veteran fighter José Sánchez in 1829 and then forced the withdrawal of a combined Monterey–San Francisco expedition led by Mariano Guadalupe Vallejo. Estanislao was pardoned thereafter and continued to live at Mission San José until his death. (Holterman, "Revolt of Estanislao"; Osio, *History of Alta California*, 89–94)

JOSÉ MARIANO ESTRADA (1784–?) was born in Loreto, Baja California and came to Alta California in the late 1790s. He served in various positions at the Monterey presidio, including habilitado and acting commander, until he retired from the military in 1829. He married María Isabel Argüello, daughter of José Darío Argüello and María Ignacia Moraga, in 1807, and she bore ten children. In the early 1830s he worked briefly in the customs service but spent most of his time managing Buena Vista, his rancho outside Monterey. Bancroft was unable to place him after 1845. (Bancroft, *History of California*, 2:792–93)

VÍCTOR FAURÉ (ca. 1815–75) was born in France and became a doctor. Mariano Guadalupe Vallejo hired Fauré to manage his vineyards and wine cellars in Sonoma. (Emparán, *Vallejos of California*, 103, 117)

JOSÉ FIGUEROA (1792–1835) was born in Jonacatepec, New Spain. He participated in the wars of independence, fighting with José María Morelos and Vicente Guerrero. He served as military commander of Cuernavaca in 1823 and in the congress of the State of Mexico in 1824. Later that year he was appointed military commander of Sonora and Sinaloa, where he subdued rebellions of the Yaqui and Mayo peoples. He arrived in Alta California as governor in 1833 and served there until his death. He is best known for secularizing the missions and for his opposition to the Híjar-Padrés colonization effort of 1834. (Hutchinson, *Frontier Settlement*, 154–55)

GEORGE FOWLER (?–1846) was an American who, in 1846, was working for Thomas Knight in the Napa Valley. He became a Bear Flagger and was killed by Californios who captured him and Thomas Cowie as they were attempting to obtain gunpowder for the movement. (Warner, *Men of the California Bear Flag Revolt*, 65–66, 247)

JOHN CHARLES FRÉMONT (1813–90), born in Georgia, was a lieutenant in the United States Army Corps and made journeys to Oregon in 1842 and California in 1843 and 1844. He appeared at John Sutter's fort in the winter of 1845 and then, claiming to be short on supplies, at Monterey in January 1846. He was active in the U.S. conquest of California and accepted the surrender of Andrés Pico at Cahuenga. He served California in the U.S. Senate and was the first Republican candidate for president in 1856. After serving in the Civil War, he spent the rest of his life as a territorial governor and promoter of various western development projects. (Denton, *Passion and Principle*, 102–56)

JOHN FRISBIE (1823–1909), a native of New York, received some legal training as a young man. When the Mexico-U.S. war broke out, he joined the New York Volunteers. While stationed in Sonoma he met Mariano Guadalupe Vallejo's daughter Epifania, whom he married in 1851. Frisbie managed many of Vallejo's financial matters, not always well. After Frisbie filed bankruptcy in 1876, he determined to start anew in Mexico. Remaining there the rest of his life, he attained moderate success and eventually was able to purchase a ranch. (See chapters 5–7.)

LEVI FRISBIE (1821–92), a brother of John Frisbie's, was born in New York. He graduated from Albany Medical College in 1841 and practiced medicine in New York for the rest of the decade. He came to California in the early 1850s and married Mariano Guadalupe Vallejo's daughter Adela in 1858. He continued to practice medicine in Solano County until his death. (Munro-Fraser, *History of Solano County*, 351–52)

ARCHIBALD GILLESPIE (1812–73), born in Pennsylvania, was a lieutenant in the U.S. Marines in 1846. He arrived at Monterey in April of that year with a message to Thomas O. Larkin, appointing him a confidential agent assigned to persuade the Californios to join the United States. He also delivered secret messages to John Frémont, which appears to have encouraged Frémont to become more belligerent. Gillespie served in the military during the U.S. conquest of California. His arbitrary behavior while he was in charge of the Los Angeles garrison sparked a Californio revolt. He was wounded in the military skirmish at San Pascual during the Mexico-U.S. war. He spent most of the rest of his life in California. (Marti, *Messenger of Destiny*; Harlow, *California Conquered*, 78)

MANUEL GÓMEZ, an artillery soldier, came to Alta California in 1816 and served at San Francisco and Monterey. He was promoted to lieutenant for his part in defending Monterey from Bouchard. He returned to Mexico in 1822. (Bancroft, *History of California*, 2:470)

VALENTÍN GÓMEZ FARÍAS (1781–1858) was a liberal who served as president of Mexico in 1833–34. He introduced reforms that sought to curtail the powers of the Church and the military. The two measures that most affected Alta California were the secularization of the missions and the Híjar-Padrés colonization effort. (Fowler, "Valentín Gómez Farías"; Hutchinson, *Frontier Settlement*, 96–180)

RAFAEL GONZÁLEZ (ca. 1786–1868) came to Alta California in 1833 with José Figueroa, as customs administrator and subcomisario at Monterey, where he remained until his death. He served as alcalde at Monterey in 1835 and worked at the customs house from 1837 to 1846. He also served on the Junta Departamental from 1839 to 1843. (Bancroft, *History of California*, 3:761)

ISAAC GRAHAM (1800–63) was born in Kentucky and moved west as a fur trapper in the 1820s. He entered Alta California from New Mexico in 1833 and settled at Natividad, outside of Monterey. He seems to have operated a distillery there that catered to hunters and deserting sailors. He supported Alvarado in 1836. Accused of leading a rebellion against the Alta California government in 1840, he was sent to Mexico City for punishment. On his return he settled near Santa Cruz, where he operated a sawmill. He supported Governor Micheltorena in 1844 and 1845 and continued to live at Santa Cruz until his death. (Bancroft, *History of California*, 3:762–63)

JOHN GRIGSBY (1806–76), a Missouri farmer, came to California in 1845 with William Ide. He was an active member of the Bear Flag movement and eventually settled in Napa. He left California in the 1870s to return to Missouri, where he died. (Bancroft, *History of California*, 3:767; Warner, *Men of the California Bear Flag Revolt*, 174–88)

ANGUSTIAS DE LA GUERRA (1815–90), daughter of José de la Guerra y Noriega and María Antonia Carrillo, was born in Santa Bárbara. In 1833 she married Manuel Jimeno Casarín, who eventually served as secretary to Governors Juan Bautista Alvarado and Manuel Micheltorena. Jimeno Casarín abandoned her and their children and returned to Mexico in 1853. He died shortly thereafter. In 1856 Angustias married James Ord, with whom she had one daughter, Rebecca. They were divorced in 1875 and Angustias died in San Francisco. (Beebe and Senkewicz, *Testimonios*, 193–200)

PABLO DE LA GUERRA (1819–74) was a son of José de la Guerra y Noriega and María Antonia Carrillo. He attended his brother-in-law William Hartnell's school at Rancho Alisal and worked at the customs house in Monterey from 1838 until the American invasion. He later served in the 1849 Constitutional Convention and as a member of the California State Senate. (Bancroft, *History of California*, 3:769; Pubols, *Father of All*)

JOSÉ DE LA GUERRA Y NORIEGA (1779–1858) was born in Spain. He left for Mexico City in the 1790s to work in his uncle's store. Soon thereafter he entered the military. He arrived in Alta California in 1801 and served in Monterey until 1806. In that year he was made lieutenant at Santa Bárbara and soon moved to San Diego, where he remained until 1809. In 1804 he married María Antonia Carrillo. By acting as his uncle's commercial agent in Alta California, he was able to improve his financial condition greatly. He was promoted to commander of the Santa Bárbara presidio in 1815 and remained in that position until 1842, when he retired from the military. (Pubols, *Father of All*)

JOSÉ MARÍA GUTIÉRREZ (1801–50) was a member of the first group of Mexican Franciscan missionaries from Zacatecas who arrived in Alta California in 1833. He served at Missions San Francisco Solano, San Francisco de Asís, and San Antonio before returning to Mexico in 1846. (Geiger, *Franciscan Missionaries*, 121–22)

NICOLÁS GUTIÉRREZ came to Alta California as a captain in 1833 with José Figueroa. Promoted to lieutenant colonel in that year, he acted as comisionado for the secularization of Mission San Gabriel from 1834 to 1836. He served as acting governor from January to May 1836 and again after the expulsion of Mariano Chico the next year. Gutiérrez himself was expelled by Alvarado at the end of 1836. Little is known of his later career. (Bancroft, *History of California*, 3:772)

WILLIAM GWIN (1805–85) was born in Tennessee. After serving a term as a U.S. congressman from Mississippi in the early 1840s, he moved to California in 1849. He was elected to the U.S. Senate in 1850–55 and again in 1857–61. He was a Confederate sympathizer during the Civil War. (Hargis, "W. M. Gwin")

HENRY HALLECK (1816–72) graduated from West Point in 1839. His influential 1850 "Report on Land Titles in California" led Frederick Billings and Archibald Peachy to recruit him into a very prominent San Francisco law firm, where he worked until the U.S. Civil War began. During the Civil War he served for a time as President Lincoln's military chief of staff. After the war, he served as commander of the U.S. Army Department of the Pacific. (Bastian, "I Heartily Regret")

FRANCISCO DE HARO (1793–1849), born in Mexico, arrived in Alta California in 1819 with the reinforcements sent after the Bouchard raid. He retired from the military in 1825 and held a variety of political offices in San Francisco and elsewhere during the 1830s and 1840s. He married Emiliana Sánchez, daughter of José Sánchez and Josefa Soto, in 1822, and she bore twelve children. Two of them, Mateo Francisco and Alejo Ramón, were killed by the Bear Flaggers in 1846. (Bancroft, *History of California*, 3:776; Mutnick, *Some Alta California Pioneers*, 2:520–21)

WILLIAM EDWARD PETTY HARTNELL (1798–1854) was born in Lancashire, England. In 1819 he left for South America to clerk for the firm of Begg and Co., then arrived in California in 1822. In partnership with a fellow Begg clerk, Hugh McCullough of Scotland, he formed McCullough, Hartnell, and Co. and did profitable business with the missions in the 1820s. On April 30, 1825, he married María Teresa de la Guerra. Business reverses in the late 1820s forced the dissolution of his partnership with McCullough, and Hartnell supported himself with a variety of enterprises. He received a grant for Rancho Alisal, outside of Monterey, and in the mid-1830s opened a short-lived school at the rancho. In 1839 Alvarado appointed him visitador general of the missions. In the late 1840s and early 1850s, he was employed by the Americans as an interpreter and translator. (Dakin, *Lives of William Hartnell*)

José María Híjar (ca. 1793–1845) was born in Guadalajara and served for many years in the congress of the State of Jalisco, where he most likely became acquainted with Valentín Gómez Farías. In 1833, Híjar was appointed director of the colonization effort and also jefe político of Alta California. Political change in Mexico prevented his assuming the political office, and the colony ran afoul of Governor Figueroa and the Californios. He was sent back to Mexico in 1835. Ironically, he returned to Alta California in 1845 as a member of a Mexican commission and died in Los Angeles. (Hutchinson, *Frontier Settlement*, 184–85, 374–75)

William Brown Ide (1796–1852) was born in Massachusetts and came overland to California in 1845. He settled near Sonoma and was a leader of the Bear Flag revolt. He became bitter when John Frémont took control of the movement in the summer but served as a private in the California Battalion during the war. He returned to Sonoma and served as a surveyor there and as a public official in Colusa. (Bancroft, *History of California*, 4:688–89; Warner, *Men of the California Bear Flag Revolt*, 15–174)

Manuel Jimeno Casarín (1803–53) was born in New Spain. He came to Alta California in 1828 as subcomisario and contador at the customs house in Monterey. Two of his brothers, José Joaquín and Antonio, were Franciscan missionaries in Alta California. Manuel held numerous public offices; he was síndico and alcalde at Monterey and a member of the Diputación. After serving as Governor Alvarado's secretary, he filled the same office for Governor Micheltorena. In the early 1830s he married Angustias de la Guerra. He returned to Mexico in 1853, where he died that year. (Bancroft, *History of California*, 4:692)

THOMAS AP CATESBY JONES (1790–1859) was born in Virginia and was commander of the United States Navy Pacific Squadron in 1842. He took Monterey in that year because he thought war had broken out between the United States and Mexico. The United States apologized for the incident and briefly relieved him of command, but restored it to him quickly. He participated in the U.S. conquest of California. (Bancroft, *History of California*, 4:695)

CAYETANO JUÁREZ (1809–83), was a son of José Joaquín Juárez and María Pascuala Lorenzana. He followed his father into military service and was a member of the presidio company at San Francisco before following Mariano Guadalupe Vallejo to Sonoma. In 1836 he married María Josefa Higuera, daughter of Francisco Javier Higuera and María Mariana Navarro. The marriage produced seven children. He participated in a number of campaigns against the Indigenous peoples of the North Bay region and died in Napa. (Bancroft, *History of California*, 4:696; Northrop, *Spanish-Mexican Families*, 1:174–76; Mutnick, *Some Alta California Pioneers*, 2:576–79)

VICENTE JUÁREZ (1813–ca. 1893) was the son of Joaquín Juárez and Pasquala Lorenzana. In 1842, he married María Antonia Rosales. He served as a soldier in the San Francisco company. (Bancroft, *History of California*, 4:696; Northrop, *Spanish-Mexican Families*, 3:29)

STEPHEN WATTS KEARNY (1794–1848) was born in New Jersey. A career soldier, he served in the U.S. Army in the War of 1812 and later commanded the Army of the West in 1846. He also served as military governor at Santa Fe. After crossing overland to California, he was defeated at the Battle of San Pascual on December 6, 1846. He died two years later, in St. Louis, after serving in Mexico as governor of Veracruz and Mexico City. (Clarke, *Stephen Watts Kearny*)

THOMAS OLIVER LARKIN (1802–58) was born in Massachusetts and came to Alta California in 1832, becoming a trader in Monterey. He supported Alvarado in 1836 and was appointed U.S. consul eight years later. In 1845, President James Polk and Secretary of State James Buchanan made him a confidential agent in an unsuccessful attempt to bring Alta California peacefully into the United States. He died in San Francisco. (Hague and Langum, *Thomas O. Larkin*)

JACOB PRIMER LEESE (1809–92) was born in Ohio. He traded along the Santa Fe Trail in the early 1830s and moved to Alta California in 1834. He lived in Yerba Buena from 1836 to 1841 then moved to Sonoma. He married Rosalía Vallejo, the sister of Mariano Guadalupe Vallejo. In 1846 he was captured by the Bear Flaggers. He was vice president of the Society of California Pioneers in 1855. In 1864 he was granted almost two-thirds of Baja California as part of a colonization enterprise. After this project failed, he abandoned his family, left California in 1865, and did not return until his old age. (Bancroft, *History of California*, 4:710–11; Martínez, *Historia de Baja California*, 406–12)

ANTONIO LÓPEZ DE SANTA ANNA (1794–1876) was born in Jalapa, New Spain. After an alliance with Agustín de Iturbide during the early years of Mexican independence, he became a partisan of the liberal federalists and was elected president in 1833. After resigning, he did not approve of the liberal policies of his successor, Valentín Gómez Farías, and became an ardent centralist. He served a number of nonconsecutive terms as Mexican president until he was overthrown in 1855. After two decades in exile, he died soon after returning to Mexico. (*Diccionario Porrúa*, 3175–79)

MACAI was the name Mariano Guadalupe Vallejo gave to Peopeo Moxmox, the chief of the Walla Walla group that entered California in 1846. The Americans called him Yellow Serpent. (Hussey and Ames, "California Preparations"; Hurtado, *John Sutter*, 199–201)

José Joaquín Maitorena (ca. 1780?–1830) came to California in 1801 and served in the military in the Santa Bárbara region. In 1805 he married Isabel María Yorba. He was elected as California's deputy to the Mexican Congress in 1828 and died in Mexico. (Bancroft, *History of California*, 4:728; Northrop, *Spanish-Mexican Families*, 1:364)

Ignacio Martínez (1774–1848) was born in Mexico City and came to Alta California around 1800. He served at Santa Bárbara and San Diego before being sent to San Francisco as a lieutenant in 1817. He succeeded Luis Antonio Argüello as commander in 1822 and acted in that capacity until 1827. From 1828 to 1831 he had various stints as acting commander and commander. After retiring from the military in 1831 he held various public offices, such as alcalde of San Francisco, member of the Diputación, and regidor at San José. He owned a large ranch, Pinole, in Contra Costa, across the bay from San Francisco. (Bancroft, *History of California*, 4:733)

Richard Mason (1797–1850) was a U.S. Army colonel who was appointed military governor of Alta California at the end of May 1847. He served in that position until May 1849. A year after he left California he died of cholera. (Bancroft, *History of California*, 4:734)

Antonio Menéndez (?–1832) was a Dominican priest who served at missions on the northern frontier of Baja California beginning in 1815. As a result of Indigenous complaints about his behavior, Governor Echeandía removed him from that position in 1825 and he was transferred to Alta California to serve at various presidios. He died in Santa Bárbara. (Nieser, "Dominican Mission Foundations," 292–99; Bancroft, *History of California*, 4:738; Beebe and Senkewicz, *Lands of Promise and Despair*, 341–43)

Ezekiel Merritt (1807–49) was born in Tennessee. After spending some time trapping and trading in the New Mexico area, he arrived in California in the mid-1830s. He joined John Sutter in supporting Micheltorena in 1844. He was an early leader of the Bear Flaggers and also participated in military operations in southern Alta California in late 1846. After prospecting for a while in 1848 and 1849, he died at some point in 1849. (Warner, *Men of the California Bear Flag Revolt*, 76–82)

PRADO MESA (1806–45) was a son of José Antonio Mesa and María Francisca Linares. He followed his father into the military and served in many capacities at San Francisco and Sonoma. He also engaged in conflicts against the Indigenous peoples of the North Bay and Central Valley regions. In 1827 he married Francisca Micaela Higuera, who bore ten children. She died in 1843 and her husband died a few years later. (Northrop, *Spanish-Mexican Families*, 1:225–27, 2:125; Mutnick, *Some Alta California Pioneers*, 2:692–93)

MANUEL MICHELTORENA (ca. 1802–53) was a native of Oaxaca, New Spain. Little is known of his career before 1840, when he was involved in suppressing a revolt in Mexico City. Appointed governor of Alta California in 1842, he arrived with some three hundred soldiers, many of whom were reported to be ex-convicts and all of whom were thoroughly disliked by the Californios. He attempted to restore undistributed mission lands and property to the Church but was generally unsuccessful. He was expelled in 1845, fought against the Americans in 1846, and was a member of the Mexican Congress in 1847. In 1850 he was comandante general of Yucatán. (Bancroft, *History of California*, 4:740)

JOHN S. MISROON (1805–65), a lieutenant on the *Portsmouth* in 1846, was sent by John Montgomery to Sonoma and New Helvetia to check on the condition of the prisoners being held by the Bear Flaggers. He invested in a San Francisco lot while he was in the area. (Bancroft, *History of California*, 4:742)

John Berrien Montgomery (1794–1873) was commander of the U.S. vessel *Portsmouth*, which was stationed at San Francisco during the Bear Flag revolt. Later in life he commanded the Charlestown, Massachusetts, and Washington, D.C., navy yards. (Rogers, *Montgomery and the Portsmouth*)

Timothy Murphy (?–1853) was born in Ireland. He settled in Alta California in 1828 as a clerk for William Hartnell in Monterey, then worked for John B. Cooper. In 1836 he settled in the San Rafael area. He was a friend of Mariano Guadalupe Vallejo and became administrator of ex–Mission San Rafael. He received a land grant in the region. (Bancroft, *History of California*, 4:750)

Luis del Castillo Negrete (?–1843), a Spaniard, came to California with the Híjar-Padrés colony in 1834. He became the district judge for the territory and later served as an advisor to Nicolás Gutiérrez. He left California in 1836. He later served as an officer of the Baja California government. (Bancroft, *History of California*, 3:466)

Jasper O'Farrell (1817–75) was born in Ireland. He came to California in 1843, where he became a well-known surveyor and made a significant street survey of San Francisco. Several Mexican landowners, including Mariano Guadalupe Vallejo, ardently solicited his surveying skills. After the 1850s he lived in the North Bay. (Bancroft, *History of California*, 4:757)

José Joaquín Ortega was the son of José María Ortega and María Francisca López. He was a member of the Diputación in the early 1830s. He married María Pico, the sister of Pío and Andrés Pico. He served as administrator of Mission San Diego from 1835 to 1840 and as mayordomo of Mission San Luis Rey from 1843 to 1845. (Bancroft, *History of California*, 4:760)

ANTONIO MARÍA OSIO (1800–78) was born in Baja California. He came to Alta California in 1825, worked in the customs service in Monterey in the late 1820s, and served on the Diputación in the early 1830s. He supported the southerners against Alvarado in the mid-1830s and eventually moved back to northern Alta California, where he returned to the customs service in Monterey. After the Mexico-U.S. war, he composed a history of Alta California. Eventually he returned to Baja California, where he died. (Osio, *History of Alta California*)

JOSÉ MARÍA PADRÉS, a native of Puebla, was a member of the engineering corps in the military. He accompanied Echeandía in 1825 but was posted to Baja California rather than continuing to Alta California. In 1827 he served in the Mexican Congress. He came to Alta California in 1830 as ayudante inspector of the presidios and troops. An ardent proponent of the secularization of the missions, he was sent back to Mexico by Governor Victoria in 1831. He returned to Alta California in 1834 with the Híjar-Padrés colonizing effort initiated by Valentín Gómez Farías. After becoming embroiled in a bitter controversy with Governor Figueroa and the Californio elite, he was sent back to Mexico again in 1835. Nothing is recorded of his later life. (Hutchinson, *Frontier Settlement*, 182–84, 370–79)

ARCHIBALD PEACHY (1820–83), a native of Virginia, arrived in California in 1849. He formed a very successful law partnership with Frederick Billings and Henry Halleck. He served in the California assembly in 1852 and in the California senate in 1860 and 1862. He died in San Francisco. (Bastian, "I Heartily Regret")

COSME PEÑA, a lawyer, came to Alta California with the Híjar-Padrés colonization party in 1834, with an appointment as asesor to succeed Rafael Gómez. He sided with Alvarado in 1836 and was made his secretary. He later affiliated with Angel Ramírez and was imprisoned at Sonoma. He left Alta California in 1839. (Bancroft, *History of California*, 3:594, 4:771)

Pío Pico (1801–94), was born at San Gabriel. He served in the Diputación in 1828, and as a vocale he was one of the leaders of the opposition to Governor Victoria in 1831. He served as one of the acting governors in 1832. Serving as the administrator of Mission San Luis Rey from 1834 to 1840, he was a leader in the 1836–37 opposition to Alvarado. After Micheltorena's expulsion, he became jefe político, and in that capacity he frequently quarreled with José Castro, the jefe militar. He fled to Mexico in 1845 but returned to southern California in 1848 and lived in Los Angeles until his death. (Salomon, *Pío Pico*)

Lázaro Piña was a Mexican artillery soldier. He served at Monterey and Sonoma and was granted Rancho Agua Caliente in 1840. He married Plácida Villela in 1823. When war with the United States broke out, he returned to Mexico where, the Californios believed, he was killed at the battle of Cerro Gordo in April 1847. (Bancroft, *History of California*, 4:780)

Víctor Prudón (1809–?) was born in France and went to Mexico in 1827. He arrived in California as a teacher with the Híjar-Padrés colonization group in 1834 and married Teodosia Bojorques. He served as president of the Los Angeles vigilantes in 1836 and as Governor Alvarado's secretary in 1837 to 1838. He worked in the same capacity for Vallejo in 1841 and was Vallejo's emissary to Mexico in 1842. Bear Flag soldiers arrested him with Vallejo in 1846. His whereabouts after 1853 are not recorded. (Bancroft, *History of California*, 4:784–85; Rhoades, "Foreigners in Southern California," 70–71)

José Lorenzo de la Concepción Quijas was most likely a native of Ecuador. He entered the Franciscan Colegio de Nuestra Señora de Guadalupe in Zacatecas after having been a muleteer and trader. He came to California in 1833 and served at Missions San Francisco, San Francisco Solano, San Rafael, and San José. After being appointed vice-commissary prefect of the missions in 1843, he quickly became involved in a series of jurisdictional disputes with Bishop García Diego y Moreno. He left California in 1844. (Geiger, *Franciscan Missionaries*, 200–203)

ANGEL RAMÍREZ (?–1840) a Franciscan friar who left his order around 1820, participated in the wars of independence. Apparently a friend of Valentín Gómez Farías, he arrived in Alta California in 1834 as administrator of the customs house in Monterey. He served in that capacity until 1836, when Alvarado removed him. He was arrested in July 1837 and died at Mission San Luis Obispo. (Bancroft, *History of California*, 3:587–88)

JOSEPH WARREN REVERE (1812–80) was born in Boston and joined the U.S. Navy in 1828. He participated in deployments in the Pacific and the Caribbean. A lieutenant on the *Cyane* in 1846, he was reassigned to the *Portsmouth*. The man who raised the U.S. flag at Sonoma, he described his time in California in *A Tour of Duty in California* (1849). He later served in the Civil War. (Sullivan, foreword to Revere, *Naval Duty in California*, n.p.; Bancroft, *History of California*, 5:692)

FERNANDO DE RIVERA Y MONCADA (1724–81) was born in Compostela, New Spain. He served in the military in Baja California and was appointed commander at Loreto in 1751. In command of the first land detachment of the Portolá expedition in 1769, he spent a few more years in Baja California. In 1774, he was appointed military commander of Alta California and served in that capacity until 1777. Then, after several more years of service in Baja California, he was appointed to lead a detachment of colonists to California. He was killed in the Quechán uprising along the Colorado River. (Bancroft, *History of California*, 5:697)

ALFRED ROBINSON (1806–95) was born in Massachusetts and came to California in 1829 as a clerk for Bryant and Sturgis Co.

He engaged in the hide and tallow trade for some years and in 1836 married Anita de la Guerra, daughter of José de la Guerra y Noriega of Santa Bárbara. He returned east in 1842 and four years later anonymously published *Life in California*, which became a standard North American account of Mexican Alta California. Robinson returned to California in 1849 as an agent for the Pacific Mail Steamship Company. He lived in Santa Bárbara and San Francisco for the remainder of his life. (Bancroft, *History of California*, 5:698; Rhoades, "Foreigners in Southern California," 72–74; Brewster, "Californiana in Two Worlds")

SEBASTIÁN RODRÍGUEZ (1785–1854) served as a soldier at Monterey during the late 1820s and led some expeditions against the Indigenous people of the Central Valley during that time. He served as comisionado at Santa Cruz in 1831 and was granted Rancho Bolsa del Pájaro in 1837. (Bancroft, *History of California*, 5:701–2)

JOSÉ MARIANO ROMERO came to California with the Híjar-Padrés party in 1834. He had been a Latin instructor at a school in Mexico City and became director of a school established in Monterey. After some disagreements with the ayuntamiento over his teaching methods, he appears to have established a good relationship with students and parents. He authored the first pedagogy published in California, *Catecismo de ortología* (1836). He left California later that year. (Hutchinson, *Frontier Settlement*, 193–94; Correspondence between ayuntamiento and Romero, Monterey Collection, MR 347, HL)

JOSÉ "PEPE" DE LA ROSA came to California in 1834 with the Híjar-Padrés colony. Like many of the colonists, he settled in the Sonoma area. A printer by trade, he worked as a handyman for Mariano Guadalupe Vallejo, mending clothes and tinware. He served as Sonoma alcalde in 1845. In 1846, Vallejo sent him to Yerba Buena to alert John B. Montgomery, captain of the *Portsmouth*, about the Bear Flag incident and to seek the captain's intervention to free Vallejo. Montgomery refused to become involved. An accomplished musician, de la Rosa also spent time in the East Bay region, where he taught Mexican songs to Adelaida Cordero Kamp, who eventually recorded some of them for Charles Lummis. (Koegel, "'Canciones del país,'" 166–72; Bancroft, *History of California*, 5:704)

María Amparo Ruiz (1831–95), born in Baja California, was the daughter of Jesús Maitorena and Isabel Ruiz, who was the daughter of former Baja California governor José Manuel Ruiz. She came to Alta California with the American forces in 1848 and married one of the officers, Henry S. Burton, the next year. She left California in 1859 when her husband was assigned elsewhere. She returned to California after his death in 1869. She published two novels, *Who Would Have Thought It* and *The Squatter and the Don.* (Sánchez and Pita, *Conflicts of Interest*)

José Antonio Sánchez (?–1843), a native of Sinaloa, Mexico, was a member of the military company at San Francisco in the 1790s. He received various promotions, rising to command the San Francisco garrison from 1829 to 1833. He had a reputation as a skilled fighter against the Indigenous peoples and participated in more than twenty campaigns against them. He retired in 1836. (Bancroft, *History of California*, 5:710)

Robert Semple (1806–54), a native of Kentucky, came overland to California in 1845. He worked as a carpenter at John Sutter's fort and became a leader of the Bear Flag revolt. After the war, he became co-publisher of the *Californian*, the first newspaper published in California. He speculated in land around the San Francisco Bay Area and served as president of the Constitutional Convention in Monterey in 1849. He moved to Colusa County, where he died after a fall from a horse. (Warner, *Men of the California Bear Flag Revolt*, 107–23; Bancroft, *History of California*, 5:715)

JOSÉ SEPÚLVEDA (1803–75) married María Francisca de Paula Avila. He served on the Los Angeles ayuntamiento in 1833, as alcalde in 1837, and on the ayuntamiento again in 1839. From Alvarado he received two land grants, Ciénega de las Ranas and Rancho San Joaquín. He served as subprefect in 1845. (Bancroft, *History of California*, 5:716; Wittenburg, "Three Generations of the Sepúlveda Family," 220–43)

JOHN DRAKE SLOAT (1781–1867) was born in New York. Joining the U.S. Navy in 1800, he had risen to commander of the U.S. Pacific Fleet by 1844. He took possession of Monterey on June 7, 1846, but left the command in California to Robert Stockton at the end of July and returned east. He commanded the Norfolk navy yard from 1848 to 1850 before retiring in 1855. (Castleman, *Knickerbocker Commodore*)

PABLO VICENTE DE SOLÁ (1761–1826) was born in Vizcaya, Spain. The date of his arrival in the New World is not recorded, but he was sufficiently well established by 1805 as a captain in the military to be appointed temporary habilitado general of Las Californias. He served in that office until 1807. He rose to the rank of lieutenant colonel by the time he was appointed governor of Alta California in 1814, a post he held until 1822. After his return to Mexico, he served on the Commission for the Development of the Californias. (Bancroft, *History of California*, 2:470–73; 5:727; Geiger, *Franciscan Missionaries*, 274; Hutchinson, *Frontier Settlement*, 117)

FRANCISCO SOLANO (ca. 1791–?) was the Spanish name given to a ten-year-old Suisun boy whose Indigenous name was recorded as Sina when he was baptized at Mission San Francisco in 1801. Mariano Guadalupe Vallejo later reported that his full Indigenous name was Sem-Yeto. He moved to Mission San Francisco Solano in 1824 and quickly became a major figure both at the mission and in the surrounding Suisun communities. When Vallejo founded

Sonoma in 1835, Solano became his ally and together they fought against the Patwin Suisunes' traditional enemies to the north. He died in the early 1850s. (See chap. 3.)

JOAQUÍN SOLÍS was a leader in the 1829 revolt in which soldiers rose up to protest their lack of pay. Little is known about him. He had apparently fought in the wars of independence and then turned to crime, for which he was sentenced to California in 1825. He was living outside of Monterey at the time of the revolt. In 1830 he was sent back to Mexico. (Bancroft, *History of California*, 3:68–69)

DAVID SPENCE (ca. 1798–1875) was born in Scotland and came to Alta California in September 1824 to manage a meatpacking plant in Monterey for Begg and Co. He went into business for himself in 1827, and in 1829 he married Adelaida Estrada, daughter of Mariano Estrada. He served as alcalde of Monterey in 1835 and was on the Diputación the following year. He was juez de paz in 1839 and also served in some public offices after Alta California became part of the United States. (Bancroft, *History of California*, 5:730–31)

ROBERT FIELD STOCKTON (1795–1866) was born in New Jersey and joined the U.S. Navy as a young man. After serving in the War of 1812, he arrived in Monterey in command of the USS *Congress* in July 1846 and soon thereafter was appointed commander to succeed John Sloat. He resigned in 1847 and returned east. He served as a senator from New Jersey from 1851 to 1853. (Bancroft, *History of California*, 5:735)

SUCCARA was a chief of the Satiyomi Indigenous group, against whom Vallejo waged several campaigns. These campaigns were inconclusive, but the 1838 smallpox epidemic dramatically weakened the group. (Heizer, *Archaeology of the Napa Region*, 229–31)

JOHN AUGUSTUS SUTTER (1803–80) was born in Germany. After failing in business in Switzerland, he traveled in northern Mexico, Alaska, and Hawai'i before settling in Alta California. Seeking to check Mariano Guadalupe Vallejo's influence, Governor Alvarado gave Sutter a huge land grant in the Sacramento Valley. Using Indigenous laborers practically as serfs, he turned New Helvetia into an almost feudal estate. In 1845 he assisted Governor Micheltorena against the Californio rebels and later supported the North American invasion of California. He was a member of the Constitutional Convention in 1849, the year after gold was discovered on his property. By the mid-1850s squatters had taken most of his land, but he managed to survive on a pension from the California legislature. When the pension was terminated in 1878, he moved to Lititz, Pennsylvania, where he died. (Hurtado, *John Sutter*)

JUAN MANUEL VACA (?–1856) arrived in California in 1841. In 1843 he and Juan Felipe Peña were granted Rancho los Putos in what is now Solano County. (Bancroft, *History of California*, 5:753–54; Hoffman, *Reports of Land Cases*, app., 8–9)

IGNACIO DEL VALLE (?–1880) was the son of Antonio del Valle. He came to California in 1825 with Echeandía and served at Santa Bárbara and San Diego in the late 1820s. In 1831 and 1832 he opposed both Governor Victoria and Zamorano. In 1836 he supported Nicolás Gutiérrez against Alvarado. Two years later he supported Carlos Carrillo and had to go into a brief exile as a result. After his father's death, he lived on the family rancho and continued to fill various Mexican public offices in the 1840s and Los Angeles municipal offices in the early 1850s. (Bancroft, *History of California*, 5:755–56)

ENCARNACIÓN VALLEJO (1809–1902) was a daughter of Ignacio Vallejo and María Antonia Lugo. In 1827 she married John Cooper, a ship captain from Massachusetts who had recently settled in Alta

California. She bore seven children. Her husband became a trader in Monterey and made regular sea voyages to Mexico, Hawai'i, and China. (Woolfenden and Elkinton, *Cooper*; Bancroft, *History of California*, 2:765–66)

IGNACIO VICENTE FERRER VALLEJO (1748–1831), founder of the Vallejo dynasty in Alta California, was born in Jalisco, Mexico. He entered the army at an early age and arrived in San Diego in 1774. He worked at Missions San Luis Obispo and San Carlos in the 1780s. After reenlisting in 1787, he was promoted to corporal in 1789 and to sergeant in 1805. His wife, María Antonia Lugo, bore thirteen children. He died in Monterey. (Bancroft, *History of California*, 5:756)

JOSÉ DE JESÚS VALLEJO (1798–1882), born in San José, was a son of Ignacio Vallejo and María Antonia Lugo and the older brother of Mariano Guadalupe Vallejo. He was an active participant in the defense of Monterey against Bouchard. Later, he held various military and civilian offices in Alta California, including service as administrator of Mission San José after 1836. After the North American conquest of California, he remained at Mission San José, serving for a time as postmaster there. (Bancroft, *History of California*, 5:757)

JUAN ANTONIO VALLEJO (1816–57) was the youngest child of Ignacio Vallejo and María Antonia Lugo. He served in several minor political positions in the 1840s. Before she passed away in 1855, his mother named him as the executor of the family estate. However, his sudden death meant that his brother Mariano Guadalupe had to assume the executorship, which continued until 1864. (Bancroft, *History of California* 7:757; Emparán, *Vallejos of California*, 100–103)

ROSALÍA VALLEJO (1811–89) was a daughter of Ignacio Vallejo and María Antonia Lugo. In 1837 she married Jacob P. Leese, a native of Ohio who had established himself as a merchant at Yerba Buena. They moved to the Sonoma region in 1841, and Rosalía ultimately bore six children. They moved to Monterey in 1850 and Leese abandoned his family in 1865. (Beebe and Senkewicz, *Testimonios*, 16–24)

SALVADOR VALLEJO (1814–76), a son of Ignacio Vallejo and María Antonia Lugo and the younger brother of Mariano Guadalupe Vallejo, was born in Monterey. In 1836 his brother appointed him captain of the militia at Sonoma, and he engaged in many campaigns against the Indigenous peoples in the area. He was married to María de la Luz Carrillo. He served as juez de paz and as administrator of San Francisco Solano. He was held prisoner by the Bear Flaggers in 1846. During the Civil War he served in Arizona on the Union side. Later, he lived with his brother at Sonoma, until his death. (Bancroft, *History of California*, 5:759; McKittrick, "Salvador Vallejo"; Sánchez, "Salvador Vallejo," in Sánchez, Pita, and Reyes, *Nineteenth-Century California Testimonios*, 92)

JESÚS MARÍA VÁSQUEZ DEL MERCADO (ca. 1808–?) was born in Mexico and entered the Franciscan Order in the 1820s. He was a member of the group of Franciscans from Zacatecas who arrived in California in 1833. His first assignment was at Mission San Rafael, where he was accused by the governor of crimes against the Indigenous people. He also served at Santa Clara in the early 1840s, where he was accused of unauthorized use of mission property. He was sent back to Mexico in 1844. (Geiger, *Franciscan Missionaries*, 261–62)

PLÁCIDO VEGA (1830–78) became governor of the Mexican state of Sinaloa in 1859. A supporter of Benito Juárez, he came to San Francisco in the mid-1860s. He raised money from a number of Mexican Americans, including Mariano Guadalupe Vallejo, to support the fight against Emperor Maximilian. After his return to Mexico, Vega was accused of misappropriation of funds and became alienated from his former allies. (Miller, "Californians against the Emperor")

José Viader (1765–?) arrived in New Spain in 1795 from Catalonia, Spain, as a Franciscan. Arriving in Alta California in 1796, he was assigned to Mission Santa Clara and remained there until he returned to his native Spain in 1833. He and Magín Matías Catalá worked together for three decades. During that time, Viader was generally in charge of the temporal concerns of the mission. (Geiger, *Franciscan Missionaries*, 263–65)

Manuel Victoria was born in Tecpan, Mexico. An infantry officer, he requested an appointment in Baja California for health reasons in 1829, and he was appointed governor there. In 1830, Alta California was added to his responsibilities. He assumed office on January 31, 1831, less than a month after Echeandía's secularization decree. Immediately, he became involved in a series of disputes with the Californios, and the Diputación organized a movement against him within a few months of his arrival. He was so badly wounded at a battle at Cahuenga, near Los Angeles, in December 1831 that he had to leave for Mexico. Little is known of his later career. (Hutchinson, *Frontier Settlement*, 142–50)

G. M. Waseurtz af Sandels was a Swede who visited California in 1842–43. He kept an extensive diary and did a number of drawings and paintings, which are important sources depicting many aspects of life in Mexican California. (Sandels, *Sojourn in California*)

Mark West, an English lumberman and carpenter, arrived in California in 1832 and worked for Thomas O. Larkin in Monterey. He married Guadalupe Vásquez and was granted San Miguel rancho in 1840. He died in the early 1850s. (Bancroft, *History of California*, 5:772)

GEORGE YOUNT (1794–1865) was a trapper from North Carolina who came to Alta California in 1831. He hunted sea otters off the Santa Bárbara Channel Islands and in San Francisco Bay. He moved to the area north of San Francisco in 1835 and worked for Vallejo at Sonoma. In the following year he received a land grant, Rancho Caymus, in the Napa Valley, where he lived as a hunter and trapper until his death. (Camp, *George C. Yount*; Bancroft, *History of California*, 5:783)

AGUSTÍN VICENTE ZAMORANO (1798–1842) was born in San Agustín, Florida. His father, a soldier, was assigned in 1809 to New Spain, where Agustín entered the military in 1821. He joined the engineering corps in 1824 and accompanied Echeandía to Alta California the following year. After serving as the governor's secretary for five years, he was made commander at Monterey in 1831. After Manuel Victoria left Alta California, Zamorano was one of three de facto jefes who ruled until Governor Figueroa's arrival in 1833. He was Figueroa's secretary for two years and operated the first printing press in Alta California. In 1835 he was made commander of San Diego. He became involved in the movement against Alvarado in 1836 to 1837, and when that failed, he left for Mexico. He returned to Alta California with Micheltorena in 1842 but died shortly after arriving in San Diego. (Harding, *Don Agustin V. Zamorano*)

ZAMPAY was a chief of the Suisun ranchería of Yolotoy who instigated a revolt against Francisco Solano's authority in 1836 and 1837. Solano and Mariano Guadalupe Vallejo organized a successful expedition against him. Zampay and his family were moved to Sonoma, where he was allowed to live after pledging allegiance to Vallejo and Solano. (See chap. 3.)

Bibliography and Further Reading

PRIMARY SOURCES

The Bancroft Library, University of California, Berkeley

Archive of California. C-A 1–63.

Juan Bojorques, "Recuerdos sobre la historia de California." 1877. C-D 46.

Jacob N. Bowman, "Indices to California Land Cases." 1941 and 1964. C-R 16.

Charles Brown, "Early Events in California." 1878. C-D 53.

Documents from the Spanish and Mexican periods in California, 1780-1849. BANC MSS C-A 150.

Documents Pertaining to the Adjudication of Private Land Claims in California. Land Case Files.

John B. Frisbie, "Reminiscences." M-M 351.

C. Hart Merriam Papers Relating to Work with California Indians. BANC FILM 1022.

Thomas Savage, "Report on Archives." C-E 191.

Mariano Guadalupe Vallejo Papers. C-B 1–36.

Vallejo Family Papers. C-B 441.

Vallejo Family Papers: Additions, 1846–1950. BANC MSS 76/79c.

Mariano Guadalupe Vallejo, "Recuerdos históricos y personales tocantes a la Alta California, 1769–1849." C-D 17–21.

Mariano Guadalupe Vallejo to Thomas Savage, October 16, 1878. B-C 7, oversize box 11, folder 9.

Salvador Vallejo, "Notas históricas sobre California." 1874. C-D 22.

Salvador Vallejo, "Lo que piensa . . . sobre origen de los indios de California." 1875. C-D 157.

California Digital Newspaper Collection, University of California, Riverside
California Star
Californian
Chico Weekly Enterprise
Daily Alta California
Marysville Daily Appeal
Napa County Reporter
Sacramento Daily Union
San Diego Union and Daily Bee
Santa Barbara Weekly Press
Sonoma Democrat

California Historical Society, San Francisco
Comunicaciones del General M. G. Vallejo. Vault 979.4 v. 24.
Melville Schweitzer Collection of California Miscellany. MS Vault 55.
Sloat Collection. MS Vault 57, 146.
Mariano Guadalupe Vallejo Miscellany. MS 2204.
M. G. Vallejo's Release from Fort Sutter. PAM 4131.

California State Parks, Sonoma
Vallejo Family Papers. Collection number 243.1.

History San José, San José
Pueblo Papers

Huntington Library, San Marino
Early California Population Project
William Heath Davis Papers. DA 1–274.
Helen and Robert W. Long Collection of Moreno Documents. HLG 1–1132.
Monterey Collection. MR 1–407.
Mariano Guadalupe Vallejo Papers. VA 1–257.
Mariano Guadalupe Vallejo to Valentín Cota, January 31, 1839. IIM 38257.
Mariano Guadalupe Vallejo to Thompson and West, September 20, 1870. TW121.

Santa Bárbara Mission Archive-Library
California Mission Documents
De la Guerra Collection
De la Guerra Collection: Vallejo
Zephyrin Engelhardt Papers
Francis Guest Research Notes

Society of California Pioneers, San Francisco
Letters of M. G. Vallejo, C059027
Vallejo Scrapbook, C058528

Published Primary Sources

Alvarado, Juan Bautista. *Vignettes of Early California: Childhood Reminiscences of Juan Bautista Alvarado.* Translated by John H. R. Polt. Introduction by W. Michael Mathes. San Francisco: Book Club of California, 1982.

Ames, George Walcott. "Gillespie and the Conquest of California: From Letters Dated February 11, 1846, to July 8, 1848, to the Secretary of the Navy." *California Historical Society Quarterly* 17, part 1, no. 2 (June 1938): 123–40; part 2, no. 3 (September 1938): 271–84; part 3, no. 4 (December 1938): 325–50.

Argüello, Luis Antonio. *The Diary of Captain Luis Antonio Argüello: October 17–November 17, 1821: The Last Spanish Expedition in California.* Translated by Vivian C. Fisher. Introduction by Arthur Quinn. Berkeley: Friends of The Bancroft Library, 1992.

Arrillaga, José Joaquín. *José Joaquín Arrillaga: Diary of His Surveys of the Frontier, 1796.* Edited by John W. Robinson. Translated by Froylan Tiscareño. Los Angeles: Dawson's Book Shop, 1969.

Beebe, Rose Marie, and Robert M. Senkewicz, eds. *Lands of Promise and Despair: Chronicles of Early California, 1535–1846.* Norman: University of Oklahoma Press, 2015.

———. *Testimonios: Early California through the Eyes of Women, 1815–1848.* Norman: University of Oklahoma Press, 2015.

Browne, J. Ross, ed. *Report of the Debates in the Convention of California, on the Formation of the State Constitution, in September and October, 1849.* Washington, D.C.: Printed by J. T. Towers, 1850.

Burdett, Charles. *Life of Kit Carson: The Great Western Hunter and Guide.* Philadelphia: J. E. Potter and Co, 1862.

Camp, Charles Lewis, ed. *George C. Yount and His Chronicles of the West: Comprising Extracts from His "Memoirs" and from the Orange Clark "Narrative."* Denver: Old West, 1966.

Castillo, Edward D. "The Assassination of Padre Andrés Quintana by the Indians of Mission Santa Cruz in 1812: The Narrative of Lorenzo Asisara." *California History* 68, no. 3 (1989): 116–25.

Cerruti, Henry. *Ramblings in California: The Adventures of Henry Cerruti.* Edited by Margaret Mollins and Virginia E. Thickens. Berkeley: Friends of The Bancroft Library, 1954.

Cook, Sherburne. *Colonial Expeditions to the Interior of California: Central Valley, 1800–1820.* Anthropological Records 16, no. 6. Berkeley: University of California Press, 1960.

———. *Expeditions to the Interior of California: Central Valley, 1820–1840.* Anthropological Records 20, no. 5. Berkeley: University of California Press, 1962.

Crosby, Elisha Oscar. *Memoirs of Elisha Oscar Crosby: Reminiscences of California and Guatemala from 1849 to 1864.* Edited by Charles A. Barker. San Marino: Huntington Library, 1945.

Dana, Richard Henry. *Two Years before the Mast and Other Voyages.* Edited by Thomas Philbrick. New York: Library of America, 2005.

Davis, William Heath. *Sixty Years in California.* San Francisco: A. J. Leary, 1889.

Dixon, William Hepworth. *White Conquest.* 2 vols. London: Chatto and Windus, Piccadilly, 1876.

"Documentary: The Bear Flag Movement." *California Historical Society Quarterly* 1, no. 1 (1922): 72–95.

Drake, Daniel. *Pioneer Life in Kentucky, 1785–1800.* Edited by Emmet Field Horine. New York: H. Schuman, 1948.

Duflot de Mofras, Eugène. *Duflot de Mofras' Travels on the Pacific Coast.* Translated by Marguerite Knowlton Eyer Wilbur. Santa Ana, Calif.: Fine Arts Press, 1937.

Dunbar, Seymour, ed. *The Fort Sutter Papers with Historical and Critical Commentaries.* New York: Edward Eberstadt, 1921.

Dwinelle, John W. *Address on the Acquisition of California by the United States: Delivered before the Society of California Pioneers on September 10th, 1866.* San Francisco: Sterett and Cubery, 1866.

Figueroa, José. *Manifesto to the Mexican Republic, Which Brigadier General José Figueroa, Commandant and Political Chief of Upper California, Presents on His Conduct and on That of José María de Híjar and José María Padrés as Directors of Colonization in 1834 and 1835.* Edited by C. Alan Hutchinson. Berkeley: University of California Press, 1978.

Font, Pedro. *With Anza to California, 1775–1776: The Journal of Pedro Font, O.F.M.* Edited by Alan K. Brown. Norman: Arthur H. Clark Company, 2011.

Frisbie, John B. *Memorial and Accompanying Papers in Relation to the Soscol Ranch.* San Francisco: Commercial Steam Presses, 1862.

Gibson, James R, ed. *California through Russian Eyes, 1806–1848.* Norman: University of Oklahoma Press, 2014.

Gleeson, W. *History of the Catholic Church in California.* San Francisco: A. L. Bancroft, 1872.

Harris, Bogardus, and Labatt. *San Francisco City Directory: For the Year Commencing October 1856.* San Francisco: Whitton, Towne, 1856.

Hartnell, William E. P. *The Diary and Copybook of William E. P. Hartnell, Visitador General of the Missions of Alta California in 1839 and 1840.* Edited by Glenn J. Farris. Translated by Starr Pait Gurcke. Santa Clara: California Mission Studies Association; Spokane: Arthur H. Clark Company, 2004.

Heizer, Robert F., ed. *Collected Documents on the Causes and Events in the Bloody Island Massacre of 1850.* Berkeley: Archaeological Research Facility, Department of Anthropology, University of California, 1973.

Hoffman, Ogden. *Reports of Land Cases Determined in the United States District Court for the Northern District of California: June Term 1853 to June Term 1858, Inclusive.* San Francisco: Numa Herbert, 1862.

Journal of the Assembly during the Seventeenth Session of the Legislature of the State of California, 1867–8. Sacramento: D. W. Gelwicks, State Printer, 1868.

Journal of the Legislature of the State of California for Its Second Session, 1851. Sacramento: Eugene Casserly, State Printer, 1851.

Journal of the Senate of the State of California at their First Session. San Jose: J. Winchester, State Printer, 1850.

Khlebnikov, K. T. *The Khlebnikov Archive: Unpublished Journal (1800–1837) and Travel Notes (1820, 1822, and 1824).* Edited by L. A. Shur. Translated by John Bisk. Fairbanks: University of Alaska Press, 1990.

Lamb, Blaine. "Mariano Guadalupe Vallejo's Report on the Derivation and Definition of the Names of the Several Counties of California." *Boletín: Journal of the California Mission Studies Association* 23, no. 1 (March 2006): 50–84.

Langley, Henry G. *The San Francisco Directory: For the Year 1862.* San Francisco: S. D. Valentine & Sons, 1862.

LeCount & Strong's San Francisco City Directory: For the Year 1854. San Francisco: Printed at the San Francisco Herald Office, 1854.

Mathes, W. Michael, Glenn J. Farris, Lyn Kalani, and Sarjan Holt. *The Russian-Mexican Frontier: Mexican Documents Regarding the Russian Establishments in California, 1808–1842.* Jenner, Calif.: Fort Ross Interpretive Association, 2008.

Oak, Henry L. *"Literary Industries" in a New Light: A Statement on the Authorship of Bancroft's* Native Races *and* History of the Pacific States. San Francisco: Bacon Printing, 1893.

———. *A Visit to the Missions of Southern California in February and March 1874.* Edited by Ruth Frey Axe, Edwin H. Carpenter, and Norman Neuerburg. Frederick Webb Hodge Anniversary Publication Fund 11. Los Angeles: Southwest Museum, 1981.

Osio, Antonio María. *The History of Alta California: A Memoir of Mexican California.* Edited and translated by Rose Marie Beebe and Robert M. Senkewicz. Madison: University of Wisconsin Press, 1996.

Palóu, Francisco. *Palóu's Life of Fray Junípero Serra.* Edited and translated by Maynard J. Geiger. Washington, D.C.: Academy of American Franciscan History, 1955.

Revere, Joseph W. *Naval Duty in California: With Map and Plates from Original Designs.* Oakland: Biobooks, 1947.

———. *A Tour of Duty in California.* New York: C. S. Francis; Boston: J. H. Francis, 1849.

Reynolds, Keld J. "Principal Actions of the California Junta de Fomento, 1825–1827." *California Historical Society Quarterly,* part 1: 24, no. 4 (December 1945): 289–320; part 2: 25, no. 1 (March 1946): 57–78; part 3: 25, no. 2 (June 1946): 149–68; part 4: 25, no. 3 (September 1946): 267–78; part 5: 25, no. 4 (December 1946): 347–67.

Rivera y Moncada, Fernando de. *Diario del capitán comandante Fernando de Rivera y Moncada, con un apéndice documental.* Edited by Ernest J. Burrus. 2 vols. Madrid: Ediciones J. Porrúa Turanzas, 1967.

Robinson, Alfred. *Life in California: During a Residence of Several Years in That Territory: Comprising a Description of the Country and the Missionary Establishments, with Incidents, Observations, Etc.* New York: Wiley & Putman, 1846.

Ruiz de Burton, María Amparo. *The Squatter and the Don.* Edited by Rosaura Sánchez and Beatrice Pita. Houston: Arte Público Press, 1992.

Sánchez, Rosaura, and Beatrice Pita, eds. *Conflicts of Interest: The Letters of María Amparo Ruiz de Burton.* Houston: Arte Público Press, 2001.

Sánchez, Rosaura, Beatrice Pita, and Bárbara Reyes, eds. *Nineteenth Century Californio Testimonios.* Crítica Monograph Series 68. La Jolla: University of California, San Diego, Ethnic Studies, Third World Studies, 1994.

Sandels, G. M. Waseurtz af. *A Sojourn in California by the King's Orphan: The Travels and Sketches of G.M. Waseurtz af Sandels, a Swedish Gentleman Who Visited California in 1842–1843.* San Francisco: Printed at the

Grabhorn Press for the Book Club of California in arrangement with the Society of California Pioneers, 1945.

Shaler, William. "Journal of a Voyage between China and the North-Western Coast of America, Made in 1804." *American Register* 3 (1808): 137–75.

Shea, John Gilmary. *Catholic Missions among the Indian Tribes of the United States.* New York: Edward Dunigan & Bro., 1857.

———. *History of the Catholic Missions among the Indian Tribes of the United States, 1529–1854.* New York: Edward Dunigan & Bro., 1855.

Sherman, William T. *Memoirs of William T. Sherman.* 2 vols. New York: D. Appleton, 1875.

The Statutes of California Passed at the Ninth Session of the Legislature. Sacramento: John O'Meara, State Printer, 1858.

Sutter, John Augustus. *The Diary of Johann August Sutter.* Edited by Douglas S. Watson. San Francisco: Grabhorn Press, 1932.

Tuthill, Franklin. *The History of California.* San Francisco: H. H. Bancroft, 1866.

Upham, Samuel C. *Notes of a Voyage to California via Cape Horn: Together with Scenes in El Dorado, in the Years 1849–'50.* Philadelphia: S. C. Upham, 1878.

Vallejo, Guadalupe. "Ranch and Mission Days in California." *Century Magazine* 41 (December 1890): 183–92.

Vallejo, Mariano Guadalupe. *Francisco Solano, gefe de las tribus de esta frontera, abusando del poder.* Sonoma: self-printed, 1838.

———. *Recuerdos: Historical and Personal Remembrances Relating to Alta California, 1769-1849.* Edited and translated by Rose Marie Beebe and Robert M. Senkewicz. 2 vols. Norman: University of Oklahoma Press, 2023.

———. *Report of a Visit to Fort Ross and Bodega Bay in April 1833.* Translated by Glenn J. Farris and Rose Marie Beebe. Bakersfield, Calif.: California Mission Studies Association, 2000.

Vallejo, Platón Mariano Guadalupe. *Memoirs of the Vallejos: New Light on the History, before and after the "Gringos" Came, Based on Original Documents and Recollections.* Fairfield, Calif.: James D. Stevenson, in cooperation with the Napa County Historical Society, 1994.

Vischer, Edward. *Edward Vischer's Drawings of the California Missions, 1861–1878.* Edited by Jeanne Van Nostrand. San Francisco: Book Club of California, 1982.

Watson, Henry Bulls. *The Journals of Marine Second Lieutenant Henry Bulls Watson, 1845–1848.* Edited by Charles R. Smith. Washington, D.C.: History and Museums Division, Headquarters, U.S. Marine Corps, 1990.

White, Philo. *Narrative of a Cruise in the Pacific: To South America and California on the U.S. Sloop-of-War Dale, 1841–1843.* Edited by Charles Lewis Camp. Denver: Old West, 1965.

Wise, Henry Augustus. *Los Gringos, or, an inside view of Mexico and California, with wandering in Peru, Chile, and Polynesia.* New York: Baker and Scribner, 1850.

SECONDARY SOURCES

Agostoni, Claudia. *Monuments of Progress: Modernization and Public Health in Mexico City, 1876–1910.* Calgary: University of Calgary Press; Boulder: University of Colorado Press; Mexico City: Instituto de Investigaciones Históricas, UNAM, 2003.

Andrews, Thomas G. "Toward an Environmental History of the Book: The Nature of Hubert Howe Bancroft's Works." *Southern California Quarterly* 93, no. 1 (2011): 33–68.

Arkush, Brooke S. "Native Responses to European Intrusion: Cultural Persistence and Agency among Mission Neophytes in Spanish Colonial Northern California." *Historical Archaeology* 45, no. 4 (2011): 62–90.

Aviña, Rose H. *Spanish and Mexican Land Grants in California.* Saratoga, Calif.: R and E Research Associates, 1973.

Bakken, Gordon Morris. "Mexican and American Land Policy: A Conflict of Cultures." *Southern California Quarterly* 75, no. 3–4 (Fall–Winter 1993): 237–62.

Bancroft, Hubert Howe. *California Pastoral, 1769–1848.* San Francisco: History Company, 1888.

———. *History of California.* 7 vols. San Francisco: History Company, 1884–90.

———. *Literary Industries.* San Francisco: History Company, 1890.

———. *The Native Races of the Pacific States of North America.* 5 vols. New York: D. Appleton, 1875.

———. *Popular Tribunals.* 2 vols. San Francisco: History Company, 1887.

Barker, Charles A. "Elisha Oscar Crosby: A California Lawyer in the Eighteen-Fifties." *California Historical Society Quarterly* 27, no. 2 (1948): 133–40.

Barrett, Samuel Alfred. *The Ethno-geography of the Pomo and Neighboring Indians.* University of California Publications in American Archaeology and Ethnology 6, no. 1. Berkeley: University of California Press, 1908.

Bastian, Beverly E. "'I Heartily Regret That I Ever Touched a Title in California': Henry Wager Halleck, the Californios, and the Clash of Legal Cultures." *California History* 72, no. 4 (December 1993): 310–23.

Bean, Lowell John, and Dorothea Theodoratus. "Western Pomo and Northeastern Pomo." In *Handbook of North American Indians*. Vol. 8, *California*, ed. Robert F. Heizer, 289–305. Washington, D.C.: Smithsonian Institution, 1978.

Beebe, Rose Marie, and Robert M. Senkewicz. *Junípero Serra: California, Indians, and the Transformation of a Missionary*. Norman: University of Oklahoma Press; Oceanside, Calif.: Academy of American Franciscan History, 2015.

———. "Mariano Guadalupe Vallejo: Recovering a Californio Voice from Mexican California." In *Writing/Righting History: Twenty-Five Years of Recovering the US Hispanic Literary Heritage*, ed. Antonia Castañeda and Clara Lomas, 261–77. Houston: Arte Público Press, 2019.

Bennyhoff, James A. *Ethnogeography of the Plains Miwok*. Publication 5. Davis, Calif.: Center for Archaeological Research, 1977.

Biggs, Donald C. *Conquer and Colonize: Stevenson's Regiment and California*. San Rafael, Calif.: Presidio Press, 1977.

Brack, Gene M. *Mexico Views Manifest Destiny, 1821–1846: An Essay on the Origins of the Mexican War*. Albuquerque: University of New Mexico Press, 1975.

Brewster, Michele M. "A Californiana in Two Worlds: Anita de la Guerra Robinson, 1821–1855." *Southern California Quarterly* 102, no. 2 (2020), 101–42.

Brinckerhoff, Sidney B., and Odie B. Faulk. *Lancers for the King: A Study of the Frontier Military System of Northern New Spain: With a Translation of the Royal Regulations of 1772*. Phoenix: Arizona Historical Foundation, 1965.

California State Lands Commission. *Grants of Land in California Made by Spanish or Mexican Authorities*. Sacramento: California State Lands Commission, 1982.

Callaghan, Catherine A. "Lake Miwok." In *Handbook of North American Indians*. Vol. 8, *California*, ed. Robert F. Heizer, 264–73. Washington, D.C.: Smithsonian Institution, 1978.

Camarillo, Albert. *Chicanos in a Changing Society: From Mexican Pueblos to American Barrios in Santa Barbara and Southern California, 1848–1930*. Cambridge: Harvard University Press, 1979.

Carlson, Pamela McGuire, and E. Breck Parkman. "An Exceptional Adaptation: Camillo Ynitia, the Last Headman of the Olompalis." *California History* 65, no. 4 (1986): 238–47.

Carrico, Richard L. *Strangers in a Stolen Land: Indians of San Diego County from Prehistory to the New Deal*. San Diego: Sunbelt Publications, 2008.

Casas, María Raquel. *Married to a Daughter of the Land: Spanish-Mexican Women and Interethnic Marriage in California, 1820–80.* Reno: University of Nevada Press, 2007.

Castleman, Bruce A. *Knickerbocker Commodore: The Life and Times of John Drake Sloat, 1781–1867.* Albany: State University of New York Press, 2016.

Caughey, John Walton. *Hubert Howe Bancroft, 1832–1918: Historian of the West.* Los Angeles: University of California Press, 1946.

Cavo, Andrés, and Carlos María de Bustamante. *Tres siglos de México durante el gobierno español hasta la entrada del ejército trigarante.* 3 vols. México: Imprenta de Luis Abadiano y Valdés, 1836.

Chávez-García, Miroslava. *Negotiating Conquest: Gender and Power in California, 1770s to 1880s.* Tucson: University of Arizona Press, 2004.

Clark, Harry. "Their Pride, Their Manners, and Their Voices: Sources of the Traditional Portrait of the Early Californians." *California Historical Quarterly* 53, no. 1 (1974): 71–82.

——. *A Venture in History: The Production, Publication, and Sale of the Works of Hubert Howe Bancroft.* Berkeley: University of California Press, 1973.

Clarke, Dwight L. *Stephen Watts Kearny: Soldier of the West.* Norman: University of Oklahoma Press, 1961.

Colman, Andrew M. *A Dictionary of Psychology.* Oxford: Oxford University Press, 2015.

Comstock, Esther J. "A Day General Vallejo Never Forgot." *Pacific Historian* 17, no. 4 (September 1973): 31–34.

Cook, Sherburne. *The Aboriginal Population of Alameda and Contra Costa Counties, California.* Anthropological Records 16, no. 4. Berkeley: University of California Press, 1957.

——. *The Aboriginal Population of the San Joaquin Valley, California.* Anthropological Records 16, no. 2. Berkeley: University of California Press, 1955.

——. *The Conflict between the California Indian and White Civilization.* Berkeley: University of California Press, 1976.

——. "Smallpox in Spanish and Mexican California, 1770–1845." *Bulletin of the History of Medicine* 7, no. 2 (February 1939): 153–91.

Cosío Villegas, Daniel. *The United States versus Porfirio Díaz.* Lincoln: University of Nebraska Press, 1963.

Curry, Daniel T. "Northern California: Persistence and Property Rights in a Changing Economy, 1840–1880." *Essays in History* 49, no. 1 (2016): 1–27.

Dakin, Susanna Bryant. *The Lives of William Hartnell.* Stanford: Stanford University Press, 1949.

Denton, Sally. *Passion and Principle: John and Jessie Frémont, the Couple Whose Power, Politics, and Love Shaped Nineteenth-Century America.* New York: Bloomsbury, 2007.

Diccionario Porrúa de historia, biografía y geografía de México. 6th ed. México: Editorial Porrúa, 1995.

Downey, Joseph T. *The Cruise of the Portsmouth, 1845–1847: A Sailor's View of the Naval Conquest of California.* Edited by Howard Roberts Lamar. New Haven: Yale University Press, 1963.

Emparán, Madie Brown. *The Vallejos of California.* San Francisco: Gleeson Library Associates, University of San Francisco, 1968.

Engelhardt, Zephyrin. *The Holy Man of Santa Clara: Or, Life, Virtues, and Miracles of Fr. Magín Catalá, O.F.M.* San Francisco: James H. Barry Company, 1909.

———. *Mission San Luis Obispo in the Valley of the Bears.* Santa Barbara: Mission Santa Barbara, 1933.

———. *The Missions and Missionaries of California.* 4 vols. San Francisco: James H. Barry Company, 1908.

———. *San Antonio de Padua, the Mission in the Sierras.* Santa Barbara: Mission Santa Barbara, 1929.

———. *Santa Barbara Mission.* San Francisco: James H. Barry Company, 1923.

Eversole, Robert Wayne. "Towns in Mexican California: A Social History of Monterey, San Jose, Santa Barbara, and Los Angeles, 1822–1846." PhD diss., University of California, San Diego, 1986.

Farris, Glenn J. "A Peace Treaty between Mariano Vallejo and Satiyomi Chief Succara." Paper Presented at the Fifth California Indian Conference, Humboldt State University, Arcata, Calif., October 13, 1989.

Foucrier, Annick. "Spy or Explorer? The True Mission of Eugène Duflot de Mofras." *Californians* 9, no. 4 (January 1992): 17–26.

Fowler, Will. *Forceful Negotiations: The Origins of the Pronunciamiento in Nineteenth-Century Mexico.* Lincoln: University of Nebraska Press, 2011.

———. "Valentín Gómez Farías: Perceptions of Radicalism in Independent Mexico, 1821–1847." *Bulletin of Latin American Research* 15, no. 1 (1996): 39–62.

Francis, Jessie Hughes Davies. *An Economic and Social History of Mexican California, 1822–1846.* Vol. 1, *Chiefly Economic.* New York: Arno Press, 1976.

Gates, Paul W. "Adjudication of Spanish-Mexican Land Claims in California." *Huntington Library Quarterly* 21, no. 3 (June 1957): 213–36.

———. "The California Land Act of 1851." *California Historical Quarterly* 50, no. 4 (October 1971): 395–430.

————. "The Frémont-Jones Scramble for California Land Claims." *Southern California Quarterly* 56, no. 1 (March 1974): 13–44.

————. "The Suscol Principle, Preemption, and California Latifundia." *Pacific Historical Review* 39, no. 4 (November 1970): 453–71.

Geary, Gerald J. *The Secularization of the California Missions (1810–1846)*. Studies in American Church History 17. Washington, D.C.: Catholic University of America, 1934.

Geiger, Maynard J. *Franciscan Missionaries in Hispanic California, 1769–1848: A Biographical Dictionary*. San Marino: Huntington Library, 1969.

Genini, Ronald, and Richard Hitchman. *Romualdo Pacheco: A Californio in Two Eras*. San Francisco: Book Club of California, 1985.

Gibb, Andrew. *Californios, Anglos, and the Performance of Oligarchy in the U.S. West: How the First Generation of Mexican Americans Fashioned a New Nation*. Carbondale: Southern Illinois University Press, 2018.

Giffen, Helen S. *Trail-Blazing Pioneer Colonel Joseph Ballinger Chiles*. San Francisco: John Howell Books, 1969.

Gillis, Michael J., and Michael F. Magliari. *John Bidwell and California: The Life and Writings of a Pioneer, 1841–1900*. Spokane: Arthur H. Clark Company, 2004.

Goerke, Betty. *Chief Marin: Leader, Rebel, and Legend*. Berkeley: Heyday Books, 2007.

Gray, Paul Bryan. *A Clamor for Equality: Emergence and Exile of Californio Activist Francisco P. Ramírez*. Lubbock: Texas Tech University Press, 2012.

Gray, Paul Bryan, David E. Hayes-Bautista, and Cynthia L. Chamberlin. "'The Men Were Left Astonished': Mexican Women in *Las Juntas Patrióticas de Señoras*, 1863–1866." *Southern California Quarterly* 94, no. 2 (Summer 2012): 161–92.

Gray, Thorne B. *The Stanislaus Indian Wars: The Last of the California Northern Yokuts*. Modesto, Calif: McHenry Museum Press, 1993.

Griswold del Castillo, Richard. *The Los Angeles Barrio, 1850–1890: A Social History*. Berkeley: University of California Press, 1979.

————. *The Treaty of Guadalupe Hidalgo: A Legacy of Conflict*. Norman: University of Oklahoma Press, 1992.

Hague, Harlan, and David J. Langum. *Thomas O. Larkin: A Life of Patriotism and Profit in Old California*. Norman: University of Oklahoma Press, 1990.

Harding, George Laban. *Don Agustín V. Zamorano: Statesman, Soldier, Craftsman, and California's First Printer*. Spokane: Arthur H. Clark Company, 2003.

Hargis, Donald E. "Native Californians in the Constitutional Convention of 1849." *Historical Society of Southern California Quarterly* 36, no. 1 (1954): 3–13.

———. "W. M. Gwin: Middleman." *Historical Society of Southern California Quarterly* 40, no. 1 (1958): 17–32.

Harlow, Neal. *California Conquered: War and Peace on the Pacific, 1846–1850.* Berkeley: University of California Press, 1982.

Hart, John Mason. *Empire and Revolution: The Americans in Mexico since the Civil War.* Berkeley: University of California Press, 2002.

Hayes-Bautista, David E., Cynthia L. Chamberlin, Branden Jones, Juan Carlos Cornejo, Cecilia Cañadas, Carlos Martínez, and Gloria Meza. "Empowerment, Expansion, and Engagement: 'Las Juntas Patrióticas' in California, 1848–1869." *California History* 85, no. 1 (January 2008): 4.

Heidenreich, Linda. "The Colonial North: Histories of Women and Violence from before the U.S. Invasion." *Aztlán* 30, no. 1 (Spring 2005): 23–54.

———. *"This Land Was Mexican Once": Histories of Resistance from Northern California.* Austin: University of Texas Press, 2007.

Heizer, Robert F., ed. *The Archaeology of the Napa Region.* Anthropological Records 12, no. 6. Berkeley: University of California Press, 1953.

———. *Handbook of North American Indians.* Vol. 8, *California.* Washington, D.C.: Smithsonian Institution, 1978.

———. "Walla Walla Indian Expeditions to the Sacramento Valley." *California Historical Society Quarterly* 21, no. 1 (1942): 1–7.

Hittell, Theodore. *History of California.* 4 vols. San Francisco: Pacific Press, 1885–97.

Holden, E. D. "California's First Pianos." *California Historical Society Quarterly* 13, no. 1 (1934): 34–37.

Holterman, Jack. "The Revolt of Estanislao." *Indian Historian* 3, no. 1 (January 1970): 43–54.

Hurtado, Albert L. *Herbert Eugene Bolton: Historian of the American Borderlands.* Berkeley: University of California Press, 2012.

———. *Indian Survival on the California Frontier.* New Haven: Yale University Press, 1988.

———. *John Sutter: A Life on the North American Frontier.* Norman: University of Oklahoma Press, 2006.

———. "John Sutter and the Indian Business." In *John Sutter and a Wider West,* ed. Kenneth N. Owens, 51–75. Lincoln: University of Nebraska Press, 1994.

———. *The Scotts Valley Band of Indians and the North San Francisco Bay Region.* Request for Indian Lands Determination, Scotts Valley Band of Pomo Indians. Report Presented to the Department of the Interior, 2016.

Hussey, John Adam, and George Walcott Ames. "California Preparations to Meet the Walla Walla Invasion, 1846." *California Historical Society Quarterly* 21, no. 1 (1942): 9–21.

Hutchinson, C. Alan. *Frontier Settlement in Mexican California: The Híjar-Padrés Colony and Its Origins, 1769–1835.* New Haven: Yale University Press, 1969.

———. "An Official List of the Members of the Híjar-Padrés Colony for Mexican California, 1834." *Pacific Historical Review* 42, no. 3 (1973): 407–18.

Jameson, J. Franklin. *The History of Historical Writing in America.* Boston: Houghton Mifflin, 1891.

Johnson, Patti J. "Patwin." In *Handbook of North American Indians.* Vol. 8, *California*, ed. Robert F. Heizer, 350–60. Washington, D.C.: Smithsonian Institution, 1978.

Johnston, Andrew Scott. *Mercury and the Making of California: Mining, Landscape, and Race, 1840–1890.* Boulder: University Press of Colorado, 2015.

Jones, Oakah L. *Los Paisanos: Spanish Settlers on the Northern Frontier of New Spain.* Norman: University of Oklahoma Press, 1996.

Kanellos, Nicolás, ed. *En otra voz: antología de literatura hispana de los Estados Unidos.* Houston: Arte Público Press, 2002.

Kelly, Isabel. "Coast Miwok." In *Handbook of North American Indians.* Vol. 8, *California*, ed. Robert F. Heizer, 414–25. Washington, D.C.: Smithsonian Institution, 1978.

Kelly, Isabel T., Mary E. T. Collier, Sylvia Barker Thalman, Tom Smith, and María Copa. *Interviews with Tom Smith and Maria Copa: Isabel Kelly's Ethnographic Notes on the Coast Miwok Indians of Marin and Southern Sonoma Counties, California.* Edited by Mary E. T. Collier and Sylvia Barker Thalman. MAPOM Occasional Papers 6. San Rafael, Calif.: Miwok Archaeological Preserve of Marin, 1991.

Kimbro, Edna E., Julia G. Costello, and Tevvy Ball. *The California Missions: History, Art, and Preservation.* Los Angeles: Getty Conservation Institute, 2009.

Koegel, John. "'Canciones del país': Mexican Musical Life in California after the Gold Rush." *California History* 78, no. 3 (1999): 160–87.

———. "Mexican-American Music in Nineteenth-Century Southern California: The Lummus Wax Collection at the Southwest Museum, Los Angeles." PhD diss., Claremont Graduate School, 1994.

Komanecky, Michael. "'The Treasures of Sentiment, the Charms of Romance, and the Riches of History:' Artists' Views of California's

Missions." In *California Mexicana: Missions to Murals, 1820–1930*, ed. Katherine Manthorne, 173–95. Laguna Beach: Laguna Art Museum in association with University of California Press, 2017.

Kroeber, A. L. *Handbook of the Indians of California.* New York: Dover Publications, 1976.

———. *The Patwin and Their Neighbors.* University of California Publications in American Archaeology and Ethnology 29, no. 4. Berkeley: University of California Press, 1932.

Kryder-Reid, Elizabeth. *California Mission Landscapes: Race, Memory, and the Politics of Heritage.* Minneapolis: University of Minnesota Press, 2016.

Lamar Prieto, Covadonga. "Land Ownership as a Resource for Constructing Otherness in California." In *Otherness in Hispanic Culture*, ed. Teresa Fernández Ulloa, 387–409. Cambridge: Cambridge Scholars Publishing, 2014.

———. "The Silencing of the Californios: Tracing the Beginnings of Linguistic Repression in 19th-Century California." *Voices* 2, no. 1 (2014).

Lamb, Blaine. *The Extraordinary Life of Charles Pomeroy Stone: Soldier, Surveyor, Pasha, Engineer.* Yardley, Pa.: Westholme, 2016.

Langellier, John P., and Daniel B. Rosen. *El Presidio de San Francisco: A History under Spain and Mexico, 1776–1846.* Spokane: Arthur H. Clark Company, 1996.

Langum, David J. "Californios and the Image of Indolence." *Western Historical Quarterly* 9, no. 2 (1978): 181–96.

———. *Quite Contrary: The Litigious Life of Mary Bennett Love.* Lubbock: Texas Tech University Press, 2014.

Larkin, Thomas O. *The Larkin Papers: Personal, Business, and Official Correspondence of Thomas Oliver Larkin, Merchant and United States Consul in California.* Edited by George P. Hammond. 10 vols. Berkeley: University of California Press, 1951–64.

Levy, Richard. "Eastern Miwok." In *Handbook of North American Indians.* Vol. 8, *California*, ed. Robert F. Heizer, 398–413. Washington, D.C.: Smithsonian Institution, 1978.

Lightfoot, Kent G. *Indians, Missionaries, and Merchants: The Legacy of Colonial Encounters on the California Frontiers.* Berkeley: University of California Press, 2005.

Lightfoot, Kent G., and Sara L. Gonzalez. "The Study of Sustained Colonialism: An Example from the Kashaya Pomo Homeland in Northern California." *American Antiquity* 83, no. 3 (July 2018): 427–43.

Lindsay, Brendan C. *Murder State: California's Native American Genocide, 1846–1873.* Lincoln: University of Nebraska Press, 2015.

Lint Sagarena, Roberto Ramón. *Aztlán and Arcadia: Religion, Ethnicity, and the Creation of Place.* New York: New York University Press, 2014.

López, Marissa K. *Chicano Nations: The Hemispheric Origins of Mexican American Literature.* New York: New York University Press, 2011.

———. "The Political Economy of Early Chicano Historiography: The Case of Hubert H. Bancroft and Mariano G. Vallejo." *American Literary History* 19, no. 4 (2007): 874–904.

Lothrop, Marian Lydia. "Indian Campaigns of General M. G. Vallejo, Defender of the Northern Frontier of California." *Quarterly of the Society of California Pioneers* 9 (1932): 161–205.

———. "Mariano Guadalupe Vallejo, Defender of the Northern Frontier of California." PhD diss., University of California, Berkeley, 1926.

Lozano, Rosina A. *An American Language: The History of Spanish in the United States.* Berkeley: University of California Press, 2018.

Lynch, Robert M., and Celeste Granice Murphy. *The Sonoma Valley Story: Pages through the Ages.* Sonoma: Sonoma Index-Tribune, 1997.

Madley, Benjamin. *An American Genocide: The United States and the California Indian Catastrophe, 1846–1873.* New Haven: Yale University Press, 2016.

Magliari, Michael. "Free Soil, Unfree Labor: Cave Johnson Couts and the Binding of Indian Workers in California, 1850–1867." *Pacific Historical Review* 73, no. 3 (2004): 349–90.

Mann, Ralph. "The Americanization of Arcadia: Images of Hispanic and Gold Rush California." *American Studies* 19, no. 1 (1978): 5–19.

Manning, John. "Discipline in the Good Old Days." In *Corporal Punishment in American Education,* ed. Irwin A. Hyman and James H. Wise, 50–61. Philadelphia: Temple University Press, 1979.

Marti, Werner H. *Messenger of Destiny: The California Adventures, 1846–1847, of Archibald H. Gillespie, U.S. Marine Corps.* San Francisco: John Howell Books, 1960.

Martínez, Pablo L. *Historia de Baja California.* México: Libros Mexicanos, 1956.

Mason, William M. *The Census of 1790: A Demographic History of Colonial California.* Menlo Park, Calif.: Ballena Press, 1998.

McClellan, C. "Ethnography of the Wappo and Patwin." In *The Archaeology of the Napa Region,* ed. Robert F. Heizer, 233–43. Anthropological Records 12, no. 6. Berkeley: University of California Press, 1977.

McGinty, Brian. "The Carrillos of San Diego: A Historic Spanish Family of California." *Historical Society of Southern California Quarterly* 39, part 1, no. 1 (1957): 3–13; part 2, no. 2 (June 1957): 127–48; part 3, no. 3 (September 1957): 281–301; part 4, no. 4 (December 1957): 371–91.

McGloin, John Bernard. *California's First Archbishop: The Life of Joseph Sadoc Alemany, 1814–1888*. New York: Herder and Herder, 1966.

McKittrick, Myrtle M. "Salvador Vallejo." *California Historical Society Quarterly* 29, no. 4 (1950): 309–31.

———. *Vallejo, Son of California*. Portland: Binfords & Mort, 1944.

McLendon, Sally, and Michael J. Lowy. "Eastern Pomo and Southeastern Pomo." In *Handbook of North American Indians*. Vol. 8, *California*, ed. Robert F. Heizer, 306–23. Washington, D.C.: Smithsonian Institution, 1978.

McLendon, Sally, and Robert L. Oswalt. "Pomo: Introduction." In *Handbook of North American Indians*. Vol. 8, *California*, ed. Robert F. Heizer, 274–88. Washington, D.C.: Smithsonian Institution, 1978.

McNally, Sr. Mary Gene. "Mariano Guadalupe Vallejo's Relations with the Indians of California's Northern Frontier, 1825–1842." MA thesis, Dominican College of San Rafael, 1976.

Merriam, C. Hart. *Ethnogeographic and Ethnosynonymic Data from Central California Tribes*. Assembled and edited by Robert F. Heizer. Berkeley: Archaeological Research Facility, Department of Anthropology, University of California, 1977.

Merrill, James M. *Du Pont: The Making of an Admiral: A Biography of Samuel Francis Du Pont*. New York: Dodd, Mead, 1986.

Meyerhof, Peter G. "Dr. Robert Semple: The Personification of Benicia's Struggle with San Francisco." *Argonaut* 23, no. 1 (Spring 2012): 48.

Miller, Robert Ryal. "Arms across the Border: United States Aid to Juárez during the French Intervention in Mexico." *Transactions of the American Philosophical Society* 63, no. 6 (1973): 1–68

———. "Californians against the Emperor." *California Historical Society Quarterly* 37, no. 3 (1958): 193–214.

———. *Captain Richardson: Mariner, Ranchero, and Founder of San Francisco*. Berkeley: La Loma Press, 1995.

———. *Juan Alvarado, Governor of California, 1836–1842*. Norman: University of Oklahoma Press, 1998.

Milliken, Randall. "Ethnographic and Ethnohistoric Context for the Archaeological Investigation of the Suisun Plain, Solano County, California." Unpublished manuscript, n.d.

———. "Ethnohistory and Ethnogeography of the Coast Miwok and Their Neighbors, 1783–1840." Technical paper presented to the National Park Service, Golden Gate NRA.

———. *Native Americans at Mission San José*. Banning, Calif.: Malki-Ballena Press, Malki Museum, 2008.

————. *A Time of Little Choice: The Disintegration of Tribal Culture in the San Francisco Bay Area, 1769–1810*. Menlo Park, Calif.: Ballena Press, 1995.

Monroy, Douglas. *Rebirth: Mexican Los Angeles from the Great Migration to the Great Depression*. Berkeley: University of California Press, 1999.

Montes, Amelia María de la Luz. "*'Es necesario mirar bien'*: Letter Making, Fiction Writing, and American Nationhood in the Nineteenth Century." PhD diss., University of Denver, 1999.

Moorhead, Max L. *The Presidio: Bastion of the Spanish Borderlands*. Norman: University of Oklahoma Press, 1991.

Morton, Michelle E. "Utopian and Dystopian Visions of California in the Historical Imagination." PhD diss., University of California, Santa Cruz, 2005.

Moyano Pahissa, Angela. *La resistencia de las Californias a la invasión norteamericana (1846–1848)*. México, D.F.: Consejo Nacional para la Cultura y las Artes, 1992.

Munro-Fraser, J. P. *History of Solano County*. San Francisco: Wood, Alley, 1879.

————. *History of Sonoma County*. San Francisco: Alley, Bowen, 1880.

Mutnick, Dorothy Gittinger. *Some Alta California Pioneers and Descendants*. 5 vols. Pleasant Hill, Calif.: Contra Costa County Historical Society, 1981.

Nieser, Albert Bertrand. "The Dominican Mission Foundations in Baja California, 1769–1822." PhD diss., Loyola University, 1960.

Northrop, Marie E. *Spanish-Mexican Families of Early California, 1769–1850*. 3 vols. Burbank: Southern California Genealogical Society, 1984–2004.

Nunis, Doyce B. *The Trials of Isaac Graham*. Los Angeles: Dawson's Book Shop, 1967.

Ogden, Adele. *The California Sea Otter Trade, 1784–1848*. Berkeley: University of California Press, 1975.

Paddison, Joshua. *American Heathens: Religion, Race, and Reconstruction in California*. Berkeley: University of California Press, published for the Huntington-USC Institute on California and the West, 2012.

Padilla, Genaro M. *My History, Not Yours: The Formation of Mexican American Autobiography*. Madison: University of Wisconsin Press, 1993.

Palmer, Lyman L. *History of Napa and Lake Counties, California: Comprising Their Geography, Geology, Topography, Climatography, Springs, and Timber*. San Francisco: Slocum, Bowen, 1881.

Parker, John. "The Kelsey Brothers: A California Disaster." Paper presented to the Lake County Historical Society, November 2012, https://www.academia.edu/5539505/The_Kelsey_Brothers_A_California_Disaster.

Parkman, Francis. *The California and Oregon Trail*. New York: George P. Putnam, 1849.

———. *The Jesuits in North America in the Seventeenth Century*. Boston: Little, Brown, and Company, 1867.

Pérez, Erika. *Colonial Intimacies: Interethnic Kinship, Sexuality, and Marriage in Southern California, 1769–1885*. Norman: University of Oklahoma Press, 2018.

———. "'Saludos from Your Comadre': Compadrazgo as a Community Institution in Alta California, 1769–1860s." *California History* 88, no. 4 (September 2011): 47–62.

Pérez, Vincent. *Remembering the Hacienda: History and Memory in the Mexican American Southwest*. College Station: Texas A&M University Press, 2006.

Peterson, Charles S. "Hubert Howe Bancroft: First Western Regionalist." In *Writing Western History: Essays on Major Western Historians*, ed. Richard W. Etulain, 43–70. Reno: University of Nevada Press, 2002.

Peterson, Richard H. "Anti-Mexican Nativism in California, 1848–1853: A Study of Cultural Conflict." *Southern California Quarterly* 62, no. 4 (December 1980): 309–27.

Pfitzer, Gregory M. *Popular History and the Literary Marketplace, 1840–1920*. Amherst: University of Massachusetts Press, 2008.

Philbrick, Nathaniel. *Sea of Glory: America's Voyage of Discovery, The U.S. Exploring Expedition, 1838–1842*. New York: Penguin Books, 2004.

Phillips, George Harwood. *Indians of the Tulares: Adaptation, Relocation, and Subjugation in Central California, 1771–1917*. 2 vols. Temecula, Calif.: Great Oak Press, 2016.

Pinheiro, John C. *Missionaries of Republicanism: A Religious History of the Mexican-American War*. New York: Oxford University Press, 2014.

Pitt, Leonard. "The Beginnings of Nativism in California." *Pacific Historical Review* 30, no. 1 (1961): 23–38.

———. *The Decline of the Californios: A Social History of the Spanish-Speaking Californians, 1846–1890*. Berkeley: University of California Press, 1966.

Prescott, William Hickling. *History of the Conquest of Mexico*. 3 vols. New York: Harper and Brothers, 1843.

———. *History of the Conquest of Peru*. 2 vols. New York: Harper and Brothers, 1847.

Pubols, Louise. *The Father of All: The de la Guerra Family, Power, and Patriarchy in Mexican California*. Berkeley: University of California Press; San Marino: Huntington Library, published for the Huntington-USC Institute on California and the West, 2009.

Purcell, Fernando. "'Too Many Foreigners for My Taste': Mexicans, Chileans and Irish in California, 1848–1880." PhD diss., University of California, Davis, 2004.

Radcliffe, Zoe Green. "Robert Baylor Semple, Pioneer." *California Historical Society Quarterly* 6, no. 2 (1927): 130–58.

Raffan, James. *Emperor of the North: Sir George Simpson and the Remarkable Story of the Hudson's Bay Company*. New York: HarperCollins, 2010.

Ratto, Héctor R. *Capitán de navío Hipólito Bouchard*. Buenos Aires: Departamento de Estudios Históricos Navales, 1961.

Rawls, James J. *Indians of California: The Changing Image*. Norman: University of Oklahoma Press, 1988.

Regnery, Dorothy F. *The Battle of Santa Clara, January 2, 1847: The Only Campaign in the Northern District between the Californios and the United States Forces during the Mexican War*. San Jose: Smith and McKay, 1978.

Reich, Peter L. "Dismantling the Pueblo: Hispanic Municipal Land Rights in California since 1850." *American Journal of Legal History* 45, no. 4 (October 2001): 353–70.

Reid, Anne Marie. "Medics of the Soul and the Body: Sickness and Death in Alta California, 1769–1850." PhD diss., University of Southern California, 2013.

Rhoades, Elizabeth. "Foreigners in Southern California during the Mexican Period." MA thesis, University of California, Berkeley, 1924.

Ríos-Bustamante, Antonio José, and Pedro G. Castillo. *An Illustrated History of Mexican Los Angeles, 1781–1985*. Chicano Studies Research Center Publications. Los Angeles: University of California, Los Angeles, 1986.

Rizzo, Martin. "*Dios no manda eso*: Indigenous Community and Leadership in the Assassination of Padre Quintana in Santa Cruz, 1812." In *Evangelization and Cultural Conflict in Mexico*, ed. Robert H. Jackson, 229–60. Newcastle upon Tyne: Cambridge Scholars, 2014.

———. "Indigenous Justice or Padre Killers? Lino, Fausta, and the Assassination of Padre Quintana." *Santa Cruz County History Journal* 8 (2016): 4–15.

Rizzo-Martínez, Martin. *We Are Not Animals: Indigenous Politics of Survival, Rebellion, and Reconstitution in Nineteenth-Century California*. Lincoln: University of Nebraska Press. 2022.

Robinson, Cecil. *The View from Chapultepec: Mexican Writers on the Mexican-American War*. Tucson: University of Arizona Press, 1989.

Robinson, W. W. *Land in California: The Story of Mission Lands, Ranchos, Squatters, Mining Claims, Railroad Grants, Land Scrip and Homesteads*. Chronicles of California. Berkeley: University of California Press, 1948.

Rodríguez-Sala, María Luisa. *Los gobernadores de las Californias, 1767–1804: contribuciones a la expansión territorial y del conocimiento.* 1st. ed. México: Instituto de Investigaciones Sociales, UNAM; Zapopan: Colegio de Jalisco; Mexicali: Universidad Autónoma de Baja California, 2003.

Rogers, Fred Blackburn. *Montgomery and the* Portsmouth. San Francisco: John Howell Books, 1958.

Rosenus, Alan. *General M. G. Vallejo and the Advent of the Americans: A Biography.* Albuquerque: University of New Mexico Press, 1995.

Russell, Craig. *From Serra to Sancho: Music and Pageantry in the California Missions.* New York: Oxford University Press, 2009.

Salomon, Carlos Manuel. *Pío Pico: The Last Governor of Mexican California.* Norman: University of Oklahoma Press, 2010.

Sánchez, George J. *Becoming Mexican American: Ethnicity, Culture, and Identity in Chicano Los Angeles, 1900–1945.* New York: Oxford University Press, 1995.

Sánchez, Rosaura. *Telling Identities: The* Californio *Testimonios.* Minneapolis: University of Minnesota Press, 1995.

Sandos, James A. "Because He Is a Liar and a Thief": Conquering the Residents of 'Old' California, 1850–1880." *California History* 79, no. 2 (June 2000): 86–112.

———. *Converting California: Indians and Franciscans in the Missions.* New Haven: Yale University Press, 2004.

Sandos, James A., and Patricia B. Sandos. "Early California Reconsidered: Mexicans, Anglos, and Indians at Mission San José." *Pacific Historical Review* 83, no. 4 (2014): 592–625.

Sawyer, Jesse O. "Wappo." In *Handbook of North American Indians.* Vol. 8, *California,* ed. Robert F. Heizer, 256–63. Washington, D.C.: Smithsonian Institution, 1978.

Schell, William. *Integral Outsiders: The American Colony in Mexico City, 1876–1911.* Wilmington, Del.: SR Books, 2001.

Schneider, Tsim D. *The Archaeology of Refuge and Recourse: Coast Miwok Resilience and Indigenous Hinterlands in Colonial California.* Tucson: University of Arizona Press, 2021.

Senkewicz, Robert M. "The Inflation of an Overdone Business: Economic Origins of San Francisco Vigilantes." *Pacific Historian* 23, no. 3 (1979): 63–75.

———. *Vigilantes in Gold Rush San Francisco.* Stanford: Stanford University Press, 1985.

Shelton, Tamara Venit. *A Squatter's Republic: Land and the Politics of Monopoly in California, 1850–1900.* Berkeley: Published for the Huntington-USC

Institute on California and the West by University of California Press, 2013.

Shoup, Laurence H., and Randall T. Milliken. *Iñigo of Rancho Posolmi: The Life and Times of a Mission Indian.* Novato, Calif.: Ballena Press, 1999.

Shuck, Oscar T. *History of the Bench and Bar of California.* San Francisco: Occident Printing House, 1889.

Shumate, Albert. *Captain A. A. Ritchie, California Pioneer: An Account of His Life, Family, and Ranchos.* San Francisco: Society of California Pioneers, 1991.

Shutes, Milton H. "'Fighting Joe' Hooker." *California Historical Society Quarterly* 16, no. 4 (1937): 304–20.

Sides, Hampton. *Blood and Thunder: An Epic of the American West.* New York: Doubleday, 2006.

Silliman, Stephen W. *Lost Laborers in Colonial California: Native Americans and the Archaeology of Rancho Petaluma.* Tucson: University of Arizona Press, 2004.

Silverstein, Michael. "Yokuts: Introduction." In *Handbook of North American Indians.* Vol. 8, *California,* ed. Robert F. Heizer, 446–47. Washington, D.C.: Smithsonian Institution, 1978.

Skowronek, Russell K., Elizabeth Thompson, and Verónica LoCoco Johnson. *Situating Mission Santa Clara de Asís, 1776–1851: Documentary and Material Evidence of Life on the Alta California Frontier: A Timeline.* Berkeley: Academy of American Franciscan History, 2006.

Soulé, Frank, John H. Gihon, and James Nisbet. *The Annals of San Francisco.* New York: D. Appleton, 1855.

Spell, Lota M. "Gorostiza and Texas." *Hispanic American Historical Review* 37, no. 4 (1957): 425–62.

Spencer-Hancock, Diane, and William E. Pritchard. "El Castillo de Monterey: Frontline of Defense." *California History* 67, no. 3 (1984): 230–41.

Spier, Robert F. G. "Foothill Yokuts." In *Handbook of North American Indians.* Vol. 8, *California,* ed. Robert F. Heizer, 471–84. Washington, D.C.: Smithsonian Institution, 1978.

Summers Sandoval, Tomás F. *Latinos at the Golden Gate: Creating Community and Identity in San Francisco.* Chapel Hill: University of North Carolina Press, 2013.

Swanson, Craig Arthur. "Vanguards of Continental Expansion: Americans in Alta California, 1790–1846." PhD diss., University of Maryland, College Park, 2000.

Swasey, W. F. *The Early Days and Men of California.* Oakland: Pacific Press, 1891.

Tanghetti, Rosamaria. "Intimate Unions: Conquest and Marriage in California, 1769–1890." PhD diss., University of California, Davis, 2004.

Tays, George. "Captain Andrés Castillero, Diplomat: An Account from Unpublished Sources of His Services to Mexico in the Alvarado Revolution of 1836–1838." *California Historical Society Quarterly* 14, no. 3 (1935): 230–68.

———. "Mariano Guadalupe Vallejo and Sonoma: A Biography and a History." *California Historical Society Quarterly*, part 1: 16, no. 2 (June 1937): 99–121; part 2: 16, no. 3 (September 1937): 216–54; part 3: 16, no. 4 (December 1937): 348–72; part 4: 17, no. 1 (March 1938): 50–73; part 5: 17, no. 2 (June 1938): 141–67; part 6: 17, no. 3 (September 1938): 219–42.

———. "Revolutionary California: The Political History of California during the Mexican Period, 1822–1846." PhD diss., University of California, Berkeley, 1932.

Tennis, George. "California's First State Election November 13, 1849." *Southern California Quarterly* 50, no. 4 (1968): 357–94.

Thompson, R. A., and Thos. H. Thompson & Co. *Historical Atlas Map of Sonoma County, California.* Sanger, Calif.: Sonoma County Historical Society, 2003.

Torres-Rouff, David Samuel. *Before L.A.: Race, Space, and Municipal Power in Los Angeles, 1781–1894.* New Haven: Yale University Press, 2013.

Trapero, Maximiano. *El libro de la décima: la poesía improvisada en el mundo hispánico.* Las Palmas de Gran Canaria: Universidad de Las Palmas de Gran Canaria, 1996.

Tunnell, Ted. *Crucible of Reconstruction: War, Radicalism, and Race in Louisiana, 1862–1877.* Baton Rouge: Louisiana State University Press, 1984.

Tuomey, Honoria. *History of Sonoma County, California.* 2 vols. San Francisco: S. J. Clarke, 1926.

Tutorow, Norman E. *The Governor: The Life and Legacy of Leland Stanford, a California Colossus.* 2 vols. Spokane: Arthur H. Clark Company, 2004.

Uhrowczik, Peter. *The Burning of Monterey: The 1818 Attack on California by the Privateer Bouchard.* Los Gatos, Calif.: Cyril Books, 2001.

Voss, Barbara L. *The Archaeology of Ethnogenesis: Race and Sexuality in Colonial San Francisco.* Berkeley: University of California Press, 2008.

———. "From Casta to Californio: Social Identity and the Archaeology of Culture Contact." *American Anthropologist*, n.s., 107, no. 3 (2005): 461–74.

Wallace, William J. "Northern Valley Yokuts." In *Handbook of North American Indians.* Vol. 8, *California*, ed. Robert F. Heizer, 462–70. Washington, D.C.: Smithsonian Institution, 1978.

———. "Southern Valley Yokuts." In *Handbook of North American Indians.*

Vol. 8, *California*, ed. Robert F. Heizer, 448–61. Washington, D.C.: Smithsonian Institution, 1978.

Warner, Barbara R. *The Men of the California Bear Flag Revolt and Their Heritage.* Spokane: Arthur H. Clark Company, 1996.

Weber, David. *Bárbaros: Spaniards and Their Savages in the Age of Enlightenment.* New Haven: Yale University Press, 2005.

———. *The Californios versus Jedediah Smith, 1826–1827: A New Cache of Documents.* Spokane: Arthur H. Clark Company, 1990.

———. *The Mexican Frontier, 1821–1846: The American Southwest under Mexico.* Albuquerque: University of New Mexico Press, 1982.

Weber, David J., and David J. Langum. "Here Rests Juan Espinosa: Toward a Clearer Look at the Image of the 'Indolent' Californios." *Western Historical Quarterly* 10, no. 1 (1979): 61–69.

Weber, Francis J. *The United States versus Mexico: The Final Settlement of the Pious Fund.* Los Angeles: Historical Society of Southern California, 1969.

Wilson, Norman L., and Arlean H. Towne. "Nisenan." In *Handbook of North American Indians.* Vol. 8, *California*, ed. Robert F. Heizer, 387–97. Washington, D.C.: Smithsonian Institution, 1978.

Winkley, John W. *Dr. John Marsh, Wilderness Scout.* Martinez, Calif.: Contra Costa County Historical Society, 1962.

Winks, Robin W. *Frederick Billings: A Life.* New York: Oxford University Press, 1991.

Wittenburg, Mary Joanne. "Three Generations of the Sepúlveda Family in Southern California." *Southern California Quarterly* 73, no. 3 (1991): 197–250.

Wolfe, Patrick. *Traces of History: Elementary Structures of Race.* New York: Verso Press, 2016.

Woolfenden, John, and Amelie Elkinton. *Cooper: Juan Bautista Rogers Cooper, Sea Captain, Adventurer, Ranchero, and Early California Pioneer, 1791–1872.* Pacific Grove, Calif.: Boxwood Press, 1983.

Zollinger, James Peter. *Sutter: The Man and His Empire.* New York: Oxford University Press, 1939.

Index

366 *Index*